eat
out in
pubs

The 2007 edition of the Michelin Eating out in Pubs guide lists over 550 pubs which have all been selected for the quality of the food they serve. This is the first and overriding criterion for selection. The menus and style of cooking found in these pubs may vary considerably, reflecting the enormous diversity and choice available to the consumer today. Some concentrate on local recipes and regional specialities; some pursue an organic mission through the support of small local suppliers and there are others whose influences owe more to eclectic, contemporary cuisine. You'll find everything from classic pub grub to the more creative cooking one usually finds in restaurants and you'll discover some pubs serving their food in the bar by the fireplace with others providing a separate, quite formal dining room. However, the one factor shared by all the establishments in this guide is an understanding of what constitutes good cooking; fresh produce, careful preparation and natural flavours.

Michelin's readers contribute thousands of letters and e-mails every year, sending in praise and criticism, suggestions for the guide itself and recommendations for new entries. We hope you'll keep them coming and help us to make the next edition of Michelin Eating out in Pubs even better. You can also fill in and return the readers' questionnaire form at the back of this guide; either way, we look forward to hearing from you!

MICHELIN
A better way forward

contents

Contents

3

MIDLANDS

EAST OF
ENGLAND

LONDON

EAST

COUNTRY OR REGION & COUNTY NAMES

ONE OF OUR FAVOURITE SELECTIONS

TOWN/VILLAGE NAME

NAME, ADDRESS, TELEPHONE, E-MAIL AND WEBSITE OF THE ESTABLISHMENT

013

ENTRY NUMBER

Each pub or inn has its own entry number.

This number appears on the regional map at the start of each section to show the location of the establishment.

COLOURED PAGE BORDER

Introduction

East Midlands

East of England

London

North East

North West

South East

South West

West Midlands

Yorkshire & The Humber

Scotland

Wales

Northern Ireland

Republic of Ireland

East Midlands - Leicestershire

Stathern

013 Red Lion Inn
2 Red Lion St, Stathern LE14 4HS
Tel.: (01949) 860868 · Fax: (01949) 861579
e-mail: info@theredlioninn.co.uk · Website: www.theredlioninn.co.uk

VISA

Grainstore Olive Oil Bitter, Brewsters, Marquise, Batemans XB, Young's Special, Abbot Ale

Though it's hard to put your finger on what makes the Red Lion such a quietly likeable place, the comfortable sitting room, with today's papers over the arms of the leather sofas, is a nice, understated invitation to make yourself at home. A rural inn to the core, filled with wooden antiques, rustic ornaments and bunches of dried flowers, its able, well-priced cooking easily steps out of old pub convention and manages to keep its well-defined contemporary country style while still rotating its dishes day by day: it's a winning formula, but never comes across as formulaic. Try an appetising lemon and herb risotto or herb-crusted cod, served at neat, gingham-clad tables in what was once the pub's skittle alley, or in the little courtyard at the back.

Food serving times:
Monday-Saturday:
12pm-2pm, 7pm-9.30pm
Sunday:
12pm-4pm
Closed 25-26 December (dinner), 1 January (booking essential)
Prices:
Meals: 15.95 (lunch) and a la carte 20.00/29.00

Typical Dishes

Spiced aubergine tartlet, pan fried red mullet

Ribeye steak

Hot chocolate pudding

8mi North of Melton Mowbray by A607. Parking.

30

HOW TO FIND A PUB

There are 3 ways to search for a pub in this guide:
- use the regional maps that precede each section of the guide
- use the alphabetical list of pubs at the end of the guide or
- use the alphabetical list of place names also at the end of the guide

PUBS WITH BEDROOMS

For easy reference, those pubs that offer accommodation are highlighted in blue. This theme is continued on the regional maps that precede each section of the guide.

SYMBOLS

- Meals served in the garden or on the terrace
- A good range of wines served by the glass
- A particularly interesting wine list
- **Rest.** Non-smoking dining room
- No dogs allowed
- **VISA** Visa accepted
- **AE** American Express accepted
- **①** Diners Club accepted
- **MC** MasterCard accepted

Hough-on-the-Hill

East Midlands - Lincolnshire

016 The Brownlow Arms

High Rd, Hough-on-the-Hill NG32 2AZ

Tel: (01400) 250234

e-mail: armsinn@yahoo.co.uk

VISA **AE** **MC**

Timothy Taylor Landlord, Marston's Pedigree, Marston's Bitter

Wolds, fens and heathlands provide an atmospheric backdrop to this handsome 17C country inn located in the centre of a pretty Lincolnshire village. By no stretch of the imagination is this a typical pub. Certainly there is a bar, of cosy dimensions and charmingly wood panelled with deep armchairs and an open fire; and here you'll find locals regularly engaging in lively debate. But the bar is only a small part of the picture – it's the starting point for an experience more akin to a gracious country house. Food is what the Brownlow Arms is renowned for: the restaurant is warmly atmospheric with wood panels, big tables and very comfy chairs. Menus are full of choice and dishes are well prepared with good quality ingredients; inspirations are equally traditional and modern. Bedrooms are exquisite: decorated with considerable taste, they include flatscreen TVs and DVD players.

6mi North of Grantham by A607 to Barkston and side road North. Parking.

Food serving times:
Monday-Saturday:
6.30pm-9.30pm
Closed 25-27 December, 3 weeks in January, 1 week in summer
Prices:
Meals: 18.45 (3 course Sunday lunch) and a la carte 25.00/38.00
4 rooms : 65.00/96.00

Typical Dishes
Cheese souffle, Lincolnshire poacher
Roast ribeye of lamb
Caramelised bread and butter pudding

REAL ALES SERVED

A listing to indicate the number and variety of regular and guest cask beers usually served.

OPENING HOURS FOOD SERVING TIMES PRICES ROOMS

Approximate range of prices for a three-course meal, plus information on booking and annual closures.

Some inns offering accommodation may close in mid-afternoon and only allow guests to check in during evening hours. If in doubt, phone ahead.

Room prices range from the lowest-priced single to the most expensive double or twin.

The cup and saucer symbol and price relate to breakfast; if no symbol is shown, assume it is included in the price of the room.

Prices are given in £ sterling, except for the Republic of Ireland where €uro are quoted.

HOW TO GET THERE

Directions and driving distances from nearby towns, and indication of parking facilities and any other information that might help you get your bearings.

THE BLACKBOARD

An example of a typical starter, main course and dessert, chosen by the chef.

Whilst there's no guarantee that these dishes will be available, they should provide you with an idea of the style of the cuisine.

The Pub of the year

There are more than 550 pubs in this year's Guide; naturally enough, it's the quality of their food that's earned them a rightful place in our pages. To secure top spot, though – the Pub of the Year – an establishment has to offer a certain something extra, a magic ingredient that makes the visitor go that extra mile – maybe through twisty lanes or winding backstreets – to seek out the very best. You know it when you find it; it's not just the quality of the cuisine, the charming location or the welcoming ambience. Nor is it just the choice of beers and wines. It has to have an all-pervading aura of excellence that balances everything in perfect harmony.

The Michelin Pub of the Year sits temptingly on the Welsh border, beckoning English visitors over into the rolling Monmouthshire hills. Its proximity to castle, bridge and river can't help but tick all the right boxes; inside, its 'country meets contemporary' style shines through from every nook, cranny and immaculate turn.

The bar draws you in, not only with a strong selection of ales, and eye-catching display of flowers from the garden, but also its fine array of local information guides to be perused at gleaming polished tables. Wine here is considered very much a thing of beauty – the owner is passionate about it, and his extensive wine list reaches across the globe; the superb selection of half bottles and Cognac is quite extraordinary for a pub.

The daily changing menu specialises in seasonality and freshness and provides diners with an appetising and balanced selection of dishes - from the rustic to the more adventurous - but all prepared with care and a refreshingly unfussy approach. Names of all the local supplies are proudly displayed on the blackboard and most of the vegetables, herbs and salads come from the pub's very own kitchen garden.

It's the bedrooms, though, that can't help but entice the weary traveller. They're the epitome of luxury, from home-made biscuits to touchpad CD and DVD players. The eye for detail here even goes as far as the offer of 'turndown': you may have to pinch yourself to believe you're only staying at a pub! Set quaintly in its idyllic rural position since the 17th century, our Pub of the Year for 2007 is…

The Bell at Skenfrith
Monmouthshire, NP7 8UH
Tel: (01600) 750235 – Fax: (01600) 750525
e-mail: enquires@skenfrith.co.uk – website: www.skenfrith.co.uk

see page 585 for more details

*A*ll the pubs in this guide have been selected for the quality of their cooking. However, we feel that several of them deserve additional consideration as they boast at least one extra quality which makes them particularly special.

It may be the delightful setting, the charm and character of the pub, the general atmosphere, the pleasant service, the overall value for money or the exceptional cooking.

To distinguish these pubs, we point them out with our "We most liked" Bibendum stamp.

We are sure you will enjoy these pubs as much as we have.

Beer
in the U.K. and Ireland

As most pub-goers know, beers in Britain can be divided not only into Ales and Lagers – which differ mainly in their respective warm and cool fermentations – but also according to their means of storage. Keg beer is filtered, pasteurised and chilled, and then packed into pressurised containers from which it gets its name, while cask beer or "Real Ale", as it is often called, continues to ferment and mature in its barrel.

Brewers rightly insist that the final flavour of a beer depends on all sorts of elements, from the variety of yeast to the minerals in the local water, not to mention storage in the pub, but there are three stages of brewing which particularly influence the character of the beer in your glass.

The malting, the way the germinating barley is dried, roasted and milled to make it fermentable, affects the flavour, the 'body' and the colour of the drink: a hotter kiln means a darker malt. This malt is then soaked in hot water to form a porridge-like mash; time and temperature are crucial here. Perhaps most importantly, the addition of hops gives a familiar, faintly astringent tang, with different strains of plant lending different overtones to the final pint. For extra aroma, bunches of hop flowers, called cones, can be added to the beer later, at the end of its vat fermentation or even in the barrel, a process known as "dry hopping".

Traditional Styles

Of the several distinct beer styles in the British Isles, **bitter** is the most popular traditional beer in England and Wales, although now outsold by lager. No precise definition exists and the name is loosely used, but bitters are usually paler and dryer than Mild with a high hop content and, of course, a slightly bitter taste and bouquet, from flowery to citrus, depending on the hop variety.

Mild is largely found in Wales, the West Midlands and the North West of England. The name refers to the hop character as it is gentle, sweetish beer, generally lower in alcohol and often darker in colour.

The great dry **stouts** are brewed in Ireland and are instantly recognisable by their black colour and creamy head: they have a pronounced yeast flavour and sometimes a faint smoky taste. Reddish-black **porter** was revived by the renewed interest in real ale and is still something of

a rarity. Originally known as 'entire', this slightly lighter though still substantial beer was said to have been a favourite with London's market porters and deliverymen when it was first brewed in the 18th century.

In Scotland the beers produced are typically full-bodied and malty and are often known simply as Light, **Heavy** or **Export**, which refers to the body and alcoholic content of the ale. The old shilling taxes were levied by roughly the same scale, at rates of 60/- to 80/- and beyond, and still survive in some beer names.

The Continental Connection

Many great European styles are now imitated by UK producers, with greater or lesser success, and publicans are also becoming increasingly discerning in their choices of European imports. Drinkers in Britain's dining pubs might come across fizzy, hazy, tan-yellow **Weizenbier** from southern Germany which can accompany anything from full-flavoured white meats to seafood, or one of the crisp, bitter-edged **lagers** produced in the north, where they are sometimes served with fish.

Belgium's spontaneously fermenting **lambic** is aged in wine barrels for up to three years; when flavoured with fruit and bottle-matured it becomes **gueuze**, a sweet-sharp, bubbly beer quite unlike anything in the British Tradition. The great **abbey beers**, traditionally produced by the Belgian Trappist orders, are usually rich, effervescent and complex and need similarly robust flavours to complement them, while cloudy **white beers** make a refreshing accompaniment to light meals and summer salads. Top-fermented then cold-stored like lagers, **bières de garde** from northern France and Wallonia are sometimes sealed with a Champagne-style wired cork. These amber or nut-brown beers are typically strong and characterful and go well with cheeses or slow-cooked meats.

13

A tour of the region begins with a well-kept secret: the rural beauty of the east. Towards the coast lie acres of silent fens, the gentle countryside of the wolds, and the magnificent silhouette of Lincoln Cathedral, rising above the old city. Nottingham, Derby and the nearby towns shot to fame as centres of industry and science and remain the powerhouses of the region. With Leicester they form an old industrial heartland, regenerated by the first plantings of the National Forest and bordered by rural Rutland, "independent" again since 1997. Then to the west, sombre moors, the pretty 'White Peak' downlands, the Derwent and dramatic Dovedale form some of the country's most picture-perfect landscapes, while Peak architecture reflects every mood and era of its history: Matlock's mills and the moving monuments of Eyam village, Georgian Buxton and the stately archetypes of Chatsworth and Haddon Hall. In the region's pubs, there's a strong local flavour on tap – even Rutland brews its own beer – as well as on the plate. Bakewell tarts, or puddings, are a point of local pride, while only the rich, blue-veined cheese from three East Midlands counties can lay claim to the name of Stilton.

Ashbourne

001 Bramhall's 🛏

6 Buxton Rd, Ashbourne DE6 1EX

Tel.: (01335) 346158
e-mail: info@bramhalls.co.uk - Website: www.bramhalls.co.uk

 ✂ 🍴 **VISA** ⓜⓒ

	Bass

D on't be put off by the rather dreary façade, just off Ashbourne's cobbled market square; once inside, it's a different picture. Pick a table in one of the four or five little rooms and snugs and let a well-drilled team do the rest. Keen and helpful staff in denim uniforms serve an appetising menu rounded out with daily specials on the board: cream of white onion soup, monkfish with gnocchi and asparagus and rasperry crème brûlée are typical of a sound modern-classic style. At the back, an enclosed terrace for dining looks down over a stepped garden. If you're planning on staying the night, the usefully equipped bedrooms range from plain to contemporary.

Food serving times:
Monday-Saturday:
12pm-2.30pm,
6.30pm-9.30pm
Closed 25-26 December,
1 January for 2 weeks, Sunday dinner November to Easter
Prices:
Meals: 13.95 and a la carte 18.65/28.15
🛏 **10 rooms :** 30.00/75.00

Typical Dishes

Ham hock and bacon terrine

Rump of lamb, champ mash

Dark chocolate and ginger pot

In centre of town. Limited parking on front; also in Market Place. **➤➤**

Baslow

002 Rowley's

Church Lane, Baslow DE45 1RY

Tel.: (01246) 583880

e-mail: info@rowleysrestaurant.co.uk - Website: rowleysrestaurant.co.uk

 Bohemia and 1 guest beer

The people who run the Michelin Star-encrusted Fischer's at Baslow Hall have now 'set up shop' along the road with this classy second venture. It's based in a quiet village in one of its quietest positions: surrounded on three sides by graveyard and church! Nothing funereal about the ambience here, though: a full makeover in 2006 introduced chrome tables and chairs and large dark brown banquettes to this old stone pub. There are three dining areas and, under the watchful eye of a bubbly manager, waiting staff skim across the blond wood floors providing excellent and personable service. Dishes are in the modern British category, and most ingredients have a Derbyshire accent: matured steaks are a particular speciality. Close by is Chatsworth House, an ideal destination for anyone making a day of it in the Peak District.

Food serving times:
Tuesday-Saturday:
  12pm-2.30pm, 6pm-9.30pm
Sunday: 12pm-2.30pm
Prices:
Meals: a la carte 23.00/35.00

Typical Dishes

Salmon and haddock fish cake

Rump of lamb, chick pea cassoulet

Lemon tart

4mi North of Bakewell by A619.
Parking.

Birchover

003 The Druid Inn

Main St, Birchover DE4 2BL

Tel.: (01629) 650302
Website: www.thymeforfood.co.uk

  🍷 🥢 **VISA** **MC**

Druids Ale, Hairy Helmet, Halifax Steam, Reverend Eatons, Civvy Salvation, Leatherbritches

Taking its name from the mysterious and ancient Druid Rocks above it, the Druid Inn, in the heart of the Peak District countryside, has been a hill-walkers' landmark for many years. Much extended since the 19C, it still has plenty of true rural character in the old bar, which has kept its tiled floor, chunky furniture and flickering firelight, and is that bit more authentic-feeling than the smarter modern dining rooms. Considerate and informal staff somehow keep track of a large menu that ranges from daily pastas and risottos, hot and cold lunchtime sandwiches and pints of prawns, by way of enjoyable and substantial modern classics. This is more than food to keep the cold out: it may not be elaborate, but it's marked by true, balanced flavours and sound culinary understanding, with sensible prices to match.

Food serving times:
Monday-Saturday:
  12pm-2.30pm, 6pm-9.30pm
Sunday: 12pm-2.30pm
Closed Mondays October-March

Prices:
Meals: 16.00 (set price lunch and dinner) and a la carte 22.00/30.00

7.5 mi Northwest from Matlock by A6 and 5.5 mi from Bakewell. Parking.

Typical Dishes

Mosaic of foie gras

Rump of lamb, confit vegetables

Sticky toffee pudding

Hognaston

004 Red Lion Inn 🛏

Main Street, Hognaston DE6 1PR

Tel.: (01335) 370396 - Fax: (01335) 370396
e-mail: redlionhognaston@w3z.co.uk

 Marstons Pedigree, Burton Bitter and Derby Brewing Co and a guest ale changing weekly

Nestling in a pretty village in the foothills of the Derbyshire Peaks, this cream-washed extended late 17C inn has a cosy, comfortable appeal, typified by a bar full of objets d'art and ornaments. A 'real' pub ambience predominates, with the warmth of the surroundings enhanced with open fires and a rugged old stone floor. You'll want for nothing: the owner is chatty and enthusiastic, and very much on hand to recommend drinks or dishes from the menu. Classic pub meals here have been given a modern twist: typically, pork sausages with mustard mash and red wine jus. Dine at a candle-lit mix of older wooden tables and chairs. Stay overnight in beamed, individually decorated bedrooms.

Food serving times:
Sunday-Monday:
    12pm-2pm, 6.30pm-9pm
Tuesday-Saturday:
    12pm-2pm, 6.30pm-9.30pm
Prices:
Meals: a la carte 20.00/30.00
🛏 **3 rooms :** 65.00/90.00

Typical Dishes

Thai crab cakes

Rack of lamb, horseradish mash

Bread and butter pudding

4.5mi Northeast of Ashbourne by B5035. Parking at rear.

Hope Valley

005 The Chequers Inn

Froggatt Edge, Hope Valley S32 3ZJ

Tel.: (01433) 630231 - Fax: (01433) 631072
e-mail: info@chequers-froggatt.com - Website: www.chequers-froggatt.com

VISA AE M©

Charles Wells Bombardier, Deuchars IPA, Black Sheep

Located at the eastern end of the Peak District, and just in front of the woods that lead to Froggatt Edge, this attractively set pub - a Grade II listed building - is quite a find. It dates back to the 16C and was originally four houses; it's been extensively refurbished yet retains many period features, such as the old stables. The spacious interior has a welcoming feel, typified in the bar by a well-chosen selection of wines by the glass, chalked up on blackboard slates hung around the richly varnished panelled ceiling; chunky stone walls with antique prints all add to the rustic atmosphere. Sit at simple, polished wooden tables and tuck into tasty meals with a distinctive modern feel, backed up by efficient, friendly service. Walkers may be delighted to finish the evening tucked up in very pleasant, cosy bedrooms.

Food serving times:
Monday-Friday:
   12pm-2pm, 6pm-9.30pm
Saturday: 12pm-9.30pm
Sunday: 12pm-9pm
Closed 25 December
Prices:
Meals: a la carte 21.15/27.85
5 rooms : 95.00

Situated on the edge of the village. Parking.

Typical Dishes

Homecured salmon

Seared scallop bruschetta, creamed leeks

Raspberry pannacotta

Marston Montgomery

006 **The Crown Inn** 🛏

Riggs Lane, Marston Montgomery DE6 2FF
Tel.: (01889) 590541 - Fax: (01889) 590576
e-mail: info@thecrowninn-derbyshire.co.uk - Website: www.thecrowninn-derbyshire.co.uk

Y ⬡ ⬡ **VISA** **AE** **MC**

Pedigree, Bass, Timothy Taylor Landlord and occasional local micro-brewery beers

Just up the road from Alton Towers is a far more relaxing and certainly less energetic alternative: a pleasant pub, hidden away in the village centre. Locals are drawn by the warm and welcoming atmosphere, not to mention the splendid selection of real ales and wines by the glass; exposed rafters and an open fire all add to the happy mix. This simple, cosy interior is further enhanced by plenty of comfy seats and distressed wooden tables. The food served here, off a daily blackboard menu, seamlessly matches its surroundings: tasty and unfussy, with modern twists thrown in for good measure. Bedrooms do the trick, too: they're warm, cosy and contemporary.

Food serving times:
Monday-Saturday:
    12pm-2.30pm, 7pm-9pm
Sunday: 12pm-2.30pm
Closed 25 December
and 1 January
Prices:
Meals: 14.95 (set price lunch)
and a la carte 14.95/30.00
🛏 **7 rooms :** 50.00/75.00

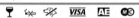

Typical Dishes

Smoked paprika goat's cheese
Supreme of Guinea fowl
White chocolate crème brûlée

7.5mi Southeast of Ashbourne by A515. Parking. ⟩⟩

Belton

007 The Queen's Head 🛏

2 Long St, Belton LE12 9TP

Tel.: (01530) 222359 - Fax: (01530) 224860
e-mail: enquiries@thequeenshead.org - Website: www.thequeenshead.org

  VISA

Marston's Pedigree, Fuller's Discovery

A renovation of the old village inn has left little if any trace of a 19C pub; even Her Majesty's severe, Penny-Black profile on the monochrome pub sign looks like a tribute to a design classic rather than a touch of Victorian detail. But it's fairer to appreciate the place for what it is. The transformation, into a smart bar, bistro and restaurant has been complete and thorough: calm whites and creams, chocolate suede and polished wood give a feeling of all-over modernity. It's no surprise to find similar attention to detail in a varied and evolving menu on different modern British themes, though you shouldn't overlook the simpler bar choice of sandwiches, salads, pastas and lunchtime specials. Bedrooms are spacious, contemporary and bright; the two in the attic share a bathroom.

Food serving times:
Monday-Thursday:
   12pm-2.30pm, 7pm-9.30pm
Friday-Saturday:
   12pm-2.30pm, 7pm-10pm
Sunday: 12pm-4pm
Closed 25 December

Prices:
Meals: 16.00 (set price lunch and dinner (except Sat dinner and Sun lunch)) and a la carte 25.00/34.00
🛏 **6 rooms :** 60.00/100.00

Typical Dishes

Marinated tuna, sesame dressing

Pot roast rack of lamb

Kirsch and cherry soufflé

6mi West of Loughborough by A6 on the B5234. On the Diseworth/Breedon rd. Parking. ❯❯

Breedon-on-the-Hill

008 **The Three Horseshoes Inn**

Main St, Breedon-on-the-Hill DE73 8AN

Tel.: (01332) 695129 - Fax: (01332) 695128

e-mail: ian@thehorseshoes.com - Website: www.thehorseshoes.com

  VISA

 Marstons Pedigree, Deuchars IPA, Theakstons Old Peculiar

A 230 year-old establishment of dubious heritage: was it an inn, a public house or maybe just houses? Whatever its provenance, The Three Horseshoes is one third of a stalwart trio in a noteworthy village, famed for its church perched atop a quarry cliff visible for miles around, and opposite an 18th Century lock-up. It's a welcoming pub: there's a locals bar with an open fire, where you can quite happily mingle and enjoy a pint. Food, though, is the main emphasis here. Apart from the bar, there are two dining areas with coir matting, walls filled with a variety of pictures, crafts and artefacts, and plenty of space to take it all in. Large mismatched dining tables and odd chairs complete the quirky picture. Nothing quirky about the menus…large blackboards offer ample choice of carefully sourced and combined ingredients in dishes more akin in style to restaurant than pub.

Food serving times:
Monday-Saturday:
    12am-2pm, 6pm-9.15pm
Prices:
Meals: a la carte 15.95/31.00

4mi Southwest of Castle Donington by Breedon rd off A453. Parking. 〉〉

Typical Dishes

Spinach, bacon and poached egg salad

Braised lamb shank

Chocolate & whisky trifle

Bruntingthorpe

009 Joiners Arms

Church Walk, Bruntingthorpe LE17 5QH

Tel.: (0116) 247 8258

e-mail: stephenjoiner@btconnect.com - Website: www.thejoinersarms.co.uk

 Greene King IPA

B e warned: you might not even recognise the Joiners Arms as a hostelry at all: its smart little whitewashed 18C exterior only bears the most discreet of pub signs. Once inside, any lingering doubts are soon banished: there's a surprising amount of contemporary design, married successfully to wooden beams, recently returned to their natural oak. Drinkers relax on velvet-upholstered furniture; diners can recline on cushioned pews at closely-spaced wood tables. The menu choice is quite small but appealingly formed, incorporating daily changing blackboard specials that are good value, tasty and accomplished, making the most of seasonal ingredients. Service is friendly and polite.

Food serving times:
Tuesday-Saturday:
  12pm-2pm, 6.30pm-9.30pm
Sunday: 12pm-2pm
Closed 25 December
and Bank Holidays
(booking essential)

Prices:
Meals: 12.95 (set price lunch)
and a la carte 22.00/29.00

Typical Dishes

Scallops bonne femme

Sea bass, pak choi, crab ravioli

Liquorice pannacotta

Between Leicester and Husbands Bosworth off A5199. Parking.

Buckminster

010 Tollemache Arms
48 Main St, Buckminster NG33 5SA

Tel.: (01476) 860007
e-mail: enquiries@thetollmachearms.com - Website: www.thetollmachearms.com

Timothy Taylor Landlord, Cooking Grainstore Brewery

In the heart of Rutland, something's cooking…and the small village of Buckminster is reaping the dividends. The Tollemache was gutted in 2004 (as were many of the villagers when it happened) but the refurbished Arms has gone a mighty long way to redress the balance. Admittedly, it now bears little resemblance to its late Victorian coaching inn origins. In fact, the wood floor, stainless steel topped bar, huge leather sofas and contemporary colour scheme are about as far removed from 'traditional' as it's possible to get. But regulars and visitors alike have taken to the 21st century version, not least due to the cooking qualities of chef Mark, who for three years was chef de partie at the famous Le Manoir in Oxfordshire. His menus are modern British, but nothing too complicated to upset a consistent level. Simple, good value rooms await those staying overnight.

Food serving times:
Tuesday-Saturday:
    12pm-2pm, 7pm-9.30pm
Sunday: 12pm-2pm
Prices:
Meals: 14.00 (set price lunch and dinner) and a la carte 21.05/35.00
5 rooms : 45.00/60.00

Off the A1 at Colsterworth, 3.75 mi West on the B676. Parking.

Typical Dishes

Mozzarella salad, avocado and chorizo

Fillet of beef with fondant potato

Hot chocolate pudding

Hallaton

011 Bewicke Arms 🛏

1 Eastgate, Hallaton LE16 8UB
Tel.: (01858) 555217 - Fax: (01858) 555598
e-mail: lottispiers@yahoo.co.uk

🚭 **VISA** Ⓜ©

🍺 *Greene King IPA and beers from the Grainstore Brewery*

Visit Hallaton on Easter Monday and you won't forget the experience in a hurry. That's the day of the annual Bottle Kicking and Hare Pie Scramble when locals jostle for pieces of pie and teams of men from Hallaton and neighbouring Medbourne engage in a manic free-for-all trying to capture three wooden casks. The 17C Bewicke Arms provides a pleasant change of pace from the strange goings-on. It is rusticity itself: solid stone floor, hop bines, open fires and exposed rafters. Produce from the region, selected on a seasonal basis, forms the hearty backbone to the weekly changing blackboard menus; chatty, friendly service is guaranteed.

Food serving times:
Monday-Saturday:
  12pm-2pm, 7pm-9.30pm
Sunday(except in winter):
  12pm-2pm
**Closed Easter Monday
(booking essential)**
Prices:
Meals: 5.95 (set price 2 course lunch) and a la carte 17.50/25.00
🛏 **3 rooms :** 40.00/55.00

Typical Dishes

Warm goat's cheese with walnuts

Cod fillet with herb and Parmesan crust

Coffee meringues

8mi Northeast of Market Harborough by B664. Parking.

Knossington

012 The Fox and Hounds

6 Somerby Rd, Knossington LE15 8LY

Tel.: (01664) 454676 - Fax: (01664) 454031
Website: www.foxandhounds.biz

  VISA

Fuller's London Pride, Pedigree

This lovely, ivy clad 18C former coaching inn makes an ideal refuelling stop after a visit to Rutland Water. Set in a small, pretty village, it's the very picture of a rural Leicestershire pub, with low ceilings, beams and wood tables at the front for al fresco meals. Drinkers relax on stools at the bar; diners make for one of two coir-carpeted rooms with polished wood tables and a choice of cushioned chairs or pew-style banquettes. Daily changing menus comprise good value, modern rustic dishes with local produce in much evidence. Try, perhaps, breast of chicken with chick peas, broad beans and lentils, or grilled calves liver with green beans and tapenade. Warm attentive service is a pleasant plus.

Food serving times:
Tuesday-Saturday:
   12pm-2.30pm, 7pm-9.30pm
Sunday: 12.30pm-2.30pm
(booking essential)
Prices:
Meals: a la carte 19.95/30.00

Typical Dishes

Terrine of confit duck and Morteau sausage

Local rib of beef

Raspberry yoghurt pannacotta

4mi West of Oakham by A606 and Braunston rd. Parking.

Stathern

013 Red Lion Inn

2 Red Lion St, Stathern LE14 4HS
Tel.: (01949) 860868 - Fax: (01949) 861579
e-mail: info@theredlioninn.co.uk - Website: www.theredlioninn.co.uk

Grainstore Olive Oil Bitter, Brewsters, Marquise, Batemans XB, Young's Special, Abbot Ale

Though it's hard to put your finger on what makes the Red Lion such a quietly likeable place, the comfortable sitting room, with today's papers over the arms of the leather sofas, is a nice, understated invitation to make yourself at home. A rural inn to the core, filled with wooden antiques, rustic ornaments and bunches of dried flowers, its able, well-priced cooking easily steps out of old pub convention and manages to keep its well-defined contemporary country style while still rotating its dishes day by day: it's a winning formula, but never comes across as formulaic. Try an appetising lemon and herb risotto or herb-crusted cod, served at neat, gingham-clad tables in what was once the pub's skittle alley, or in the little courtyard at the back.

Food serving times:
Monday-Saturday:
    12pm-2pm, 7pm-9.30pm
Sunday: 12pm-4pm
Closed 25-26 December (dinner), 1 January
(booking essential)
Prices:
Meals: 15.95 (lunch) and a la carte 20.00/29.00

8mi North of Melton Mowbray by A607. Parking.

Typical Dishes

Spiced aubergine tartlet, pan fried red mullet

Ribeye steak

Hot chocolate pudding

Thorpe Langton

014 ## The Bakers Arms

Main St, Thorpe Langton LE16 7TS

Tel.: (01858) 545201
Website: www.thebakersarms.co.uk

 VISA

 Langton Bakers Dozen Bitter

This pleasantly relaxed pub hidden away in a Leicestershire village has a wonderfully appealing 16C thatched appearance; inside, the appeal also harks back to olden days. Scrubbed pine tables - candlelit in the evenings - exposed timbers, pew seats, oriental rugs, all of them surrounded by rich red walls, ensure that the atmosphere is intimate and most convivial. It's not really a drinker's pub, though if you want a pint, you're certainly welcome. The Bakers is aimed more for the dining fraternity, who, judging by their numbers, are well satisfied by their experience here. Menus are innovative and well executed, with good use made of seasonal Leicestershire ingredients.

Food serving times:
Tuesday-Friday:
6.30pm-9.30pm
Saturday-Sunday:
12pm-2pm
Closed Monday,
Sunday evening, weekday lunchtimes
(booking essential)
Prices:
Meals: a la carte 20.00/30.00

Typical Dishes

Pan fried scallops, honey dressing

Breast of duck with spiced roast parsnips

Vanilla brûlee

3.75mi North of Market Harborough by A4304 via Great Bowden. Parking

Belchford

015 The Blue Bell Inn

1 Main Rd, Belchford LN9 6LQ
Tel.: (01507) 533602

✄ ✗ ***VISA*** ●③

Black Sheep, Timothy Taylor Landlord and one guest beer

Nobody really knows how old this pub is; they're even less sure about the origins of the huge blue bell that hangs outside the place. Either way, it adds a unique dimension to the pretty exterior. Run by a friendly husband and wife team (he cooks, she looks after customers), the Blue Bell's a warm and inviting place in the heart of the Wolds. Clearly, this is a dining pub, though you'll still see locals at the bar at weekends when all the fuss over lunch and dinner has died down. Comfy armchairs in front of the bar provide a relaxing place to peruse the menu: you can choose to stay where you are and eat at the bar or go through to the similarly decorated restaurant. Take your time over the blackboards – there are six in all! – and you'll find a healthy share of accomplished and adventurous modern British dishes amongst the standard pub favourites.

Food serving times:
Tuesday-Saturday:
  11.30am-2pm, 6.30pm-9pm
Sunday: 11.30am-2pm
Closed 2nd and 3rd weeks in January
Prices:
Meals: a la carte 14.45/24.40

Typical Dishes

Crab meat, chervil mayonnaise

Saddle of wild fallow venison

Dark chocolate & pecan nut brownie

In the centre of the village. Parking. ▶

Hough-on-the-Hill

016 **The Brownlow Arms**

High Rd, Hough-on-the-Hill NG32 2AZ

Tel.: (01400) 250234
e-mail: armsinn@yahoo.co.uk

Timothy Taylor Landlord, Marston's Pedigree, Marston's Bitter

Wolds, fens and heathlands provide an atmospheric backdrop to this handsome 17C country inn located in the centre of a pretty Lincolnshire village. By no stretch of the imagination is this a typical pub. Certainly there is a bar, of cosy dimensions and charmingly wood panelled with deep armchairs and an open fire; and here you'll find locals regularly engaging in lively debate. But the bar is only a small part of the picture – it's the starting point for an experience more akin to a gracious country house. Food is what the Brownlow Arms is renowned for: the restaurant is warmly atmospheric with wood panels, big tables and very comfy chairs. Menus are full of choice and dishes are well prepared with good quality ingredients; inspirations are equally traditional and modern. Bedrooms are exquisite: decorated with considerable taste, they include flatscreen TVs and DVD players.

Food serving times:
Monday-Saturday:
6.30pm-9.30pm
Closed 25-27 December,
3 weeks in January, 1 week
in summer

Prices:
Meals: 18.45 (3 course Sunday lunch) and a la carte 25.00/ 38.00

4 rooms : 65.00/96.00

Typical Dishes

Cheese soufflé, Lincolnshire poacher

Roast ribeye of lamb

Caramelised bread and butter pudding

6mi North of Grantham by A607 to Barkston and side road North. Parking.

Lincoln

017 Wig & Mitre

First Floor, 30-32 Steep Hill, Lincoln LN2 1TL

Tel.: (01522) 535190 - Fax: (01522) 532402
e-mail: email@wigandmitre.com - Website: www.wigandmitre.com

Black Sheep Special, Batemans XB, Milestone Rich Ruby

Superior and diverse: two words which readily spring to mind when describing this 14C hostelry, now a most welcoming café, bar and restaurant. It's close to the cathedral, a natural resting place after climbing Steep Hill, where it's perched. Walk in past the handsome broad-windowed exterior to the relaxed café: newspapers to read, sofas and pews to lounge in, exposed stone walls, oak floorboards, simple tables, appealing bistro style menus. Upstairs, the dining room has a medieval air about it, with an open fire, shelves of old books, antique prints and banquette seats. Wide ranging menus with much appeal might include roast sausages with garlic and black pudding mash and apple cream sauce; or steamed brill with red wine butter.

Food serving times:
Monday-Sunday:
8am-12am

Prices:
Meals: 13.95 (set price lunch) and a la carte 22.00/36.50

Close to the Cathedral. Parking in Castle car park in Castle Square.

Typical Dishes

Baked cheese and pea souffle

Fillet steak with black pudding

Raspberry brûlee

Surfleet Seas End

018 **The Ship Inn**

154 Reservoir Rd, Surfleet Seas End PE11 4DH

Tel.: 01775 680547 - Fax: 01775 680541
e-mail: moil@shipinnsurfleet.com - Website: www.shipinnsurfleet.com

  VISA **AE** **D** **MC**

 Adnams Bitter and 3 other guest ales - Batemans, Gales HSB, Banks, SA Brains Selection, Marstons, Slaters, Cottage Breweries

Despite the name of its location, The Ship's actually a dozen or so miles from the briny! Newly rebuilt, it stands on the 17C foundations of a pub once used by Irish navvies building local drains, and offers good views over the surrounding creek and Fenland. As such, this is a busy meeting place for sailors and walkers alike. The popular pubby bar on the ground floor has nautical paraphernalia; upstairs a slightly more formal 'restaurant' boasts a wonderful balcony where you can eat and watch the boats. The best time to come and eat here is the winter, when an adventurous menu is based around very seasonal, well-sourced local ingredients. The bedrooms are large, comfy and up-to-date – best of all, they have long-distance views over the Fens.

Food serving times:
Tuesday-Saturday:
           12pm-2pm, 7pm-9pm
Sunday: 12pm-2pm
Prices:
Meals: a la carte 20.00/30.00
4 rooms : 50.00/65.00

Typical Dishes

Duck terrine

Fillet of beef stuffed with Colton Basset cheese

Raspberry and pistachio Bakewell tart

4mi North of Spalding by A16. Parking.

Woolsthorpe-by-Belvoir

019 ## The Chequers

Main Street, Woolsthorpe-by-Belvoir NG32 1LU

Tel.: (01476) 870701

e-mail: justinnabar@yahoo.co.uk - Website: www.chequers-inn.net

Timothy Taylor Landlord, Hardy & Hanson, Olde Trip

In the gentle Lincolnshire countryside near 19C Belvoir Castle, this sizeable old coaching inn is made up of lounges, snugs and a bar with original features but all furnished in a modern style, as well as a slightly more formal restaurant. The same menu is served throughout, the variations on a classic British theme together with more contemporary offerings; it's worth asking about the lunchtime set menu. A gravel petanque strip in the back garden should stimulate some healthy competition, and the cricket pitch in the pub grounds hosts village matches from May to September. Alternatively, friendly local staff can also point you in the right direction for a walk towards Grantham. Out in the converted stable block, four neat, pine-furnished rooms in cottage patterns offer useful facilities.

Food serving times:
Monday-Sunday:
  12pm-2.30pm, 6pm-9.30pm

Closed 25 and 26 December (pm) Sunday dinner in winter

Prices:
Meals: 12.50/15.00 and a la carte 22.00/35.00

4 rooms : 49.00/59.00

7.5mi West of Grantham by A607. Parking.

Typical Dishes

Smoked and poached salmon terrine

Roasted rump of lamb

Hot chocolate fondue

Lowick

020 The Snooty Fox

16 Main St, Lowick NN14 3BH
Tel.: (01832) 733434 - Fax: (01832) 733931
e-mail: thesnootyfox@btinternet.com

VISA

Green King IPA, Moorland Original, Fuller's London Pride, Ruddles Rumpus, Old Speckled Hen, Summer Lightening

This spacious inn dates back to 16C; it started life as the local Manor House, and is reputedly haunted by a horse and its rider killed in the Battle of Naseby, a dozen or so miles to the west. Its carved beams are of particular note, but then again, for those who've tasted them, so are the locally renowned rotisserie grill menus and home-made favourites like pasties and cottage pies. You can eat around the sizable bar or in the elegant main dining room. If you're going for meat, select the size of your cut from a nicely stocked chilled cabinet, but if you're after the vegetarian option, then you won't be disappointed either. Prices are keen and the cooking's very good. It's all run, most unsnootily, by experienced and welcoming owners.

Food serving times:
Monday-Sunday:
    12pm-2pm, 6pm-9.30pm
Closed dinner 25-26
December and 1-2 January
Prices:
Meals: 14.90 (set price lunch) and a la carte 20.00/28.00

Village off A6116. Parking.

Typical Dishes

Iberico ham, wood roast peppers

Blade of Aberdeenshire beef, foie gras

Caramelised apple tart

Oundle

021 # The Falcon Inn

Fotheringhay, Oundle PE8 5HZ

Tel.: (01832) 226254 - Fax: (01832) 226046

e-mail: falcon@cyberware.co.uk - Website: www.huntsbridge.co.uk

Adnams Best, Greene King IPA and 1 guest beer

Richard III and Mary Queen of Scots aren't a bad couple of names to help draw in the punters: one was born here, one died here (not in the pub, you understand, but in the village of Fotheringhay). Those not aware of the history will still succumb to the warmth of this characterful place, run with professionalism and great personality. Though modernised, it still feels like an all-round good pub: open fires, spindle back chairs, fresh flowers, framed prints picking up on the history, and tubby wood tables. A spacious conservatory offers a formal air, Lloyd Loom chairs, and some impressive cooking from the modern British repertoire: Greek feta burger with light raita and crisp chips, or smoked haddock with potato and chive tart.

Food serving times:
Monday-Sunday:
12pm-2.15pm,
6.15pm-9.30pm

Prices:
Meals: a la carte 25.00/35.00

Typical Dishes

Soup of spring pea, mint and pancetta

Grilled John Dory, capers and olives

Pannacotta and cherries

3.75mi North of Oundle by A427 off A605. Parking.

Caunton

022 Caunton Beck

Main St, Caunton NG23 6AB

Tel.: (01636) 636793 - Fax: (01636) 636828

 Milestone Loxley, Black Sheep Bitter, Batemans XB

With the parish church opposite and the beck itself running alongside, this end of Caunton wouldn't look quite right without a neat village pub to complete the picture. Spacious and airy, with exposed brick walls, open fires and a big counter bar, this sympathetically designed modern place is actually bigger than it looks; a smart dining room offering a more formal alternative and soundly prepared lunches and dinners on a traditional base. A typical selection might take in leek and cheese soufflé or monkfish with crispy pancetta, but don't overlook the bar menu, particularly if you're after something a bit lighter or simpler: a keen young team are on hand if you just can't decide.

Food serving times:
Monday-Sunday:
8am-12am

Prices:
Meals: 13.95 (set price lunch and dinner) and a la carte 22.50/32.00

Typical Dishes

Smoked trout rillette

Fillet of beef with tarragon

Warm dark chocolate tart

On A616, 6mi past the sugar beet factory. Parking.

Colston Bassett

023 **The Martins Arms**

School Lane, Colston Bassett NG12 3FD

Tel.: (01949) 81361 - Fax: (01949) 81039

 Bass, Black Sheep, Adnams, Abbott Ale, Greene King IPA, T Taylor Landlord, Pedigree, Fuller's London Pride

Blessed indeed are the cheesemakers, for we're right in the heart of "Stilton country", and the owners of the Martins Arms are as proud as anyone of Nottinghamshire's most famous culinary export. Tucked away at the heart of this sleepy rural village, the big pub with the warm and welcoming atmosphere varies its appealing modern menu with the seasons, but cheese connoisseurs will want to try the generous ploughmans lunches or a tasty starter of Stilton rarebit: other dishes from a wide-ranging repertoire, generally with a more complex and contemporary edge, might include pigeon with mushroom ravioli or strawberry mousse. Lunches and dinners are served in a smart, semi-panelled dining room with lovely Queen Anne style chairs, but the spacious bar is equally appealing, with a carved wooden fireplace and rustic brickwork and furnishings.

Food serving times:
Monday-Saturday:
12pm-1.30pm, 7pm-9pm
Sunday: 12pm-1.30pm
Closed dinner 25 December
Prices:
Meals: a la carte 21.00/35.00

East of Cotgrave off A46. Parking (35 spaces only).

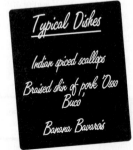

Typical Dishes

Indian spiced scallops

Braised skin of pork 'Osso Buco'

Banana Bavarois

Halam

⟨024⟩ Waggon and Horses

Mansfield Rd, Halam NG22 8AE

Tel.: (01636) 813109 - Fax: (01636) 816228
e-mail: info@thewaggonathalam.co.uk - Website: www.thewaggonathalam.co.uk

 ⚒rest 🚳 **VISA** **MC**

🍺 *Thwaites Bomber, Thwaites Original, Thwaites Smooth, Thoroughbred*

Between Nottingham and Mansfield, just to the east of Sherwood Forest, the Waggon and Horses draws in an appreciative mix of East Midlanders and passers-by, many of whom have heard about its good local reputation. It's no more than due recognition for the owners, who are members of the Campaign for Real Food and try to offer as much fresh, local produce as possible. The pub itself is quite small with low-beamed ceilings and heavy wooden tables; cricket memorabilia betrays the fact you're not so far from Trent Bridge. The dining area, adjacent to the bar, is the place to try out extensive menus: blackboard specials change daily, and the modern, style of the cuisine, allied to the freshness of the ingredients, guarantees a legion of fans.

Food serving times:
Monday-Saturday:
  12pm-2.30pm, 6pm-9.30pm
Sunday: 12pm-2.30pm
Closed 25-26 December
and 1 January

Prices:
Meals: 14.50 (set price lunch and dinner (6-7pm)) and a la carte 23.00/28.00

1.75mi West of Southwell, opposite the school. Parking. ➤

Typical Dishes

Pears roasted with grain mustard

Venison shank, roasted beetroot

Vanilla pannacotta

Normanton-on-the-Wolds

025 The Plough

Old Melton Rd, Normanton-on-the-Wolds NG12 5NN

Tel.: (0115) 937 2401 - Fax: (0115) 937 2401

 ♿ ✂ ***VISA***

Theakston's Best, Adnam's and guest beer changing monthly

Driving on the A606 from Nottingham, your attention might well be caught by this attractive, creeper-clad country pub on the edge of an affluent little village. You won't be the first. In summertime, the large rear garden here is a popular place for eating, mucking about – and playing pétanque (there are a couple of pitches). Sunday night is barbeque night. The outdoor life is advisable at The Plough, as the interior's a bit on the small side. There's not an immense amount of traditional pub character, save for all those lovely open fires to light up greyer days. Dining's the priority here: there's a cosy little restaurant with six tables, blue and white cloths giving it a slightly formal air. Simple lunchtime fare gives way in the evenings to a more adventurous modern British menu, full of tasty local ingredients.

Food serving times:
Monday-Sunday:
11am-3pm, 6pm-10.30pm
Prices:
Meals: 12.95 and a la carte
12.95/30.00

Typical Dishes

Terrine of local game
Breast of duck, poached figs
Banana tart Tatin

7mi Southeast of Nottingham by A606. Parking.

Nottingham

026 Cock and Hoop

25 High Pavement, Nottingham NG1 1HE

Tel.: (0115) 852 3231 - Fax: (0115) 852 3223

e-mail: cockandhoop@lacemarkethotel.co.uk - Website: www.cockandhoop.co.uk

 VISA **AE** **MC**

 *Deuchars IPA, Fuller's London Pride, Greene King, Abbot Ale,
Nottingham Rock Bitter, Adnams Best*

Known by many names over the last two centuries, the Cock and Hoop has at last come full circle. The cobbled streets of the redeveloped Lace Market have had a change in fortune too, and the refurbished pub fits in well: an old-fashioned front of mullioned windows and brick-and-timber between two dignified 18C neighbours. Inside is a clutch of tables by a brass-edged bar and, downstairs, a much larger lounge and dining area, panelled in pale modern wood. The familiar modern British cuisine works in a few daily variations, but the core of the menu is tasty and substantial cooking in fair quantity – it's the kind of place where you can have one or two courses and feel well satisfied. Pleasantly chatty staff, all in black, keep the place running smoothly.

Food serving times:
Monday-Sunday:
   12pm-3pm, 5.30pm-9.30pm
Closed 25-26 December
and 1 January
Prices:
Meals: a la carte 17.90/22.00

Typical Dishes

Soup of the day

*Flame grilled home-made
beefburger*

Citrus marcarpone cheesecake

Adjacent to Lace Market Hotel. NCP
Stoney St and free on-street parking
after 6pm.

Barrowden

027 Exeter Arms

28 Main St, Barrowden LE15 8EQ

Tel.: (01572) 747247 - Fax: (01572) 747247
e-mail: joeallsopp@aol.com - Website: www.exeterarms.com

VISA MC

Wide range of real ales produced on site and guest ales

Handily placed just off the A47, this family run pub exudes much of the rural charm associated with the area close to Rutland Water. It's a 17C inn of light stone idyllically rooted in a sleepy village overlooking the green with its little pond and duck house. Inside is warm and welcoming: the yellow painted walls see to that. Beers here are a must. They come from the pub's own micro-brewery housed in an old rear barn, and you can't sup them anywhere else in the country. If you're eating you can choose a seat wherever takes your fancy, be it the stone-walled dining room or the bar with its cosy open fire. Either way, you won't forget where you are, as old photos of the pub crop up on all walls. You'll remember this hostelry, too, for its well-executed cuisine, classic dishes given an updated, international twist, with Asian influences inspiringly conspicuous. Three neat and tidy bedrooms offer pleasant country views.

Food serving times:
Tuesday-Saturday:
12pm-2pm, 7pm-9pm
Sunday: 7pm-9pm
Prices:
Meals: a la carte 20.00/30.00
3 rooms : 35.00/70.00

11mi Southwest of Oakham by A6003 and A47. Parking.

Typical Dishes

Smoked goose breast

Local venison fillet en croûte

Roast plum bruschetta

Clipsham

028 **The Olive Branch**

Main St, Clipsham LE15 7SH

Tel.: (01780) 410355 - Fax: (01780) 410000
e-mail: info@theolivebranchpub.com - Website: www.theolivebranchpub.com

     VISA ***MC***

Grainstore Olive Oil, Elgood Old Wag, Abbot Ale

Gourmets will have their taste buds suitably satiated at this rurally located inn. But, as Rutland residents have appreciated for some years now, there's so much more to this cosy firelit pub than the admittedly first-rate cooking. For instance, the neat pergola doubles as a terrace in good weather, while back inside there's an irresistible mix of country style attractions – church pew seats, open wood fires, and roughly painted walls with sepia prints, cookery books and assorted curios. And the food? Perfectly judged, seasonally inspired dishes – a flavourful mix of the old and new, with plenty of flexibility and originality in the end result. Three charmingly endowed dining areas enrich the enjoyment factor. Six bedrooms are now available in the house opposite.

Food serving times:
Monday-Sunday:
    12pm-2pm, 7pm-9.30pm
Closed 25 (dinner),
26, 31 (lunch) December
and 1 January
(booking essential)
Prices:
Meals: 16.00 and a la carte
20.00/31.50
🛏 **6 rooms :** 95.00/150.00

Typical Dishes

Tempura battered tiger prawns, sweet chilli dip

Braised oxtail, horseradish gratin, mashed carrots

Belvoir marmalade pudding

9.5mi Northwest of Stamford by B1081 off A1. Parking.

Glaston

029 The Old Pheasant

Main Rd, Glaston LE15 9BP

Tel.: (01572) 822326 - Fax: (01572) 823316
e-mail: info@theoldpheasant.co.uk - Website: www.theoldpheasant.co.uk

Pheasant Ale (brewed for The Old Pheasant by Grainstore Brewery), Everards Original and guest ales

Rutland Water is a fine place to go for fly-fishing, sailing and cycling enthusiasts, and this former 18C coaching inn, completely refurbished in 2004, is an ideal spot to rest tired limbs. The modernisation has been done in keeping with the age of the building: stone walls, wood flooring and rafters with dried hops evoke the rustic spirit of the past, no less than a cosy seating area by the inglenook, with small leather Chesterfield and wood-burning stove. You can dine here, though most choose the Gun Room restaurant. A compact menu opts for the traditional, with pub classics using a good range of Rutland ingredients: there's a blackboard selection too. Bedrooms have good facilities and extra homely touches.

Food serving times:
Monday-Saturday:
    12pm-2pm, 6.30pm-9pm
Sunday: 12pm-2pm
Closed 25 December
Prices:
Meals: a la carte 19.85/29.95
🛏 **9 rooms :** 45.00/100.00

Typical Dishes

Home cured salmon

Fillet of beef, fondant potatoes

Chocolate marquise, caramel sauce

2.5mi east of Uppingham on A47. Parking.

Hambleton

030 Finch's Arms

Ketton Rd, Hambleton LE15 8TL
Tel.: (01572) 756575 - Fax: (01572) 771142
e-mail: finchsarms@talk21.com - Website: www.finchsarms.co.uk

    VISA **MC**

Timothy Taylor Landlord, Greene King, Abbot Ale, Oakham Ales JHB, Hudson Bitter

It doesn't matter why you come to the Finch's; you're not likely to find the experience unrewarding. Some tourists want to see its location: alone, surrounded by the vast expanse of Rutland Water. Others want to relax on the splendid hillside terrace and check out the views from another angle. But many arrive wanting to enjoy the pub's atmosphere: an inviting rusticity in keeping with its surroundings; there are open fires, coir carpets, scrubbed, candle-lit wooden tables, and pew-style benches. The more formal rear dining room has solid stone-topped tables. Rather complex menus have an appealing quality full of fresh, seasonal ingredients: typically, ballottine of guinea fowl with prunes. A weekly changing blackboard menu is more down-to-earth. Impressive bedrooms have a French country feel.

Food serving times:
Monday-Sunday:
12pm-2.30pm, 6.30pm-9.30pm
Closed 25 December
Prices:
Meals: 11.50 (set price lunch) and a la carte 16.95/26.95
6 rooms: 65.00/75.00

Typical Dishes

Twice baked cheese souffle
Pan fried fillet of beef with spinach
Lemon and lime tart

3mi East of Oakham by A606. Parking.

Lyddington

031 Old White Hart

51 Main Street, Lyddington LE15 9LR

Tel.: (01572) 821703 - Fax: (01572) 821965
e-mail: mail@oldwhitehart.co.uk - Website: www.oldwhitehart.com

VISA MC

 Greene King IPA, Greene King Abbott, Fullers London Pride

Among the happy throng of drinkers at this wonderfully unstuffy, unfussy pub you'll find a surprising number of petanque players, drawn by the – probably unique – 10-lane boules court. Of course, you don't need to be a sporty type to appreciate the delights of this pretty Rutland village inn. The gardens offer plenty of outdoor seats, but in winter you'll prefer the roaring fires, welcoming beamed bar and nice feeling of intimacy which ensues. When you're hungry, dine on good value lunch menus or, later, a seasonal à la carte with plenty of choice. The daily changing blackboard fish specials are tasty and renowned: try, perhaps, the Grimsby haddock or mussels in white wine and garlic. Well-kept bedrooms await those staying overnight.

Food serving times:
Monday-Saturday:
    12pm-2pm, 6.30pm-9pm
Sunday: 12pm-2pm
Closed 25 December
Prices:
Meals: 12.95 and a la carte 18.75/32.15
6 rooms : 55.00/85.00

1.5mi south of Uppingham off A6003. By the village green. Parking.

Typical Dishes

Seared foie gras with fresh fig

Fried Grimsby haddock with homemade chips

Crème brûlée

Stretton

032 The Jackson Stops Inn

Rookery Rd, Stretton LE15 7RA

Tel.: (01780) 410237 - Fax: (01780) 410237

Oakham Ales JHB, Whychwood Hob Goblin, Timothy Taylor Landlord

When estate agent Jackson Stops sold off the Stretton Estate in 1955, their sign was outside what was then The White Horse pub for so long that it became known as the Jackson Stops. An interesting little anecdote which goes some way to explaining why a 17C, rurally set thatched inn should end up with such an unusual name. It's a wonderfully characterful place, rustic down to its Rutland wellies; a low wooden bar is frequented by regulars, but this then gives way to, surprisingly, four dining areas, minimalist with plain décor and vintage scrubbed tables, silver chargers glinting in welcome. A very pleasant atmosphere prevails; the constantly evolving menus offer good value, rustic British cooking.

Food serving times:
Tuesday-Saturday:
　　　　12pm-2pm, 7pm-10pm
Sunday:　　　　　　12pm-2pm
Closed 25 December to 3 January
Prices:
Meals: a la carte 21.00/27.00

Typical Dishes

Sauteed king prawns, sauce vierge

Rump of beef, oxtail suet pudding

Apple tart Tatin

8mi Northwest of Stamford by B1081 off A1. Parking.

Wing

033 The Kings Arms

13 Top St, Wing LE15 8SE

Tel.: (01572) 737634 - Fax: (01572) 737255
e-mail: info@thekingsarms-wing.co.uk - Website: www.thekingsarms-wing.co.uk

room **VISA** **AE** **MC**

 Grainstore Cooking, Timothy Taylor Landlord, Marston Pedigree, and 1 guest ale

Built in the early days of Cromwell's Britain, this delightful place gave the Restoration time to settle before becoming "The Kings Arms", but the cosy bar can't have changed much over the last 350 years or so. Flagstone floors, ancient beams and a big open fire lend true period warmth, while more recent prints and paintings of Rutland and around reflect a local pride that comes across just as clearly on the menu. Fresh and substantial dishes on a traditional base make good use of seasonal produce from our smallest county, and the landlord and team chip in well with relaxed, conversational service. All well away from the main bar, the bedrooms are warm and immaculately kept. Rutland Water is a short drive away.

Food serving times:
Monday-Sunday:
12pm-2pm, 6.30pm-9.30pm
Closed Monday (lunch)
November-March
Prices:
Meals: a la carte 17.00/32.00
8 rooms : 60.00/75.00

Typical Dishes

Pheasant breast, apple & celeriac

Venison tenderloin, roast roots

Caramelised pears

5mi South of Oakham by A6003.
Parking.

Little Red Riding Hood

But Little Red Riding Hood had her regional map with her, and so she did not fall into the trap. She did not take the path through the wood and she did not meet the big bad wolf. Instead, she chose the picturesque touring route straight to Grandmother's house, and arrived safely with her cake and her little pot of butter.

The End

With Michelin maps,
go your own way.

MICHELIN
A better way forward

*W*ith culinary tastes ranging from fresh samphire-shoots to cockles, smoked eel and Cromer crab, it's easy to get a flavour of the East of England. It's a region with strong brewing traditions and some of England's most charming pubs, but it's also a place of rich historic roots and a deep attachment to rural life. Here you'll find the medieval wool towns of Lavenham, Coggeshall and Saffron Walden and the old trading centres of Norwich and King's Lynn, Ely's distant tower and the Palladian splendour of Holkham Hall. Be part of the world-famous Aldeburgh music festival or the first Classics of the racing season at Newmarket; cast off into the waterways of the Norfolk Broads or lie back in a punt and drift down the Cam past the beautiful Cambridge colleges. Stroll through the fields of a lavender farm or strike out into the wilds, under the great open sky of the coast and the salt marshes, and spot basking seals, a flight of curlew or the rare wildlife of the broadland meadows. Wherever you go exploring, it's bound to be an inspiration. "They made me a painter and I am grateful", Constable once said of the walks along the Stour near his boyhood home. We can't guarantee the same for everyone, but you'll certainly work up an appetite along the way…

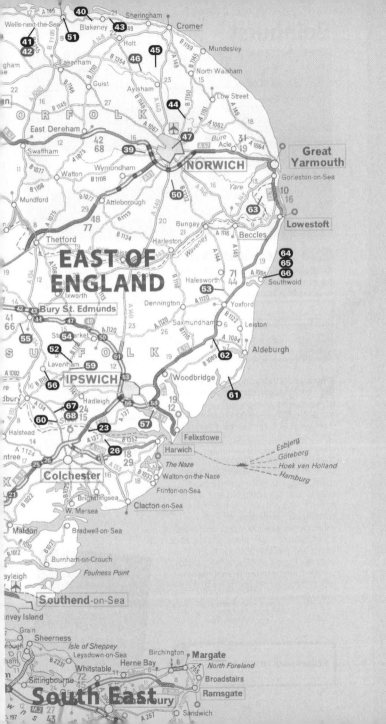

Bolnhurst

001 # The Plough at Bolnhurst

Kimbolton Rd, Bolnhurst MK44 2EX

Tel.: 01234 376274

e-mail: theplough@bolnhurst.com – Website: www.bolnhurst.com

Village Bike Potters Brewery, Batemans XB, Fullers Discovery

Razed to the ground nearly two decades ago, the pure white Plough has been lovingly and sympathetically restored to something like its original 14th century glory and was reopened in the summer of 2005. The charming interior offers an inglenook, thick rustic walls, and wood and stone floors in three main seating areas with reassuringly low ceilings and exposed beams. You can't help but feel utterly relaxed. Step outside and there's a duck pond, spacious gardens and two extensive terraces. Local produce is keenly sought and carefully prepared on menus which also pay due homage to the seasons. There's an eclectic feel to what's on offer: amongst the modern dishes, look out too for old favourites that have stood the test of time.

Food serving times:
Tuesday-Saturday:
   12pm-2pm, 7pm-9.30pm
Sunday: 12pm-2.30pm
Closed from 29 December
for 2 weeks, also Monday
Prices:
Meals: 15.00 (fixed price lunch)
and a la carte 20.22/35.00

Typical Dishes

Buffalo ricotta gnocchi

Braised oxtail with creamed carrots

Hot chocolate fondant

South of village on B660. Parking.

Houghton Conquest

002 Knife and Cleaver

The Grove, Houghton Conquest MK45 3LA

Tel.: (01234) 740387 - Fax: (01234) 740900
e-mail: info@knifeandcleaver.com - Website: www.knifeandcleaver.com

  ✗rest **VISA** **AE**

Village Bike - Potton Brewery, Batemans XB

This 17C redbrick inn is situated right opposite the church. It's lovely on a July day, when those in the know find a white metal table out in the garden, but the bar is also most inviting with a warm log fire, deep purple décor and black timbers - settle down on mahogany chairs, stools or even a small sofa. The area at the side – the old darts room – now looks rather contemporary, and minimalist, too, with just four tables. Menus go across the board from traditional to modern, light to substantial. Alternatively, a conservatory restaurant, which overlooks the garden, offers a fine choice of fish from an altogether more serious selection. Best produce is paramount. Pleasant bedrooms, in former stables, are individually styled and carefully furnished.

Food serving times:
Monday-Saturday:
 12pm-2.30pm, 7pm-9.30pm
Sunday: 12pm-2.30pm
Closed 27-30 December
(set price dinner Monday-Friday only; a la carte menu Monday-Saturday only)

Prices:
Meals: 15.95/22.50 (set price lunch / dinner) and a la carte 22.00/34.00

9 rooms : 59.00/84.00

6.5mi South of Bedford by A6. Near All Saints Church. Parking.

Typical Dishes

King scallops, pepper sauce

Rack of lamb, creamed broad beans

Chocolate mousse

Milton Bryan

003 The Red Lion

Toddington Rd, Milton Bryan MK17 9HS

Tel.: (01525) 210044

e-mail: paul@redlion-miltonbryan.co.uk - Website: www.redlion-miltonbryan.co.uk

 Greene King IPA, Abbot Ale, Old Speckled Hen and 1 guest ale in summer

You can't miss this place in early summer, when the white-gabled, redbrick pub is polka-dotted with a truly extravagant show of overflowing hanging baskets: the old English pub in Glorious Technicolor. Inside, the wood-floored, bare-brick public bar offers a tasty lunch menu of all-time pub favourites, but there's greater seasonal variety in the more formal restaurant, the friendly tenants gladly going the extra mile to find good ingredients for their Thai fishcakes, pheasant confit and a crisp and creamy leek and goat's cheese tart. For friendly neighbourhood atmosphere, it takes some beating, and there's real warmth and thoughtfulness to the service, too.

Food serving times:
Monday-Saturday:
12pm-2.30pm, 7pm-9.30pm
Sunday: 12pm-2.30pm
Closed 25-26 December and 1 January
Closed Monday in winter
Prices:
Meals: a la carte 25.00

Milton Bryan is South of Woburn by A4012. Parking.

Typical Dishes

Twice baked goat's cheese souffle

Grilled lemon sole

Pecan nut and Jack Daniels tart

Old Warden

004 Hare & Hounds

The Village, Old Warden SG18 9HQ
Tel.: (01767) 627225 - Fax: (01767) 627588

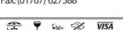

Eagle IPA, Old Speckled Hen, Charles Wells Bombardier

Such a sincerely friendly welcome at the bar is always a good sign: you'd be welcome to stop here for a pint, but such enjoyable and fairly-priced food is just too good to miss. Three chic but cosy country dining rooms, decorated in tweeds, floral patterns and soft autumnal colours, are an appropriate setting for rustic cooking with a good modern and traditional balance. Plentiful and full-flavoured dishes come and go – it all depends on the season and a handful of trusted local suppliers – but appealing blackboard specials supplement the menu: try a rich, crisp spiced duck confit with lentils and bacon or the Shuttleworth pork plate of fillet, belly and sausage. It's the staff who really make the difference, though: discreetly attentive and genuinely enthusiastic about the dishes they serve.

Food serving times:
Tuesday-Saturday:
    12pm-2pm, 6.30pm-9.30pm
Sunday: 12pm-2pm
Closed Monday except Bank Holiday Mondays
Prices:
Meals: a la carte 20.00/25.00

Typical Dishes

Crab spring rolls
Sirloin steak, hand-cut chips
Sticky toffee pudding

3.5mi West of Biggleswade by A6001 off B658. Parking and at Village Hall.

Shefford

005 **The Black Horse**

Ireland, Shefford SG17 5QL

Tel.: (01462) 811398
Website: www.blackhorseireland.com

Greene King IPA, Fuller's London Pride, Village Bike - Potton Brewery

Y ou'd be hard put to find fault with this 17C white pub not far from the A1. For starters, it boasts a charming garden with bench seats and stylish patio, while inside the feel is no less comfortably rustic. The front bar's old and new beams are warmly off set by polished tables; an adjacent dining room boasts a stylish country feel. Main dining is at the rear in a 21C extension: again, very cool and contemporary, with an African theme predominating. The same menu is served throughout and changes every three months. Well-executed, modern dishes with a classic base ensure the Black Horse retains a serious dining tag. Two bedrooms, neat, up-to-date and compact, guarantee the satisfaction factor remains high.

Food serving times:
Monday-Saturday:
12pm-2.30pm, 6.30pm-10pm
Sunday: 12pm-5pm
Closed 25-26 December
and 1 January
Prices:
Meals: 24.95 (set price lunch)
and a la carte 22.00/29.00
⊨ **2 rooms :** 55.00

Typical Dishes

Spicy Moroccan gambas

Braised lamb shoulder

Chocolate brownie

1.75mi Northwest of Shefford by B658 and Ireland Rd. Parking.

Steppingley

006 The French Horn

Church End, Steppingley MK45 5AU

Tel.: (01525) 712051 - Fax: (01717) 334305
e-mail: info@thefrenchhorn.com - Website: www.thefrenchhorn.com

Old Speckled Hen, IPA

The pretty hamlet of Steppingley boasts this late 18th century pub that features a beautiful period restaurant from the 1950s that's metamorphosed via a super recent makeover. Original character remains in the front bar, where flag flooring and rustic beams are the order of the day. But it's the main dining room that's taken the regulars by pleasant surprise. There are stylish dark leather chairs, dark varnished solid wood tables, bright, modern oil paintings and contemporary lighting. The food is very well regarded. Menus change seasonally and skilfully combine a classic base with the chef's individual flair. Presentation is strong and flavours intense, raising the standard to above the pub norm. To build up a hunger before your visit, take a leisurely stroll through the glories of nearby Woburn Park.

Food serving times:
Monday-Saturday:
12pm-2.30pm,
6.30pm-9.30pm
Sunday: 12pm-2.30pm
Booking essential
Prices:
Meals: a la carte 24.00/50.00

Typical Dishes

Quail with mustard, apple salad

Rack of lamb

Mixed berries tiramisu

4.5 miles from Woburn through The Park. Between junctions 12 and 13 of M1. Parking.

Woburn

007 The Birch

20 Newport Rd, Woburn MK17 9HX
Tel.: (01525) 290295 - Fax: (01525) 290899
e-mail: etaverns@aol.com - Website: www.birchwoburn.com

Fuller's London Pride, Adnams

This established dining pub, like much else in Woburn, sits confidently in the superior category. Locals and visitors mingle contentedly in an establishment that offers a very agreeable ambience, from the pleasant outside decking terrace to the stylish mix of furnishings within; these include mosaic and pine tables and rugs on the floors. At the back, the dining area covers two levels, not counting the conservatory extension: Mediterranean style décor gels comfortably with wooden chairs and tables. All eyes are on an open kitchen in the corner, where the satisfying modern dishes, particularly meat and fish, are conjured up from the grill. An interesting evening à la carte menu is balanced with lighter lunchtime dishes.

Food serving times:
Monday-Saturday:
 12pm-2.45pm, 6.30pm-10pm
Sunday: 12pm-2.45pm
Closed 25-26 December and 1 January
(booking essential)
Prices:
Meals: a la carte 17.95/23.95

Typical Dishes

Seared scallop with balsamic

Grilled fillet steak

Passion fruit and Grand Marnier soufflé

0.5mi North on A5130. Parking.

Broughton

008 The Crown

Bridge Rd, Broughton PE28 3 AY

Tel.: (01487) 824428 - Fax: (01487) 824912
e-mail: simon@thecrownbroughton.co.uk - Website: www.thecrownbroughton.co.uk

  VISA

 Greene King IPA, Potton Shambles, City of Cambridge Hobson's Choice

This soft-hued brick pub nestles in the archetypal English country village scenario: next to the church, surrounded on all sides by rustic repose. Owned by the village, it boasts a large lawned garden and paved terrace with benches. Inside, the 21C has come calling: it's essentially one room divided by a fireplace, with modern tiled floor, pine furniture, bare tables and farmhouse chairs. The clean, uncluttered ambience is enhanced with bright bay windows, mustard walls and golden wood beams which create a sunny, open feel. Menus – which change monthly and feature blackboard specials at lunch and dinner – are keenly priced and modern with a classic French base.

Food serving times:
Wednesday-Sunday:
   12pm-2pm, 6.30pm-9pm
Closed 1st week in January
Prices:
Meals: 13.50 (set price lunch) and a la carte 19.50/27.00

Typical Dishes

Marinated feta cheese

Venison with bubble and squeak

Lime tart with crème fraîche

6mi Northeast of Huntingdon by B1514 off A141. Opposite the village church. Parking.

Elton

009 The Crown Inn

8 Duck St, Elton PE8 6RQ
Tel.: (01832) 280232

3-5 real ales offered - Crown Inn Glory in summer

Situated in a honey pot village overlooking the village green, the Crown could hardly nestle in a finer, more rewarding spot. This is a charming 17C thatched mellow stone inn: try and grab yourself a place at the small seven-tabled front terrace. It's an enviable place to sit and sup. Super keen owners add a friendly and cordial tone to the place: Mr Lamb is meticulous about his beers, and serves a wide range from all over the UK, not just Cambridgeshire. You can sample them in a beamed and thoroughly engaging bar boasting a feature log fire. Blackboard menus offer an interesting mix, underpinned by a strong seafood base. Printed menus at dinner highlight how seriously food is taken here – cooking is strong, tasty and fresh.

Food serving times:
Tuesday-Saturday:
12pm-2.30pm, 6.30pm-9pm
Sunday and Bank Holiday Monday:
12pm-3pm
Closed 25 December (except drinks 12pm-2pm); also 1-2 weeks January or February
Booking essential for dinner
Prices:
Meals: a la carte 18.00/32.00

Typical Dishes

Pan-seared king scallops

Roast rack of lamb, rosemary jus

Vanilla cheesecake

6mi Southwest of Peterborough by A1139, A605 and minor road North. Parking.

Fowlmere

010 The Chequers

High St, Fowlmere SG8 7SR

Tel.: (01763) 208369 - Fax: (01763) 208944
e-mail: info@thechequersfowlmere.co.uk - Website: www.thechequersfowlmere.co.uk

 Adnams, Bass, Archers, Nethergate

There's history at every turn in this fascinating 16C inn, built into the timbers and displayed on the walls: Spitfires and Mustangs are frozen in time in old photographs of Fowlmere airfield and even the colours of the sign comemmorate the pub's finest hour, mirroring the chequerboard insignia of the British and American fighter squadrons who made this their local during the Second World War. Sound, satisfying cooking on a traditional base includes Dover sole, a hearty smoked haddock, cheese and tomato bake and homemade date pudding; you can eat in the conservatory, overlooking the garden, in the beamed and galleried dining room or in the bar itself. After dinner, settle down by the fire and try one – or more – of the thirty malt whiskies: the long-standing owners will be happy to recommend a personal favourite.

Food serving times:
Monday-Saturday:
    12pm-2pm, 7pm-9.30pm
Sunday: 12pm-2pm,
        7pm-9pm
Closed 25 December, dinner
26 December and 1 January
Prices:
Meals: a la carte 21.50/33.50

8mi South of Cambridge by A10 and B1368. Parking.

Typical Dishes

Baked smoked haddock

Char grilled venison liver

Pan fried figs laced with amaretto

Great Staughton

011 The Tavern on the Green
12 The Green, Great Staughton PE19 5DG
Tel.: (01480) 860336
e-mail: thetavernonthegreen@btinternet.com - Website: www.thetavernonthegreen@btinternet.com

     VISA AE MC

> *Green King IPA, Village Bike, Fuller's London Pride, Abbot Ale, Old Speckled Hen, Summer Lightening*

A note on the bottom of the menu says: "Taxis are very scarce around here – book in advance." They could just as easily be offering advice to prospective diners, because the Tavern on the Green's reputation is spreading fast. Close to Grafham Water, it's a pleasant pub, the hub of a proudly rural village. Any claims to traditionality, though, disappear once inside: the open interior has a distinctively modern feel, enhanced by comfy leather tub chairs and effusive arrangements of lilies. There are three main dining areas with wood tables and a warm, relaxing ambience. Chilled meat is on display: you can buy steak dishes by 25 gram weight, and there's a wide selection. If your tastes differ, very good value daily set menus are also on offer, supplemented by blackboard specials. The seasonal, modern dishes are underscored by a host of favourites.

Food serving times:
Monday-Sunday:
12pm-2pm, 6.30pm-9.30pm
Closed dinner 25 December and 1-2 January
Prices:
Meals: 15.00/19.45 (set price lunch/dinner certain days only) and a la carte 20.00/26.00

Typical Dishes
Deep fried Brie de Meaux
Slow roast scrag of lamb
Calvados soaked spotted dick

On A45 northwest of St Neots. Parking.

Hemingford Grey

012 The Cock

47 High St, Hemingford Grey PE28 9BJ

Tel.: (01480) 463609 - Fax: (01480) 461747
e-mail: cock@cambscuisine.com - Website: www.cambscuisine.com

🍷 🥢 *VISA* 💳

Wolf Brewery Golden Jackal, Woodfordes Wherry, Earl Soham Victoria Bitter, Nethergate Monks Habit

This lovely 17C village pub has been stripped back to basics by its owners, and given a new lease of life in the process. Locals flock to the pubby part, which revels in its original simplicity. A separate room, it specialises in real ale, and has won several accolades in this department. Don't expect food at the bar: if you're here to satisfy an appetite rather than slake your thirst, step into the main dining area, spacious and soft-toned with wooden floors and comfy, traditional tables and chairs. A wood burning stove crackles, and saleable oil paintings might tempt you into a purchase. The menu is individual and offers a good choice of British and European dishes, on top of a well-priced light lunch selection. Specialities are fresh fish blackboard specials, and the hallmark sausage board.

Food serving times:
Monday-Friday:
  12pm-2.30pm, 6.30pm-9pm
Saturday-Sunday:
  12pm-2.30pm,
  6.30pm-9.30pm

Prices:
Meals: 12.95 (set price lunch) and a la carte 19.85/29.40

Typical Dishes

Duck parcel

Rare breed loin of lamb, pea & mint blini

Fig and Muscat crème brûlée

5mi South East of Huntingdon by A1198 off A14. Parking. ➤

Horningsea

013 Crown and Punchbowl 🛏

High St, Horningsea CB5 9JG

Tel.: (01223) 860643 - Fax: (01223) 441814
e-mail: crown@cambscuisine.com - Website: www.cambscuisine.com

 VISA **AE** **MC**

🍺 | *City of Cambridge ales*

When is a pub not a pub? Answer: when it comes in the guise of the Crown & Punchbowl. This marriage of two buildings, one 17C, the other 19C, looks and feels like a pub, but doesn't actually have a bar, so anyone revisiting from 200 years ago would wonder what had happened to the village inn. It's certainly been given a modern makeover: wooden floors, farmhouse tables and chairs, rattan seats, neutral décor, contemporary lighting. Lovely old beams will take you back, though. Menus are a mixture of traditional, modern and international; favourite features include the sausage mix and match board and fresh fish blackboard. Clean, modern bedrooms keep the modish feel intact.

Food serving times:
Monday-Thursday:
  12pm-2.30pm, 6.30pm-9pm
Friday-Saturday:
  12pm-2.30pm,
  6.30pm-9.30pm
Sunday: 12pm-3pm
Closed 26-28 December
Prices:
Meals: a la carte 20.00/30.00
🛏 **5 rooms :** 69.95/89.95

Typical Dishes
Smoked salmon salad
Breast of pigeon with broad bean, bacon and pea
British and Continental cheeses

4mi Northeast of Cambridge by A1303 and B1047 on Horningsea rd. Parking.

Keyston

014 The Pheasant

Village Loop Road, Keyston PE28 0RE

Tel.: (01832) 710241 - Fax: (01832) 710340
e-mail: thepheasant@cyberware.co.uk - Website: www.huntsbridge.co.uk

Adnams Best and 2 guest ales

A tip for drivers tearing along the A14 on the Cambridgeshire and Northamptonshire borders: turn off at Keyston and sample a taste of this gloriously thatched inn. A dining pub writ large, The Pheasant consistently serves a range of good value, eclectic dishes in three agreeable dining areas. Regulars mingle in the airy, timbered bar with its open fire, muskets on the wall and well-spaced wooden tables, but if the going gets too busy there, then the rear section – decorated with a mix of pictures and prints - is just as pleasant a place to eat. Interesting, modern à la carte menus with international influences are never less than accomplished and offer plenty of balanced flavour. Helpful, efficient service is a given wherever you decide to eat.

Food serving times:
Monday-Sunday:
12pm-2pm, 6.30pm-9.30pm
Closed dinner Sunday
October-April
(booking essential)
Prices:
Meals: a la carte 24.00/29.00

Typical Dishes

Brandade with poached egg

Braised ox cheek with Dauphinoise and greens

Crème brûlée

3.5mi Southeast of Thrapston by A14 on B663. Parking.

Little Wilbraham

015 The Hole in the Wall

2 High St, Little Wilbraham CB1 5JY

Tel.: (01223) 812282

 Courage Best and 3 changing guest ales - City of Cambridge, Hobsons Choice, Golden Newt Elgoods Brewery, Oakham Ales JHB

The people who made Herefordshire's Lough Pool Inn such a welcoming destination have turned their attention to this pretty little extended cottage on a country road at the edge of a pretty village outside Cambridge. The pub's nomenclature is of pleasing origin: when the ale house was first built in the 15th century, the local farm workers would pass their empty jugs through a hole in the wall on their way to work. These were filled during the day and left in the hole for the workers to collect on their way home. The firmly traditional timbered qualities of 'The Hole' have rightly been left alone, with modernisation principally taking place where many might say is most important: in the kitchen. There's a small bar, two dining rooms in rustic style with exposed beams and real fires, and, as at Lough Pool, an interesting and well-priced modern menu.

Food serving times:
Tuesdays-Saturdays:
12pm-2pm, 7pm-9pm
Sunday and Bank Holiday Monday:
12pm-2pm
Closed 25 December, dinner 26 December and 2 weeks in January
Prices:
Meals: a la carte 20.00/30.00

Typical Dishes

Smoked mackerel

Dingley Dell bacon collar

Warm treacle tart

5mi East of Cambridge by A1303 and minor road South. Parking.

Madingley

016 The Three Horseshoes

High St, Madingley CB3 8AB

Tel.: (01954) 210221 - Fax: (01954) 212043
e-mail: 3hs@btconnect.com - Website: www.huntsbridge.com

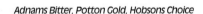

Adnams Bitter, Potton Gold, Hobsons Choice

This picture-perfect thatched pub is an ideal bolt-hole for visitors slightly overwhelmed by tourist numbers in Cambridge. It's located in a village just to the west of the city, and presents an elegant, centuries-old exterior to the world: it used to be the local smithy. The interior, though, comes right up to date. There's a stylish, airy ambience, attributable in part to the pale floorboards, modern log fire and sage green walls, though the alert service has something to do with it too. Eat in the bar - which does a well-priced, short grill menu - or in the smartly set conservatory at the back. It has painted chairs and stylish cloth-clad tables, and menus are innovative, full of interesting combinations with an Italian bias.

Food serving times:
Monday-Saturday:
12pm-2pm, 6.30pm-9.30pm
Sunday: 12pm-2pm,
6.30pm-8.30pm
Closed 1-2 January
Prices:
Meals: a la carte 20.00/40.00

Typical Dishes

Portland crab salad

Char grilled fillet of Aberdeen beef

Caramelised lemon tart

4.5mi West of Cambridge by A1303.
Parking.

Spaldwick

017 George Inn

5 High St, Spaldwick PE28 0TD

Tel.: (01480) 890293 - Fax: (01480) 896847

Fuller's London Pride, Greene King IPA, Adnams Broadside

This early 16C inn is defined on the exterior by its characterful, crooked appearance, but inside refurbishment has been going on apace, and the renovated airy interior now has a bold, clean and uncluttered contemporary look. Lilac and aubergine walls blend with exposed black beams, tiled and wood floors, scrubbed wood tables, and leather armchairs around a lovely fireplace, with the inn's history framed above. The restaurant – also spacious – blends old ceiling timbers with pink hued leather banquettes and rich oil paintings: a stylish statement indeed. Menus here are modern European with solid British classics. You can also take your pick from the blackboard.

Food serving times:
Monday-Sunday:
    12pm-2.30pm, 6pm-9.30pm
Closed dinner 25-26 December and 1 January

Prices:
Meals: 9.95 (set price 2 course lunch) and a la carte 20.00/ 32.00

Typical Dishes

Butternut squash ravioli

Pan roast woodpigeon

Warm Bakewell tart

7.5mi West of Huntingdon by A141 off A14. Parking.

Stilton

018 Village Bar (at Bell Inn) 🛏

Great North Rd, Stilton PE7 3RA

Tel.: (01733) 241066 - Fax: (01733) 245173
e-mail: reception@thebellstilton.co.uk - Website: www.thebellstilton.co.uk

Greene King IPA and Abbot Ale, Fuller's London Pride, Oakham Ales - JHB and guest beers

You know you're in for a cheery experience the moment you come upon this part 16C inn with garden: its swinging red bell pub sign almost beckons you in off the street. The separate Village Bar is the heart and soul of the place, charmingly rustic in its appeal: rough stone walls, flag flooring, large wooden tables with benches and a mix of chairs. Local memorabilia all adds to the characterful mix. It shares its menu with the adjoining Courtyard bar. Expect robust cooking, international influences embellishing a firm traditional base. Hearty portions are guaranteed, and Stilton cheese turns up in soups, dumplings, quiche and dressings. Bedrooms are in the Bell Inn proper: some are deluxe, all are individually styled and well kept.

Food serving times:
Monday-Friday:
12pm-2pm, 6.30pm-9.30pm,
Saturday: 6.30pm-9.30pm,
Sunday: 7-9pm

Closed 25-26 December

Prices:
Meals: 25.95 and a la carte 17.50/24.95
🛏 **22 rooms :** 72.50/99.50

In centre of village. Parking. ➤

Typical Dishes

Stilton and leek soup

Wild boar sausages on parsley mash

Quenby Hall Stilton

Sutton Gault

019 The Anchor Inn

Sutton Gault CB6 2BD

Tel.: (01353) 778537 - Fax: (01353) 776180

e-mail: anchorinn@popmail.bta.com - Website: www.anchorsuttongault.co.uk

City of Cambridge Hobson's Choice, Boathouse Bitter

Standing by the bridge over the New Bedford River, this lovely, ever-popular inn can claim to be as old as the Levels landscape itself: the story goes that it was built to house Vermuyden's navvies, who ditched and drained the Cambridgeshire marshes back in the 1650s. Today, gas lamps and open fires light several charming little rooms, and a strong local reputation rests on the tasty cooking. Blackboard specials have a particularly seasonal flavour and the Modern British repertoire finds room for some ambitious Mediterranean touches: typical dishes include Cromer crab, halibut with spinach and artichoke risotto, and sticky toffee pudding with rum and raisin ice cream. Conscientious and personable staff certainly know their regulars, but see to it that everyone is well looked-after.

Food serving times:
Monday-Sunday:
    12pm-2pm, 7pm-9pm
Closed 26 December
(fixed price lunch Sunday only)
Prices:
Meals: a la carte 15.00/35.00
4 rooms : 55.00/150.00

Typical Dishes

Grilled dates wrapped in bacon

Loin of venison, cassis jus

Cinnamon pannacotta

Off B1381; follow signs to Sutton Gault from Sutton village. Pub is beside the New Bedford River. Parking.

Blackmore

020 Leather Bottle

The Green, Blackmore CM4 0RL

Tel.: (01277) 823538

e-mail: leatherbottle@tiscali.co.uk - Website: www.theleatherbottle.net

Adnams, Broadside, Timothy Taylor Landlord, Crouch Vale Brewers Gold Extra

A pleasant, well-run place and something of a family enterprise, the Leather Bottle has that confidence-inspiring neighbourhood feel to it: the guest beer mats decorating the walls of the little public bar will be invitation enough to any real ale converts and, in these welcoming surroundings, even sceptics might be tempted to try a half. Diners arriving in good time can choose between a table in the simply styled conservatory overlooking the garden or near the wood burner in the front bar, where a frequently changing menu blends traditional British and eclectic Mediterranean styles, with satisfying results: simple snacks and a handful of daily specials lend a touch of variety. Smooth but unpretentious service.

Food serving times:
Monday-Saturday:
12pm-2pm, 7pm-9pm
Sunday: 12pm-4pm
Prices:
Meals: 8.95 (2 course lunch) and a la carte 17.50/30.00

Typical Dishes

Chicken and roasted pepper terrine

Roast duck breast, marmalade sauce

Bread and butter pudding

2.75mi Southeast of High Ongar by A414. Parking in front of the pub.

Chelmsford

021 The Alma

37 Arbour Lane, Chelmsford CM1 7RG

Tel.: (01245) 256783 - Fax: (01245) 256793

e-mail: the_alma@hotmail.com - Website: www.thealma.biz

 ♈ ✂ *VISA* Ⓜ️

Greene King IPA, Spitfire, Crouchvale, Brewers Gold, Nethergate Suffolk County - usually 3 of these and others

Go into the suburbs of Chelmsford to find this very popular place. You can't miss it – it has an immaculately yellow painted façade, and you get to the entrance via a terrace of crazy paving. Its brightly lit windows are a welcoming sight in the dark. If you're here to drink, sit on a stool at the informal front bar; diners in this section have the benefit of high-backed black leather chairs. Everyone can make use of a flat-screen TV on the wall. The rear of The Alma, meanwhile, becomes something else again: a very smart formal restaurant, where the décor is stylish to a tee. Even the loos boast piped episodes of TV comedy programmes. Menus offer an accomplished a la carte of modern dishes on a classic base (restaurant and bar) or popular pubby favourites (bar only). Check them out for regular theme and quiz nights.

Food serving times:

Monday-Sunday:
12pm-2.30pm, 6pm-9.30pm

Closed dinner 25 December, 26 December

Prices:

Meals: 14.95/18.50 (set price lunch/dinner) and a la carte 16.95/24.95

Typical Dishes

Grilled sardines

Duck breast, parsnip tart, Port glazed onions

Tangy lemon tart

East of town centre; off northside of Springfield Road (A1099). Parking.

Clavering

022 The Cricketers

Clavering CB11 4QT

Tel.: (01799) 550442 - Fax: (01799) 550882
e-mail: cricketers@lineone.net - Website: www.thecricketers.co.uk

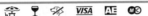

Adnams Broadside, Greene King IPA, Adnams

How many landlords could get Jamie Oliver to do the washing-up for pocket money? Mr and Mrs Oliver have been running this well-established local since The Naked Chef was in short trousers and not much has changed over the years: old beams, velour seats, a few newspaper cuttings and a lot of satisfied regulars. Gastro-pilgrims expecting an audioguide and photos of Jamie's dad inventing the Botham Burger will just have to like it for what it is, though that's easily done, and a nicely balanced menu is bound to put a smile on their faces – dishes range from dependable classics to a few recipes from the local hero. If you'd like to stay the night, the bedrooms in the pavilion are traditionally styled and those in the courtyard are more modern.

Food serving times:
Monday-Sunday:
    12pm-2pm, 7pm-10pm
Closed 25-26 December
Prices:
Meals: 26.00 (set price dinner) and a la carte 21.00/26.00
🛏 **14 rooms :** 70.00/100.00

On B1038; Southwest of Saffron Walden. Parking.

Typical Dishes

Mille feuille of blue cheese

Braised oxtail

Fresh fig and frangipane tart

Dedham

023 The Sun Inn 🛏

High St, Dedham CO7 6DF

Tel.: (01206) 323351

e-mail: info@thesuninndedham.com - Website: www.thesuninndedham.com

✗room **VISA** **MC**

Adnams Broadside, Brewers Gold, Earl Soham Victoria,
Grasshopper from Green Jack

Opposite its contemporary, the 15C village church, this handsome inn is an understated blend of tradition and up-to-date style; despite recent renovations, it still feels surprisingly unspoilt. Behind a suitably cheery sunshine-yellow façade, polished period oak and bright modern bouquets fill the spacious front and back rooms. Pick a table, then choose from an affordable, well-sourced menu which changes day by day, adopting an original approach to Italian, Spanish and Maghreb traditions; antipasti platters are good for sharing, but you may find it hard to part with a forkful of chicken tagine, Tuscan sausage on spicy black beans or light and juicy cannellini and sage risotto. Thoughtfully appointed modern rooms include one with a four-poster bed. Walks up to the River Stour and Constable's beloved Flatford start right outside the door.

Food serving times:
Monday-Saturday:
12pm-2.30pm,
6.30pm-9.30pm
Sunday: 12pm-2.30pm
Closed 25-27 December
Prices:
Meals: a la carte 15.00/25.00
🛏 **5 rooms :** 55.00/150.00

In the centre of the village opposite the church. Parking. **➤➤**

Typical Dishes

Ricotta bruschetta

Gloucester Old Spot pork
belly 'Arista', roast potatoes

Baked chocolate cake

High Ongar

024 The Wheatsheaf

King St, High Ongar CM5 9NS
Tel.: (01277) 822220 - Fax: (01277) 822441

 Greene King IPA and Leffe

Pretty and well-restored it may be, but The Wheatsheaf wouldn't be half the place it is without its hard-working staff; cordial, well-informed and eager to please, but in a very genuine, down-to-earth way. They serve four rooms – decorated with ornaments, bric-a-brac and floral fabrics – surrounding a central bar, but if you feel like an open-air summer lunch, ask them if there's a free table in the garden. A classically based British menu, notable for its well-combined but nicely defined flavours, varies from one day to the next, but past dishes have included a rich and fluffy goat's cheese and pecan soufflé, cod with a cheese and bacon crumble crust and rhubarb jelly and ice cream, with caramelised oranges for a zingy foil.

Food serving times:
Tuesday-Friday:
12pm-1.30pm, 6.45pm-8.45pm
Saturday: 12pm-1.30pm, 6.30pm-9.30pm
Sunday: 12pm-2.30pm
Closed from 26 December for 2 weeks, 1 week May and 1 week October
(booking essential)

Prices:
Meals: 8.95 (1 course lunch with wine Tuesday-Saturday) and a la carte 21.40/35.40

Typical Dishes

Onion and goat's cheese tart
Honey roast guinea fowl
Tangy lemon tart; rhubarb sorbet

2mi East by A414 on Blackmore rd. Parking.

Horndon-on-the-Hill

025 ## The Bell

High Rd, Horndon-on-the-Hill SS17 8LD

Tel.: (01375) 642463 - Fax: (01375) 361611
e-mail: info@bell-inn.co.uk - Website: www.bell-inn.co.uk

 VISA **AE** **MC**

Greene King IPA, Bass, Crouchvale Brewers Gold, Shepherd Neame Spitfire

Monkfish with veal and snail fritters, ox cheek ravioli with crab sauté and truffle froth: there's no doubting the high culinary ambition behind The Bell's daily-changing modern European menu. At its most complex, the cooking can seem a little overwrought, but there's no denying that the extra effort and attention raise simpler dishes – like Caesar salad or ribeye with parsley sauce – comfortably above pub average. The rather serious approach to good eating sits surprisingly well with the comfy, traditional décor and a long family history, and this characterful and well-established place is efficient, upbeat and busy, particularly at lunchtime.

Food serving times:
Monday-Sunday:
12pm-1.45pm,
6.30pm-9.45pm
Closed 25-26 December and Bank Holiday Mondays
Prices:
Meals: a la carte 21.00/27.95
5 rooms : 85.00
4.00

Typical Dishes

Saute scallops, pancetta

Rib eye of beef, garlic button mushrooms

Maple crème brûlée

3mi Northeast of Grays by A1013 off A13. Parking.

Mistley

026 The Mistley Thorn 🛏

High Street, Mistley CO11 1HE

Tel.: (01206) 392821 - Fax: (01206) 390122
e-mail: info@mistleythorn.com - Website: www.mistleythorn.com

  VISA **MC**

Greene King IPA, Adnams, Deuchar's

Though the exceptionally likeable young staff are only too happy for people to drop in for a drink – and maybe a plate of oysters – you're missing a real treat if you don't stay for dinner in the strikingly contemporary setting of this restyled Georgian pub. Well-composed menus of carefully presented cooking – with conspicuous depth and freshness of flavour – make a strong case for sourcing imaginatively, locally and organically, and include dishes like East Anglian asparagus, shrimp and herb mousse, tender lamb chops on a borlotti and artichoke stew, and a light Chez Panisse chocolate cake: the owner's cookery classes in "the Mistley Kitchen" reveal some, but not all of the secrets. Of the five bedrooms, two front-facing ones look out towards the Stour.

Food serving times:
Monday-Sunday:
　　　　　　12pm-2.30pm,
　　　　　　6.30pm-9.30pm

Prices:
Meals: 13.95 (set price lunch) and a la carte 16.00/23.00
🛏 **5 rooms :** 70.00/85.00

Typical Dishes

Calamari, lemon chilli, garlic & coriander

Tuna steak with ginger vinaigrette

Sherri's Mum's cheesecake

On B1352 not far from Mistley Towers. Parking.

Thundersley

027 The Woodmans Arms

Rayleigh Rd, Thundersley SS7 3TA

Tel.: (01268) 775 799 - Fax: (01268) 590 689

e-mail: thewoodman@hotmail.co.uk

Various guest ales - Bombardier, Theakstons Old Peculiar, Courage Best, Courage Directors, Old Speckled Hen and Young's Special

The Woodmans Arms is something of a desert oasis. In an area crying out for a stylish venue to eat and drink, it ticks a lot of the right boxes. Set on a busy main road – admittedly not the most attractive location – it's a Victorian stalwart that's been modernised to a good standard, with etched and frosted bay windows and smart, wood-furnished al fresco terraces. A snazzy little lounge bar with squashy brown leather sofas and low tables is reserved for drinkers. The remainder of the pub is given over to diners, and locals are making the most of the stylish modern surroundings: each area is separated by screens and highlighted by warm modern colours. There are some old photos of the pub as it was in its former days. Good-sized menus have an international flavour, with, typically, Thai and French dishes mingling alongside the British selection. These are supplemented by simpler daily specials, prepared to a good standard.

Food serving times:
Monday-Sunday:
12pm-9pm

Prices:
Meals: a la carte 17.00/25.00

Between Basildon and Southend-on-Sea off A127. Parking.

Typical Dishes

Fried whitebait

Pie of the day

Homemade puddings

Aldbury

028 The Valiant Trooper

Trooper Rd, Aldbury HP23 5RW

Tel.: (01442) 851203 · Fax: (01442) 851071
Website: www.valianttrooper.com

 Fullers London Pride, Tring Brewery, Oakham JHB and 2 changing guest beers

This is another traditional pub that benefits from its close proximity to the Ridgeway Path, so a healthy gathering of walkers can be guaranteed at most times. Even closer than the Ridgeway is the local duck pond; the pub's red, black and white bulk is a short walk away. The rustic bar boasts not only a real fire but also a welcoming wood burner; quarry tiled floors and scrubbed tables and chairs enhance the effect. Dining happens in an area at the back, which has seen a modicum of modernisation: the newer feel is accentuated by minimalist décor. Blackboard plaques announce traditional menus with some international influence, at a reasonable price. There's a good selection of lighter dishes, too: many a rambler has felt the benefit of one of the pub's hearty jacket potatoes.

Food serving times:
Tuesday-Saturday:
   12pm-2pm, 6.30pm-9.15pm
Sunday-Monday:
                  12pm-2pm
Closed 25 December
Prices:
Meals: a la carte 12.50/21.50

In centre of village. Parking.

Typical Dishes

Goat's cheese and sun dried tomato tart with pesto dressing

Natural smoked haddock thermidor

Chocolate and Brandy torte

Cottered

029 The Bull of Cottered

Cottered SG9 9QP
Tel.: (01763) 281243

Greene King IPA and Abbot Ale

In a pretty village blighted by a busy A road, you need somewhere to keep your spirits up. The Bull is that place: a well looked-after and neighbourhood pub in the old tradition that's genuinely eager to please and worth a visit for its understated friendliness and recently extended and refurbished to provide a more stylish and comfortable dining environment. If you're stopping by at lunchtime, expect anything from homemade burgers, ploughman's or jacket potatoes to full meals – good "beer-friendly" pub meals, in other words. Dinner, though, sees the addition of tasty and sustaining seasonal British dishes like steak, calves' livers with Roquefort cheese or rack of lamb, plus a couple of daily specials.

Food serving times:
Monday-Sunday:
  12pm-2pm, 6.30pm-9.30pm
Prices:
Meals: 18.00/30.00 (dinner - booking essential) and a la carte 17.00/30.50

On A507 in the centre of the village. Parking at the front of the pub.

Typical Dishes

Wild mushroom and Parmesan risotto

Loin of lamb, rosemary gravy

Selection of cheeses

Frithsden

030 The Alford Arms

Frithsden HP1 3DD

Tel.: (01442) 864480 - Fax: (01442) 876893
e-mail: inn@alfordarmsfrithsden.co.uk - Website: www.alfordarmsfrithsden.co.uk

 Brakspear, Flowers Original, Marstons Pedigree, Marlow Rebellion IPA

The quiet hamlet of Frithsden has a frequent tendency to see its population inflate like the hot-air balloons floating over its beautiful surrounding countryside. This is due in part to the popularity of this attractive brick pub, which is based quite close to the Ridgeway Path and regularly offers pints, sustenance and a comfy seat to walkers and saddle-sore cyclists. It's a small and stylish inn, and a good neighbourhood feel pervades the place with a confident, modern gastropub style much in evidence. There's a "free-for-all" drinking area at the front bar, but tables are reserved in the rear dining area. Well-priced menus change seasonally, and the fresh ingredients are evident in a tasty, varied dining pub selection.

Food serving times:
Monday-Saturday:
   12pm-2.30pm, 7pm-10pm
Sunday: 12pm-4pm,
             7pm-10pm

Prices:
Meals: a la carte 18.00/26.00

4.5mi Northwest of Hemel Hempstead by A4146. By the village green. Parking.

Typical Dishes

Smoked bacon, bubble & squeak

Pancetta wrapped cod fillet

Brioche chocolate doughnuts

Harpenden

031 The Fox

469 Luton Rd, Kinsbourne Green, Harpenden AL5 3QE

Tel.: (01582) 713817 - Fax: (01582) 765306
Website: www.thefoxharpenden.co.uk

Bass Ale, IPA Bitter

The Fox is another of Harpenden's recent influx of hostelries worthy of investigation. The reason for the excitement is an overhaul of recent vintage which has transformed it into a smart, comfy and characterful place to be, made up of various rooms that impress equally with rafters, country styling and interesting ornaments of wood and stone. Two rooms are given over to the drinking crowd; elsewhere, diners are catered for at heavy wood tables and chairs giving the whole place a robust, rustic ambience. An appealingly eclectic menu offers something for everyone with a mix of styles and cooking: the rotisserie is a very popular choice here. Brisk, attentive service from waiting staff used to being on their toes.

Food serving times:
Monday-Saturday:
    12pm-2.30pm, 6pm-10pm
Sunday :   12pm-7pm
Prices:
Meals: a la carte 24.00/30.00

Typical Dishes

Crispy duck salad

Pork belly with 'five spice', honey and soy sauce

Sticky toffee pudding

2.5mi northwest on A1081. Parking.

Harpenden

032 The Three Horseshoes

136 East Common, Harpenden AL5 1AW

Tel.: (01582) 713953 - Fax: (01582) 764090
e-mail: satta13easy@yahoo.com - Website: www.3horseshoes.net

   VISA **MC**

Greene King IPA, Fuller's London Pride

Locals will know where to find the Three Horseshoes, but anyone from outside the Harpenden postcode may have to ask for directions to the wooded environs of East Common. This smart-looking pub has had a stylish and tasteful conversion, but there are reminders that it dates back 400 years; for instance, a large inglenook dominates the small sofa furnished bar dedicated for drinkers. Not that too many customers hang around this area for long – after making the effort to get here, most punters have built up a decent hunger. The lovely rustic interior is certainly conducive to good dining, and the extensive a la carte menu is more restaurant than pub oriented; service is renowned for being pacy and attentive. The versatile range of modern European dishes benefit from a herb garden, which is handily placed right outside the kitchen.

Food serving times:
Monday-Saturday:
  12pm-2.30pm, 6pm-9.30pm
Sunday: 12pm-2.30pm
Prices:
Meals: a la carte 23.65/31.70

Typical Dishes

Wild mushroom on toasted brioche

Roast partridge, juniper jus

Apple and blackberry crumble

Southeast 1.75mi by A1081 and Cross Lane, turning right at crossroads. Parking.

Harpenden

033 The White Horse

Hatching Green, Harpenden AL5 2JP
Tel.: (01582) 713428 - Fax: (01582) 460148
e-mail: info@atouchofnovelli.com - Website: www.atouchofnovelli.com

 VISA AE M©

 Fuller's London Pride, Brock Bitter

P art owned by TV's very own Jean Christophe Novelli, The White Horse has some pretty ambitious foody aspirations on show. Set in an immaculately whitewashed pub with 17C origins, the past soon gives way to a sleek modernity, typified by modern art and brash 21C décor. You can have a drink in the pub part of the building, where there's a wood-topped bar and some original beams, but most people come here for the cuisine, served in the large dining room with its A-framed beamed ceiling and open kitchen. Jean Christophe has a major input on the menus; these are most definitely not of the traditional type. In fact, the original dishes are quite complicated and ambitious, with French influences overlaying the well-used local ingredients. Friendly, organised service completes the picture. This is a very busy destination pub: remember to book well in advance.

Food serving times:
Monday-Sunday:
12pm-3pm, 6pm-10pm
Closed 24-25 December
Prices:
Meals: a la carte 20.00/30.00

Typical Dishes

Escabeche of mackerel with scallop brochette

John Dory, paprika galette

Honeycomb parfait

1mi southwest by A1081 on B487. Parking.

Hertford

034 The Hillside

45 Port Hill, Bengeo, Hertford SG14 3EP

Tel.: (01992) 554556 - Fax: (01992) 583709
e-mail: justin624@hotmail.com - Website: www.thehillside.co.uk

No real ales offered

Put on the brakes as you head out of Hertford and pay a visit to this cosy, intimate, recently refurbished 17C pub, nestling contentedly – as its name suggests – on a hillside. The small beamed bar with comfy leather sofa is a charming haven for drinkers; for diners, there's a sunny, surprisingly airy restaurant with leather banquettes and bare tables decorated with bright flowers. Paintings – for sale – brighten the walls. Contemplate what takes your fancy while waiting for chef's cheery wife to serve a modern menu of brasserie dishes with pronounced global reach alongside more traditional staples. There's also an interesting little organic deli and farm shop next door.

Food serving times:
Monday-Saturday:
    12pm-2.30pm,
    6.30pm-9.30pm
Sunday: 12pm-2.30pm
Prices:
Meals: a la carte 30.00/45.00

Typical Dishes

Smoked eel, horseradish

Rack of veal with veal kidneys

Pot au chocolat with biscotti

North 0.25mi on B158. Parking.

Hunsdon

035 Fox and Hounds

2 High St, Hunsdon SG12 8NH

Tel.: (01279) 843999 - Fax: (01279) 841092

e-mail: info@foxandhounds-hunsdon.co.uk - Website: www.foxandhounds-hunsdon.co.uk

 Adnams Bitter and Broadside, Timothy Taylor Landlord, Tring Brewery Beers, Red Squirrel guests

300 years old in parts, this is a village pub with a great rural ambience not too many miles from the teeming streets of north London. Outside is a spacious garden and paved patio for summer solipsism. Inside, it's basically one long room with a beamed bar counter in the centre, a crackling log fire with sofa seating at one end and a cosy dining area at the other. A smart dining room sits to the rear. Books, guides and magazines are dotted around too. The earnestly rustic character isn't above its cheeky side: loos are accessed through false bookcases. There's nothing fake about the food. Accomplished, classically based, robust dishes encompass a global range: the well-priced two course early evening set menus are worth investigating.

Food serving times:
Tuesday-Saturday:
12pm-3pm, 6pm-10pm,
Sunday: 12pm-3pm

Closed 26 December, 1 January, 2 weeks January-February

Prices:
Meals: 14.50/17.50 (3 course Sunday lunch £21.50) and a la carte 21.50/35.00

Typical Dishes

Seared scallops, blood orange beurre blanc

Côte de boeuf

Poached champagne rhubarb

5mi East of Ware by B1004 to Widford and B180 South. Parking.

Reed

036 The Cabinet at Reed

High St, Reed SG8 8AH

Tel.: (01763) 848366 - Fax: (01763) 849407
e-mail: thecabinet@btinternet.com - Website: www.thecabinetatreed.co.uk

🍷 🍇 ⇆ **VISA** ⓂⒸ

Greene King IPA, Old Speckled Hen and a guest beer

This pretty 16C clapboard inn suits Reed to perfection, but since its refurbishment it's more than just a village pub in the traditional sense. So while the bar proper still has all the charm of a rustic local, with a little snug to one side, the real focal point is the quietly chic, contemporary dining room beyond, with elegant tables featuring outsize glassware – the red wine glasses actually hold a whole bottle, although that's not really the idea. The interesting, upmarket Modern British menu would not look out of place in a West End restaurant.

Food serving times:
Monday-Saturday:
12.30pm-2.30pm,
7pm-9.30pm

Prices:
Meals: 18.50/25.50 (set price lunch/dinner) and a la carte 22.00/41.00

Typical Dishes

Cornish crab tian and avocado

Rack of lamb with colcannon mash

Apple tarte Tatin

3mi South of Royston, just off the A10 London to Cambridge road. Parking.

Ware

037 Jacoby's

Churchgate House, 15 West St, Ware SG12 9EE

Tel.: (01920) 469181 - Fax: (01920) 469182
e-mail: info@jacobys.co.uk - Website: www.jacobys.co.uk

VISA AE M©

 No real ales offered

Carefully renovated into a modern bar and restaurant, this Grade II listed timber framed house, dating back to the late 15C, boasts tremendous history and character: in its time, it's been an inn, a bakery and maltings and even a motorcycle repair shop. It stands opposite St Mary's church; in the summer, you'll want to look for a place on the pleasant pavement terrace which faces the square. The stylish front bar has leather armchairs and sets a buzzy tone for the rest of the place. Dining is on two levels: go upstairs for the more intimate tables. Menus change frequently, providing well-executed, mix and match options: good British classics with strong Mediterranean influences alongside dishes with a wider global reach. Service is prompt, young and keen; booking's advisable at weekends.

Food serving times:
Tuesday-Sunday:
  12am-3pm, 6pm-11pm
Prices:
Meals: 7.95 (2 course lunch) and a la carte 25.00/40.00

Typical Dishes

Foie gras and chicken liver parfait

Roast half Barbary duck

White chocolate crème brûlée

In the town centre, just off the High St. Public car park (Library) opposite.

Willian

038 The Fox

Willian SG6 2AE

Tel.: (01462) 480233 - Fax: (01462) 676966
e-mail: restaurant@foxatwillian.co.uk - Website: www.foxatwillian.co.uk

Adnams Bitter, Fuller's London Pride, Woodeforde's Wherry and guest ales - St Peter's Golden Ale, Wye Valley The Stick

Pretty Willian had two of the three boxes ticked: a church to the rear and a pond to the front. To complete the 'archetypal English village' equation, its pub – set between the two – was gutted in 2004 and then refurbished with an extension to the rear, a spacious restaurant whose attractive pitched ceiling windows gave it the feel of a conservatory. With third tick firmly in place, locals now swarm to the rejuvenated Fox to sample its delights. Summer dining is enhanced by a pretty little terrace which can be completely covered with an extendable awning. The airy modern bar area comes complete with its own substantial dedicated menu – and a conspicuous plasma TV to share it with, should the feeling take you. For more serious diners, there's an interestingly extensive restaurant menu with an emphasis on fish and shellfish imported from Norfolk.

Food serving times:
Monday-Saturday:
  12pm-2pm, 6.45pm-9.15pm
Sunday: 12pm-2pm
Prices:
Meals: a la carte 25.00/36.00

Village signposted off A1 (m), junction 9. Parking.

Typical Dishes

Goat's cheese tempura

Mustard brushed lemon sole

Lemon thyme crème brûlée

Bawburgh

039 Kings Head

Harts Lane, Bawburgh NR9 3LS

Tel.: (01603) 744977 - Fax: (01603) 744990
e-mail: anton@kingshead-bawburgh.co.uk - Website: www.kingshead-bawburgh.co.uk

Woodfordes Wherry, Adnams and guest beers - Augustinian, Old Speckled Hen

Only a short drive out of Norwich but already well into the countryside, this traditional place has plumped for Edward VII as its royal figurehead, the under-represented pub monarch perhaps getting the nod here for his generous appetite and his Sandringham connections. The old bon vivant would be baffled by the fruit machines, but drawn instinctively to the casual but comfortable dining room leading off from one side of the main bar. The daily changing menu blends modern European with traditional dishes: an equal mix of traditional and modern recipes might offer anything from bangers and burgers to potted crab, chicken salsa verde with pasta and peppers or maple and pecan cheesecake. Once the woodburning stove is fired up on winter afternoons, it's also pleasant enough for a quiet pint.

Food serving times:
Tuesday-Saturday:
    12pm-2pm, 7pm-9.15pm
Sunday: 12pm-2.30pm
Monday: 12pm-2pm
Closed 25 December, dinner 26 December,
dinner 1 January
Prices:
Meals: a la carte 23.50/33.00

5mi Northwest of Norwich by B1108. Parking.

Typical Dishes

Thai fish cakes

Plaice with brown shrimps, gremolata

Baked ginger pudding

Blakeney

040 **White Horse**

4 High St, Blakeney NR25 7AL

Tel.: (01263) 740574 - Fax: (01263) 741339

e-mail: enquiries@blakeneywhitehorse.co.uk - Website: www.blakeneywhitehorse.co.uk

  ⊬rest **VISA**

Adnams, Woodfordes Wherry, Greene King IPA, Abbott Ale

Estuary, saltings, quayside, and a gaggle of tourists from the Capital make up much of the character of 21C Blakeney. It's further defined by this popular part-17C pub of flint-and-brick which draws in the locals and weekenders a-plenty. They gather round a split-level bar and sup good real ale at wooden tables, chairs and banquettes – an appealing conservatory provides a smart alternative. Go to the rear, to the former stables, to eat: the food is proudly local in nature and naturally enough, seafood is the staple here. For those not climbing back into their 4X4s, there's the option of small, cosy bedrooms.

Food serving times:
Monday-Sunday:
  12pm-2.15pm, 7pm-9pm
Prices:
Meals: a la carte 15.00/25.00
⊨ **9 rooms :** 40.00/130.00

Typical Dishes

Bruschetta of smoked salmon

Gressingham duck with Asian coleslaw

Chocolate marquise

Off A149 following signs for the Quay, beside the church. Parking.

Burnham Market

041 The Hoste Arms ⇤

The Green, Burnham Market PE31 8HD
Tel.: (01328) 738777
e-mail: reception@hostearms.co.uk - Website: www.hostearms.co.uk

Woodfordes Wherry, Norfolk Nog, Greene King, Abbott Ale, Adnams Best

The popularity of this bright yellow coaching inn has almost come to define the charming north Norfolk town of Burnham Market: set on the picturesque Green, its 17C quirks have been fully restored; in startling contrast, there's an intriguing wing decorated in Zulu style, and a new Moroccan garden terrace. The bar is an invariably bustling place, and the sound of champagne corks popping is not uncommon; you'll find similar levels of volume and bonhomie in the restaurant. The staff respond well to being busy, and are invariably attentive and friendly, with good attention to detail. Fairly-priced menus offer a mix of global styles, with much local produce in evidence. There's an excellent wine selection featuring 180 bins.

Food serving times:
Monday-Sunday:
    12pm-2pm, 7pm-9pm
(booking essential)
Prices:
Meals: a la carte 23.00/42.00
⇤ **36 rooms :** 88.00/260.00

Typical Dishes

Smoked Gressingham duck salad

Roast cod, ham hock ravioli

Dark chocolate fondant

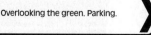

Overlooking the green. Parking.

Burnham Thorpe

042 The Lord Nelson

Walsingham Rd, Burnham Thorpe PE31 8HL

Tel.: (01328) 738241 - Fax: (01328) 738241
e-mail: enquiries@nelsonslocal.co.uk - Website: www.nelsonslocal.co.uk

Greene King IPA, Abbot, Woodfordes Wherry, Nelsons Revenge, Fox Brewery Nelson's Blood Bitter (all direct from the cask)

Named in honour of Burnham Thorpe's most illustrious son, and perhaps Britain's first modern celebrity, this 17C inn honours the Victor of the Nile with just enough in the way of pictures and memorabilia: too much swashbuckling nauticalia would clutter up this shipshape little place. Three low-ceilinged parlours, one with a Battle of Trafalgar mural, lead off from a firelit taproom with a tiny cubby-hole of a bar: the landlord opens up the timbered barn, with chunky pine tables and benches, if the pub itself starts to feel overcrowded. Simple, fresh, good-value dishes, both classic and modern, could include grilled red mullet with tapenade or chicken with a red wine and parsley sauce.

Food serving times:
Monday-Saturday:
  12pm-2.30pm, 7pm-9.30pm
Sunday: 12pm-2.30pm
Closed Monday October-June except Bank Holidays, school holidays and half term holidays

Prices:
Meals: a la carte 15.00/28.30

Typical Dishes

Seared scallops, pineapple salsa

Tornedos of venison, truffle sauce

Chocolate fondant

2mi South of Burnham Market by B1355. Parking.

Cley-next-the-Sea

043 The George

High St, Cley-next-the-Sea NR25 7BY

Tel.: (01263) 740652 - Fax: (01263) 741275
e-mail: thegeorge@cleynextthesea.com - Website: www.thegeorgehotelcley.com

Greene King IPA, Abbot, Yetmans (Holt)

There are two imposing buildings in Cley: the famous windmill which can be viewed from miles around, and the rather grand-looking George, its red-brick Victorian/Edwardian façade providing a solid security to this charming little coastal village. Etched frosted windows and plenty of hanging baskets add lustre to the ornate exterior. Inside, there's an individual style to the place. Three rooms are divided into a bar and two dining areas, decorated in warm coloured wallpapers, and enhanced by wood-burning stoves. A large book on a brass pulpit records bird sightings from the nearby bar: whether these are influenced by pints consumed, you decide! Weighty menus make great use of local mussels and oysters, while the village smokehouse supplies other seafood. Rustic modern British cooking is tasty and accomplished. Bedrooms come in various configurations: the superior version, on the top floor, has finer views over the marshes.

Food serving times:
Monday-Sunday:
    12pm-2pm, 6.30pm-9pm
Prices:
Meals: a la carte 20.50/27.00
12 rooms : 70.00/140.00

1.5mi east of Blakeney on A149. Parking.

Typical Dishes

Local moules marinière
Grilled fish of the day
Orange bread and butter pudding

Coltishall

044 **King's Head** 🛏

26 Wroxham Rd, Coltishall NR12 7EA

Tel.: (01603) 737426

🍷 🍴 *VISA* AE MC

Adnams Best, Courage Best, Marstons Pedigree

One of the nicest things about this rather ordinary looking pub in deepest Norfolk is its attractive setting – diners with window tables can look out onto the meandering River Bure. Elsewhere within, a relaxed air pervades. Open fires crackle beneath solid timbers and pieces of fishing and boating memorabilia hang from the ceiling, lending a particularly atmospheric air at night: meals can be ordered in the bar as well as the dining room. Seafood specialities take pride of place with the Norfolk catch freshly served each day or, as an alternative to fish, chef's special meat dishes.

Food serving times:
Monday-Sunday:
12pm-2pm, 7pm-9pm
Closed 26 December
and 1 January
Prices:
Meals: 9.95 and a la carte
22.50/30.50
🛏 **4 rooms :** 27.00/59.00

Typical Dishes

Pan fried herring roes

Sea bass with scallops

Hot chocolate fondant

7mi North of Norwich on B1150. Parking. ⟩

Erpingham

045 **The Saracen's Head**

Wolterton, Erpingham NR11 7LX
Tel.: (01263) 768909 - Fax: (01263) 768993
Website: www.saracenshead-norfolk.co.uk

 ←room *VISA* AE M●

Adnams Best Bitter, Woodfordes Wherry

Charmingly faded and quirky by turns, this individualistic 19C former coaching inn is in the middle of nowhere and loses nothing by its isolation. It contains an impressive walled garden and courtyard set back from two busy, bustling bar rooms and a boldly red-painted parlour filled with odd pictures, bric-a-brac and little wooden tables and chairs with plastic tablecloths. Traditional dishes come dressed in local ingredients such as mussels from Morston and crab from Cromer: unpretentious, country dishes that draw in regular shoals of satisfied customers from miles around. Bright, modest bedrooms nevertheless share the owner's mild and endearing eccentricity.

Food serving times:
Monday-Sunday:
12.30pm-2pm, 7.15pm-9pm
Closed 25 December and dinner 26 December
Prices:
Meals: a la carte 20.00/28.50
🛏 **6 rooms :** 50.00/85.00

Typical Dishes

Morston mussels (in season)

Medallions of venison

Brown bread and butter pudding

West 1.5mi on Wolterton Hall rd. Parking.

Itteringham

046 Walpole Arms

The Common, Itteringham NR11 7AR
Tel.: (01263) 587258 - Fax: (01263) 587074
e-mail: goodfood@thewalpolearms.co.uk - Website: www.thewalpolearms.co.uk

🏠 🍷 *VISA* ⓂⒸ

 Adnams Bitter, Broadside, Woodfordes Wherry, Walpole Ale

Blickling Hall sets an awesome architectural benchmark in this part of Norfolk; in its more modest way, the nearby part-18C Walpole Arms reaches out in empathy. It's hugely characterful and inviting, with a warm ambiance, roaring fires, exposed brick walls and heavy timbers marking out the bar as a great place for modern dining. New, varied menus are devised daily; the accomplished kitchen interweaves Italian and Spanish ideas. Extensive use is made of local and seasonal ingredients; the owners heartily take on board recommendations from their fishmonger and game supplier. There's a more formal restaurant beyond the bar, but no let-up on the character front, with linen-clad tables and exposed roof trusses lending it an appealing air.

Food serving times:
Monday-Saturday:
12pm-2pm, 7pm-9pm
Sunday: 12pm-2pm
Closed 25 December
Prices:
Meals: a la carte 21.50/25.00

Typical Dishes

Mediterranean fish soup

Warm salad of pigeon

Pear, prune and frangipane tart

5mi Northwest of Aylsham by B1354. Signed The Common. Parking.

Norwich

047 1 Up at the Mad Moose Arms

2 Warwick St, Norwich NR2 3LD

Tel.: (01603) 627687
e-mail: madmoose@animalinns.co.uk

 Greene King IPA, Adnams Broadside, Wolf Brewery Golden Jackal, Mad Moose Ale

Just eccentric enough to stand out from the suburban herd, this Victorian tavern wears its bright, cheerful modern refit surprisingly well, particularly in the simply styled first-floor dining room, which feels a little cut off, for better or worse, from the young, full-volume crowd in the bar downstairs. Flavourful modern cooking at a fair price takes in dishes like seared scallops with chilli jam, roast duck in cinnamon jus, served on spring greens, and banana tart – if you've ever eaten at the Wildebeest Arms across the city, you'll have an idea of what to expect. The chatty service from a smart, black-shirted team is well organised and evenly paced.

Food serving times:
Monday-Saturday:
7-10pm, Sunday: 12pm-3pm,
Closed 25 December
Bar meals only Saturday lunch and Sunday dinner
Prices:
Meals: 18.50 (Dinner) and a la carte 20.00/28.00

In residential area West of city centre. Designated parking bays lunchtime, street parking in the evening.

Typical Dishes

Smoked duck, marinated beetroot

Pan fried halibut, Vermouth veloute

White chocolate pannacotta

Ringstead

048 The Gin Trap Inn

6 High St, Ringstead PE36 5JU

Tel.: (01485) 525264 - Fax: (01485) 525321
e-mail: gintrapinn@keme.co.uk - Website: www.gintrapinn.co.uk

🍴 🍷 ⤢ **VISA** ⓂⒸ

Adnams, Woodfordes Wherry

Two old iron ploughs crown the modest doorway of this whitewashed inn, which dates back to 1667. In all those years it can rarely have looked and felt so inviting: a proper country pub, warm and comfortable, with a real fire stoked up in the stove on frosty winter evenings. The bar, with its glossy wood-topped tables, and the smartly set dining room feel like two halves of the same whole: the modern British restaurant dishes are well prepared and full of flavour, but no less care goes into a really appealing choice of generous pub classics, good and simple. If you're thinking of staying the night and exploring Hunstanton and the coast in the morning, this could be the place: the bedrooms are a very tasteful blend of subtle country patterns, and two bathrooms have luxurious roll-top baths.

Food serving times:
Moday-Sunday:
      12pm-2pm, 6pm-9pm
Prices:
Meals: a la carte 17.00/36.00
🛏 **3 rooms :** 80.00/170.00

Typical Dishes
Grilled sardines
Prawn and monkfish brochette
Dark chocolate fondant with tarragon ice cream

3,25 miles East of Hunstanton by A149. Parking.

Snettisham

049 The Rose and Crown

Old Church Rd, Snettisham PE31 7LX

Tel.: (01485) 541382 - Fax: (01485) 543172
e-mail: info@roseandcrownsnettisham.co.uk - Website: www.roseandcrownsnettisham.co.uk

   room *VISA* *MC*

Adnams Bitter, Adnams Broadside, Greene King IPA

A buzzing, convivial place at its best, though first-time guests may struggle to get their bearings in a maze of cosy, rustic bars and brightly styled rooms, where quirky decorative details and bric-a-brac give just a hint of well-composed muddle. Whatever you do, don't plan on a quick dinner – for all its good intentions, the service can start to unravel on busy evenings, leaving some diners feeling slightly lost – but go prepared to flag down waitresses and allow time for a drink and a chat between courses. The menu is a conversation piece in itself. Asian influences mingle with Modern European dishes and the out-and-out traditional. There is a well-priced lunch menu and good choice on the à la carte. Tidy, interestingly appointed bedrooms, in a colourful style you'll recognise from downstairs, and good breakfasts.

Food serving times:
Monday-Thursday:
 12pm-2pm, 6.30pm-9pm
Friday-Saturday:
 12pm-2pm, 6.30pm-9.30pm
Sunday: 12pm-2.30pm,
 6.30-9pm

Prices:
Meals: a la carte 17.00/25.00
16 rooms : 50.00/95.00

11mi North of King's Lynn by A149. Parking.

Typical Dishes

Caramelised onion and feta cheese tart

Confit fillet of salmon, sorrel butter

Warm pecan pie

Stoke Holy Cross

050 Wildebeest Arms

82-86 Norwich Rd, Stoke Holy Cross NR14 8QJ

Tel.: (01508) 492497 - Fax: (01508) 494946

e-mail: wildebeestl@animalinns.co.uk

   VISA AE MC

Adnams Best Bitter

Dark wooden furniture and sunny yellow ragwashed walls, allied to soft lighting and a slight African theme, lend a homely, comfortable feel to this smoothly run rural pub. The invariably friendly and efficient service is a notable plus; meals are served at substantially proportioned "tree-trunk" tables or, if preferred on brighter days, in the garden. If reputation is everything, then these days The Wildebeest has it in spades: cooking from the open kitchen is of a modern style and has both the quality and price to bring in punters from miles around East Anglia. Menus are exceptional for a pub; they're particularly well-compiled, blending a classic base with French and British elements. Wines, too, are eye-catchingly well-priced. Because of its high regard locally, this is a pub where booking is essential, especially for dinner.

Food serving times:
Monday-Sunday:
        12pm-3pm, 7pm-10pm
Closed 25-26 December

Prices:
Meals: 15.95/18.95 (set price lunch/dinner) and a la carte 25.00/35.00

5.75 mi South of Norwich by A140. Parking.

Typical Dishes

North Norfolk crab tian

Rosemary marinated chump of spring lamb

Strawberry Eton mess

Wells-next-the-Sea

051 The Globe Inn 🛏

The Buttlands, Wells-next-the-Sea NR23 1EU

Tel.: (01328) 710206 - Fax: (01328) 713249
e-mail: globe@holkham.co.uk - Website: www.globeatwells.co.uk

Woodfordes Werry, Adnams Best, Broadside, Mayday, Nelsons Revenge adn Great Eastern

Just a five-minute stroll from the harbour - where fishermen set out for inshore crab, whelk, sea trout and bass – this renovated inn boasts its own charming position, overlooking the town's leafy Georgian square. Sun-filled courtyards surround its whitewashed exterior, and brews drift by along the breezes of the north Norfolk coast. Inside, all is neat, tidy and spruce. 'Front of house' is the more characterful part of the pub, where a log-burning stove churns out winter warmth, and brick faced walls add rustic flavour to wood tables and chairs. Beyond, the airy, neutral dining area is enlivened by excellent, blown up local photos on the walls. Everywhere you go, daily papers lie around for you to pick up and peruse. Menus are a mixture of modern British and classic pub dishes, washed down by local Adnams and Woodfordes beers. Bedrooms, too, charmingly merge the contemporary with the past.

Food serving times:
Monday-Sunday:
    12pm-2.30pm, 7pm-9pm
Prices:
Meals: a la carte 15.00/25.00
🛏 **7 rooms :** 40.00/105.00

Typical Dishes

Prawns with lemon and herb mayonnaise

Deep fried haddock

Apple and rhubarb crumble

In town centre. Parking. ❯❯

Bildeston

052 The Bildeston Crown

104 High Street, Bildeston IP7 7EB

Tel.: (01449) 740510 - Fax: (01449) 741843

e-mail: hayley@thebildestoncrown.co.uk - Website: www.thebildestoncrown.co.uk

VISA AE MC

Adnams, Greene King IPA, Mauldons

15C origins, a part-timber frontage and a smart yellow finish announce this extremely popular hostelry in the heart of Suffolk. Smart modern styling mixes well with the traditional appeal of the exterior, as exemplified by the bar area, where delightful inglenook, beams and heavy wood furniture evolve into comfy sofas in an adjacent room. The old and the new also rub shoulders in the dining room – the whole pub boasts a well-integrated feel. Locals enjoy a drink in the popular bar, and if you choose, you can eat here as well as sup. Good-sized menus are of two types: the Crown Classic, which is mainly traditional, or the dinner menu, which offers more elaborate temptations. Overnighters have made a sound choice: bedrooms are very strong here: individually styled, they merge pleasant traditional features with up-to-date facilities like Wi-Fi.

Food serving times:
Monday-Sunday:
   12pm-3pm, 7pm-10pm
Prices:
Meals: a la carte 28.00/50.00
10 rooms : 55.00/150.00

Typical Dishes

Crown Hors d'oeuvres

Rabbit, tarragon gnocchi

Study in citrus

On B1115 in village centre. Parking.

Bramfield

053 Queen's Head

The Street, Bramfield IP19 9HT

Tel.: (01986) 784214 - Fax: (01986) 784797
e-mail: qhbfield@aol.com - Website: www.queensheadbramfield.co.uk

 rest *VISA* AE MC

Adnams Bitter, Broadside

Organic food is the name of the game at this neat and tidy, 'proper' pub not far from Southwold and the Suffolk coast. Nobody seems to know quite how old the Queens Head is, but going by the exposed roof trusses and mighty fireplaces in one of the hugely rustic rooms – a former barn – we're talking about a few hundred years at least. Good value menus take a particular delight in showing off the organic nature of extremely local ingredients: pork, venison and beef are from nearby farms. Settle down to eat at scrubbed pine tables and chairs. In the summer months, the pretty garden is worth discovering with its dome-shaped willow bower, but at colder times of the year settle down in front of a blazing fire with a pint of ale from down the coast road.

Food serving times:
Monday-Saturday:
12pm-2pm, 6.30pm-10pm
Sunday: 12pm-2pm,
7pm-9pm
Closed 26 December
Prices:
Meals: a la carte 16.85/23.95

3mi South of Halesworth on A144. Parking.

Typical Dishes

Grilled dates wrapped in bacon

Smoked haddock, Welsh rarebit

Tunisian orange and almond cake

Buxhall

054 The Buxhall Crown

Mill Road, Buxhall IP14 3DW

Tel.: (01449) 736521 - Fax: (01449) 736425
e-mail: trevor@buxhallcrown.fsnet.co.uk - Website: www.thebuxhallcrown.co.uk

VISA AE MC

*Greene King IPA, Buxhall brewed 'Old Mill', Tindalls Ale,
Woodfordes Wherry*

Without a sixth sense for country pubs, you'd do well to find the Crown by chance, but all the more reason to seek it out, especially on a quieter weekday. One half of the pub is always set for dining, with plenty of intimate corners and a big fire, but you can also eat in the classic old bar, where many of the regulars drop in for a pint of the usual and a quiet smoke. There's an almost homely, family feeling to the place as gently helpful staff shuttle between the bar and kitchen, bringing out well-heaped plates of hearty cooking: notwithstanding a few modern touches, it's the traditional foundations that come across in dishes like Bailey's cheesecake with strawberries and raspberries or thick, pink lamb cutlets with pea purée and plenty of seasonal veg.

Food serving times:
Tuesday-Saturday:
12pm-2pm, 6.30pm-9pm
Sunday: 12pm-2pm
Closed 25-26 December
Prices:
Meals: a la carte 25.00/35.00

Typical Dishes

Pigeon breast, curried lentils
Lamb fillet with pea purée
Malva pudding

2mi West of Stowmarket by B1115; follow the road to Buxhall across Rattlesden Junction. Parking.

Horringer

055　The Beehive

The Street, Horringer IP29 5SN

Tel.: (01284) 735260 - Fax: (01284) 735532

 　VISA　MC

Greene King IPA, Abbot, Old Speckled Hen

Staggeringly rich and deeply eccentric, even by the standards of the Regency gentry, the 4th Earl of Bristol spared no expense on Ickworth House and its Italianate gardens, now owned by the National Trust. His ideal local would probably have been a neoclassical gastro-folly, but The Beehive, just down the road, brings us back down to earth in the very best sense. An attractive, traditional brick and flint house, its old timbers and flagstones set off nicely with a bright, modern décor, it always seems to have one last inviting corner waiting and an old wooden table free. A good-sized blackboard menu, with its share of lighter dishes, combines predominantly British themes with a subtle taste for the modern and the exotic – perhaps His Lordship would have approved after all. Well run by long-standing landlords.

Food serving times:
Monday-Saturday:
　　12pm-2pm, 7pm-9.30pm
Sunday:　　　　12pm-2pm
Closed 25-26 December
Prices:
Meals: a la carte 18.00/25.00

Typical Dishes

Ballontine of salmon

Roast belly of pork with Bramley apple gravy

Date and toffee pudding

3.5mi South West of Bury St Edmunds by A143. Parking.

Lavenham

056 The Angel 🛏

Market Pl, Lavenham CO10 9QZ

Tel.: (01787) 247388 - Fax: (01787) 248344
e-mail: angellav@aol.com - Website: www.theangelhotel.co.uk

    VISA

 Adnams, Greene King IPA, Nethergate Suffolk County, Adnams Broadside

History's timbered face appears at every turn in the gorgeous old town of Lavenham, and the Angel wears one of its more delightful countenances. This charming inn has stood in the market square since 1420 and receives a never-ending stream of curious tourists and relaxed locals. There's a pubby bar with several dining areas including lots of timbers, simple wooden tables and a log fire. On the first floor is the Solar, which contains a rare fully pargetted ceiling constructed in the early 1600s, featuring the remains of early wall paintings on some of its beams. This has great views of the Guildhall and Church and is now a residents' sitting room. Hearty, varied menus employ seasonal, local produce, while well-kept bedrooms provide effortlessly comfortable accommodation.

Food serving times:
Monday-Sunday:
12pm-2.15pm,
6.45pm-9.15pm
Closed 25-26 December
Prices:
Meals: a la carte 15.00/25.00
🛏 **8 rooms :** 55.00/80.00

Typical Dishes

Roast stuffed tomato

Braised shank of lamb

Steamed syrup sponge with custard

In town centre. Parking.

Levington

057 The Ship Inn

Church Lane, Levington IP10 0LQ
Tel.: (01473) 659573

 VISA

Adnams Best, Broadside, Greene King IPA

In an age of rebranding, some pub names still go deeper. The salt of the Suffolk marshes is in the very timbers of this part 14C thatched inn, which stands in sight of the estuary. Though built from the broken-up hulks on the coast and full of seafaring pictures, curiosities and keepsakes, it now feels just too neat and cosy ever to have been a smugglers' haunt, but read the old newspaper cutting on the wall and you'll find the atmosphere of excisemen and contraband hangs about you a little more thickly. Relaxed, smiling and attentive service recalls you to the present for an appetizing menu with a good balance tilted in favour of the traditional: seafood includes Cromer crab and fresh griddled plaice with crispy salad. Save a space for homemade puddings like apple and rosemary crumble with custard.

Food serving times:
Monday-Sunday:
12am-2pm, 6.30pm-9.30pm
Closed 25-26 December
and 1 January
Prices:
Meals: a la carte 16.00/25.00

Typical Dishes

Seared local wood pigeon

Prawn and potato cake with seared scallops

Brown bread ice cream

6mi Southeast of Ipswich by A14. Parking.

Lidgate

058 **The Star Inn**

The Street, Lidgate CB8 9PP
Tel.: (01638) 500275 - Fax: (01638) 500275

   VISA

Greene King IPA, Abbot Ales and Ruddles

This part 16C village inn may just prove the point: any fusion of traditions will work if you understand both well enough. Its three intimate rooms and snugs are full of restful, old-English charm, braced with ancient beams worn smooth and warmed by drowsy inglenooks. Absolutely the last place, in fact, that you would expect to find sparklingly fresh Iberian cooking. The day's menu comes on blackboards that offer a good variety of simply stated Spanish and Mediterranean dishes. Even locally sourced wild boar and venison are prepared to authentic recipes: at once hearty, piquant and satisfyingly different. Suffolk summers seldom feel properly continental: even so, the terraced garden is very pleasant once the weather finally gets it right.

Food serving times:
Monday-Saturday:
    12pm-3pm, 7pm-10pm
Sunday: 12pm-3pm
Closed 25-26 December
and 1 January
Prices:
Meals: 12.50 (fixed price lunch)
and a la carte 26.00/30.00

Typical Dishes

Moules marinières

Paella

Treacle tart

7mi southeast of Newmarket on B1063. Parking.

Monks Eleigh

059 The Swan

The Street, Monks Eleigh IP7 7AU

Tel.: (01449) 741391

e-mail: swan@monkseleigh.com - Website: www.monkseleigh.com

 Adnams Best and Broadside

Heading, perhaps, for the Tudor delights of Lavenham, there's every chance you'll come across this attractive little 16C roadside pub with its thatched roof and honey yellow façade. Stop off and step inside. The interior is as fresh as the country air, with rustic olive tones and shiny wooden floors. It's a charming mix of the old and the new, undertaken with understated style. You won't be let down by the food, either. The chef and landlord specialises in innovative menus that treat local ingredients with the utmost respect: fish, for instance, is the day's catch from the coast. Early dinners come at bargain prices – a great time to sample the homemade seasonal game dishes. When you've left the pub, remember to look round the quaint little streets of Monks Eleigh itself.

Food serving times:
Wednesday-Sunday:
    12pm-2pm, 7pm-9.00pm
Closed 25-26 December
and 1 January
Prices:
Meals: a la carte 18.50/32.00

Typical Dishes

Lasagne of Parma ham

Sea bass on char-grilled vegetables

Pannacotta with grappa

3.5mi Southeast of Lavenham on A1141. Parking.

Nayland

060 **White Hart Inn**

11 High Street, Nayland CO6 4SF

Tel.: (01206) 263382 - Fax: (01206) 263638
e-mail: nayhart@aol.com - Website: www.whitehart-nayland.co.uk

  ⌀room *VISA*

 No real ales offered

Floodlit at night, this very pleasant, well-run part-15C former coaching inn has a charming position on the high street of a typically homely Suffolk village, amid colour washed houses, overhanging timbers and patches of cobblestone. Dining is really what the White Hart is all about, and the smooth, considerate service certainly reflects this as much as the layout. Exposed beams divide the welcoming, terracotta-tiled dining room into three distinct areas, with a cosy back bar for pre-prandial relaxation. Menus are modern and accomplished, and may include millefeuille of baby spring vegetables with tomato and basil butter sauce, or rolled loin of suckling pig with seasonal greens and Calvados sauce; the bread and butter pudding is made to the chef's mother's own secret recipe! Beamed bedrooms are pleasantly creaky but very comfortable.

Food serving times:
Tuesday-Sunday:
12pm-2.30pm,
6.30pm-9.30pm
Closed 26 December
to 10 January
Prices:
Meals: 15.50 (set price lunch)
and a la carte 20.00/32.00
6 rooms : 69.00/110.00

Opposite the church. Parking.

Typical Dishes

Twice baked cheese with
fresh tomato sauce

Casserole of tender lamb
with spring vegetables

Pistachio crème brûlée

Orford

061 Crown and Castle

Orford IP12 2LJ

Tel.: (01394) 450205

e-mail: info@crownandcastlehotel.co.uk - Website: www.crownandcastle.co.uk

 Greene King IPA

Very much a bar with strong restaurant sensibilities, The Trinity sits smartly within the confines of the Crown and Castle hotel, in the wonderfully isolated village of Orford, right next to the 12C castle and within wading distance of the eerie Ness. The sleek and stylist bar and lounge has an easy, relaxed ambience with dark wood tables, log fire and banquettes. You can eat, too, in a rather bohemian three-roomed area with brick walls and oak panelling. Keen pricing has earned The Trinity a Bib Gourmand, though it's fair to say lunches are more keenly priced than dinners. Constantly evolving menus include much skilfully employed local produce, carefully prepared by chef and co-proprietor Ruth Watson, who, apart from keeping a watchful eye over the Trinity with husband David, also writes award-winning food books and presents Channel 5's 'The Hotel Inspector'.

Food serving times:
Monday-Sunday:
12pm-2.15pm,
6.45pm-9.30pm
Closed 19-22 December and 3-4 January
Booking essential
Prices:
Meals: 35.00 (Dinner Saturday and bank holidays only) and a la carte 23.50/31.50
18 rooms: 72.00/145.00

11mi East of Woodbridge by A1152 and B1084. Parking.

Typical Dishes

Chicken liver parfait

Orford caught skate with brown shrimps

Chocolate soufflé cake

Snape

062 **The Crown Inn**

Bridge Rd, Snape IP17 1SL
Tel.: (01728) 688324

   room **VISA**

Adnams Explorer, Admans Broadside, Adnams Old Ale, Tally Ho! (seasonal)

This gem of a Suffolk pub, with its origins firmly entrenched in the 15C, draws in visitors from upmarket Aldeburgh and The Maltings. They come for the Suffolk ale, the pubby atmosphere enhanced enormously by standing timbers and rafters, old brick flooring and horseshoe-shaped high-backed settles around a grand brick inglenook, and the heart-warming popular dishes served from the blackboard menu. These have a sharp emphasis on fresh fish, game and organic vegetables supplied by local producers. Quaint bedrooms continue the aged theme, complete with sloping floors, beams and some low, low doorways.

Food serving times:
Monday-Sunday:
12pm-2.15pm, 7pm-9.15pm
Closed 25 December
and dinner 26 December
Prices:
Meals: a la carte 18.00/26.00
3 rooms : 70.00/80.00

Typical Dishes

Seared jumbo scallops

Fillet of halibut on wilted spinach

Lemon posset

6mi West of Aldeburgh by A1094 on B1069. Parking.

Somerleyton

063 **Duke's Head**

Slugg's Lane, Somerleyton NR31 5QR

Tel.: (01502) 730281 - Fax: (01502) 733931
e-mail: dukeshead@somerleyton.co.uk - Website: www.somerleyton.co.uk

 Adnams IPA, Woodfordes and guest beers - Brewer's Gold, Oulton Ales Orange Wheat Beer

Up the coast and inland a bit from Lowestoft stands one of Suffolk's finest stately homes, Somerleyton Hall, and its watering hole has a friendly and welcoming feel about it. Located in the unfortunate sounding Slugg's Lane, it's not the prettiest of pubs, but its setting, down by the river, and its super sun-drenched terrace, enhance the feeling that all is not lost. The characterful interior is thronged with locals and visitors to the Hall, and there are regular live music evenings as well as 'big screen' events. A spacious, simply furnished restaurant stands by the bar, and this is home to some appetising grub at very digestible prices. Simply prepared, well executed dishes are full of tasty, fresh ingredients originating from, or around, the estate, with Cromer crab and brown shrimps a couple of tasty possibilities.

Food serving times:
Monday-Sunday:
12pm-3pm (restaurant), all day (bar snacks)

Prices:
Meals: a la carte 20.00/30.00

Typical Dishes

Potted brown shrimps

Skate wing, brown butter and caper sauce

Norfolk whipped syllabub

6mi Northwest of Lowestoft by B1074. Parking.

Southwold

064 **The Crown**

90 High St, Southwold IP18 6DP

Tel.: 01502 722275 - Fax: 01502 727263
e-mail: crown.hotel@adnams.co.uk - Website: www.adnamshotels.co.uk

 Adnams Ales

The sophisticated elegance of The Crown sits easily within the beguiling surrounds of delightful Southwold. Its mellow yellow tones have graced the high street for many a year, standing proudly adjacent to the Adnams Sole Bay brewery. This smart, intimate old coaching inn is the ideal stopping-off point for a pint with the Suffolk locals in the compact oak-panelled rear bar where, not surprisingly, a nautical edge permeates. Get to the front bar early if you want to bag a seat for dining: it can get packed in there. Or choose a more formal option in the intimate, linen-clad restaurant. The same daily changing menu is served throughout: a well-established and well-prepared mix of modern and more classical dishes, which find favour with East Anglians and the metropolitan influx alike. Individually styled bedrooms.

Food serving times:
Monday-Sunday:
12pm-2pm-7pm-9.45pm

Prices:
Meals: 29.00 (set price dinner) and a la carte 25.00/29.00
14 rooms : 80.00/180.00

In the centre. Parking.

Typical Dishes

Norfolk smoked eel

Lamb shank, roasted root vegetables

White chocolate brownie

Southwold

065 The King's Head

25 High Street, Southwold IP18 6AD

Tel.: (01502) 724517

e-mail: reception@southwoldkingshead.co.uk - Website: www.southwoldkingshead.co.uk

VISA MC

Adnam's Broadside, The Bitter, Explorer, Mayday, Regatta

Up the road from its stable mate The Randolph and just five minutes from the beach, this is an attractive 19C pub that's felt the positive effects of a recent injection of cash allied to large doses of TLC. As the wind whips in from the North Sea, you'll feel the benefits of the comforting old fire as you share a pint of frothing Adnams with the locals in the busy bar. Take your pick from two dining areas with mix and match furniture, or a private dining room, smartly decked out with original tiles and blond wood tables and chairs. Appealing menus are the same wherever you land up, from the 'Black Slate' sharing platters, to a range of locally sourced classics, to lunchtime 'lite bites' and hearty Sunday roasts. There are three well priced, comfortable and spacious bedrooms whose bright, fresh looks complement the gleaming Sole Bay sunrise.

Food serving times:
Monday-Sunday:
    12pm-2.30-pm, 6pm-9pm
Prices:
Meals: a la carte 18.00/25.00
3 rooms : 50.00/100.00

Typical Dishes

Thai style salmon kebabs

Grilled sea bass, avocado salsa

Rhubarb fool with sable biscuit

Near the centre. Parking outside or on Southwold Common.

Southwold

066 The Randolph

41 Wangford Rd, Reydon, Southwold IP18 6PZ

Tel.: (01502) 723603 - Fax: (01502) 722194
e-mail: reception@therandolph.co.uk - Website: www.therandolph.co.uk

Adnams Bitter, Broadside and 1 regularly changing ale

It's a wrench setting foot out of glorious Southwold, but a mile up the road is this sturdy old Victorian stalwart, built by the grandfather of the chairman of the local brewery. It's been given a startling and successful 21C makeover, the big, open-plan bar is suffused with light and furnished with contemporary wicker chairs and leather sofas; deep, bold colours lead you into the dining room where the emphasis is on extremely local produce: those who supply fish, game and the like often stay on for a pint of ale in the bar. Food is traditional and robust: apart from the aforementioned, you might tuck into steaks or toad-in-the-hole. If you're not staying in one of the comfy bedrooms, then what could be better than a post-prandial walk round the greens, beach huts and lighthouse of Suffolk's finest…

Food serving times:
Monday-Sunday:
12pm-2pm, 6.30pm-9pm
Prices:
Meals: a la carte 25.00/30.00
🛏 **10 rooms :** 55.00/105.00

2mi North West of Southwold by A1095 and B1126. Parking.

Typical Dishes

Tartlet of goat's cheese

Confit of duck leg, Oriental noodles

Vanilla cheesecake

Stoke-by-Nayland

067 The Angel Inn

Polstead St, Stoke-by-Nayland CO6 4SA

Tel.: (01206) 263245 - Fax: (01206) 263373
e-mail: the.angel@tiscali.co.uk - Website: www.horizoninns.co.uk

VISA AE M©

Greene King IPA and Abbot, Adnams Best Bitter

Parts of this 16C inn in the heart of Constable country creak with age: not surprisingly, a traditional air is worn with pride. It's heavily beamed and timbered, with exposed brickwork and roaring fires, and a cheerily informal bar that leads through to a sitting room where you can recline in deep sofas. Dine in the main bar or repair to the Well Room, which contains the house's original well and a superb beamed ceiling. Menus here are the same as elsewhere, but the pervading atmosphere is a touch more tranquil and formal. Seasonally influenced dishes abound with locally sourced meat, fish and game prepared in a modern British style. It's the kind of place you might not want to leave, so stay on in one of the traditionally and individually styled bedrooms.

Food serving times:
Monday-Saturday:
12pm-2pm, 6.30pm-9.30pm
Prices:
Meals: a la carte 16.00/25.00
6 rooms : 70.00/85.00

Typical Dishes

Chicken liver pate

Rosette of salmon with a duo of sauces

Bread and butter pudding

On B1068. Parking.

Stoke-by-Nayland

068 The Crown

Stoke-by-Nayland CO6 4SE

Tel.: (01206) 262001 - Fax: (01206) 264026
e-mail: thecrown@eoinns.co.uk

  VISA ⓂⒸ

 Greene King IPA, Adnams BB, Old Hooky, Landlord, Golden Best, Harvieston, Fuller's London Pride, HSB, Batemans XXXB

"1530" is stamped on the outside of this promising-looking pub, but its comfortable and stylish interior – with a mis-match of sofas, leather armchairs and farmhouse chairs at broad tables – owes much to a recent sympathetic refit. Such is its local reputation that several spacious dining rooms soon fill with a mix of couples, friends and families, particularly for long lunches at weekends and holidays, so booking really is a must. With a new menu every fortnight, the hearty cooking keeps pace with the seasons and brings a regional touch to a couple of daily specials – plus a catch of the day – and a wider range of surefire gastropub classics: a handful of these come in either starter or main portions. The Crown is owned by a firm of wholesale vintners, and its wine shop sells an interesting selection, as well as local homemade chocolates.

Food serving times:
Monday-Thursday:
  12pm-2.30pm, 6pm-9.30pm
Friday-Saturday:
  12pm-2.30pm, 6pm-10pm
Sunday: 12pm-9pm
Closed 25-26 December
(booking essential)
Prices:
Meals: a la carte 17.85/27.70

Village centre at the junction of B1068 and B1087. Parking.

Typical Dishes
Smoked eel salad
Garlic herb stuffed suckling pig
Vanilla & Sauternes poached pear

It's Britain's cultural centre, a business superpower and a fashionista's paradise, but where do you go to find the heart of London itself? Amid the money and the power of Westminster and the City, the mini-Manhattan of Canary Wharf or the bars and studios of Shoreditch and Hoxton in between? Down by Tate Modern and The Globe on rejuvenated Bankside, in the Thames meadows of Richmond and Kew or at the top of the London Eye? The boutiques on New Bond Street or the market stalls of Borough and Billingsgate? Dreaming in the Pavilion End at Lord's or paddling on the Serpentine? In leafy Greenwich, chic Kensington and Chelsea or the glitzy streets of Soho? Wherever you start within this changing patchwork of neighbourhoods, somewhere between The Mall and Metroland, the capital's pubs are moving with the times. Away from the bright lights, brassy Victorian gin-palaces, quiet mews bars and old local boozers are being restored and reborn as London's newest gastronomic gems, bringing good-value informal dining closer to home…

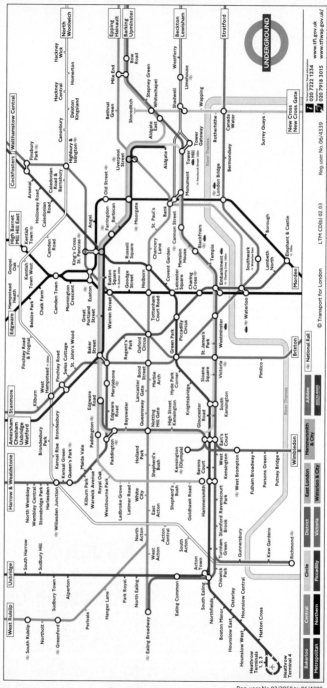

Reg. user No 03/3850 to 06/4399

Kensal Rise

001 The Greyhound

64-66 Chamberlayne Road, Kensal Rise NW10 3JJ

Tel.: (020) 8969 8080 - Fax: (020) 8969 8081
e-mail: thegreyhound@needtoeat.co.uk

  VISA **M©**

Adnams Bitter

Once the London campus for the School of Hard Knocks, Kensal Rise is on the up, helped along by enterprising efforts like this. The old neighbourhood pub stood derelict for a year before a group of young friends – with a big picture of a greyhound, but nowhere to hang it – set to work on its restoration. To one side it's a bar, with club chairs and comfy chesterfields for slow drinking and snacking, and on the other side, it's more like a classic gastropub, with reclaimed furniture and black leather banquettes setting a slightly more formal tone. Enjoyable cooking in tried-and-tested, Modern British style takes in crispy belly pork, roast cod on pea purée and caramelised pork chops with lemon and rosemary. Sheltered rear terrace.

Food serving times:
Tuesday-Saturday:
  12.30pm-3pm,
  6.30pm-10.30pm
Sunday: 12.30pm-6.30pm
Monday: 6.30pm-10.30pm
Closed 25-26 December
and 1 January
Prices:
Meals: a la carte 16.00/27.00

Typical Dishes

Potato scones, smoked salmon

Gloucester Old Spot pork chop

Apple crumble

⊖ Kensal Green.

Willesden Green

002 The Green

110 Walm Lane, Willesden Green NW2 4RS

Tel.: (020) 8452 0171 - Fax: (020) 8452 0774
e-mail: info@thegreennw2.com

 No real ales offered

Actually a converted Conservative Club snooker room, The Green has kept its airy period proportions, but green baize is out and leather banquettes and stripped wood are in: a bustling but pleasantly low-key bar in the modern gastropub manner, its dining room a touch smarter than out front. The chef and co-owner's Caribbean heritage and an Anglo-French fine dining apprenticeship are both discernable in the generous modern cooking, but the influence is more subtle, and the balance more natural, than you might expect: bream with fried plantain and salsa appears next to duck confit on pak choi or chicken liver parfait, while the lighter selection served in the bar and on the front terrace might feature jerk chicken and coleslaw or gastropub staples like Caesar salads and steak sandwiches. Bright, spontaneous and "au fait" service.

Food serving times:
Monday-Sunday:
11am-10.30pm
Closed 1 January
Prices:
Meals: 17.50 (set price lunch and dinner) and a la carte 25.00/40.00

Typical Dishes

Chicken liver parfait
Jerk chicken with plantain
Apple and raspberry crumble

↔ Willesden Green. 〉〉

Belsize Park

003 The Hill

94 Haverstock Hill, Belsize Park NW3 2BD

Tel.: (020) 7267 0033

e-mail: thehill@geronimo-inns.co.uk - Website: www.geronimo-inns.co.uk

 VISA

Fuller's Organic Honeydew

Haverstock Hill, to be precise, where this substantial Victorian pub has been turned around from a workaday drinking haunt to something far trendier: strings of fairy lights twinkle against oxblood-red walls and stylish twentysomethings make themselves at home in old armchairs and sofas. One half of the big, high-ceilinged bar is given over to dining and a smaller room to one side – with one wall covered in black and white photos – is also just for food. Chatty, T-shirted staff serve a good choice of modern Mediterranean cooking with the odd Far Eastern touch: tiger prawns are mixed with coriander and paw-paw salad; prosciutto-wrapped chicken and mozzarella comes with tasty Parmentier potatoes. Laid-back yet lively – a good evening out.

Food serving times:
Monday-Wednesday:
7pm-10pm
Thursday-Saturday:
12pm-3pm, 7pm-10.30pm
Sunday: 12.30pm-9pm
Closed 25 December
Prices:
Meals: a la carte 18.00/25.00

Typical Dishes

Rye bruschetta, smoked duck

Pan fried salmon, wilted bok choy

Lemon cake

⊖ Belsize Park/Chalk Farm.

Hampstead

004 The Magdala

2A South Hill Park, Hampstead NW3 2SB

Tel.: (020) 7435 2503 - Fax: (020) 7435 6167

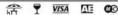

 3 real ales which change seasonally

A stroll on Hampstead Heath reaches a perfect finale with a visit to this deliciously characterful pub, with its two surprisingly rustic bars, appealing neighbourhood ambience - and one rather dark secret, in that it's the place in the 1950s where Britain's last execution victim, Ruth Ellis, shot her lover. Original stained glass windows allow the sunshine to flood through; flickering candles lend a more romantic evening glow. You can eat downstairs or up: the former has an open kitchen, the latter an elegant, formal feel, but it's only open at weekends. Interesting, honest cooking with well-sourced ingredients provides the backbone of a solid dining-pub menu.

Food serving times:
Monday-Friday:
    12pm-2.30pm, 6pm-10pm
Saturday-Sunday:
    12pm-9.30pm
Closed 25 December
Prices:
Meals: a la carte 20.00/25.00

Typical Dishes

Pan fried scallops with citrus salsa

Lamb rump with Harissa spiced couscous

Orange crème brûlée

⊖ Belsize Park. Street parking in South Hill Park or nearby Heath car park.

Hampstead

005 **The Wells**

30 Well Walk, Hampstead NW3 1BX

Tel.: (020) 7794 3785 - Fax: (020) 7794 6817
e-mail: info@thewellshampstead.co.uk - Website: www.thewellshampstead.co.uk

 Abbot Ale

This attractive 18C inn sits very easily in a smart part of Hampstead equidistant between the High Street and the Heath. Wander in and relax instantly into one of the dark leather sofas arranged in cosy corners; drinks are ordered from a smart modern bar running centrally across the room. Upstairs it's a bit more formal, with three adjoining rooms linked by burgundy walls and linen covered tables. Menus are from a classical French repertoire, carefully prepared and well balanced. Recent recommendations include roast monkfish minestrone or loin of hare with red cabbage and celeriac purée. What we have here is not quite a pub, not quite a restaurant, but something satisfying in-between.

Food serving times:
Monday-Friday:
 12pm-3pm, 7pm-10pm
Saturday-Sunday:
 12pm-4pm, 7pm-10pm
Closed 1 January
Prices:
Meals: a la carte 17.00/22.00

Typical Dishes

Pan-fried scallops, crispy pancetta

Sea bass, sesame, ginger and garlic

Chocolate pots

Hampstead. Limited metered parking on Christchurch Hill.

Primrose Hill

006 The Engineer

65 Gloucester Ave, Primrose Hill NW1 8JH
Tel.: (020) 7722 0950 - Fax: (020) 7483 0592

 Ⅳ 🍷 *VISA* Ⓜ️©

Charles Wells Bombardier, Hook Norton

Amid tall terraces in an ever-smarter part of town, this elegantly remodelled Victorian tavern is a neighbourhood pub of a very modern kind. Locals lounge over late lunch and pints in a front bar, filled with light from the broad windows, and even with the intimacy of linen and candlelight, there's an easy, come-as-you-are style about the chic dining room. There's also a little walled terrace at the back. Eclectic cooking, in gratifyingly massive portions, draws freely on global influences: dishes with a robust Pacific Rim or Modern European edge might include quail with polenta or squid on papaya, cucumber and mint salad. Efficient and friendly service.

Food serving times:
Monday-Friday:
9am-12pm, 12.30pm-3pm,
7pm-11pm
Saturday-Sunday:
9am-12pm, 12.30pm-4pm,
7pm-11pm
Closed 25-26 December
Prices:
Meals: a la carte 18.00/45.00

Typical Dishes

Tequila cured salmon

Miso marinated cod, taro crisps

Balsamic strawberries with lemon sorbet

⊖ Camden Town/Chalk Farm. Parking meters outside. 》

Primrose Hill

007 **The Queens**

49 Regent's Park Rd, Primrose Hill NW1 8XD
Tel.: (020) 7586 0408 - Fax: (020) 7586 5677
Website: www.geronimo-inns.co.uk

Youngs Special and Ordinary

C hief among the places that defined the style, and substance, of the capital's gastropubs, this surprisingly down-to-earth local landmark continues as buzzing as ever, and not dining out on past successes, either. With its gauze of hazy blue-grey smoke and the Premiership highlights on in the corner, the bar remains an everyday-chic, urbanite drinking den and upstairs the balcony overlooking Primrose Hill is still one of the most popular square metres in North London. In the dining room, simple, close-set linen and paper-clad tables give half a glimpse of jars and rolling pins in the open kitchen, which serves up robust, almost rustic, modern classics like steak and chips and moules portugaise: a regularly changing choice is chalked up on the boards.

Food serving times:
Monday-Thursday:
    10am-3pm, 7pm-10pm
Friday-Saturday:
    10am-3pm, 7pm-10.30pm
Sunday: 10am-4pm,
                        7pm-9pm

Closed 25 December
Prices:
Meals: a la carte 20.00/26.00

Typical Dishes

Crisp pancetta and Nuremburg sausage

Fish soup

Red wine poached pear and flapjack

⊖ Chalk Farm. Parking meters in High Street.

Tufnell Park

008 Junction Tavern

101 Fortess Rd, Tufnell Park NW5 1AG

Tel.: (020) 7485 9400 - Fax: (020) 7485 9401
Website: www.junction.junctiontavern.co.uk

  VISA

4 different guest ales changing weekly

Halfway between Tufnell Park and Kentish Town stands this noble Victorian edifice, now given a modern makeover, guaranteeing swarms of North Londoners making a beeline for its doors: it's become so popular that it could be worth booking at weekends. This is a typical grand 19C metropolitan pub, with a high ceiling and ornate wood panelling and though it still has its split, two-room bar, you're free to eat in either. One is more an informal bar with a conservatory extension; the other a proper dining area with a stainless-steel, open-plan kitchen and array of mis-matched tables. Cheerful young staff serve generous portions of robust dishes with tasty, fresh ingredients sourced from local markets.

Food serving times:
Monday-Friday:
 12pm-3pm, 6.30pm-10.30pm
Saturday: 12pm-4pm,
 6.30pm-10.30pm
Sunday: 12pm-4pm,
 6.30pm-9.30pm
Closed 24-26 December
and 1 January
Prices:
Meals: a la carte 20.00/30.00

Tufnell Park. Residents only parking until 6.30pm Monday-Friday; on-street parking after 6.30pm Monday-Friday.

Typical Dishes

Pan fried scallops, minted pea purée

Daube of Highland venison

Russet apple tart

City of London

009 **The White Swan**

108 Fetter Lane, City of London EC4A 1ES

Tel.: (020) 7242 9696 - Fax: (020) 7404 2250

e-mail: info@thewhiteswanlondon.com - Website: www.thewhiteswanlondon.com

Deuchars IPA, Adnams Broadside

Just off Fleet Street, the old Mucky Duck has completed an elegant transformation. A lively, free-spending after-work crowd can make the ground floor a busy press of suits and pints, but the vast mirror, reflecting the white sweep of the mezzanine and the big blackboards, makes this handsome, part-panelled bar feel bigger than it really is. In the quieter dining room upstairs, a long mirrored ceiling again gives a sense of space, while elegant, close-set tables and low-backed leather chairs lend a smart brasserie atmosphere. The bar menu with pub classics and a few earthier Old English dishes – pheasant pie, pork cheeks on mash and pints of prawns – makes way for a European and British daily repertoire that might include monkfish fricassee or lamb with gnocchi and root veg. Tidy if rather formal service. Good value for The City.

Food serving times:

Monday:	12pm-3pm
Tuesday-Friday:	
	12pm-3pm, 6pm-10pm

Closed 24-26 and 31 December, 1 January and Bank Holidays

Prices:

Meals: 25.00 (set price lunch) and a la carte 20.00/30.00

Typical Dishes

Seared foie gras, truffle ice cream

Lemon sole à la meunière

Praline and coffee parfait

⊖ Chancery Lane. NCP car park nearby or free on street parking after 6pm.

Acton Green

010 The Bollo

13-15 Bollo Lane, Acton Green W4 5LR

Tel.: (020) 8994 6037

e-mail: sullivanashley@hotmail.com

Greene King IPA, Abbot Ale

Already a popular neighbourhood meeting-place, this handsome redbrick tavern is at its best on bright summer days, when a buoyant crowd of drinkers and diners fill the spacious bar and make themselves at home on the terrace. There's a slightly smarter rear dining room – its wood panelling, burgundy walls and tan leather banquettes rather suit the pub's Victorian dimensions – but the full menu is served throughout. A core of suitably generous gastropub favourites needs no introduction, but the daily changing menu finds room for more eclectic and original dishes in the same forthright, full-flavoured style: their tasty, medium-rare tuna with braised peas, chorizo and celery is worth looking out for.

Food serving times:
Monday-Sunday:
10am-6pm (bar only),
6pm-10.30pm
Closed 25 December
Prices:
Meals: a la carte 18.00/30.00

Typical Dishes

Deep fried brie with red onion marmalade

Sea bass cartoccio with watercress

Pannacotta

⊖ Chiswick Park. Parking meters outside.

Ealing

011 The Ealing Park Tavern

222 South Ealing Rd, Ealing W5 4RL

Tel.: (020) 8758 1879 - Fax: (020) 8560 5269

  VISA **AE** **MC**

Fuller's, Young's, Grand Union and Crane Breweries; also Timothy Taylor, Wadworth 6X, Itchen Valley, Adnams Ales

The M4 thunders along close by, but visitors to the Ealing Park Tavern are oblivious to its presence. This typically Victorian pub looks large on the outside, and is cavernous within. It's split into two, with a large, pubby bar, and a high-ceilinged dining area, and light floods through large windows looking out onto the road. Despite its London location, there's a modern-rustic flavour to the cooking, which lures the locals in droves. The buzzy atmosphere is enhanced with an open-plan kitchen, old wooden tables and chairs and colourful modern artwork on the walls. Daily changing menus might offer goats cheese with mixed bean salad for a starter, with rump of lamb, rösti and rosemary jus next up.

Food serving times:
Monday: 6pm-10.30pm
Tuesday-Sunday and Bank Holiday Monday:
           12pm-3pm, 6pm-10.30pm
Closed 25-26 December
Prices:
Meals: a la carte 20.00/25.00

Typical Dishes

Globe artichoke and Hollandaise sauce

Treacle cured pork with sage mash

Spotted dick and custard

⊖ South Ealing. On street parking.

Hackney

012 **Cat & Mutton**

76 Broadway Market, Hackney E8 4QJ

Tel.: 020 7254 5599

e-mail: info@catandmutton.co.uk - Website: www.catandmutton.co.uk

♀ **VISA** **AE** **M⊘**

Adnams , Timothy Taylor Landlord

In Broadway Market's trendier moments, Hackney's old drinking habits feel a world away and, to most of the Cat and Mutton's regulars, the names of Carrington and Toby, etched on its windows, must seem about as up-to-date as medieval stained glass. It still looks like a Victorian corner pub on first sight, but inside it's one large space: the plain, clean lines of the counter, the brick walls, the open kitchen, and the retro school chairs are lit up by those massive windows. A slate board announces the day's menu: snackier at lunchtime, with rarebit or hot sandwiches next to more substantial dishes. All in all, the cooking is robustly tasty; produce from the Saturday farmers' market is worked in well, and anyone showing up for a late, late Sunday lunch, deep into the afternoon, could find themselves staying for the live DJ in the evening.

Food serving times:
Tuesday-Saturday:
  12pm-3pm, 6.30-10.30pm
Sunday: 12pm-3pm
Closed 25-26 December
Prices:
Meals: a la carte 19.00/29.00

Typical Dishes

Smoked ham and foie gras ballottine

Poached halibut, purple sprouting broccoli

Chocolate fondant cake

⊖ London Fields (rail). Parking Pay and Display outside. ⟩⟩

Shoreditch

013 The Fox

28 Paul St, Shoreditch EC2A 4LB

Tel.: (020) 7729 5708
e-mail: fox.ph@virgin.net

VISA · AE · MC

Charles Well's Bombardier

On the Islington/Hackney borders, this is a 'back-to-basics' pub with rough décor typified by thick yellowing paint. You could hardly describe the tables and chairs as 'shabby chic', just shabby. Yet the clientele is often three deep at the bar, ranging from locals to business suits. So what's the secret? It's hinted at downstairs in succulent salt beef sandwiches and Kirkham Lancashire Ploughmans; the real answer lies upstairs, in the much more serene dining room. Ornate silver cutlery, bone-handled knives and grannies china indicate that something rather special is going on here. To describe the menus as terse would be an overstatement: what they say is what you'll get. Chef cooks in a no-nonsense, unfussy style, producing flavours that are bold, seasonal and fresh; combinations have been carefully thought-through, reflecting a contemporary European style. Quite simply, this is a rough and ready East End pub with a great menu.

⊖ Old Street, Moorgate.

Food serving times:
Monday-Friday:
12.30pm-3pm, 6.30pm-10pm
Closed 27 December
to 3 January, Easter
and Bank Holidays
Prices:
Meals: 21.50 (set price lunch
and dinner)

Typical Dishes

Pork and chicken liver terrine

Onglet, roasties and Bearnaise sauce

Chocolate pudding

Shoreditch

014 The Princess

76-78 Paul St, Shoreditch EC2A 4NE

Tel.: (020) 7729 9270

e-mail: theeaston@btconnect.com

Timothy Taylor Landlord, Fuller's London Pride

A traditional Victorian pub which has travelled the modernist path of others within this trendy postcode, The Princess announces its gastro credentials atop an iron staircase within an eye-catchingly stylish first floor setting. Here you'll find bold wallpaper, oil paintings, sash windows and very comfortable leather cushioned chairs arranged at dark wooden tables. Rather than a lengthy list of dishes, chef concentrates on a concise menu, and the choice is invariably interesting and original. And well priced, to boot. The style is international, with Mediterranean combinations particularly to the fore. Waiters are friendly and efficient, and obviously used to being busy. This is a well-run pub that's strong in every aspect, and great to visit after a trip to nearby Spitalfields Market or Columbia Road flower market.

Food serving times:

Sunday-Friday:
12.30pm-3pm,
6.30pm-10.30pm

Saturday: 6.30pm-10.30pm

Closed 24 December to 8 January and Bank Holidays

Prices:

Meals: a la carte 22.00/26.00

Typical Dishes

Zucchini, leek and Gruyère tart

Sea bream, aïoli

Meringue with whipped passion fruit curd

⊖ Old Street. Parking meters outside in the street.

Fulham

015 The Farm

18 Farm Lane, Fulham SW6 1PP

Tel.: (020) 7381 3331
e-mail: info@thefarmfulham.co.uk - Website: www.thefarmfulham.co.uk

 Adnam's Broadside, Fuller's London Pride

Don't misjudge The Farm by its offer of a football lunch menu, served before match-days at nearby Stamford Bridge: The Farm sums up the "nouveau" pub as much as Chelsea stand for "nouveau" football. Lustrous dark wood, dark-chocolate leather and subtle, sidelong lighting give the bar and dining room an ultra-stylish look, particularly at the back where smartly set tables aspire to the height of chic. Confident and flavoursome cooking introduces a French and Italian tone to a steady Modern British style; service is efficient, and its element of restaurant poise hardly feels out of place. It's just what the locals wanted: a good-spirited pub-full of them can always be found doing justice to the well-composed cocktail list, enjoying a few bar snacks or meeting up for dinner.

Food serving times:
Monday-Sunday:
  10am-6pm (bar only),
  6pm-11pm
Closed 25 December
Prices:
Meals: a la carte 18.00/35.00

Typical Dishes

Crumbled goat's cheese salad

King prawns and linguine, wild garlic

Crème brûlée

⊖ Fulham Broadway. Difficult street parking.

143

Hammersmith

016 Anglesea Arms

35 Wingate Rd, Hammersmith W6 0UR

Tel.: (020) 8749 1291 - Fax: (020) 8749 1254
e-mail: anglesea-events@gmail.com

 VISA **MC**

Fuller's London Pride, Greene King IPA, Old Speckled Hen, Adnams Broadside

Though hidden away in deepest Hammersmith, the secret of one of London's original gastropubs is long since out, and a wait at the bar, and at table, is not uncommon on busier days, though decent service smooths things over well. Undoubtedly food-focused, there's still something of the residential street-corner pub about the place, with a sizeable bar at the centre and its dozen close-spaced dining tables kept off to one side, expectantly facing a bustling open kitchen. Capable and full-flavoured cooking in distinctly modern style encompasses dishes like home-cured gravadlax, duck with roast figs and celery and a smooth summer fool with biscotti.

Food serving times:
Monday-Saturday:
12.30pm-2.45pm, 7pm-11.45pm
Sunday: 7pm-10pm
Closed 23-29 December
(bookings not accepted)
Prices:
Meals: 12.95 (set price lunch) and a la carte 20.00/35.00

Typical Dishes

Warm squid saladt

Roast cod fillet, snail bourguignon

Vanilla crème brûlee

Ravenscourt Park/Goldhawk Road.

Shepherd's Bush

017 The Havelock Tavern

57 Masbro Rd, Brook Green, Shepherd's Bush W14 0LS

Tel.: (020) 7603 5374 - Fax: (020) 7602 1163
e-mail: info@thehavelocktavern.co.uk - Website: www.thehavelocktavern.co.uk

Brakspear's, Fuller's London Pride, Marston's Pedigree

It may not look too enticing on the corner of this unassuming West London street, but inside, the Havelock is buzzing. Formerly two shops, there are still big windows looking out onto the street. It gets very, very busy here, so for drinkers or diners, the message is simple: arrive early. Many come for the rather classy food to be had, and most tables are snapped up by seven o'clock. Menus change daily and might include pork with lentils, spinach and mash; Thai fish cakes with chilli dipping sauce; or smoked salmon with soft flour tortillas, avocado salsa, coriander and lime. Despite the bustling atmosphere, staff are friendly and attentive and obviously used to being at full stretch.

Food serving times:
Monday-Saturday:
12.30pm-2.30pm, 7pm-10pm
Sunday: 12.30pm-3pm,
7pm-9.30pm

**Closed 22-26 December
and Easter Sunday
(bookings not accepted)**
Prices:
Meals: a la carte 21.00/26.00

Typical Dishes

Steamed mussels with thyme

Slow roast belly of pork

Norfolk apple and treacle tart

⊖ Kensington Olympia. Pay and display parking during the week, free parking at weekends.

Highgate

018 The Bull

13 North Hill, Highgate N6 4AB

Tel.: (0845) 456 5033 - Fax: (0845) 456 5034
e-mail: info@inthebull.biz - Website: www.inthebull.biz

  VISA

Highgate IPA, Timothy Taylor Landlord

Since the spring of 2005, denizens of one of London's most sought-after areas have been flocking to this smart Grade II listed pub standing proudly on North Hill. The building dates only from 1906 but the earliest recorded date for a pub here is 1765. There is dining on both floors; upstairs, together with the small bar, there are striking floor to ceiling windows, a real fire and a relaxed style of décor; the art on the walls is for sale. Downstairs you eat at banquette seats in a smart, spacious area with good views of the chefs at work in the open kitchen. Menus are very appealing: simple European dishes, mostly English with a strong Gallic undercurrent, all home-made using top quality seasonal ingredients.

Food serving times:
Monday: 6pm-10.30pm
Tuesday-Friday:
12pm-2.30pm, 6pm-10.30pm
Saturday-Sunday:
12pm-3.30pm,
6.30pm-9.30pm (10.30pm Sat)
Closed 25 and 26 December.
Prices:
Meals: 17.95 (set price lunch)
and a la carte 27.00/40.00

Typical Dishes

Roast scallops, sauce Nero

Monkfish, jamon de pata negra

Chocolate and almond pudding

⊖ Highgate. Free parking on road outside pub.

Chiswick

019 **The Devonshire House**

126 Devonshire Rd, Chiswick W4 2JJ

Tel.: (020) 8987 2626 - Fax: (020) 8995 0152

e-mail: info@thedevonshirehouse.co.uk

 VISA **AE** **MC**

 Fuller's London Pride

At the quiet residential end of a West London road close to the A4, this Victorian pub has reaped the benefits of a pleasant conversion: a young crowd creates a bustling atmosphere in what is now a stylish dining pub. Some of the original character is retained by way of the high ceiling and large windows. Elsewhere, the feeling is contemporary and spacious, with wooden floors, navy blue banquettes and chocolate brown leather chairs. Interesting, contemporary menus offer a succinct but balanced choice and might include, for starters, summer salad with smoked haddock brandade, tomato and chive vinaigrette; for mains, escalope of pork Milanese; and, as a refreshing dessert, nougatine glace with fresh raspberries. Obliging and efficient service.

Food serving times:
Tuesday-Friday:
    12pm-2.30pm, 5pm-12am
Saturday-Sunday:
    12pm-3.30pm, 5pm-12am
Closed 24-30 December
Prices:
Meals: a la carte 14.95/25.95

Typical Dishes

Tagliatelle of oxtail ragout
Paillards of chicken
Waffles with caramelised banana

⊖ Turnham Green. Parking available on the street.

Archway

020 St John's

91 Junction Rd, Archway N19 5QU

Tel.: (020) 7272 1587 · Fax: (020) 7687 2247

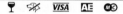

Deuchar's IPa, Timothy Taylor's Landlord, Brakspear Special

This one-time scruffy, edgy boozer, down from Archway tube, looks sharp and bright again as a smartly run gastro-local. Broad picture windows light up the long counter bar, its real buzz provided by a lively mix of regulars and others at stools and scrubbed tables, but squeeze your way through to the big double doors on the right to see the place at its best. The high-ceilinged former snooker hall, in fine period proportion, is now a bustling dining room and open kitchen, hung with tall mirrors and big blackboard menus; laid-back, convivial and modestly stylish, it's just the place for varied, fresh-tasting dishes in decent quantity, including some tasty chargrills. Spirited staff in t-shirts and aprons shuttle to and fro with baskets of fresh bread, providing swift and friendly service.

Food serving times:
Monday-Thursday:
6.30pm-11pm
Friday-Saturday:
12pm-3.30pm, 6.30pm-11pm
Sunday: 12pm-4pm,
6.30pm-9.30pm
Closed 25-26 December and 1 January
Prices:
Meals: a la carte 20.00/30.00

Typical Dishes

Pork, rabbit, chorizo and black pudding terrine

Baked bream, basil oil

Plum and apple crumble

 Archway. Street parking free after 6.30pm.

Canonbury

021 **The House**

63-69 Canonbury Rd, Canonbury N1 2DG

Tel.: (020) 7704 7410 - Fax: (020) 7704 9388
e-mail: info@inthehouse.biz - Website: www.inthehouse.biz

VISA ◐ ◍

 Adnams ales

Around the back of the Town Hall in residential Islington, a pleasant and unassuming bar which is popular with the locals. There's a subtle change of tone in the dining room, however: smart linen, flowers, candlelight and even the artwork should prepare you for similar aspiration and attention to detail in a menu that shows the chef's West End restaurant experience. From the open kitchen come carefully composed and full-flavoured dishes: good-sized slices of crispy duck on a soy-dressed watercress salad, herb-crusted cod with noodles and a creamy mustard and chive velouté, and rich, smooth chocolate and orange parfait. A lunchtime list includes shepherd's pie and a modern take on the all-day breakfast.

Food serving times:
Monday: 12pm-2.30pm
Tuesday-Friday:
 12pm-2.30pm, 6pm-10.30pm
Saturday-Sunday:
                12pm-3.30pm,
 6pm-10.30pm(9.30pm Sun)
Closed 24-26 December
Prices:
Meals: 17.95 (fixed price lunch)
and a la carte 45.00/66.00

Typical Dishes

Crab and ginger spring rolls

Rib of beef with a shallot crust

Chocolate pudding, vanilla ice cream

⊖ Highbury and Islington. Parking meters outside or free after 6.30pm.

Clerkenwell

022 **The Coach & Horses**

26-28 Ray St, Clerkenwell EC1R 3DJ

Tel.: (020) 7278 8990 - Fax: (020) 7278 1478

e-mail: info@thecoachandhorses.com - Website: www.thecoachandhorses.com

 Adnams, Fuller's London Pride, Timothy Taylor Landlord

Tucked away off the Farringdon Road, this is an establishment that delights in its self-confidence. Its ornate brick exterior is clothed in red and cream, and a cheeky sign might entice followers of Cinderella. Located off the 'main drag', it tends not to get as busy as most – the unaware are missing out on a certain element of eccentricity, not least from the chef who's called Scott Welsh and hails from Ireland! His dishes are fiercely seasonal and carefully compiled from painstakingly sourced suppliers. There aren't too many ingredients or unnecessary garnishes; you might even detect an influence from the nearby St John oozing from the rustic fare - for example: snipped pig's ear on split pea soup. No shortage of bare tables and chairs to sit at in the down-to-earth interior; in good weather, head for the sunny 'Back Room' terrace.

Food serving times:
Monday-Friday:
12pm-3pm, 6pm-10pm
Saturday: 6pm-10pm
Closed Christmas to New Year, Easter weekend and Bank Holidays
Prices:
Meals: a la carte 20.00/28.00

⊖ Faringdon. Parking meters across the road.

Typical Dishes

Broccoli with a boiled duck egg

Goosnargh duck breast with pommes Sarladaise

Mrs Allen's carrageen moss pudding

Finsbury

023 The Peasant

240 St John St, Finsbury EC1V 4PH

Tel.: (020) 7336 7726 - Fax: (020) 7490 1089
e-mail: eat@thepeasant.co.uk - Website: www.thepeasant.co.uk

Charles Wells Bombardier and 1 monthly changing guest ale

No-one charting the rise of the gastro-revolution could miss out The Peasant. This upmarket founding father between Smithfield and The Angel is a landmark pub in more ways than one, and if the cooking has evolved over time, the recipe for success has stayed the same: daily changing menus of robust, well-presented cooking combine fresh ingredients and a marked Mediterranean influence; brunch on Sunday. The pub's original glory days came over a century ago and hints of handsome, high-Victorian style remain, from the broad arched windows and lofty ceilings to the tiled floor, but the defining quality is the bustling atmosphere of happy Londoners at full volume. Even when it's packed out, more often than not, well-organised staff keep their cool and their smiles, but head for the linen-laid tables upstairs if you want quieter, more intimate dining. In fine weather a dozen diners can enjoy the garden patio.

Food serving times:
Monday-Sunday:
    12pm-4pm, 6pm-10.30pm
(booking essential)
Prices:
Meals: a la carte 35.00/45.00

Typical Dishes

Grilled kangaroo, oyster mushrooms

Roast lamb chump

Piernik cake with rote grötze

↦ Farringdon/Angel. Parking meters opposite.

Finsbury

024 The Well

180 St John St, Finsbury EC1V 4JY

Tel.: (020) 7251 9363 - Fax: (020) 7404 2250
e-mail: drink@downthewell.co.uk - Website: www.downthewell.co.uk

 No real ales offered

Finsbury locals may not glance twice as they pass this predictable looking pub-on-a-corner in a trendy part of St John Street not unacquainted with food-and-drink destinations. But regulars in The Well know they're on to a good thing here. Big blue canopies hang out over the pavement providing shelter for drinkers at al fresco benches next to slide-open screen windows. Inside, it's small, busy and buzzing: all around is the ambience of the metropolitan gastropub with wooden floorboards, exposed brickwork and mismatched wood furniture. It's the food that lifts it above the average, with everything from the 'pie of the week' to sophisticated, accomplished dishes in the modern British vein: all the fish and shellfish is from Billingsgate. Downstairs a sexy lounge with fish tanks and brown sofas draws a more louche crowd.

Food serving times:
Monday-Friday:
   12pm-3pm, 6pm-10.30pm
Saturday: 10.30am-10.30pm
Sunday: 10.30am-10pm
Closed 24-26 December
Prices:
Meals: a la carte 18.00/25.00

Typical Dishes
Foie gras and chicken liver parfait
Rump of lamb
Valrhona chocolate cake

⊖ Farringdon, Barbican, Angel. Parking in the street outside.

Islington

025 The Barnsbury

209-211 Liverpool Rd, Islington N1 1LX

Tel.: (020) 7607 5519 - Fax: (020) 7607 3256
e-mail: info@thebarnsbury.co.uk - Website: www.thebarnsbury.co.uk

Timothy Taylor Landlord, Fuller's London Pride and 1 monthly guest ale

A block or so back from busy Upper Street, The Barnsbury takes things at a more laid-back pace than its larger neighbours. Easy to spot in summer, with a line of flowering lavender fringing the front railings, this agreeable gastrobar keeps up the same downplayed chic on the inside. It's appealingly simple, with a central counter bar surrounded by pews, old stripped tables and chairs, cool cut-glass goblet chandeliers and quarterly changing tableaux on the walls, which are painted in signature shades of dusky duck-egg blue. Genuinely helpful staff, as smiling and at ease as the regulars, happily make the effort to talk you through the menu, a selection of robust modern pub dishes served in unstinting portions.

Food serving times:
Monday-Sunday:
    12pm-3pm, 6.30pm-10pm
Closed 24-26 December
and 1 January
Prices:
Meals: a la carte 21.00/30.00

Typical Dishes

Chilli pickled oranges with feta cheese

Veal chop, porcini sauce

Mango and raspberry semifredo

⊖ Highbury and Islington. On-street parking after 6.30pm.

Islington

026 The Drapers Arms

44 Barnsbury St, Islington N1 1ER
Tel.: (020) 7619 0348 - Fax: (020) 7619 0413
e-mail: info@thedrapersarms.co.uk - Website: www.thedrapersarms.co.uk

Old Speckled Hen, Courage Best and 1 monthly guest ale

An impressive and substantial stone façade announces this proud looking Georgian pub tucked away in one of fashionable Islington's quiet side streets. It was once a ramshackle boozer, but in the last few years has undergone something of a "gastropub" rebirth: rough wooden floors, plenty of space to air-kiss, shiny leather sofas, tables and booths sited along walls made over with a contemporary palette. A delightful rear courtyard terrace is great for summer smooching, and food comes with the guarantee of a light, precise touch: white gazpacho with chilli tiger prawns; gnocchi with Gorgonzola; salmon and cod fishcake with spinach and tartare sauce.

Food serving times:
Monday-Saturday:
    12pm-3pm, 7pm-10.30pm
Sunday: 12pm-5pm
Closed 24-28 December
Prices:
Meals: a la carte 22.00/35.00

Typical Dishes

Chicken livers, poached egg

Moroccan chicken, spiced couscous

Bitter chocolate tart

⊖ Highbury and Islington.

Islington

027 The Northgate

113 Southgate Rd, Islington N1 3JS
Tel.: (020) 7359 7392 - Fax: (020) 7359 7393

 Fuller's London Pride, Deuchars IPA and regularly changing guest ales

The Northgate looks like the kind of ordinary corner pub you walk past every day, but ask around and you won't want to pass up a visit to this neighbourhood stalwart. A traditionally proportioned front room mixes scrubbed tables and wood floors with eye-catching works of modern art; a big central bar separates it from a slightly smarter dining room to the back. There's no hard and fast split, though, and locals who pull up a stool for a half may well end up staying for one of the daily specials; you can also eat out on the street-side terrace. Blackboard menus offer a cross-section of modern cooking, often working in Mediterranean ideas and flavours to good effect: unusually for a London pub, they also bake their own bread.

Food serving times:
Monday-Friday:
6.30pm-10.30pm
Saturday: 12pm-4pm,
6.30pm-10.30pm
Sunday: 12pm-4pm,
6.30pm-9.30pm
Closed 25 December
Prices:
Meals: a la carte 18.00/24.00

Typical Dishes

Tiger prawns with chilli and garlic

Lamb shank, spiced couscous

Vanilla pannacotta

Essex Road/Canonbury (rail).
Unrestricted street parking Sunday,
after 6.30pm Monday-Saturday.

Chelsea

028 Builders Arms

13 Britten St, Chelsea SW3 3TY
Tel.: (020) 7349 9040

 Deuchar's IPA, Fuller's London Pride, Adnams Best Bitter

Down a quiet Chelsea side street, just off the King's Road, this neat and tidy cream-washed terraced bar can seem impossibly crowded in the early evening, but squeeze through to the less smoky back rooms and a more orderly sense prevails: here you can find bookshelves, wing-back armchairs and slightly surreal oil paintings which create an easy, offbeat lounge ambience for the young King's Road set. There are warming colours everywhere, enhanced by an open fire, and matted flooring adds to the contemporary feel. Relaxed but super-efficient staff haven't let the pub's popularity go to their heads, serving up modern dishes in endless succession, and somehow it all works. Lunch times are much quieter than evenings so arrive early for dinner. And bear in mind that Sundays in this part of the world are particularly busy so do plan ahead.

Food serving times:
Monday-Wednesday:
12pm-2.30pm,
7.15pm-10.15pm
Thursday-Saturday:
12pm-2.30pm,
7.15pm-11.15pm
Sunday: 12pm-4pm,
7.15pm-9.15pm
Closed 25 December and 1 January
(bookings not accepted)
Prices:
Meals: a la carte 22.00/40.00

⊖ South Kensington. Parking meters available on adjacent roads.

Typical Dishes

Eggs Benedict

Soused mackerel fillets with beetroot salad

Sherry trifle

Chelsea

029 Chelsea Ram

32 Burnaby St, Chelsea SW10 0PL

Tel.: (020) 7351 4008
e-mail: bookings@chelsearam.co.uk

 VISA

Youngs Bitter, Youngs Special and seasonal ales such as Waggledance

Standing out like a hardy reminder of old London near the rather soulless enclaves of Chelsea Harbour, this solid citizen of a dining pub draws in the punters like a magnet: it's on a corner so it's hard to miss it. Walk in and a feeling of good cheer is instantly awakened. This could be something to do with the bright, airy interior with warm yellow hued walls, or the light that pours in through the etched glass windows. Maybe it's just the knowledge that good beer is on handpump and interesting menus lurk round the back in intimate dining alcoves - an internationally influenced choice of dishes is up for grabs: start off, maybe, with Thai duck salad and follow it up with smoked haddock, black pudding and crushed potato. The shelves of old books might serve to remind you that in a past incarnation this was a junk shop.

Food serving times:
Monday-Saturday:
    12pm-3.30pm,
    6.30pm-10.30pm
Sunday: 12pm-4pm,
    7pm-10pm

Prices:
Meals: a la carte 16.00/24.50

Typical Dishes

Asparagus and smoked salmon salad

Chelsea Ram salad

Pear and cinnamon crumble

⊖ West Brompton. Pay and display parking available nearby.

Chelsea

030 Lots Road Pub & Dining Room

114 Lots Rd, Chelsea SW10 0RJ

Tel.: (020) 7352 6645

London Pride, Wadworth 6X, Adnams, Hook Norton

Tucked away between Chelsea Harbour's flats and offices and the old gasworks, this refitted gastropub is a friendly, informal and surprisingly busy place – if you happen to be passing, the logic seems to go, you've every right to make yourself at home. Old schoolroom chairs and tables follow the curve of a quadrant-shaped bar-room, and while you can also get a good plate of something and a cold beer sitting at the metal counter, the most intimate place to dine is easily missed, with smart tables off to the other side; a few deep armchairs also beckon for a slow drink. Young, T-shirted staff stay on the move from table to open kitchen, serving a daily changing menu of contemporary dishes like sea bream with fennel.

Food serving times:
Monday-Sunday:
    12pm-5.30pm, 6pm-10pm
Prices:
Meals: a la carte 35.00/60.00

Typical Dishes

Smoked haddock fish cake with tartar sauce

Lots Road burger with big chips

Rocky Roads chocolate

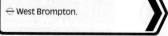

⊖ West Brompton.

Chelsea

031 Swag and Tails

10-11 Fairholt St, Knightsbridge, Chelsea SW7 1EG

Tel.: (020) 7584 6926 - Fax: (020) 7581 9935
e-mail: theswag@swagandtails.com - Website: www.swagandtails.com

Charles Wells Bombardier, Adnams

Just a two-minute walk from Harrods, down a charming mews, hides this cosy little inn with its colourful hanging baskets and smart blue shutters. It makes a neat contrast to the more garish pubs in this part of London. Despite the compact proportions, it falls into two distinct sections: a front half, embellished with wood and pine, brick walls and eponymous swagged curtains; and a rear tiled conservatory with imposing posters and swish down-lighting. Seasonal modern dishes please sophisticated palates while simpler, more popular items are also available.

Food serving times:
Monday (except Bank Holidays) to Friday:
   12pm-3pm, 6pm-10pm
Closed 1 week Christmas to New Year
Prices:
Meals: a la carte 21.25/32.00

Typical Dishes

Pan seared foie gras

Lamb's liver with warm salad of Jersey Royals

Vanilla and yoghurt pannacotta

⊖ Knightsbridge. Parking meters at the end of the street, or on single yellow line after 6.30pm.

Chelsea

032 **The Admiral Codrington**

17 Mossop St, Chelsea SW3 2LY

Tel.: (020) 7581 0005 - Fax: (020) 7589 2452
e-mail: admiralcodrington@longshotplc.com - Website: www.theadmiralcodrington.co.uk

Charles Wells Bombardier, Greene King IPA

This well-established, fashionably located pub is something of a traditional gathering point for the well-heeled neighbours. Its main bar is invariably packed in the evenings, when a pair of shoulder pads can prove a useful fashion accessory. Lightly push your way to the back and you'll find a very pleasant small dining area with wood floor, soft lighting and even a retractable glass roof. Large banquettes, in a modern floral fabric resembling tapestry, can be a haven after the scrum through the bar. The menus are changed quarterly and provide a very good choice: there's strength in depth in the fine range of modern dishes. Pleasant, efficient service is a certainty.

Food serving times:
Monday-Friday:
12pm-2.30pm, 6.30pm-11pm
Saturday: 12pm-3.30pm, 6.30pm-11pm
Sunday: 12pm-4.30pm, 6.30pm-10pm
Closed 24-26 December
Prices:
Meals: a la carte 22.95/31.15

Typical Dishes

Diver caught scallops, pea purée

The Admiral's cod

Passion fruit cheesecake, mandarin sorbet

⊖ South Kensington.

Chelsea

033 The Cross Keys

1 Lawrence St, Chelsea SW3 5NB

Tel.: (020) 7349 9111 - Fax: (020) 7349 9333
e-mail: cross.keys@fsmail.net - Website: www.thexkeys.co.uk

 VISA **AE** **①** **M©**

Courage Best, Directors

A t a fashionable address just up from Cheyne Walk, this is more than just a local pub, whatever the inn sign and 200 year-old façade might suggest on first sight. A spacious bar, brightened by tall windows, mirrors and a curly iron chandelier and open to the gallery above, caters well for drinkers, but the glass–roofed dining room is in a style of its own: tables are spread beneath the branches of a tree, while wicker hurdles, sheaves of grass and a frieze of farming tools are best described as Chelsea Ironic-Rustic. Upstairs, you'll either love or try to ignore a faintly kitsch mix of modern and neo-Classical: the gaping Bacchus-head fireplace on the top floor is particularly impressive. More importantly, though, flavourful, generous standards and specials from the open kitchen strike a real chord with a smart crowd of local diners.

Food serving times:
Monday-Friday:
12pm-3pm, 7pm-10.45pm
Saturday: 12pm-4pm,
7pm-10.45pm
Sunday: 12pm-4pm,
7pm-10pm
Closed 24-30 December and Bank Holidays

Prices:
Meals: 12.50 (set price lunch (except Sunday)) and a la carte 20.65/27.80

Typical Dishes

Smoked duck breast, rocket salad

Seared king scallops in Parma ham

Sticky toffee pudding

⊖ Sloane Square.

Chelsea

034 The Phoenix

23 Smith St, Chelsea SW3 4EE

Tel.: 020 7730 9182

e-mail: thephoenix@geronimo-inns.co.uk - Website: www.geronimo-inns.co.uk

Adnams Best Bitter, Deuchars IPA, Sharp's Doombar

E ven the most "comfortable" of London neighbourhoods has need of a superior kind of local, and the Phoenix gets the full approval of a friendly young crowd, all shopped-out from an afternoon on the King's Road or just kicking back on a balmy weekend evening. A retro tweak or two stops the stylish bar from feeling too uncongenially modern: only in Chelsea could this be thought of as 'shabby chic', but suede, stripped-back floorboards and some suitably clunky old wooden chairs give it a nicely lived-in feel. It's never less than pleasantly busy and, unlikely as it seems, the street-side seats have become one of the area's alternative "destinations". Extensive Modern British menus and a few specials serve their public well. Service is polite, friendly and never off-hand.

Food serving times:
Monday-Sunday:
12pm-2.45pm, 7pm-10pm
Closed 25-26 December
Prices:
Meals: a la carte 15.00/25.00

Typical Dishes

Red pepper and goat's cheese salad

Salmon and tiger prawn gratin

Hot chocolate pudding

 Sloane Square. Parking meters.

Chelsea

035 The Pig's Ear

35 Old Church St, Chelsea SW3 5BS

Tel.: 020 7352 2908 - Fax: 020 7352 9321
e-mail: thepigsear@hotmail.co.uk - Website: www.thepigsear.co.uk

Uley Brewery 'Pigs Ear', Deuchars IPA, Adnams

Around the corner from the King's Road, the lightly refurbished Pig's Ear still mixes in plenty of traditional style in a likeable ground-floor bar, with the odd pig-themed picture and ornament here and there. They're also represented on the menu – pigs' ears are not unknown as a starter, and are one of the more extreme examples of a taste for slightly uncommon but properly used ingredients. The bar menu works equally well if you want a set lunch or just a main course, though be warned that it can get very busy in here: you may need a little luck or determination to grab a space. If the panelled first-floor dining room offers more peace and quiet, and a more structured menu, the style of cooking carries over – hearty cuisine with a rustic edge.

Food serving times:
Monday-Friday:
 12.30pm-3pm, 7pm-11.30pm
Saturday: 12.30pm-3pm,
 7pm-10.30pm
Sunday: 12.30pm-4pm
Closed 25-26 December
and 1 January
Prices:
Meals: a la carte 22.00/35.75

Typical Dishes

Salad of baby octopus

Fillet of turbot, pommes chateau

Lemon and goat's cheese tart

Sloane Square (25 mins. on foot).

Earl's Court

036 Hollywood Arms

45 Hollywood Rd, Earl's Court SW10 9HX
Tel.: (020) 7349 7840 - Fax: (020) 7349 7841

Y   VISA   AE   MC

    Fuller's London Pride, Hogsback TEA

An intelligent renovation of this handsome old pub seems to have struck just the right balance: original glasswork has been preserved while fine fabrics, neo-Gothic arches and even the period-patterned wallpaper pay discreet modern homage to the more restrained school of Victorian design. Beyond the stylish bar - polished tables and club chairs - is a softly lit dining room serving a concise, Mediterranean influenced menu with some original touches: flavourful dishes include tender veal with a piquant lemon and caper sauce and a warm salad of artichokes, butter beans, aïoli and soft-boiled egg. Smooth, helpful service really adds to the enjoyment.

Food serving times:
Monday-Saturday:
12pm-10pm
Sunday: 12pm-5pm
Closed 23 December to 2 January
Prices:
Meals: a la carte 18.00/25.00

Typical Dishes

Steamed prawn dim sum

Crab ginger and lemon confit salad

Chocolate fondant

West Brompton. Pay and display parking nearby.

Wimbledon

037 The Fire Stables

27-29 Church Rd, Wimbledon SW19 5DQ

Tel.: (020) 8946 3197 - Fax: (020) 8946 1101
e-mail: thefirestables@thespiritgroup.com

Fuller's London Pride

Amongst the trendy natives of Wimbledon, this is seen as a rather smart and stylish addition to the eateries of SW19. They're not wrong: The Fire Stables is handily set in the centre of the village, and is a dining pub writ large, the contemporary décor being modish but not clinical. There's a high vaulted ceiling with a startling abstract painting on the wall. Furniture is a pleasing mix of modern and retro: leather sofas, dark wooden artefacts and floorboards, a coal fire. The rear restaurant serves locally renowned, heart-warming menus. How about the moist, fresh, tasty lamb burger with herbs, light mayonnaise and thick cut, home cooked chunky chips? Followed by feather light panna cotta with caramelised blood orange salad? Enough people are smitten, even though it's not the cheapest place around, so get there early.

Food serving times:
Monday-Sunday:
 12pm-4pm, 6pm-10.30pm
Prices:
Meals: 15.50 (set price lunch) and a la carte 22.00/33.00

⊖ Wimbledon. Pay and display parking outside.

Typical Dishes

Seared scallops, minted pea purée

Herb crusted rack of lamb

Chocolate torte

Barnes

038 The Bridge

204 Castelnau Road, Barnes SW13 9DW
Tel.: (020) 8563 9811 - Fax: (020) 8748 50096
e-mail: thebridgeinbarnes@btinternet.com - Website: www.thebridgeinbarnes.co.uk

 rest VISA AE ① ⓂⒸ

Adnams Broadside, Ruddles Best, Charles Wells Bombardier

Smartly refurbished a few years back, The Bridge's smart gold lettering and sign proclaim a welcome change of direction for this reformed boozer. With polished tables and chairs dotted around a horseshoe counter bar, the original proportions remain, while the old fireplace and the arch of the ceiling fit the cool but casual look of the retro lounge and its palms, leather sofas and chandelier. Even in the more formal dining area, however, the hint of smartness is less important than the approachable, pleasantly lived-in feel of the place. There's also a neat decked terrace set aside for summer dining and a light seasonal shift in the menu of contemporary gastropub favourites. Though it's set back from the river, don't go expecting a slow, peaceful pint on Boat Race day!

Food serving times:
Monday-Saturday:
 12pm-3pm, 5.30pm-10.30pm
Sunday: 12pm-9.30pm
Closed 25 December
Prices:
Meals: 18.50/25.00 (set price lunch/dinner) and a la carte 21.00/30.00

Typical Dishes

Asparagus and chicken liver terrine

Halibut fillet, saffron bouillabaisse

Bread and butter pudding

Hammersmith. Near Hammersmith Bridge, opposite Lonsdale Road. Parking in Arundel Terrace.

East Sheen

039 The Victoria

10 West Temple Sheen, East Sheen SW14 7RT

Tel.: (020) 8876 4238 - Fax: (020) 8878 3464
e-mail: bookings@thevictoria.net - Website: www.thevictoria.net

    VISA **AE** **MC**

Old Speckled Hen

The age-of-empire pub sign still hangs outside The Victoria, but any resemblance to a suburban boozer stops at the door. Restyled in clean lines and natural colours, a conservatory with linen-clad tables leads out to a terrace and children's play area: it's ideal for diners who like a quick slide or clamber between courses, but a post-lunch family ramble across nearby Richmond Park is better for really letting off steam. Daily changing evening menus combine traditional and Mediterranean-inspired dishes like walnut and rocket penne, brandade-stuffed peppers and sea bass with a bouillabaise sauce; there are one or two weekend lunch specials and understanding staff can suggest a few smaller failsafe options for young gastronomes. It's worth knowing that they're also open for morning coffee and buns: a big hit with mums and toddlers alike.

Food serving times:
Monday-Friday:
    12pm-2.30pm, 7pm-10pm
Saturday: 12pm-3pm,
    7pm-10pm
Sunday: 12pm-4pm,
    7pm-9pm
Closed 24-27 December
Prices:
Meals: a la carte 25.00/35.00
7 rooms : 108.50

Typical Dishes

Chicken and pork terrine

Charolais rib eye steak

Chocolate pot

⊖ Mortlake/North Sheen (rail). Parking.

Bermondsey

040 The Hartley

64 Tower Bridge Road, Bermondsey SE1 4TR

Tel.: (020) 7394 7023

e-mail: enquries@thehartley.com - Website: www.thehartley.com

 VISA AE ◑ 🅜🅒

 No real ales offered

It's already a bit of a sleeper hit with the upwardly mobile young neighbours and local after-work diners, and Bermondsey may soon wonder how it ever got on without the new version of this Victorian redbrick pub, a little one-room place with close-set, rickety bistro tables, an open kitchen and a lightly quirky taste in decoration. No points for guessing the origin of the name: the converted Hartley's factory across the road is remembered in old nanny-knows-best adverts, black and white photos showing a hard day at the marmalade vats and even jars of jam above the spirits rack. Fight down the urge to order toast and choose instead from a concise menu – terrines, steaks, roast poussin and salsa rosso, salmon cakes and chips – or half a dozen daily specials. Friendly staff, and efficient with it.

Food serving times:
Monday-Friday:
        12pm-3pm, 6pm-10pm
Saturday: 11pm-4pm,
        6pm-10pm
Sunday: 12pm-7pm
Closed 25-27 December and 1 January
(Sunday lunch - roast menu only)
Prices:
Meals: a la carte 16.00/30.00

Typical Dishes

Sherry glazed foie gras

Chargrilled Springbok steak

Lemon mousse brûlée

⊖ Borough. On street parking (meters).

Waterloo

041 The Anchor & Hope

36 The Cut, Waterloo SE1 8LP
Tel.: (020) 7928 9898 - Fax: (020) 7928 4595

Charles Wells Bombardier, Eagle IPA and weekly changing guest ale

Those in the know queue round the bar to eat here so arrive early to avoid waiting. Close to the Young Vic Theatre, this place is noisy and has a real buzz. This is one of London's most talked-about dining pubs, where a stylish and convivial no-frills attitude extends to communal tables and boiled eggs and celery salt on the bar, yet avoids the charge of inverse pretension: the patrons serve out front, behind the bar and also do the cooking. A tiny open kitchen serves up simply presented but very satisfying cooking which is indebted to the French regional traditions and the earthy, rustic cuisine of St John, Clerkenwell, but remains seriously original for all that. When you add impressively calm, well-timed service, even under pressure, and wines by the tumbler and carafe, this represents conspicuously good value for money.

Food serving times:
Tuesday-Saturday:
 12pm-2.30pm, 6pm-10.30pm
Monday: 6pm-10.30pm
Closed 25 December to 1 January and Bank Holidays
Prices:
Meals: a la carte 18.00/35.00

Typical Dishes

Smoked sprats

Bottled rabbit, white beans, tomatoes and rocket

Walnut pick-me-up

⊖ Southwark.

169

Canary Wharf

042 The Gun

27 Coldharbour, Canary Wharf E14 9NS
Tel.: (020) 7515 5222 - Fax: (020) 7515 4407
e-mail: info@thegundocklands.com - Website: www.thegundocklands.com

 Youngs Ordinary, Adnams Broadside, Brakspear Honeycomb

Restored after a fire, The Gun might have played more on an authentic naval heritage that begins in the era of the Blackwall cannon-foundry, the India Docks and that most saleable of maritime heroes, Lord Nelson. Thank goodness it didn't. The "Horatio" and "Emma" signs on the toilets are a small price to pay: relaid oak, polished black bar panels and white walls, and a print of a magnificent Dreadnought-era destroyer at full steam give it all the maritime London look it needs. Even the charming terrace keeps it real with a view of the Dome and the cement works. Blackboard specials make the most of nearby Billingsgate market, a great local source of fresh fish, and the modern cooking on a classic French base strikes a good balance between finesse and bold pub style. Keen service is neat and well-timed.

Food serving times:
Monday-Friday:
    12pm-3pm, 6pm-10.30pm
Saturday: 10.30am-4pm,
        6pm-10.30pm
Sunday: 10.30am-4pm,
        6pm-9.30pm
Closed 26 December
Prices:
Meals: a la carte 22.00/35.00

Typical Dishes

Omelette cradinal

Poached guinea fowl with sauteed foie gras

Crème brûlee

⊖ Blackwall (DLR). Street parking.

Battersea

043 The Greyhound

136 Battersea High St, Battersea SW11 3JR

Tel.: (020) 7978 7021 - Fax: (020) 7978 0599
e-mail: eat@thegreyhoundatbattersea.co.uk - Website: www.thegreyhoundatbattersea.co.uk

No real ales offered

The owner's knowledge and experience, gained as a sommelier, is given full rein in The Greyhound's superb wine list, but its concise contemporary menu deserves to be at least as well known in this corner of South West London. Behind its neat, tile-and-glass frontage in navy and gun-metal grey, the comfortably remodelled pub divides into a stylish bar and a cosy, nicely lit dining room which opens on to a courtyard: great to have up your sleeve in summer. Even if you're not eating, there's an understated buzz out front, not to mention some interesting beers, but with such a well-priced set lunch on offer, plenty of people take them up on the deal. As in the evening, dishes make use of carefully selected, largely organic produce.

Food serving times:
Tuesday-Saturday:
    12pm-2.45pm, 7pm-10pm
Sunday: 12pm-2.45pm
Closed 24-27 December and 31 December to 3 January

Prices:
Meals: 27.00/31.00 (set price dinner) and lunch a la carte 14.00/16.00

Typical Dishes

Calves liver, anchovy apple

Cornish hake fillet, fennel, tomato and olive salad

Pistachio pannacotta

⊖ Clapham Junction (rail). Parking in Simpson Street.

Putney

044 The Spencer Arms

237 Lower Richmond Road, Putney SW15 1HJ

Tel.: (020) 8788 0640 - Fax: (020) 8780 0816

VISA **MC**

Fuller's London Pride, Adnam's Broadside, Adnam's Explorer, Pride Honeydew

If you're not drinking, you can go for a stroll on adjacent Putney Common. If you're not strolling, you can take in the more sedentary charms of this attractive Victorian corner pub, which, on a warm day, offers visitors smart pavement seating and a pint of Fuller's London Pride. Inside, the dining pub transformation is total. Left of the main entrance is an enticing 'library' area with leather sofas – lose yourself here amongst a plethora of books and games - a fireplace and plasma TV. Over the other side, the hungry are catered for in a rustic bar-cum-restaurant: scrubbed tables and mix-and-match chairs exert an old church/ old school charm. Blackboard menus are concise - six starters, six mains, three puds the max - ranging from the likes of home-made soups to duck pie to Dundee cake with rhubarb compote…maybe the stroll should wait till this point.

Food serving times:
Monday-Friday:
12pm-2.30pm, 6.30pm-10pm
Saturday: 12pm-3pm, 6.30pm-10pm
Sunday: 2pm-3pm, 6.30pm-9.45pm
Closed 25-26 December
Prices:
Meals: a la carte 20.00/27.50

Typical Dishes

Warm goat's cheese and crayfish with rocket

Steak and chips

Bananas and custard

⊖ East Putney. Parking at top of Putney Common and in nearby streets.

Bayswater and Maida Vale

045 The Waterway

54 Formosa St, Bayswater and Maida Vale W9 2JU

Tel.: (020) 7266 3557

e-mail: info@thewaterway.co.uk - Website: www.thewaterway.co.uk

Fuller's London Pride

With bright-painted barges moored along the canal, the trees in full leaf and the church spire beyond, the deck terrace of this smart gastrobar seems far removed from the pressures and cares of Travelcard zones 1 and 2. Cool young locals chat, clink beers and Pinot Grigio and relax on garden chairs and slatted benches; heaters take the last chill out of the spring air. To the right of the bar, a smart team provides relaxed and efficient restaurant-style service, coasting around a chic dining room where leather banquettes, blond wood and elegant lights set the tone. A concise but nicely weighted modern menu offers dishes like braised lamb with Parmesan polenta, crisp, golden salt cod cakes with aioli, or coffee and praline brulée. Civilised fun.

Food serving times:
Monday-Sunday:
12.30pm-3.30pm,
6.30pm-10.30pm

Prices:
Meals: a la carte 20.00/28.00

Typical Dishes

Terrine of confit duck

Pan fried sea bass, risotto of mussels

Selection of French cheeses

⊖ Warwick Avenue. Parking.

Regent's Park & Marylebone

046 The Salt House

63 Abbey Road, St John's Wood, Regent's Park & Marylebone NW8 0AE

Tel.: (020) 7328 6626 - Fax: (020) 7604 4084

e-mail: jackwesthead@majol.co.uk

 ___VISA___ (i) (m)(c)

Greene King IPA and Abbot Ale

Just down the road from the recording studios made famous by the Beatles is this rather grand gastropub. Its corner location guarantees conspicuousness; so does its striking columned façade. A patio terrace with wooden benches, canopy and heaters brings out summer drinkers in swarms. Inside, the bustling front bar leads through to a snazzy cream main dining room, with high ceiling and French posters: large windows let you see on to the terrace. Modern menus are in the Mediterranean style; on Sundays a roast and brunch is up for grabs. Everyday dishes might include courgette and pine nut ravioli with saffron for starters, followed by roast cod with mixed pepper coulis and spinach; to finish, perhaps, deliciously moist chocolate torte.

Food serving times:
Monday-Saturday:
    10am-6pm (bar only),
    6pm-11pm
Closed 25 December
Prices:
Meals: a la carte 18.00/30.00

⊖ St John's Wood/Maida Vale. Some on-street parking, free after 6.30pm.

Typical Dishes

Cornish crab with avocado, ginger and pink grapefruit

Prime South Dakota ribeye steak au jus

Hazlenut ice cream

Victoria

047 The Ebury

Ground Floor, 11 Pimlico Rd, Victoria SW1W 8NA

Tel.: (020) 7730 6784 - Fax: (020) 7730 6149
e-mail: info@theebury.co.uk - Website: www.theebury.co.uk

Fuller's London Pride

The ground floor of this refurbished Victorian redbrick pub is now a rather smart meeting place, with floor-to-ceiling windows looking out to the pavement, and a striking and sizable walnut bar being the centre of attention for those who want to look in: it does have just a hint of the "place to be seen" about it. Much of the space is laid out as a comfortably modern room with stylish tables and chairs, but one end is set aside with small leather sofas, another has become a smart seafood bar. Cooking covers the spectrum, and you can get anything from Welsh rarebit and salads to full modern menus blending the continental brasserie and Modern British kitchen. Service is attentive and quite formal, but pleasantly so. More metropolitan good living from the people who brought you The Wells and The Waterway.

Food serving times:
Monday-Sunday:
    12pm-3pm, 6pm-10.30pm
Closed 25-26 December
Prices:
Meals: a la carte 23.00/29.00

⊖ Sloane Square. On street parking after 6.30pm.

Typical Dishes

Goat's cheese mousse

Roast saddle of lamb, shallot purée

Chocolate fondant, salt caramel

Victoria

048 ## The Thomas Cubitt

44 Elizabeth Street, Victoria SW1W 9PA

Tel.: (020) 7730 6060 - Fax: (020) 7730 6055

e-mail: reservations@thethomascubitt.co.uk - Website: www.thethomascubitt.co.uk

Old Speckled Hen, Adnam's Ale, (John Smiths)

This sizable Georgian pub has been converted and renamed after the famous master builder, who would have approved of its elegant and well-furnished style. There's a split personality here: downstairs is where the drinkers gather and where those wanting pie of the day can repair to rustic tables at the back. Upstairs, however, it's a different story. The dining room is divided into three, with fine period detail at every turn, including edging to the ceilings, marble fireplaces, wooden laid floor, huge floral arrangements and chic grey painted walls. For the sheer sake of a talking point, wall pictures are hung upside down! Unobtrusive service is nevertheless warm and friendly. Time is spent sourcing suppliers, and the modern British dishes are appealingly seasonal.

Food serving times:
Monday-Saturday:
         12pm-3pm, 6pm-10pm
Sunday: 12pm-10pm
Closed 25 December,
1 January, Good Friday
to Easter Monday
Prices:
Meals: 21.50 (set price lunch)
and a la carte 26.50/47.00

Sloane Square. Parking meters in Elizabeth Street and adjoining streets.

Typical Dishes

Seared tuna, grilled asparagus

Loin of lamb, semi dried tomato relish

Lemon tart

Personalized gifts are an important part of any relationship.

Your company's name here

For reaching your customers, driving sales to your business, go for Michelin customized road maps and travel guides. Contact us via **www.b2b-cartesetguides.michelin.com** and we will work out with you a business solution to meet your needs.

A better way forward

*S*trengthened by the iconic BALTIC Centre, the Millennium Bridge and the Angel of the North, the sense of identity which binds Newcastle, Gateshead and the region around them has made northeastern unity a modern reality. In the days of the mighty border fiefdom, Northumbria's independent spirit took shape in the castles of Bamburgh and Alnwick and the splendour of Durham Cathedral, though the most celebrated symbols of the region date back still further. The ruins of Lindisfarne Priory and lonely Inner Farne, just off the beautiful Northumberland coast, recall the austerity and learning of the first monastic settlers, and from Housesteads to Wallsend, Hadrian's Wall is the cornerstone of Northern history. But the North East doesn't stop here – to the surprise of many visitors from further south! Some of England's most impressive working countryside can be found in the vast man-made pinewoods of Kielder Forest and the rolling line of the Cheviots: these weathered volcanic slopes are renowned for flavourful Cheviot lamb, while Kielder is known for its venison. Other specialities include fresh and smoked fish and, of course, Newcastle's famous Brown Ale, the national beverage of the "Geordie Nation"!

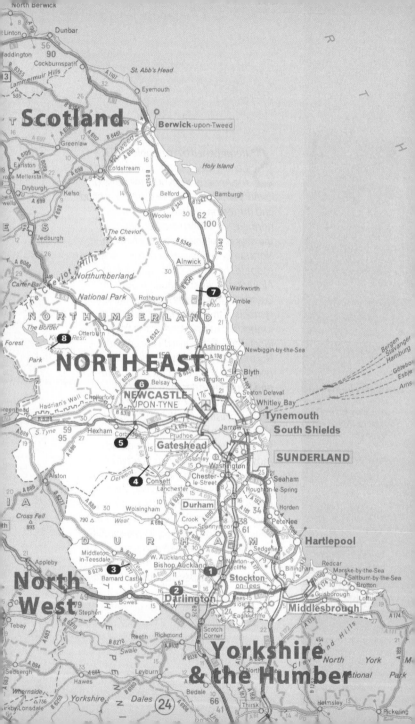

Aycliffe

001 The County

13 The Green, Aycliffe DL5 6LX
Tel.: (01325) 312273

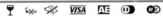

Charles Wells Bombardier, Acorn Brewery Barnsley Bitter, Hambleton Ales

Attention to detail comes first in what must surely be one of Northumbria's most keenly run pubs: that's clear from the warm welcome and the pub itself – four neat, cheerfully coloured rooms with chairs and two-seater pews at polished pine tables, overlooking the village green. There's further proof in the seasonally changing cooking, as the landlord leads by example in the kitchen, producing classic pub and modern British cuisine. Well-drilled staff with a spring in their step are always discreetly helpful, and make the whole thing seem even more of a bargain.

Food serving times:
Monday-Saturday:
12pm-2pm, 6pm-9pm
Closed 25-26 December
(booking essential)
Prices:
Meals: a la carte 17.00/30.00

Typical Dishes

Wild mushroom and pea risotto

Braised oxtail with roasted root vegetables

Tiramisu

5.5mi North of Darlington off A167. Parking.

Hutton Magna

002 Oak Tree Inn

Hutton Magna DL11 7HH

Tel.: (01833) 627371
Website: www.elevation-it.co.uk/oaktree

 VISA **M©**

 Charles Wells Bombardier, Timothy Taylor Landlord, Black Sheep Best Bitter

Personally run by an amiable couple, this whitewashed part-18C inn fits in perfectly in this unpretentious little village on Hutton Beck. Its simple interior – beamed ceiling, leather-seated pews and food-themed pictures on the walls – gives it an intimate atmosphere, helped along by some keen and friendly service. The blackboard changes daily, but there's a consistent theme to the robust cooking: British classics with an understated modern twist. Books, guides and a supply of newspapers available to read.

Food serving times:
Tuesday-Sunday:
6.30pm-8.30pm
Closed 25-26 December and 1 January
Dinner only. Booking essential.
Prices:
Meals: a la carte 24.00/32.50

Typical Dishes

Fettuccini of Shetland mussels
Casserole of local venison
Hot chocolate fondant

6.5mi Southeast of Barnard Castle by B6277 off A66. Parking.

Romaldkirk

003 Rose and Crown

Romaldkirk DL12 9EB

Tel.: (01833) 650213 - Fax: (01833) 650828
e-mail: hotel@rose-and-crown.co.uk - Website: www.rose-and-crown.co.uk

  VISA

Theakstons Best, Black Sheep

Our 2006 Pub of the Year was built in 1733 and bears its age with much dignity, and not a little ivy cladding. The inn's stone features sit in the centre of a pretty, unspoilt village, staring out over the green which still boasts original stocks and water pump. Everything revolves around the charming bar with its reassuring grandfather clock, Jacobean oak settle, ancient farm tools and log fire, which roars magnificently, even in May! This is a deliciously relaxing spot to eat, but you can also choose two other rooms to dine in: the formal, oak-panelled, linen-clad restaurant, or red-walled, brasserie-styled Crown Room. Cuisine counts for much here: daily changing menus reflect the seasons, with local meat and game forming the core of English dishes cooked with culinary good sense. Relax afterwards in the snug, lounge, or slip upstairs to superior bedrooms that strike the right balance between chintzy allure and restful country style.

Food serving times:
Monday-Sunday:
  12pm-1.30pm, 7.30pm-9pm
Closed 24-26 December
a la carte in the bar only

Prices:
Meals: 17.25/26.00 (set price Sunday lunch/4 course dinner) and a la carte 16.45/25.25
12 rooms : 75.00/140.00

3.5mi Southeast of Middleton-in-Teesdale on B6277. On the village green, next to the church. Parking.

Typical Dishes

Potted smoked trout

Confit of duck leg, Le Puy lentils

Hot Calvados and apple cobbler

Carterway Heads

004 **Manor House Inn** 🛏

Carterway Heads DH8 9LX

Tel.: (01207) 255268

🍷 ✂ **VISA** **AE** **MC**

Theakstons Best, Courage Directors, Charles Wells Bombardier and locally brewed guest ales

A personally owned and run pub with a growing reputation for good, honest homecooked food: a separate dining room overlooking the countryside allows you to forget the inn's on a busy road, but you'll find more of a local atmosphere in the trim little wood-fitted bar – good for a pint and a game of darts with the locals if you're feeling confident; a characterful lounge with comfy banquettes and views over the fields has the best of both worlds. Amiable staff serve a mix of popular pub dishes and robust British classics. Pleasant, conveniently appointed bedrooms make a handy stopover if you're heading on north of the border, while a deli shop at one end of the restaurant sells local farm produce and home-made goodies. A short drive west takes you to Derwent Reservoir, with lakeside walks through rolling moorland and pine forest.

Food serving times:
Monday-Sunday:
12pm-2.30pm, 7pm-9.30pm
Closed dinner 25 December
Prices:
Meals: a la carte 17.00/25.00
🛏 **4 rooms :** 33.00/60.00

Typical Dishes

Chicken liver pate

Pan fried scallops with chilli jam

Sticky toffee pudding

3mi West of Consett at junction of B6278 and A68. Parking.

Corbridge

005 The Angel Inn 🛏

Main St, Corbridge NE45 5LA
Tel.: (01434) 632119

🍷 ✂ ✗ *VISA* 💳

Timothy Taylor's Landlord and five other ales usually locally brewed

This 18C coaching inn took on a new lease of life when it was refurbished in the not-too-distant past. It's now the focal point of a pretty, riverside village and quite rightly so. At the entrance, the warm, wood-panelled lounge is furnished with leather Chesterfield and comfy chairs and would be a nice place to settle into, if it weren't for counter claims in other parts of the establishment. A rather charming bar has coil flooring, whitewashed walls, beams and open fires - in other words, a winning mix of rustic and contemporary – while a modern, split-level restaurant sources elaborate weekend meals. During the week, like the bar, it proffers good-sized menus, classical in style with modern twists, on which Northumbrian produce is proudly served at good value prices. Stay overnight in rooms whose taste harmonises with the age of the inn; those at the front boast Tyne Valley views.

Food serving times:
Monday-Saturday:
    12pm-3pm, 6pm-9pm
Sunday: 12pm-3pm
Prices:
Meals: a la carte 16.00/30.00
🛏 **5 rooms :** 60.00/85.00

Typical Dishes

Seared king scallops

Tuna with honey and soy dressing

Raspberry and rhubarb compote

In the town centre. Parking.

Great Whittington

006 Queens Head Inn

Great Whittington NE19 2HP
Tel.: (01434) 672267

 VISA MC

Queens Head Bitter, Black Sheep Bitter

In the beautiful rolling wooded countryside near Hadrian's Wall lies this attractive, quiet, stone-built village and its characterful pub, proudly and personally run for over 20 years. Exposed stone walls and old-English fixtures and fittings give the firelit bar a unpretentious, well-ordered atmosphere, and a neat dining room with a mix of banquettes, pews and old spokeback chairs has the same feeling of everything neatly in its place. Character and charm are equally matched. Suitably traditional cooking has a real Northumbrian flavour to it and the service is as polite as you could possibly wish.

Food serving times:
Tuesday-Saturday:
    12pm-2pm, 6.30pm-9pm
Sunday: 12pm-2pm
Closed 1 week in Spring
and 1 week in Autumn
Prices:
Meals: a la carte 19.50/25.00

Typical Dishes

Chicken liver & bacon pate

Pot roasted guinea fowl

Iced nougatine served with a fruit coulis

6mi North of Corbridge by A68 off B6318. Parking.

Newton on the Moor

007 The Cook and Barker Inn 🛏

Newton on the Moor NE65 9JY

Tel.: (01665) 575234 - Fax: (01665) 575234
Website: www.cookandbarkerinn.co.uk

Black Sheep, Bass, Timothy Taylor Landlord, Theakston's XB, Theakston's Best, Fuller's London Pride

To recommend The Cook and Barker simply as a useful stop for motorists ploughing up and down the A1 doesn't do justice to this big, friendly pub, which has been run by the same team for over 15 years. Traditional country style extends through a series of split-level rooms, main bar and a spacious restaurant, and onto an extensive menu. There's nothing revolutionary here and while a blackboard of daily specials rings the changes, most people seem happy with something classic, served by a considerate and friendly local team who are clearly used to being kept busy. You may choose to eat informally in the bar or opt for the more formal atmosphere in the linen-laid restaurant. Bedrooms vary in size and style, but all are comfy, modern and fairly priced.

Food serving times:
Monday-Sunday:
12pm-2pm, 7pm-9pm
Prices:
Meals: 25.00 (set price dinner menu) and a la carte
25.00/32.00
🛏 **19 rooms :** 47.00/75.00

Typical Dishes

Pressed ham terrine

Roast maigret of duck breast with Asian spices

Nougatine parfait

5mi South of Alnwick by A1. Parking.

Stannersburn

008 The Pheasant Inn

Falstone, Stannersburn NE48 1DD

Tel.: (01434) 240382 - Fax: (01434) 240382
e-mail: enquiries@thepheasantinn.com - Website: www.thepheasantinn.com

*Timothy Taylor Landlord, Black Sheep Bitter, Wylam Brewery
'Whistle Stop'*

This impressive, ivy-clad inn boasts 17C origins; its neighbour can claim even earlier roots, but then that neighbour is the Northumberland National Park. Tradition is a byword at the Pheasant Inn: the owners have been here for nearly 20 years, and run it as keenly now as the day they arrived. There's a two-roomed bar with low beamed ceiling, polished wood tables, cluttered knick-knacks reflecting local history, and the glint of lovingly cared-for brass. The pine furnished dining room is the place for good, old fashioned, tried-and-tested cooking, where you can expect grand portions of popular favourites such as fish from North Shields quay or home-made game and mushroom pie. An old barn conversion next door has been turned into simply furnished, comfy bedrooms.

Food serving times:
Monday-Sunday:
    12pm-2pm, 7pm-9pm
Closed 25-26 December, Monday and Tuesday November-Easter
Prices:
Meals: a la carte 14.00/23.00
🛏 **8 rooms :** 45.00/85.00

Typical Dishes

Red onion and goat's cheese tartlet

Slow roasted Northumbrian lamb

Rhubarb and ginger crumble

0.5mi Northeast crossing North Tyne river. Parking.

*S*tretching from the Cheshire plains to the Solway Firth, this region defies all easy definitions. Roman Chester, the busy Pennine market towns and the peaceful and scenic West Cumbrian coast are North-West England at its most traditionally picturesque, though there's a very different history to be traced in the decline and renewal of Liverpool's Albert Dock and in the shimmering modern metal of Salford Quays. Lancashire's towns, built for industry and "King Cotton", are now at least as well-known for their cross-Pennine rivalries in football, rugby and the Roses Match as for Lowry's busy cityscapes. Most famous by far, though, is Cumbria's Lake District which, at its best and quietest, remains both a challenging wilderness and a picture of serenity. Bikes, boats, trains, bridle paths and hiking trails will all get you closer to the beauty of Derwentwater and Buttermere and the bleak grandeur of Striding Edge. Local specialities like hot pot, black pudding, Morecambe shrimps, Cumberland sausage, Cumberland sauce and air-dried ham, sticky toffee pudding and Cheshire cheese have all spread well beyond the bounds of the region, but taste as good as ever after all that fresh North Country air…

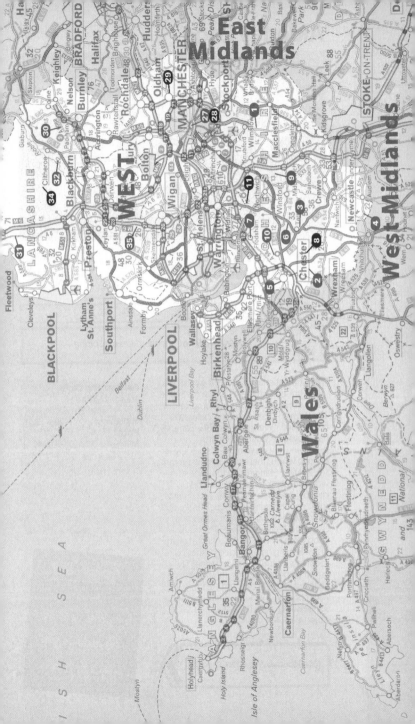

Alderley Edge

001 **The Wizard**

Macclesfield Rd, Alderley Edge SK10 4UB
Tel.: (01625) 584000 - Fax: (01625) 585105

   VISA

 Marstons Ashes, Shepherd Neame Spitfire

The National Trust has a good presence in these parts in the shape of Hare Hill and the local watermill. The Wizard – named after a children's book called "Wizard of Alderley Edge" – has proved an institution worth preserving in its own right. It's a 200 year-old pub which, these days, has restaurant sensibilities. Standing on the edge of a woodland park with superb walks clsoeby, it earns a tick in the box on most rustic counts: beamed, flagged and wood floors, with heavy wooden tables and chairs located everywhere. The menu - good value lunches and evening à la carte - is wide ranging and eclectic; the cooking's interesting and precise. Try grilled black pudding on mash with poached egg and mustard cream, cod with buttered spinach and salsa verde, or sea bass with red chard, avocado salad, lemongrass and coriander.

Food serving times:
Tuesday-Saturday:
        12pm-2pm, 7pm-9pm
Sunday: 12pm-2pm
Prices:
Meals: a la carte 20.00/40.00

Typical Dishes

King scallops, lobster bisque
Herb crusted cod fillet
Sticky toffee puddding

1.25mi Southeast on B5087. Parking.

Aldford

002 **The Grosvenor Arms**

Chester Rd, Aldford CH3 6HJ

Tel.: (01244) 620228 - Fax: (01224) 620247
e-mail: grosvenor-arms@brunningandprice.co.uk - Website: www.grosvenorarms-aldford.co.uk

   Deuchars IPA, Weetwood, Brains SA, Kodiak Gold

V ictorian visitors to the then recently built Grosvenor Arms would find it hard to relate their experience with a modern day excursion. They might recognise the lawned gardens of this spacious, red brick establishment, set in a rural village close to the River Dee, but the bustling, wood-furnished outside dining terrace and conservatory extension would be an eye-opener, to say nothing of the huge, modern interior and busy comings-and-goings of the ever-friendly staff. The Grosvenor owes much of its recent reputation not only to its period charm but also to interesting blackboard menus, which combine contemporary and rustic cooking, as typified by butterbean, bacon and watercress soup, duck breast with herb potato cake and sweet and sour beetroot, or parsnip, red onion and goats' cheese tart. What would the Victorians have made of all that and the daily specials?

Food serving times:
Monday-Saturday:
12pm-10pm
Sunday and Bank Holidays:
12pm-9pm
Closed for dinner 25-26 December and 1 January
Prices:
Meals: a la carte 14.40/29.45

Typical Dishes

Corned beef hash cake with poached egg

Braised half shoulder of lamb with redcurrant sauce

Classic crème brûlée

3.5mi South of Chester by B5130. On the main village road. Parking.

Bunbury

003 Dysart Arms

Bowes Gate Rd, Bunbury CW6 9PH
Tel.: (01829) 260183 · Fax: (01829) 261286
e-mail: dysart.arms@bruningandprice.co.uk

  VISA ⓂⒸ

 Thwaites Original, Weetwood Eastgate, Phoenix Arizona and regularly changing guest beers

Next to the impressive part-14C parish church, this trim, redbrick house, standing four-square by a little lane, is handsome enough in itself, particularly when floodlit at night. Away from the central bar, Victorian portraits, engravings and memorabilia line the white walls and polished wood, Persian rugs and floor-to-ceiling bookshelves give the place a spacious, country feel: broad French windows flood the back room with sunlight on bright days and lead out to benches and tables on the lawn. Fresh, tasty cooking ranges from pie and ploughmans to dishes with a more modern edge, including sweet potato and pepper tarte Tatin and seafood casserole. Though busy with eaters and drinkers in the early evening, it's usually a little quieter after 8.30.

Food serving times:
Monday-Sunday:
12pm-9.30pm
Closed 25 and 31 December
Prices:
Meals: a la carte 17.20/27.70

3.25mi South by A49 then take Bunbury Mill Rd. Parking.

Typical Dishes
Sate king prawns
Seared red bream with saffron mash
Raspberry Bakewell tart

Burleydam

004 ## The Combermere Arms

Burleydam SY13 4AT

Tel.: (01948) 871223 - Fax: (01948) 661371
e-mail: combermere.arms@brunningandprice.co.uk - Website: www.combermerearms-burleydam.co.uk

 Derby Just for You, Flowers Original, Green King IPA, Woodlands Oak Beauty, Storm Silk of Amnesia, Beeching Axe Ale, Old Rosie

A clever merging of styles allows the old and the new to link stylistic arms here. There are old beams on view as you step inside, but beyond them the adjoining rooms have been opened up around the central bar, and skylights added, so that everything's open and airy, although you can still find a snug spot if that's what you're after. Walls are covered in pictures of every style and hue. There's an informal menu, and you can eat anywhere you like: lots of choice right across the board means a good selection from sandwiches to more substantial dishes; the wine list is worthy of note, too. This is the ideal dining spot for bigger parties, as some truly cavernous tables are up for grabs. Service is efficient from staff who are used to being busy.

Food serving times:
Monday-Sunday:
12pm-9.30pm
Prices:
Meals: a la carte 17.65/26.90

Typical Dishes

Black pudding with mustard sauce

Monkfish on pea mash

Bakewell tart with custard

4.25mi East of Whitchurch on A525. Parking.

Chester

005 Old Harkers Arms

1 Russell St, Chester CH3 5AL

Tel.: (01244) 344525 - Fax: (01244) 344812
e-mail: harkers.arms@brunningandprice.co.uk - Website: www.brunningandprice.co.uk

 VISA AE MC

Flowers Original, Wapping Bitter, Thwaites Original, Weetwood Cheshire Cat and 6 guest ales changing daily

Although not in the city centre, this big, friendly canalside bar is especially busy on Saturday nights. It's hard to believe that not so many years ago the building was half-derelict. Steel beams, brick pillars and tall sash windows hint at its past as a Victorian warehouse and the heavy restoration, from the ground up, kept the long, open-plan interior, adding hundreds upon hundreds of old framed cuttings, period prints, cover pages and photographs. It has just the atmosphere for just meeting up for drinks, though a large blackboard menu covers lunchtime sandwiches, snacks and tasty, modern food, including chicken stuffed with spinach and ricotta and seared salmon on chive and yoghurt mash.

Food serving times:
Monday-Saturday:
12pm-9.30pm
Sunday:
12pm-9pm
Closed 25 December
Prices:
Meals: a la carte 20.00/28.00

Between A51 and the canal. Limited parking in City Rd; NCP car park round the corner.

Typical Dishes

Farmhouse terrine

Braised lamb shoulder, roast vegetables

Selection of mature cheeses

Cotebrook

006 Fox and Barrel

Forrest Road, Cotebrook CW6 9DZ
Tel.: (01829) 760529 - Fax: (01829) 760192

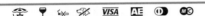

Jenning's Cumberland, Marston's Pedigree, John Smiths Best

It may look pretty ordinary on the outside, but step into the neat front bar and you'll recognise the atmosphere of a personally run pub with a friendly husband and wife team keeping things ticking over, pulling pints and pointing out any daily specials to the diners. They certainly know what their regulars like: as well as light meals and sandwiches, there's a traditional menu built around sound, substantial English dishes, and while this still offers decent variety, you can't go far wrong with braised beef on horseradish mash, followed by a trifle. The panelled, open-plan dining room can feel a bit less intimate than the lounge, but there's plenty of likeable neighbourhood spirit here too, especially when the local jazz quintet play New Orleans classics on Monday nights.

Food serving times:
Monday-Saturday:
  12pm-2.30pm, 6pm-9.30pm
Sunday: 12pm-8pm
Closed 25 December
Prices:
Meals: 14.50 (set price meal Sunday only) and a la carte 15.95/22.25

Typical Dishes

Tempura king prawns, red pepper jam

Ribeye steak, roast tomato

Strawberry roulade

1.5mi Northeast of Tarporley by A49. Parking.

Frodsham

007 Netherton Hall

Chester Road, Frodsham WA6 6UL

Tel.: 01928 732342 - Fax: 01928 739140

e-mail: sharter@btconnect.com - Website: www.nethertonhall.com

rest · VISA · AE · MC

Timothy Taylor Landlord

Hiding under its all-enveloping greenery, Netherton Hall is a large Georgian farmhouse, its interior now converted into three relaxing and pleasantly busy dining areas. Books and knick-knacks line the walls throughout and a collection of mix and match wooden tables seem to add the warm homely atmosphere; the personal hand of the patron is everywhere in evidence. It's also worth knowing that there's plenty of room to eat in the spacious garden. Food is definitely the focus here, with an unusually large choice written up on the blackboards: it's all freshly prepared, and the list can change twice a day. A freely ranging mix of traditional and European ideas guarantees plenty of good, sustaining cooking. The steady, well-run atmosphere of the place is most noticeable in the service, which is invariably alert and smooth.

Food serving times:
Monday-Thursday:
12pm-2.30pm, 6pm-9pm
Friday-Saturday:
12pm-2.30pm, 6pm-9.30pm
Sunday: 12pm-8pm
Closed 25-26 December and 1 January
Prices:
Meals: a la carte 21.00/29.50

0.75 miles Southwest of Frodsham on A56. Parking.

Typical Dishes

Seared king scallops, watercress salad

Lamb noisettes, pepper sauce

Glazed lemon tart

Higher Burwardsley

008 The Pheasant Inn

Higher Burwardsley CH3 9PF

Tel.: (01829) 770434 - Fax: (01829) 771097
e-mail: info@thepheasantinn.co.uk - Website: www.thepheasantinn.co.uk

Weetwood ales and one changing guest beer

There's been an inn on this elevated site since the 17C; certainly, few pubs can enjoy such enviable views as those afforded from The Pheasant. Its appealing sandstone and timber frame sits atop the Peckforton Hills, giving it astonishing vistas over the Cheshire Plain to Liverpool and the Welsh Hills. Whilst beamed and open-fired, it also boasts a smart, modern feel after refurbishment a few years ago; everyone's made to feel welcome, particularly the many walkers who pass this way. Food is hearty and nourishing, ideal if you've been working up a hiker's hunger. Among the seasonal fare are lots of favourites such as steak and kidney pie. Sandwiches have a modern twist; more accomplished dishes boast interesting and original combinations. An adjacent sandstone barn now houses attractively furnished bedrooms, and, yes, they all enjoy the excellent view.

Food serving times:
Monday-Thursday:
12pm-9.30pm
Friday-Saturday:
12pm-10pm
Sunday:
12pm-8.30pm
Prices:
Meals: a la carte 22.00/30.00
12 rooms : 65.00/130.00

2.5mi Southeast of Tattenhall. Parking.

Typical Dishes

Monkfish and tiger prawns in sweet chilli jam

Beef medallions, smoked bacon sauce

Bakewell tart

Lach Dennis

009 Duke of Portland

Penny's Lane, Lach Dennis CW9 7SY

Tel.: (01606) 46264 - Fax: (01606) 41724

e-mail: info@dukeofportland.com - Website: www.dukeofportland.com

Pedigree, Jennings, Banks, Samuel Adnams, Weetwood

The Belle Epoque in Knutsford is not an oxymoron: it's a restaurant that's been a renowned local stalwart for 30 years, and its long-standing owners have built up a solid reputation. Good reason, then, for a visit to the rurally set Duke of Portland, seven miles away, now overseen by those same owners, the Mooney family. There's a nice rustic feeling of space inside, accentuated by two airy lounges where low-level sofas are a good place to peruse the menus. Adjacent dining areas feature natty wooden balustrades; in summer months, visitors often prefer to tuck in on the smart outdoor terrace or in the garden. Frequently changing menus offer a very well priced and eclectic mix of modern and traditional dishes: local favourites are the delicious homemade burgers or hotpot. Drinkers are well catered for with an impressive range of real ales and wines by the glass.

Food serving times:
Monday-Friday:
   12pm-2.30pm, 6pm-9.30pm
Sunday: all day

Prices:
Meals: a la carte 15.00/20.00

3.5mi West of Northwich by B 5082. Parking.

Typical Dishes

Black pudding, onion compôte

Rump of lamb, red wine jus

Iced strawberry terrine

Little Barrow

010 The Foxcote

Station Lane, Little Barrow CH3 7JN
Tel.: (01244) 301343 - Fax: (01244) 303287

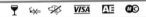

No real ales offered

From the outside, this traditional looking inn certainly gives the impression of being somewhere to sink a pint. Wrong! This is now a dining pub, pure and simple, though the courteous, friendly staff and relaxed atmosphere certainly create a very gentle, local feel. The Foxcote is in a tiny Cheshire village off the beaten track, its interior given over to dining tables with gingham cloths; seafood and country prints line the walls; fine view of the Cheshire countryside from the side room. A vast number of blackboards greet you upon arrival: they mostly list seafood dishes featuring a broad variety of ingredients prepared in an accomplished, modern manner. Vegetarians and meat eaters are not forgotten, though, and are well catered for on the blackboards.

Food serving times:

Monday-Friday:	12pm-2pm, 6pm-9.30pm
Saturday:	12pm-2pm, 6pm-10pm
Sunday:	12pm-2pm

- Seafood -

Prices:
Meals: 9.95 (fixed price lunch) and a la carte 15.00/25.00

6.5mi Northeast of Chester by A56 on B5132. Parking.

Typical Dishes

Avocado, crab and brown shrimp salad

Half lobster Thermidor

Caramelized banana, honeycomb ice cream

Lower Whitley

011 Chetwode Arms

Street Lane, Lower Whitley WA4 4EN

Tel.: (01925) 730203 - Fax: (01925) 730870
e-mail: info@chetwodearms.com - Website: www.chetwodearms.com

Jennings Cumberland, Adnams Broadside, Pedigree, Bank's Original

Popularity is clearly nothing new to this neighbourhood favourite, where a brisk, personally led team are well used to a full house of contented diners. The 17C brick-built former coaching inn still welcomes its regulars for a pint, and there are few better places for it than the inviting front bar: old framed prints, real fires, even the Victorian style tiled floor all add to the unassuming charm. The three bedrooms are equipped in the same homely style. Find a simply set table in one of the three former bar-parlours and choose from a blackboard menu which lists a few dishes reflecting the patrons' links with South Africa as well as Bury black pudding with mustard mash or liver and onions: honest, unfussy and full of appetising Northern flavour. If ever there was cooking tailor-made for a decent local ale, this is it.

Food serving times:
Monday-Sunday:
    12pm-3pm, 6pm-10pm
Closed 25 December
and 1 January
Prices:
Meals: 20.00 (set price lunch and dinner) and a la carte 20.00/35.00
3 rooms : 60.00/120.00

6.5mi Northwest of Northwich by A533 off A49. Parking.

Typical Dishes

Warm king prawn and avocado salad

Pork fillet, roasted root vegetables

Banoffee cheese cake

Ambleside

012 **Drunken Duck Inn** 🛏

Barngates, Ambleside LA22 0NG

Tel.: (01539) 436347 - Fax: (01539) 436781
e-mail: info@drunkenduckinn.co.uk - Website: www.drunkenduckinn.co.uk

🍷 ✕rest *VISA* AE 🅜🅔

Barngates Brewery - Tag Lag, Catnap, Westmorland Gold, Red Bull Terrier, and also 1 guest ale

A handsome inn that takes its name from a story involving a 19C landlady, a leaky barrel and a gaggle of unsteady ducks: true local history or an old taproom canard? Either way, this trusty Lakeland landmark still marks the old crossroads, in the midst of stunning fell and high peak scenery. Its lovely rustic bar with open fire is a haven for walkers, particularly those who like real ale, as The Duck has an on-site micro-brewery producing four beers on handpump, and local waterfowl are kept well away these days. The beers can be enjoyed in one of the cosy, beamed rooms which radiate from the bar, while meals are served in two pleasant dining rooms with polished wooden tables: a modern style menu has a seasonal base and an elaborate, eclectic range. Bedrooms are snug and of fine quality; they all boast the excellent view.

Food serving times:
Monday-Sunday:
    12pm-2.30pm, 6pm-9pm
Closed 25 December
Prices:
Meals: a la carte 26.00/32.00
🛏 **16 rooms :**
165.70/220.95

Typical Dishes

Mussels cooked with garlic, white wine and cream

Venison fillet, chestnut polenta

Vanilla brûlée

3mi Southwest of Ambleside by A593 and B5286 on Tarn Hows road. By the crossroads at the top of Duck Hill. Parking.

Beetham

013　Wheatsheaf Inn

Beetham LA7 7AL

Tel.: (01539) 562123 - Fax: (01539) 564840
e-mail: wheatbeeth@aol.com - Website: www.wheatsheafbeetham.com

Jennings Cumberland, Tirrel Bragham, Tirrel Old Faithful and weekly changing guest ale

Stained glass windows, old prints of country life and prize sportfish from the Cumbrian rivers and lakes, mounted in glass cases, all add to the genuine charm of this part-16C inn with its warm and bustling atmosphere. The front lounge bar, set with polished tables and spokeback chairs, has exposed beams and joists; there is a real fire in the recently refurbished main bar. An extensive menu – served downstairs and in the quieter first floor dining rooms – begins with reliable pub standards and interesting sandwiches, but also finds room for a few more dishes with a modern edge. Pastel-toned bedrooms with neat fittings and tapestry-style fabrics are all named after nearby areas: even if local geography isn't your strong point you should find them homely and practical.

Food serving times:
Monday-Sunday:
　　12pm-2pm, 6pm-9pm
Closed 25 December
and 8-18 January
Prices:
Meals: 12.95 (set price dinner until 7.45pm) and a la carte 17.50/28.00
6 rooms : 55.00/95.00

Typical Dishes

Sauteed tiger prawns

Noisettes of Silverdale lamb

Rich chocolate pot with a sable biscuit

Off the A6, 1mi South of Milnthorpe. Parking.

Cartmel Fell

014 The Masons Arms

Strawberry Bank, Cartmel Fell LA11 6NW

Tel.: (015395) 68486 - Fax: (015395) 68780
e-mail: info@masonsarms.com - Website: www.strawberrybank.com

 Hawkshead Bitter, Hawkshead Gold, Black Sheep, Timothy Taylor Landlord

The characterful downstairs bar and its layout of little snugs, parlours and open fires in the old ranges are all clues to the history of the Masons Arms, originally built as a cottage and converted in the 1800s. This smaller, family scale can make it feel a little crowded at the busiest times, so head upstairs to the restaurant if you want a touch more comfort and formality, or take a seat outside. From the heights of Strawberry Hill there are charming views to be had from the rear garden or the front terrace, handsomely equipped with broad canopy parasols, lights and heaters to bring a hint of café culture to the Lakes. A popular menu – the same at lunch and dinner – combines British standards like Stilton mousse and chutney or chicken, leek and ham pie with international favourites like Caesar salad, lasagne and barbecue ribs.

Food serving times:
Monday-Friday:
12pm-2pm, 6pm-9pm
Saturday-Sunday:
12pm-9pm

Prices:
Meals: a la carte 20.00/30.00

Typical Dishes

Black pudding, poached egg, red wine jus

Warm salad of seared tuna

Cumberland Dairy cheeses

3.75mi North East of Newby Bridge by A590 off A592. Parking.

Casterton

015 The Pheasant Inn 🛏

Casterton LA6 2RX
Tel.: (015242) 71230 - Fax: (015242) 74267
e-mail: pheasantinn@fsbdial.co.uk - Website: www.pheasantinn.co.uk

 ✗-rest ✗ **VISA** **MC**

Dent Aviator, Theakston Best Bitter, Timothy Taylor Landlord, Westmorland Ale

Halfway between the Lake District and the Dales lies the agreeable little village of Casterton and, at its centre, this traditional 18C inn at the foot of the fell. With its easy pace and a very open and natural warm welcome, it seems to draw on the best of the village's character, and its collection of local artefacts and farming prints are reminders that this part of Cumbria still earns part of its living from the land. There's a room set aside for dining, but you can also choose from a full menu - with surprisingly varied daily specials – in the three traditionally appointed bars and lounges: very comfortable, especially when they stoke up the fires. Tasty, homely dishes, from sandwiches, grills and filling stews to baked crab and honey-roast ham, seem entirely in keeping here. Inviting, good-sized bedrooms.

Food serving times:
Sunday-Thursday:
12pm-2pm, 6pm-9pm
Friday-Saturday:
12pm-2pm, 6pm-9.30pm
Closed 2 weeks mid January
Prices:
Meals: a la carte 12.70/26.60
🛏 **10 rooms :** 37.00/100.00

Typical Dishes

Warm goat's cheese, char grilled vegetables

Sea bass baked in olive oil

Baileys cheesecake

In the centre of the village. Parking.

Castle Carrock

016 **The Weary at Castle Carrock**

Castle Carrock CA8 9LU

Tel.: (01228) 670230 - Fax: (01228) 670089
Website: www.theweary.com

 VISA AE MC

Cask ale changed regularly

Two minutes' drive from the beauty spot of Talkin Tarn, this white-painted pub looks the picture of pretty Lake District gentility – until you open the front door. Striking modern lighting, chic wood and slate and dashes of zingy modern colour make the restyled front bar look anything but weary: you can take a seat on the sofa and dine here, or head through to the conservatory and a smart walled terrace. With a nod to local tradition, a sizeable modern menu finds room for toffee pudding or a starter of black pudding and apple mash with whisky sauce, but also takes in vegetable tempura, chilli and garlic sea bass and a Pernod parfait with cassis pear. Fine bedrooms certainly don't let the side down, with more bold colourways plus stylish bathrooms and flat-screen televisions.

Food serving times:
Tuesday-Sunday:
    12pm-2pm, 6pm-9pm
Monday residents only
Prices:
Meals: a la carte 14.50/35.00
5 rooms : 65.00/105.00

Typical Dishes

Chorizo and black pudding stack

Fillet of red snapper

Ravioli of chocolate truffle

4mi south of Brampton on B6413. Parking.

Coniston

017 Black Bull Inn 🛏️

1 Yewdale Rd, Coniston LA21 8DU

Tel.: (015394) 41335 - Fax: (015394) 41168
Website: www.conistonbrewery.com

 Bluebird Bitter, Bluebird XB, Opium Old Man Ale, Blacksmiths Ale and changing guest ales, lagers and fruit beers

There's no mistaking this sizeable 16C coaching inn at the foot of the Old Man, not with the sign of a hefty-looking bull hanging below the eaves. From blackened timbers to stone floor, it's a decent, personally run inn of the old school, though with far more depth of character than most. The pleasant dining room is neatly kept, but the bar itself just edges it for warmth and personality, and beer experts will waste no time in pulling up a stool and ordering its great speciality. Of the pints produced on-site, none is more renowned than Bluebird: it shares its name with Donald Campbell's record breaking hydroplane and a memento recalls the triumph and loss of the speed-king on nearby Coniston Water. With its true local flavours, honest and homely Lakeland cooking makes a fine accompaniment to an ale; try local beef followed by apple pie.

Food serving times:
Monday-Sunday:
    12pm-9.30pm (restaurant 6pm-9.30pm)
Closed 25 December
Prices:
Meals: a la carte 15.00/20.00
🛏️ **15 rooms :** 35.00/99.00

Typical Dishes

Sauteed goose livers

Bluebird Bitter steak and ale pie

Marmalade bread and butter pudding

On A593. Parking. ⟫

Crosthwaite

018 The Punch Bowl Inn

Crosthwaite LA8 8HR

Tel.: (01539) 568237 - Fax: (01539) 568875
e-mail: info@the-punchbowl.co.uk - Website: www.punchbowl.co.uk

Barngates Brewery Tag Lag and Cracker, Black Sheep

Seasonal ingredients and a traditional base define the menu in this part 17C Cumbrian inn. The fine balanced cuisine draws out robust, pronounced flavours from classic combinations - at good value prices - and among the best are a satisfyingly meaty pea and ham soup, crisp, juicy beetroot tart with goat's cheese, honey and mustard chicken and chocolate and ginger tart served with honey ice cream. Framed menus from around the world decorate three dining areas, including a raised gallery, and the friendly, efficient service would be worthy of a restaurant, but the Punch Bowl is still recognisably a neighbourhood pub, with locals propping up the front bar. In the fells and banks of the Lake District, there's no shortage of after-lunch walks in the area, and the road running west leads on to Windermere. The bedrooms have modern facilities and each is individually designed.

5.25 West of Kendal by A11 Hallows Lane. Next to the church. Parking.

Food serving times:
Tuesday-Sunday:
     12pm-2pm, 7pm-9pm
Prices:
Meals: a la carte 30.00/45.00
🛏 **9 rooms :** 75.00/160.00

Typical Dishes

Tart Tatin of goat's cheese

Fillet of Galloway beef,
Shiraz jus

Hot dark chocolate fondant

211

Great Salkeld

019 The Highland Drove Inn

Great Salkeld CA11 9NA

Tel.: (01768) 898349 - Fax: (01768) 898708
e-mail: highlanddroveinn@btinternet.com - Website: www.highland-drove.co.uk

 John Smiths Cask, Theakstons Black Bull and various guest ales

Approaching the Lake District from the north, this is an ideal stop-off point before the inevitable encounter with the tourist masses. It's a pleasant whitewashed pub in a tiny village in the heart of the Eden valley, and dates back hundreds of years. There are beams and a good selection of cask ales, but what really catches the eye is the content of the menus. Dishes are changed on a daily basis and revolve around local meat, game and fish. Sea bass, salmon fillet and brill regularly share the honours with mallard duck, rack of lamb and spiced Elizabethan pork; look out too for the steaks from herds reared in Cumbria. Suitably replenished, you'll need no reminding that you're in first-class walking country. Comfy bedrooms await those staying on.

Food serving times:
Tuesday-Sunday:
 12pm-2pm, 6.30pm-9pm
Monday: 6.30pm-9pm
Closed 25 December
Prices:
Meals: a la carte 14.95/28.75
🛏 **5 rooms :** 32.50/60.00

Typical Dishes

Homecured Bresaola

Sachete salmon, saffron mussel sauce

Pannacotta of Victoria plums

6.75mi North of Penrith by A686. Parking.

Loweswater

 020 Kirkstile Inn 🛏

Loweswater CA13 0RU

Tel.: (01900) 85219 - Fax: (01900) 85239
e-mail: info@kirkstile.com - Website: www.kirkstile.com

   VISA **MC**

Melbreak, Grasmoor, Rannerdale and Kirkstile Gold brewed on site; also Yates Bitter and Coniston Bluebird

A part-16C inn in a picture-perfect setting: an isolated and beautiful valley between Loweswater and Crummock Water. If you can tear yourself away from the view, head inside to the welcoming beamed bar or a more formal dining room and choose a lighter lunch – from sandwiches upwards – or more substantial cooking at dinner. Fresh Cumbrian produce, organic where possible, is the cornerstone of their traditional cooking: decent, substantial dishes like Lakeland rump steak or beef and ale pie – plus a couple of specials – find favour with locals and visitors and certainly suit the home-brewed beers. Simple tidy accommodation with lovely hill views; two rooms suitable for families. Needless to say, there's good climbing and walking nearby.

Food serving times:
Monday-Sunday:
   12pm-2pm, 6pm-9pm
Closed 25 December
Prices:
Meals: a la carte 14.00/19.00
🛏 **11 rooms :** 55.00/79.00

Typical Dishes

Croftan goat's cheese with sun dried tomato and pine kernels

Steak and kidney pudding

Cumberland rum Nicky

Located between Loweswater and Crummock Water. Parking.

Portinscale

021 The Farmers

Portinscale CA12 5RN

Tel.: (017687) 73442

e-mail: lynnerowe@ukonline.co.uk - Website: www.tp-inns.co.uk

Jennings Bitter, Cumberland Ale, Jennings Fish King, Jennings Crag Rot; also Banks Original, IPA, Pedigree

n the face of it, this slate-built village pub looks much the same as it ever was: a few tables out front, a tiny beer garden behind and a neat, stone-flagged bar with stools and tables occupied by the regulars, who make up the backbone of the pub's darts and quiz teams and sup their pints to the quiet click of dominoes. But the remainder of the pub, decorated in bright Mediterranean tones, is given over to dining; besides the lunchtime ciabattas, galettes, ploughmans and homemade breads, a more adventurous main menu offers pancetta wrapped salmon on olive ratatouille, and rhubarb and white chocolate fool. Very helpful service binds together this deserving combination of the modern and the traditional.

Food serving times:
Monday-Sunday:
 12pm-2pm, 6pm-9pm
Prices:
Meals: a la carte 19.00/26.00

Typical Dishes

Tomato and olive bruschetta

Roast lemon and pepper monkfish

Hot coffee pancakes

1.5 miles West of Keswick by A66. Limited parking in street.

Tirril

022 The Queens Head Inn

Tirril CA10 2JF

Tel.: (01768) 863219 - Fax: (01768) 863243
e-mail: bookings@queensheadinn.co.uk - Website: www.queensheadinn.co.uk

 Tirril Brewery: Bewshers, Old Faithful, Academy, and 1 guest ale

When not wandering lonely as a cloud, the great William Wordsworth also dabbled in the more profitable world of property management. God's gift to the Lakes Tourist Board signed away the family's stake in this charming 18C inn in 1836 and the contract still hangs in the atmospheric bar, along with such un-Wordsworthian curios as a hunting horn, a First World War shell and a diving helmet. Ullswater trout and local lamb feature on a hearty but carefully prepared menu which works much better on the plate than on the page: lamb and rosemary pie and steak and ale pudding show the same full-flavoured style. The pub also hosts a Cumbrian Beer and Sausage weekend every August. Four rooms for dining include a pleasant conservatory, ideal in summer.

Food serving times:
Monday-Sunday:
12pm-2.30pm,
6.15pm-9.15pm

Prices:
Meals: a la carte 15.00/30.00
🛏 **7 rooms :** 40.00/70.00

Typical Dishes

Rosettes of Scottish salmon

Fillet of beef, swede purée

Cointreau and orange cheesecake

3mi South West of Penrith by A6 on B5320. Parking.

Troutbeck

023 Queens Head

Troutbeck LA23 1PW

Tel.: (015394) 32174 - Fax: (015394) 31938
e-mail: enquiries@queensheadhotel.com - Website: www.queensheadhotel.com

 room **VISA**

Hawkshead Best, Tirrel Academy, Jennings Cockerhoop

Not many pub bars are built around superbly carved Elizabethan four-poster beds. In fact, this 400 year old posting inn boasts probably the only one in the country. The place has charm and character to spare. You might get lost in the warren of beamed and panelled rooms, in which cobwebbed musical instruments hang, and beribboned stuffed beasts gaze. You'll come across old cushioned settles, stone walls and a roaring open fireplace. The upstairs dining room has capacious windows for even bigger views over valley and moor. Settle down at scrubbed oak tables and extinguish countryside appetites with imaginative, well-cooked, tasty Northern food with traditional and modern options, served by staff eager to please. You might want to stay the night: bedrooms boast antique furnishings and terrific views.

Food serving times:
Monday-Sunday :
 12pm-2pm, 6.30pm-8.45pm
Closed 25 December
Prices:
Meals: 15.50 (fixed price) and a la carte 22.00/29.00
16 rooms : 67.50/150.00

4mi North of Ambleside by A592. Parking.

Typical Dishes

Confit of duck leg

Loin of venison, roast roots, garlic froth

Soft centre hot chocolate pudding

Ulverston

024 The Bay Horse 🛏

Canal Foot, Ulverston LA12 9EL

Tel.: (01229) 583972 - Fax: (01229) 580502
e-mail: reservations@thebayhorsehotel.co.uk - Website: www.thebayhorsehotel.co.uk

⚄-rest **VISA** **AE** **MC**

 Pendle Witches Brew, Cocker Hoop, Cumberland, Blond Witch, Moorhouses

ommanding views of the Lancashire and Cumbria Fells are just one reason to recommend this well-established little inn by Ulverston Sands. The bar area, well known for its capacious horse's head of stone, has a smart ambience, afforded by plush built-in wall banquettes, stylish wooden armchairs, beams and open fire. An adjacent conservatory houses a more formal linen-clad restaurant, which boasts fine views over Morecambe Bay. Tasty, effectively prepared cooking finds favour with appreciative diners, who have long admired the flavourful, seasonal menus, typified by roast fillet of halibut, or Cumberland sausage with date chutney, cranberry and apple sauce. Bedrooms - snug and with a host of extras - have the enviable coastal view.

Food serving times:
Monday:
12pm-2pm, at 7.30pm
Tuesday-Sunday:
12pm-2pm, at 7.30pm
**One sitting for dinner
7.30pm for 8pm**
Prices:
Meals: 31.50 (set price dinner menu) and a la carte 21.00/40.00
🛏 **9 rooms:** 80.00/117.50

2.25mi East of Ulverston by A5087, turning left at Morecambe Tavern B&B and beyond industrial area, on the coast. Parking.

Typical Dishes

Morecambe Bay potted shrimps

Fillet steak, ginger and soy sauce

Profiteroles filled with praline cream

Watermillock

025 **Brackenrigg Inn**

Watermillock CA11 0LP

Tel.: (017684) 86206 - Fax: (017684) 86945
e-mail: enquiries@brackenrigginn.co.uk - Website: www.brackenrigginn.co.uk

🍷 ⋈rest 🚭 **VISA** Ⓜ︎©

Tirril Old Faithful, Coniston Bluebird, Black Sheep and others

Commanding fine views of the lakes and mountains, the Brackenrigg Inn is sure to appeal to Lakeland pub lovers, for many reasons. Its open main bar has changed a little since it welcomed the post coach in the 18C, but its comfy seats, dartboard and promising line of bar taps still sends the right message to the tired traveller. Meals are also served in two more formal adjoining rooms and the appealing, full-flavoured cooking casts its net surprisingly wide. They aim to offer something for everyone, serving potato, chorizo and trout salad or salmon with basil and asparagus alongside well-known favourites, snacks and daily specials. Well marshalled service directed by the experienced patrons – still as keen and amiable as ever – binds the whole place together.

Food serving times:
Monday-Sunday:
  12pm-2.30pm, 6.30pm-9pm
**Accommodation rates
include dinner.**
Prices:
Meals: 12.95/24.95 (set price Sunday lunch/dinner) and a la carte 16.00/24.95
🛏 **17 rooms :** 33.00/118.00

Typical Dishes

Black & white pudding and haggis in ale batter

Cumberland sausages

Treacle pudding

On A592 beside Ullswater. Parking.

Yanwath

026 **The Yanwath Gate Inn**

Yanwath CA10 2LF

Tel.: (01768) 862386 - Fax: (01768) 899892
e-mail: enquiries@yanwathgate.com - Website: www.yanwathgate.com

⇖⇒rest   ⓘ

Hesket Newmarket Doris 90th birthday ale, Tirril Bewshers and regular Cumbrian guest beers

This charming drovers' inn, built back in 1683, takes its name from the tollgate which once stood outside. If you're unfortunate enough to be caught by a Lakeland downpour, or find yourself cold and lunchless on the hills, this is the kind of place you dream of finding. The old taproom, in the light of candles and an open fire, looks wonderfully inviting, with scrubbed wooden tables and thoughtful, welcoming service from behind the bar, but the panelled dining room beyond is no less pleasant – the friendly owner willingly takes a hand in both to keep things going according to plan. Seasonal cooking is never less than generous, concentrating on nourishing, substantial recipes and organic or free-range ingredients. Good value pub food with a sound slice of local character.

Food serving times:
Monday-Sunday:
    12pm-2.30pm, 6pm-9pm
Prices:
Meals: a la carte 24.00/36.85

Typical Dishes

Black pudding and haggis

Wild rabbit braised with rosemary and cream

Chocolate pot

2.5mi Southwest from Penrith by A6 and B5320. Parking.

Chorlton-cum-Hardy

027 Marmalade

60 Beech Road, Chorlton Green, Chorlton-cum-Hardy M21 9EG

Tel.: (0161) 862 9665

e-mail: jqmarmalade@tiscali.co.uk - Website: www.mymarmalade.co.uk

No real ales offered

Don't get the impression that this neighbourhood hostelry deals only in charming knick-knacks. Yes, there are things like silver three-tier cake stands, wall-hung antique suitcases and framed replicas of Manchester buses. You can even buy a jar of the eponymous sticky stuff which gives the pub its name. All of which could sidetrack you from the fact that, most of all, John the owner and Phil the chef want you to enjoy the serious food served here. Seasonally changing menus have a strong British accent, from the cracking Lancashire hotpot to mouth-watering mussels and lobster from Wales. Mature ribs of local beef are hung for 42 days and served with home-made chips; everything is freshly cooked on the premises, and the result is well-executed, tasty fare, eaten at simple wooden tables.

Food serving times:
Monday-Wednesday:
5.30pm-10pm
Thursday-Sunday:
12pm-3pm, 5.30pm-10pm
closed 25-26 December

Prices:
Meals: 11.95/14.95 (set price dinner) and a la carte 17.95/25.00

Typical Dishes

Welsh mussels with cider leeks

Slow roast Aylesbury duck

Mixed fresh berry crumble

3mi South of Manchester by A5103 and minor road west.

Manchester

028 **The Ox**

71 Liverpool Rd, Castlefield, Manchester M3 4NQ

Tel.: (0161) 839 7760

e-mail: gmtheox@barbar.co.uk - Website: www.theox.co.uk

Joseph Holts, Deuchars IPA, Boddingtons, Timothy Taylor's Landlord

The pub's proximity to Castlefield Heritage Park, the Science Museum and the local Granada studios provides a steady flow of drinkers and diners to The Ox, as well as incognito appearances by a few television celebrities. Apart from the massive, block-bold "OX" monogram, stamped like a cattle-brand between the eaves and glowering in at the windows, it's an understated corner pub, more pleasant and homely than the logo suggests. An open though still intimate-feeling bar room leads on to a traditionally styled dining area, and this is where The Ox sets itself apart from its neighbours: the menu has an unmistakeably eclectic touch, with a number of lightly fusion-influenced dishes in among the more familiar favourites. Fresh and popular food served unpretentiously.

Food serving times:
Monday-Sunday:
    12pm-3pm, 5.30pm-9.30pm
Prices:
Meals: 12.95/15.00 (set price lunch/dinner) and a la carte 19.00/25.00
9 rooms : 44.95/49.95
3.95

Centre of the City. Street parking meters and NCP car park.

Typical Dishes

Pigeon breasts, spinach, foie gras

Roast cod, pea and mint purée

Passion fruit and orange tart

Oldham

029 ## The White Hart Inn

51 Stockport Rd, Lydgate, Oldham OL4 4JJ

Tel.: (01457) 872566 - Fax: (01457) 875190
e-mail: bookings@thewhitehart.co.uk - Website: www.thewhitehart.co.uk

VISA AE MC

Timothy Taylor Landlord, JW Lees, Tetleys, Copper Dragon

Between the town centre and Saddleworth Moor, this great local favourite - built in 1788 to provide hospitality for cross-Pennine travellers - remains ever-popular; in part a tribute to the attentive staff who provide a pleasant but quite formal style of service. The rural setting and 12 comfy bedrooms are an additional inducement to stay overnight. Two rooms off the main bar – one larger and slightly more comfortable – are set aside for lunch and dinner, but share the same simple décor of bricks, beams and open fires. New to the White Hart in 2005 is the lavish Oak Room, proof of the inn's increasing appeal. There's a friendly mix of drinkers and diners but the focus is definitely on the owner's locally renowned cooking: full-flavoured dishes in the Modern British vein. The same menu is served throughout the house; it's good value with occasional special set-price lunches and early evening deals.

Food serving times:
Monday-Sunday:
  12pm-2.30pm, 6pm-9.30pm
(booking essential)
Prices:
Meals: 18.00/35.00 (set price lunch/dinner) and a la carte 24.00/31.00
12 rooms : 90.00/135.00

Typical Dishes

Moules marinière

Grilled sea bream, lemongrass tagliatelle

Baked lemon tart

3mi East of Oldham by A669 on A6050.
Parking.

Fence

030 The Forest Inn

Cuckstool Lane, Fence BB12 9PA

Tel.: (01282) 613641 - Fax: (01282) 698140
Website: www.forestinn.co.uk

 ⇆ **VISA** **MC**

Thwaites, Moorhouses IPA

Fresh-tasting and seasonal in character, the food at the Forest Inn has plenty of generous country flavour to it. Lighter, simpler lunches and more substantial dinners, most with a hearty, traditional base, are prepared with equal care, and it's no surprise that word has reached well beyond the little Lancashire village. If the setting of fields and trees comes as a relief after the madness of the M65, the plain-fronted inn looks respectable but nondescript. A contemporary interior, however, complete with comfortable leather chairs, blond wood dining tables, modern art and hushed, neutral colours feels much less stark than it sounds and the service lends real warmth to the place: a dedicated local team is never short on friendliness or effort when helping out the family owners.

Food serving times:
Tuesday-Sunday and Bank Holiday Monday:
    12pm-2.30pm, 5pm-9pm
Prices:
Meals: 9.95 (set price dinner) and a la carte 9.95/27.00

3mi Northeast of Padiham by A6068, then 0.5mile southwest by A6248. Parking.

Typical Dishes

Cornish crab cakes, lemon mayonnaise

Roast duck, crushed potatoes

Lemon posset

Forton

031 Bay Horse Inn

Bay Horse Lane, Forton LA2 0HR

Tel.: (01524) 791204 - Fax: (01524) 791204
e-mail: bayhorseinninfo@aol.com - Website: www.bayhorseinn.com

 Lancaster Bomber, Pendle Witches Brew, Black Sheep

With service from a cheery local team, enthusiastic, all-action management from the chef, well-chosen regional produce and big helpings of homemade everything, this hidden 18C inn has personality in abundance. A lovely rustic bar, filled with framed menus and sporting memorabilia and warmed by an open fire, leads into an airy dining room. Pick whichever suits you best and choose from a quarterly menu, a list of chalkboard specials or the daily-changing sandwich board: Lancashire hotpot terrine, Morecambe Bay shrimps and Cumbrian roast beef sum up an appealing modern-rustic range with a forthright Lancastrian flavour; everything is homemade.

Food serving times:
Tuesday-Saturday:
   12pm-1.30pm, 7pm-9.30pm
Sunday: 12pm-1.30pm
Closed 25 December,
1 January
Prices:
Meals: 17.90 (set price Sunday lunch) and a la carte 20.00/ 30.00

Typical Dishes

Seared scallops, truffle oil

Cumbrian mutton shank

Sherry trifle

1.25mi North by A6 on Quernmore Rd. Parking.

Mitton

032 The Three Fishes

Mitton BB7 9PQ

Tel.: (01254) 826888 - Fax: (01254) 826026
Website: www.thethreefishes.com

Thwaites Original, Thwaites Bomber, Bowland Brewery Hen Harrier

Pies and hotpots, platters of tongue and brisket, black pudding and potted Morecambe shrimps – a look at the Three Fishes menu is the stuff of northern dreams. It's rare to find cuisine so thoroughly rooted in a region, but the richly savoury and heartening Lancastrian recipes are given pride of place here, prepared in a kitchen which is stocked by a host of hand-picked local suppliers, and served in a very spacious, modern and totally non-smoking pub. There is a special menu for children but the dairy specials are for all. Find a table then order at the bar – this is such beer-friendly food that it's worth trying a north-western cask ale to go with it. This updated and professionally run pub has come a long way since it served passengers from the river Ribble ferry, but its change of tack has been a definite success, so be warned: it gets very busy.

Food serving times:
Monday-Friday:
    12pm-2pm, 6pm-9pm
Saturday: 12pm-2pm,
    5.30pm-9pm
Sunday: 12pm-8.30pm
Closed 25 December
Prices:
Meals: a la carte 18.00/23.00

2.5mi Northwest of Whalley on B6246. Parking.

Typical Dishes

Buttered crumpet, Lancashire curd

Bowland lamb, Lancashire hotpot

English custard, mulled pears

Tunstall

033 The Lunesdale Arms

Tunstall LA6 2QN

Tel.: (01524) 274203 - Fax: (01524) 274229
e-mail: info@thelunesdale.co.uk - Website: www.thelunesdale.co.uk

📷 🍷 *VISA* ⓂⒸ

Black Sheep and 1 guest ale - Aviator

This rural dining pub with Cumbria to the north and Yorkshire to the east is making friends across the board, and across the borders. What was probably once a licensed room of the old village hall now feels pleasantly, deliberately modern; uncluttered and bright with chunky tables and chairs dotted around, squashy sofas facing a vast fireplace and a combined family and games room for post-lunch pool or table football. Eat – or drink – where you like: a blackboard menu changes as seasons and local suppliers dictate, but sharp, simple, flavourful dishes like spinach, pea and mint soup with homemade bread, goujons of cod, or broccoli, mustard and cheese tart make good, nourishing lunches, while a larger dinner selection could take in chicken with pesto or herb-crusted fennel with garlic butter.

Food serving times:
Tuesday-Friday:
    12pm-2pm, 6pm-9pm
Saturday-Sunday and Bank Holiday Monday:
    12pm-2.30pm, 6pm-9pm
Closed 25-26 December
Prices:
Meals: a la carte 18.25/23.50

4mi South of Kirkby Lonsdale on A683. Parking.

Typical Dishes

Purple sprouting broccoli with mustard sauce

Steak and kidney pie with vegetables and chips

Cappuccino crème brûlée

Whitewell

034 The Inn at Whitewell

Whitewell BB7 3AT

Tel.: (01200) 448222 - Fax: (01200) 448298
e-mail: reception@innatwhitewell.com - Website: www.innatwhitewell.com

 VISA

 Timothy Taylor, Bowland Brewery, Copper Dragon

A delightful location in a river valley in the Forest of Bowland means that a visit is always going to be special. The pub itself is an extended 14C cottage which once served as a coaching inn; nowadays it's very personally run with an endearing eccentricity which surfaces at the unlikeliest moments! It has considerable charm downstairs with a lovely faded bar full of eyecatching curios, a reception-cum-shop and an intimate restaurant overlooking the River Hodder and Trough of Bowland. Dishes have a traditional base and make good use of sound Lancastrian produce: just pull up a chair in the bar for a hearty meal or ask for a table in the restaurant for a more formal occasion. The large, comfortable bedrooms, whether traditional or modern, boast plenty of style, with good views and, in some cases, real peat fires. All have CD players and fittings that touch on the highest inn standards.

Food serving times:
Monday-Sunday:
   12pm-2pm, 7.30pm-9.30pm
Prices:
Meals: a la carte 15.50/35.00
23 rooms : 70.00/96.00

6mi Northwest of Clitheroe by B6243.
Parking.

Typical Dishes

Crumbed & fried goat's cheese

Whitewell fish pie

Lancashire and other British cheeses

Wrightington Bar

035 ## The Mulberry Tree

Wrightington Bar WN6 9SE

Tel.: (01257) 451400 - Fax: (01257) 451400

  VISA

 Boddington's Original, Greene King IPA

Not a pub for the traditionally-minded lover of beams and foaming ale. Nevertheless, what it lacks in traditional character, it makes up for in ample size and ultimately in the quality of the food. The rather cavernous open plan interior has a spacious bar with simple tables and chairs occupying one end, and a large, more formal, and slightly more expensive, linen-clad restaurant at the other. Both share a warm, buzzy atmosphere as well as the same range of specials, and this is where the pub comes into its own: the satisfying modern cooking demonstrates sound experience and culinary know-how and portions are, by any standards, generous. Local, seasonal ingredients are to the fore in the quality cuisine which pays due homage to global influences. Keenly-priced menu with a strong Lancashire base and plenty of choice.

Food serving times:
Monday-Thursday:
    12pm-2pm, 6pm-9.30pm
Friday-Saturday:
    12pm-2pm, 6pm-10pm
Sunday: 12pm-9.30pm
Closed 26 December
and 1 January
Prices:
Meals: a la carte 25.00/45.00

3.5mi Northwest of Standish by A5209 on B5250. Parking.

Typical Dishes

Black pudding and Lancashire cheese tart

Confit belly pork

Melting chocolate pudding

*N*ot content with seven historic counties, the South East has always looked further for inspiration. This, after all, is the region that gave the world a prince's Indian pavilion facing the Brighton seafront, the pretty redbrick streets of Sandwich, bridging the Channel to Holland and Germany, and Waddesdon Manor, a perfect Loire Chateau just off the A41. Yet these are as much an image of "Englishness" as the domes and spires of Oxford or Kent's white-capped oasthouses amid the hop-poles and apple orchards of the Weald. Here in the South East you'll find the start of the Cotswolds and the freedom of the South Downs Path, the ancient vantage of White Horse Hill and the rural calm of Royal Berkshire's riverside villages, while Canterbury and Winchester, Blenheim, Chartwell and Windsor all have their special place in British history. For a change of pace, fast or slow, the quiet countryside or the colourful cultural life of Brighton are both within an hour from the capital. The South East is also a place to dine well: Whitstable oysters, delicately flavoured Romney Marsh lamb and Aylesbury duck, not to mention a long brewing tradition, are just some of its specialities.

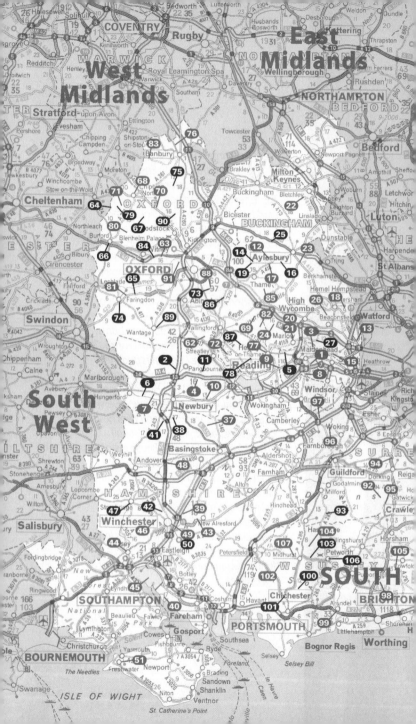

Bray-on-Thames

001 The Hinds Head

High St, Bray-on-Thames SL6 2EB

Tel.: (01628) 626151 - Fax: (01628) 623394
e-mail: info@hindsheadhotel.co.uk - Website: www.thehindshead.com

 Green King IPA, Abbot Ale and 2 changing guest ales

C ross Heston Blumenthal's dedication with the warm, true-grained charm of the English pub and you have a recipe for success. The ground-breaking modern cuisine of the Fat Duck, four doors away, is little reflected in the pub's menu, but the team at the Hind's Head do share the owner's fascination with the lost glories of English cookery: try a glass of pear cider or a sip of mead with satisfying and full-flavoured dishes that include pies and puddings, syllabubs and trifles. The most imaginative choices are based on favourites from the old royal kitchens downriver at Hampton Court. The pub itself has its origins in the 1600s – with its beams, panelled walls and real fire, it feels wonderfully inviting – but it's more used to keeping up with 21C demand, so arrive early.

Food serving times:
Monday-Saturday:
    12pm-2.30pm,
    6.30pm-9.30pm
Sunday: 12pm-3pm
Closed 25-26 December
Prices:
Meals: a la carte 25.00/45.00

Typical Dishes

Pea and ham soup
Oxtail and kidney pudding
Quaking pudding

1mi South of Maidenhead by A308.
Parking across the road.

Chieveley

002 The Crab at Chieveley 🛏

Wantage Rd, Chieveley RG20 8UE

Tel.: (01635) 247550 - Fax: (01635) 248440
e-mail: info@crabatchieveley.com - Website: www.crabatchieveley.com

No real ales offered

D own a country road, surrounded by waving fields of wheat and well-ordered countryside, The Crab doesn't look like the kind of place to rock the boat, but country pub preconceptions are best forgotten here. The old fishing nets give you a clue to the menu – an extensive choice of seafood served in the more casual Fish Bar and a surprisingly formal dining room. The real surprise, though, is reserved for diners who decide to stay the night. Ten bedrooms in the modern annex eclipse the average inn for originality and luxury. Decorated in the style of famous hotels from Raffles to Sandy Lane in Barbados and La Mamounia in Marrakesh, each one is equipped with DVD players and other delightful extras: ground floor rooms have their own private terrace with a hot tub!

Food serving times:
Monday-Sunday:
   12pm-2.30pm, 6pm-10pm
- seafood -
Prices:
Meals: 16.50/19.50 (fixed price 2/3 course lunch and dinner before 7pm) and a la carte 19.50/35.00
🛏 **17 rooms :** 100.00/170.00

Typical Dishes

Caulflower risotto

Pan fried sea bass, red onion pommes Lyonnaise, Shiraz jus

Raspberry and white chocolate tower

2.5mi West of Chieveley by School Road on B4494. Parking.

Cookham

003 **The Ferry**

Sutton Rd, Cookham SL6 9SN

Tel.: (01628) 525123
Website: www.theferry.co.uk

  rest **VISA**

Timothy Taylor Landlord, Adnams, Fullers London Pride

In terms of location, it's hard to imagine a pub more enviably situated than The Ferry, which stands alongside the meandering Thames overlooking Cookham Bridge. It even has its own landing stage for those who like to arrive in a bit of style. Some don't even make it inside, but are tempted to linger on the lovely wood furnished dining terrace, but those who do venture through the front doors are hardly short-changed. The pub boasts a part-14th century interior, and its recent restoration offers modernised, rustic charm. There's a smart snug with leather seats, a bar with sofas to snuggle into, and two restaurants with good views over the river. Appealing menus wander through the gastro universe, from snacks to pasta and pizza, and on to rotisserie and grill, all of which can be walked off afterwards with a nice stroll along the Thames Path.

Food serving times:
Monday-Sunday:
12pm-2.30pm, 6pm-9.30
Prices:
Meals: a la carte 21.00/30.00

By the river 2 mins walk from the centre of the village. Parking.

Typical Dishes

Mushrooms and smoked goat's cheese

Spit roast chicken

Sticky toffee pudding

Frilsham

004 The Pot Kiln

Frilsham RG18 0XX

Tel.: (01635) 201366
e-mail: info@potkiln.co.uk - Website: www.potkiln.co.uk

Brick Kiln, Mr Chubbs, Maggs Mild (West Berkshire Brewery), Morlands and changing guest ales

Hard to believe that dull roar you hear in the background is the M4. This 350 year-old brick built house – a former brick makers' - transports you to a quieter age. Run by TV chef Mike Robinson, you enter into a tiny, wonderfully characterful front bar that's wood floored with benches unchanged for over a century. You might be tempted to eat here, but most prefer the dining area through a door, complete with chunky pine tables and chairs. "Locally caught" is the absolute principle here. Game is from the nearby Berkshire countryside, wild mushrooms come from the woods, and herbs and salad leaves travel all the way from the back garden. Filled roll or roasted game dish, you're sure of a good mouthful, washed down by wine from the excellent list, or a pint from the West Berkshire Brewery – it's based at the bottom of the garden!

Food serving times:
Monday-Saturday:
12pm-2pm, 7pm-9pm
Sunday: 12pm-2pm
Restaurant closed 25 December
Prices:
Meals: 16.50 (set price lunch Monday-Friday) and a la carte 23.00/28.00

6mi North East of Newbury by B4009 to Hermitage and minor road. Parking.

Typical Dishes

Warm salad of wood pigeon

Braised wild rabbit with rosemary

Tarte Tatin

Hurley

005 **Black Boys Inn**

Henley Rd, Hurley SL6 5NQ

Tel.: 01628 824212

e-mail: info@blackboysinn.co.uk - Website: www.blackboysinn.co.uk

Brakspears Bitter

This part-16C inn is already showing the benefits of a thorough-going renovation: it's intimate, relaxing, and obviously run with real pub know-how. A delightful, soft-toned main bar centres on an open stove. True to form, the gently helpful, conversational service strikes just the right note: the friendly team are justifiably proud of their good food and will talk you through the daily specials, which might include fresh Newlyn fish, salt-marsh lamb and good seasonal game. The concern for fine ingredients is typical of a pub which even draws its water from its own well, but the result is the sort of flavourful, well-prepared cooking which is very easy to enjoy. Extremely comfortable and pleasantly furnished modern bedrooms – some in converted outbuildings – really stand out for value.

Food serving times:
Tuesday-Saturday:
12pm-2pm, 7pm-9pm
Sunday: 12pm-2pm
Closed 1 week from 24 December, 17-25 April, last week in August
Prices:
Meals: 19.95 (set price Sunday lunch) and a la carte 22.50/31.70
8 rooms: 65.00/105.00

Typical Dishes

Salcombe crab, pink grapefruit gelee

Petit sale duck leg

Rhubarb and marzipan fritter

1.5 miles Southwest on A4130. Parking.

Kintbury

006 **The Dundas Arms**

Station Rd, Kintbury RG17 9UT

Tel.: (01488) 658263

e-mail: info@dundasarms.co.uk - Website: www.dundasarms.co.uk

Adnams Bitter, Ramsbury Gold, Sharp's Eden, West Berks Mr Chubb's Lunchtime Bitter

After supplying Kintbury with sustaining dinners and its daily pint for over three decades, the long-standing landlord knows he's among friends in the bar. Never ones to pass up a good thing, the locals arrive on the dot for filling dishes like fried skate with capers and jacket wedges or roast duck with apple and cider sauce, and a friendly, familiar atmosphere prevails. It can get just a little too busy and smoky for some tastes, in which case the trick is to ask if they're opening the rear restaurant, usually reserved for more formal dinners. But on a summer afternoon, there's only one place to be. A lovely double terrace borders the edge of the Kennet and the canal: watch the narrowboats passing the lock as the stopping trains roll away to Bedwyn and the Wessex Downs. Five neat, light bedrooms face the river.

Food serving times:
Monday: 12pm-2pm
Tuesday-Saturday:
            12pm-2pm, 7pm-9pm
Closed 25-26 December
Prices:
Meals: a la carte 17.00/26.00
🛏 **5 rooms :** 80.00/90.00

3.5mi East of Hungerford by A4. Parking.

Typical Dishes

Dressed crab salad

Fried calves liver with bacon

Chocolate pavé with coffee bean sauce

Marsh Benham

007 **The Red House**

Marsh Benham RG20 8LY

Tel.: (01635) 582017 - Fax: (01635) 581621
e-mail: cyrilgrell@btconnect.com - Website: www.theredhousepub.com

 No real ales offered

Once inside this well cared-for thatched inn, there's a choice to be made. To the front, the more casual bar: grab one of several tables by the old mullioned windows, if you can. To the back, pleasant countryside views, courteous, attentive service, smartly set dining tables polished to a high sheen and the option of an à la carte or prix-fixe bistro menu. A classical French influence comes through in rather delicate, carefully presented dishes like chicken and wild mushroom terrine with brioche or a buttery asparagus risotto; they're also very proud of their banoffee pie with cinnamon and nut crumble.

Food serving times:
Monday-Saturday:
11.30pm-2.30pm,
7pm-9.30pm
Sunday: 11.30pm-2.30pm
Closed 25-26 December
Prices:
Meals: a la carte 19.45/32.95

Typical Dishes

Duck terrine

Roast rack of lamb, herb crust

Warm chocolate and redberry fondant

Off the A4 between Newbury and Hungerford. Parking.

Paley Street

008 The Royal Oak

Paley Street SL6 3JN

Tel.: (01628) 620541
e-mail: see website - Website: www.theroyaloakpaleystreet.com

Fuller's London Pride

A pleasant, proudly preserved village pub, but with a difference: framed photos of the owner's father, chatshow legend Michael Parkinson, and his showbiz friends beam affably from the wattle and timber walls. Attentive staff share Parky's talent for putting guests at their ease and serve up classically tasty, no-nonsense cooking with proper seasonal character: dishes could include chicken parfait and grilled sole with asparagus, followed by a lemon tart. A smart yet cosy bar, complete with dedicated regulars, offers a fine selection of wines and real ales and a quietly convivial atmosphere.

Food serving times:
Monday-Saturday:
12pm-2.30pm,
6.30pm-9.30pm
Sunday: 12pm-2.30pm
Closed
27 December-2 January
Prices:
Meals: 19.50 (set price lunch) and a la carte 20.00/30.00

Typical Dishes

Pan fried scallops, rocket, spinach

Sea bass, Chinese vegetables

Poached pear with chocolate sauce

3.5 mi Southwest of Bray-on-Thames by A308, A330 on B3024. Parking.

Wargrave

009 St George & Dragon

High Street, Wargrave RG10 8HY

Tel.: (0118) 940 5021 - Fax: (0118) 940 5024
Website: www.stgeorgeanddragon-wargrave.co.uk

Timothy Taylor's Landlord, Fuller's London Pride

Summer visitors to this delightfully modern and relaxed pub should make sure they arrive early: the enviably located raised deck terrace is a perfect spot to watch life go by on the neighbouring River Thames, but a place here is at a premium. Don't worry if your best bet is to stay inside – this is a textbook contemporary pub with a central bar, copper topped tables, tub chairs and several inviting log fires on colder days. To make the most of the river views, the main restaurant with open kitchen is around the side: heavy wood tables, fine glassware and interesting, modern specialities from the wood-fired oven and spit roast, alongside other up-to-date, globally inspired dishes at a keen price.

Food serving times:
Monday-Sunday:
12pm-2.30pm, 6pm-9.30pm
Closed 25-26 December
Prices:
Meals: a la carte 20.00/30.00

Typical Dishes

Baked Camembert

Salmon, Parma ham, pesto and new potatoes

Sticky toffee pudding

Moorings on the River Thames, at the end of the garden. Parking.

Woolhampton

010 ## The Angel

Bath Rd, Woolhampton RG7 5RT

Tel.: (0118) 971 3307
Website: www.a4angel.com

  VISA **MC**

Fuller's London Pride

A first impression of the Angel – green window frames in a curtain of ivy – offers no hint of the highly personalised design inside. Tropical plants, flowers, hops and yet more ivy set off some eye-catching modern art and photographs in a series of intimate, candlelit rooms: burgundy, green and ochre, with rows of wine bottles glinting between the beams. Fish and chips aside, much of an ambitious modern repertoire takes French culinary style as its starting point, and delicately presented starters and mains might include tuna on salad niçoise or prawns in lobster broth. Compiling the wine list is clearly a labour of love: some rare vintages – like the empties on the ceiling – may be out of reach to most of us, but the selection includes a more accessible range by the glass and even a homemade sloe gin.

Food serving times:
Tuesday-Sunday:
11.30pm-2.30pm,
6.30pm-10pm
closed Christmas week
Prices:
Meals: a la carte 19.00/25.00

Typical Dishes

Carpaccio of beef with horseradish

Fried trout, lemon and tomato

Warm chocolate fondant

On A4 between Reading and Newbury. Parking.

Yattendon

011 The Royal Oak 🛏

The Square, Yattendon RG18 0UG

Tel.: (01635) 201325 - Fax: (01635) 201926

e-mail: info@royaloakyattendon.com - Website: www.royaloakyattendon.com

West Berkshire Good Old Boy and Mr Chubbs

Though not a million miles from the roaring intensity of the M4, this very pleasant redbrick former coaching inn could inhabit another age. Sympathetically set in a picture postcard village, its well-appointed lounge with real fire sets the scene, evoking English country house style at its more comfortable and unassuming. Choose from two dining rooms, one in smart, classic style with cloth-clad tables and fine quality cover, the other more pubby and relaxed. Menus, invariably with plenty of choice, change every two and a half months but never stray far from a confidently executed classic base with distinctly modern overtones, their influences stretching globally. Comfortable, pretty bedrooms, with a rather chintzy quality, beckon upstairs.

Food serving times:

Monday-Friday:
12pm-2.15pm, 7pm-9.30pm

Saturday: 12pm-2.15pm, 7pm-10pm

Sunday: 12pm-3.30pm, 7pm-9pm

Closed 1 January

Prices:

Meals: 15.00 (lunch weekdays only) and a la carte 24.00/35.00

🛏 **5 rooms :** 85.00/130.00

Typical Dishes

Carpaccio with mustard glaze

Fillet of venison, rosemary jus

Chocolate crème brûlée

In the village centre. Parking.

Cuddington

012 The Crown

Aylesbury Rd, Cuddington HP18 0BB

Tel.: (01844) 292222
e-mail: david@anniebaileys.com

 VISA AE MC

Fuller's London Pride, Adnams

Locals swarm to this highly renowned village pub, and not just because it's 16C, Grade II listed, and thatched to boot. The interior is a most welcoming place to be, with subdued lighting, small windows and several period fireplaces, though the collection of Victorian prints reveal a lightly quirky side, too. There are four areas in which to relax and mingle; the two most sought-after being around the bar, near the fires, though you can eat wherever you like. Menus mix pub staples, like steaks and lamb casserole, with more contemporary dishes, such as scallops and chilli jus, or chicken saltimbocca with sweet potato mash, while puddings come under the heading 'heart-warming'. Enthusiastic, down-to-earth service is entirely in keeping for a pub with the true "local" ambience.

Food serving times:
Monday-Sunday:
12pm-2.15pm,
6.45pm-9.30pm
Closed 25 December
Prices:
Meals: a la carte 17.00/23.00

Typical Dishes

Scallops, pancetta, truffle oil dressing

Calves liver, sweet potato mash

Bread and butter pudding

West of Aylesbury by A418. Some parking spaces available.

Denham

013 The Swan Inn

Village Rd, Denham UB9 5BH
Tel.: (01895) 832085 - Fax: (01895) 835516
e-mail: info@swaninndenham.co.uk - Website: www.swaninndenham.co.uk

Courage Best, Wadworth 6X, Marlow Rebellion IPA

Very much at the heart of one of the loveliest villages in Buckinghamshire, the pretty, ivy-clad Swan Inn is half bar, half restaurant, but it's run in such a pleasant, accommodating spirit that everyone feels welcome; drinkers and diners mingle under the broad umbrellas on the terrace, which leads into a spacious garden. Choose from a menu with a modern edge or daily changing blackboard specials which reflect the season; typical of these are tasty black and white puddings with crispy pancetta, halloumi with saffron vegetables and couscous and a subtly flavoured elderflower and lavender crème brulée.

Food serving times:
Monday-Saturday:
  12pm-2.30pm, 7pm-10pm
Sunday: 12pm-4pm, 7pm-10pm
Closed 25-26 December
(booking essential)
Prices:
Meals: a la carte 19.00/27.75

Typical Dishes

Crab gnocchi with peas

Grilled seabass fillets, brown shrimp butter

Warm chocolate brownie

In the centre of the village on the north side of the road. Small car park.

Easington

014 Mole & Chicken

The Terrace, Easington HP18 9EY

Tel.: (01844) 208387 - Fax: (01844) 208250
e-mail: shanepellis@hotmail.com - Website: www.moleandchicken.co.uk

Hook Norton, Ruddles, Greene King IPA, Vale Best

The bend in the road of a tiny Buckinghamshire hamlet provides the cosy backdrop to this attractive, wisteria clad country pub. There's a really comfortable ambience here, highlighted by the carefully chosen fabrics in pretty country pub style, roaring fires, beams, decorative candles and scrubbed pine tables and chairs: it's a cosy and intimate place. Menus are changed regularly (apart from the well-established favourites the regulars won't allow to go!). Good modern dishes are served in hearty sized portions: originality is the keyword. Service is locally renowned: staff are known for their enthusiasm. Adjacent cottages provide bright, modern bedrooms, some with countryside views.

Food serving times:
Monday-Sunday:
12pm-2pm, 7pm-9pm
Closed 25 December
(booking essential)
Prices:
Meals: a la carte 22.00/30.00
5 rooms : 50.00/65.00

Typical Dishes

Homemade soup of the day

Chicken breast en croute, spring onion and cheese sauce

Baileys crème brûlée

2.5mi Northwest of Thame by B4011. Parking.

Farnham Royal

015 ## The King of Prussia

Blackpond Lane, Farnham Royal SL2 3EG

Tel.: (01753) 643006
Website: www.thekingofprussia.com

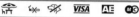

Fuller's London Pride

Perched between the M4 and the M40, not far 'up' from Windsor and just 'down' from Burnham Beeches, Farnham Royal is a smart village that now boasts an equally smart country dining pub. Part-owned by TV chef Phil Vickery, the King of Prussia presents a shiny, cream-washed appearance to visitors and its part 17C credentials lose nothing by the bright lick of exterior paint. The impressive interior is rich in character, exemplified by beamed ceilings, wood floors and panels. Take your choice from three dining areas: either around or off the bar, or in a wonderfully welcoming barn conversion with rafters. The modern cooking is constantly evolving and benefits from an unfussy approach. Top English produce is used to fine effect; effortless service – keen and organised – completes a smooth picture.

Food serving times:
Monday-Saturday:
12pm-2.15pm,
6.30pm-9.30pm
Sunday: 12pm-2.15pm
Closed Sunday dinner
Prices:
Meals: 19.95 (set price Sunday lunch) and a la carte 23.00/28.00

Typical Dishes

Onion tart with goat's cheese

Roast cod, prawn colcannon

Bread and butter pudding

3mi Northwest of Slough by A4 and A355. Parking.

Ford

016 Dinton Hermit

Water Lane, Ford HP17 8XH

Tel.: (01844) 347100 - Fax: (01296) 748819
e-mail: colinswooddeb@aol.com - Website: www.dinton-hermit.com

Brakspears, Young's 6X

Although it's much less secluded than the name suggests – surely the only hermit with an extensive car park – the gently firelit bar of this listed pub does provide a lovely, if temporary, retreat from the world. Burnished benches, cane-backed chairs, whitewashed walls with bricks and beams make it recognisably traditional in spirit, but there's also a modern sense of clutter-free space about the place. Neatly set dining rooms are in similar style, and the upfront country flavours in a modern pub menu seem to go down well: try braised ham with tarragon and Cheddar sauce or pot-roast guinea fowl with a nutty, zesty sauce. The restored outbuilding now houses the inn's bedrooms: two have Jacobean style four-posters, the others have a pleasing modern look: bright, tidy and individual.

Food serving times:
Monday-Saturday:
12pm-2pm, 7pm-9pm
Sunday: 12pm-4pm
Closed 25-26 December and 1 January
Prices:
Meals: a la carte 22.00/31.00
13 rooms : 72.00/125.00

Typical Dishes

Pan fried sea bass, chilli cream sauce

Calves liver, port jus

Passion fruit crème brûlée

5.5mi Southwest of Aylesbury by A418. Parking.

Haddenham

017 **Green Dragon**

8 Churchway, Haddenham HP17 8AA

Tel.: (01844) 291403 - Fax: (01844) 299532

e-mail: peteandsue@pmoffat.freeserve.co.uk - Website: www.eatatthedragon.co.uk

IPA, Deuchars, Wadsworth 6X and local guest ale Wychert

Personally run with an affable ease which seems to spread through the place, the well looked-after Green Dragon has a reputation for good food, one which now reaches far beyond the picturesque village it still serves so well. An extensive menu – with a few unexpected combinations – ranges from partridge with parsnips and pear sauce or scallops with white wine and vanilla dressing to a few simple but carefully sourced pub classics like chicken and wild mushroom pie and steak and kidney pudding with local ale. Haddenham was once as famous for its ducks as nearby Aylesbury and they still have quite a taste for them here, so look out for confits or roasts among the specials. Light lunches and dinners are served at the same neatly set tables, laid out all around the central bar.

Food serving times:
Monday-Saturday:
11pm-2pm, 6.30pm-9.30pm
Sunday: 11pm-2pm
Closed 25 December
and 1 January
(booking essential)

Prices:
Meals: 12.95/19.95 (2 course dinner Tuesday and Thursday; 3 course Sunday lunch) and a la carte 24.50/32.00

By the Green and St Mary's Church. Parking.

Typical Dishes

Salmon and prawn fishcakes

Calves liver and bacon

Pinacolada pannacotta

Little Chalfont

018 ## Sugar Loaf Inn

Station Road, Little Chalfont HP7 9PN

Tel.: (01494) 765579
e-mail: info@thesugarloafinn.com - Website: www.thesugarloafinn.com

Adnams, Wychert and regularly changing guest ales - Adnams Broadside

The nearby railway station of Chalfont and Latimer once disgorged thirsty commuters to the Sugar Loaf hotel, a classic 30s hostelry. Rundown at the turn of the Millennium, it's now evolved into a vibrant establishment in a very attractive part of the world; the Chilterns form a leafy backdrop and the popular Chess Valley isn't far away. Despite the extensive refit, the interior is surprisingly characterful: the original oak-panelled walls have been given prominence, while wood floors, moody lighting and blinds help create a distinctive gastro feel. There's a good mix of contemporary and original furniture, typified by polished tables and rustic high-backed chairs. Cooking is fresh and unfussy with a modern British edge: the menu is quite concise, but all the better for it, with shanks of local lamb, risotto and heartwarming puds getting the diners' vote. Keen, attentive and well-meaning service.

Food serving times:
Monday-Friday:
    12pm-3pm, 6pm-10.30pm
Saturday: 12pm-4pm,
                6pm-10.30pm
Sunday: 12pm-4pm, 6-10pm
Closed 26 December
and 1 January
Prices:
Meals: a la carte 20.00/26.00

2mi East of Amersham by A404.
Parking.

Typical Dishes

Smoked haddock & parsley fishcakes

Gressingham duck, Cassis jus

Apple tart Tatin

Long Crendon

019 **Angel**

47 Bicester Rd, Long Crendon HP18 9EE

Tel.: (01844) 208268 - Fax: (01844) 202497
e-mail: angelrestaurant@aol.co.uk

♨ ♟ ✟room ✗ **VISA** **MC**

Fuller's London Pride, Hook Norton, Bombardier

This attractive part-16C inn is now most assuredly in the quality restaurant-with-rooms category, but qualifies in the pub league due to its bright and cheery bar area with leather sofas. This is where the regulars gather to pay homage to the local beer on draught. Characterful dining areas lead off from here, defined by tiled flooring, bare wood tables and crisp linen napkins. To the rear an air-conditioned conservatory adds another enticing option. Seasonally changing, modern, creative menus have assured the Angel of a grand reputation, enhanced by daily changing fish specials. The word has spread, too, about the bedrooms here. They're decorated on a lavish scale with rich fabrics and wrought iron beds. One even allows you the luxury of a roll-top bath.

Food serving times:
Monday-Saturday:
  12pm-2.30pm, 7pm-9.30pm
Sunday: 12pm-2.30pm
Prices:
Meals: 19.95 (fixed price lunch) and a la carte 30.00/45.00
🛏 **3 rooms :** 65.00/85.00

Typical Dishes

Roast pigeon breast, rocket salad

Honey roast pork fillet

Iced cappuccino soufflé

1.5mi Northwest of Thame by B4011. Parking.

Marlow

020 The Hand and Flowers

126 West St, Marlow SL7 2BP

Tel.: (01628) 482277
Website: www.thehandandflowers.co.uk

  VISA

Green King IPA, Abbot Ale

The Hand and Flowers was originally a pretty row of period cottages, dating back at least to the 1800s by the look of their black and white timbered facades. A necessary modicum of modernisation inside has left it feeling nice and unspoilt: beams, rough plasterwork and chunky wooden tables in the original bar blend perfectly with modern art and vases of elegant lillies. The classically based cuisine is an equally good balance, excellent in sourcing and preparation and full of richly appealing, sophisticated flavours: professional but unstuffy service helps the enjoyment no end. Any off-hand Gallic shrugs or feigned unconcern are far more likely to be found on the petanque pitch in the back garden, where the pub team enjoys a bit of good-natured competition.

Food serving times:
Monday-Sunday:
12pm-2.30pm and 7pm-10pm
Closed 24-26 December
Prices:
Meals: a la carte 20.00/50.00

Typical Dishes

Potted crab

Braised shin of beef with bone marrow

Vanilla crème brûlée

From town centre follow Henley signs West on A4155. Pub on right after 350metres. Parking.

Marlow

021 The Royal Oak

Frieth Rd, Bovingdon Green, Marlow SL7 2JF
Tel.: (01628) 488611 - Fax: (01628) 478680
e-mail: info@royaloakmarlow.co.uk - Website: www.royaloakmarlow.co.uk

 Fuller's London Pride, Brakspear's Original, Marlow Rebellion IPA

Though it remains every inch the rural pub, from the old beams to the logs stacked by the wood burners, plenty of well thought-out details lend the Royal Oak an eclectic, but well-adapted, modern atmosphere. A bright conservatory bar feels clean and airy: barmen, spotting the regulars arriving, can get pouring before they've even walked through the door! Beyond, salvaged antique chairs and tables and fine tableware invite an easygoing attitude to good eating, and the charming staff do the same, carrying off what's actually very efficient, personalised service with breezy friendliness. Offering great value for this part of the world, ably judged dishes share a fresh, seasonal, classically balanced taste.

Food serving times:
Monday-Saturday:
12pm-2.30pm, 7pm-10pm
Sunday: 12pm-4pm, 7pm-10pm
Closed 25-26 December
Prices:
Meals: a la carte 18.00/26.75

Typical Dishes
Bubble & squeak, poached egg
Crispy duck leg, white bean cassoulet
Pear tart Tatin

From Marlow town centre head towards Bovingdon Green; pub is on the left as you leave the woods. Parking.

Newton Longville

022 Crooked Billet

Newton Longville MK17 0DF

Tel.: (01908) 373936
e-mail: john@thebillet.co.uk - Website: www.thebillet.co.uk

 VISA **AE** **MC**

White Star Titanic, Morland Original, Old Speckled Hen, Hobgoblin, Ruddles County, IPA

The Crooked Billet's phenomenal wine list, chosen with passionate connoisseurship to include over 300 wines by the glass, makes remarkable reading and very enjoyable drinking. With their typically helpful friendliness, the owner and his staff are happy to recommend a good match for lunch or dinner, and the well-judged modern cooking does it justice. In fact, it's hard to fault this smoothly run, ever welcoming pub with its thatched roof and pretty gardens: a spacious firelit bar still attracts its locals — you're welcome for a pint or a lunchtime sandwich if that's all you feel like — while the comfortable dining room with a hint of 16C character is a lovely setting for a dinner at leisurely pace.

Food serving times:
Monday: 7pm-10pm
Tuesday-Saturday:
        12pm-2pm, 7pm-9.30pm
Sunday: 12pm-3pm
Closed 25-26 December
Prices:
Meals: a la carte 25.00/40.00

Typical Dishes

Roast squab, baby beet risotto

Seared yellowfin tuna

Mango crème brûlee, mango sorbet

6mi Southwest of Milton Keynes by A421. Parking.

Stoke Mandeville

023 **The Wool Pack**

21 Risborough Road, Stoke Mandeville HP22 5UP

Tel.: (01296) 615970 - Fax: (01296) 615971

Fuller's London Pride and one guest ale

An object lesson in how to bring an old pub up to date, the low-ceilinged but now very contemporary bar of this part-thatched pub seems to get more cosy as the night draws in, especially if you've bagged one of the leather tub chairs and copper topped tables, or a spot near the fire. At the back is a sizeable dining room with French doors leading out onto the terrace, and this is where the contemporary influence is really brought to bear. Dishes like duck confit with pak choi and chilli are the exceptions in a repertoire which is more likely to turn to Italian cuisine for its subtle fusion twists: fresh, tasty stone-baked pizzas, grills and dessert treats like lemon polenta cake are all prepared with understanding and care and served by knowledgeable, spontaneous staff who seem genuinely happy to be there.

Food serving times:
Monday-Saturday:
12pm-2.30pm, 6pm-9.30pm
Sunday: 12pm-3.30pm,
6-9pm

Prices:
Meals: a la carte 15.00/45.00

Typical Dishes

Rocket and Parmesan garlic pizette

Calves' liver, caramelised onion jam

Mixed cheeses

South of town on A413 close to the hospital. Parking.

Turville

024 The Bull & Butcher

Turville RG9 6QU

Tel.: (01491) 638283 - Fax: (01491) 638836
e-mail: info@thebullandbutcher.com - Website: www.thebullandbutcher.com

 Brakspears Bitter and special breweries - Hooky Dark

Built in the mid-16C, this handsome, half-timbered pub served its first ales to the workmen restoring nearby St Mary's church. Tasty, tried-and-tested bar dishes can be as simple as ploughman's, fish and chips or a "Farmer's Supper and pint", while the table d'hôte might offer confit of duck or shellfish cakes with spicy lentils, unless it's time for a themed dinner: the "Bangers", "South Africa" and "Beaujolais" nights all went down well. Menus and specials are served in the restaurant and in the bar, where a semi-circular table centres on the rediscovered pub well. The charming village of Turville is worth an after-dinner stroll: fans of "The Vicar of Dibley" may find that it all looks strangely familiar…

Food serving times:
Monday-Saturday:
12pm-2.30pm,
6.30pm-9.30pm
Sunday and Bank Holidays:
12pm-4pm, 7pm-9pm
Prices:
Meals: a la carte 21.00/28.00

Typical Dishes

Duck liver pate
Slow cooked lamb shank
Cream tea cheesecake

5mi North of Henley-on-Thames by A4130 off B480. Parking.

Waddesdon

025 The Five Arrows

High St, Waddesdon HP18 0JE

Tel.: (01296) 651727 - Fax: (01296) 658596
e-mail: bookings@thefivearrowshotel.fsnet.co.uk - Website: www.waddesdon.org.uk

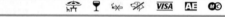

VISA AE MC

Fuller's London Pride

Certainly not your everyday local, this delightful late 19C inn is part of a magnificent estate built by Baron Rothschild, complete with attractive gardens and courtyard terrace, and close to Waddesdon Manor, now a National Trust property. Numerous comfy dining rooms centre on a charming bar; they're undeniably characterful and period features like wood panelling and parquet floors fit the studied country-house style to the last detail. Extensive menus offer a mix of British classic and contemporary, and though the service has an element of restaurant smartness, this aristocrat among pubs wears its hint of formality with good grace. As might be expected, very spacious bedrooms offer some stylish touches, along with an almost de rigeur four-poster. It's all very impressive, though maybe not for those who want to "pop out for a swift half."

Food serving times:
Monday-Saturday:
  12pm-2.30pm, 7pm-9.15pm
Sunday: 12.30pm-7pm
Prices:
Meals: 19.50 (set price lunch)
and a la carte 20.00/36.00
🛏 **11 rooms :** 75.00/150.00

Typical Dishes

Scallops, tarragon butter

Braised oxtail, red wine jus

Quince and lemon steamed pudding

9.5mi Northwest of Aylesbury on A41. Parking.

Winchmore Hill

026 **The Plough**
The Hill, Winchmore Hill HP7 0PA

Tel.: (01494) 721001
e-mail: plough.amersham@btconnect.com

 Courage Best, Greene King IPA

Those smart Buckinghamshire towns Amersham and Beaconsfield cradle the peaceful village of Winchmore Hill, where this neatly whitewashed establishment overlooks the green. There's no stinting on genuine rustic character here: the wood burning stove's orange glowing heart pumps a gentle rhythm in keeping with a flagged-floored, low-beamed ambience. The bar-top glints stainless steel. Modernity takes a bow in the form of comfy leather suites and sofas, much frequented by an appreciative local crowd. There's a split-level dining area, modern artwork lighting up its walls. Menus evolve on a daily basis, with cooking based upon British classics, rustic yet quite refined in style: sort of pub favourites meet fine dining. There are super value lunch menus; midweek evenings, too.

Food serving times:
Monday-Sunday:
  12pm-2.30pm, 6pm-10pm
Prices:
Meals: 11.00 (set price lunch)
and a la carte 20.00/30.00

Typical Dishes

Confit duck, black fig purée

Ribeye beef, triple cooked chips, Bearnaise sauce

Hot chocolate fondant

2mi Southwest of Amersham by A416 off A404. Parking.

Wooburn Common

027 **Chequers Inn**

Kiln Lane, Wooburn Common HP10 0JQ

Tel.: (01628) 529575 - Fax: (01628) 850124

e-mail: info@chequers-inn.com - Website: www.chequers-inn.com

 Ruddles County, Abbot Ale, Greene King IPA, Rebellion Smuggler

You're looking for a handsome redbrick inn, but alternatively you could just follow your nose: the famous garden barbecues at The Chequers do all their own advertising, and if you arrive on a sunny evening, your mouth may be watering by the time you reach the front door. Bring your elbows to make your way through a well-dressed knot of post-commute drinkers until around eight, but you should be able to grab a table for sandwiches or a full meal in the bar, or something a touch more adventurous in the restaurant at the back: favourites include ribeye and chips and almond and pear tart with crème anglaise. Bedrooms are perfect for anyone who wants pretty, cottage-style furnishings, but can't be without modems and satellite television. A well run place with real personality.

Food serving times:
Monday-Sunday:
  12pm-2.30pm, 7pm-9.30pm
Closed dinner 25 December and dinner 1 January

Prices:
Meals: 19.95 (set price lunch menu) and a la carte 30.00/45.00

17 rooms : 99.50/107.50

Typical Dishes

Cornish crab tian

Char grilled beef fillet, fondant potato

Rich chocolate mousse

3.5mi Southwest of Beaconsfield by A40. Parking.

Alfriston

028 **The George Inn**

High St, Alfriston BN26 5SY

Tel.: (01323) 870319

e-mail: info@thegeorge-alfriston.com - Website: www.thegeorge-alfriston.com

VISA **MC**

Greene King IPA, Abbott Ale, Old Speckled Hen and 1 guest ale - Riddley's Prospect

The most charming sight on Alfriston's pretty High Street, the overhanging front of the listed, brick-and-timber-built George Inn looks the picture of a good, old-fashioned English pub, and first impressions are confirmed in the front bar, with its strings of hops and its flickering fire. There's even some original 15C art on the walls. A relaxed landlord succeeds in making everyone feel properly at home, from the South Downs walkers who come for pints and ploughmans to a good crowd of locals – many pub cricket club and panto society members among them. Tasty dishes with an international or Asian touch offer plenty of choice and put their faith in the local greengrocer and butcher. The refurbished bedrooms have antique furniture but modern facilities; at the front, the sound of traffic to and fro on a weekday is noticeable, but no more than that.

Food serving times:
Sunday-Thursday:
    12pm-2.30pm, 7pm-9pm
Friday-Saturday:
    12pm-2.30pm, 7pm-10pm
Closed 25-26 December
Prices:
Meals: a la carte 19.00/27.00
6 rooms : 50.00/120.00

Two public car parks 150 metres and street parking.

Typical Dishes

Mushrooms with smoked bacon and goat's cheese

Poached cod in red wine with spiced pear

Fresh raspberry crème brûlée

Bodiam

029 The Curlew

Junction Rd, Bodiam TN32 5UY

Tel.: (01580) 861394

e-mail: enquiries@thecurlewatbodiam.co.uk - Website: www.thecurlewatbodiam.co.uk

 Hall and Woodhouse Badger Best and guest ales - Fursty Ferret, Everards Tiger, Harveys

A pub of two halves, but the warm ambience ensures this is a local favourite either way: choose from a good list of snacks and simpler meals in the main bar, its timbers edged with beardy fringes of Sussex hops, or a thoughtfully composed menu on a classic base. Smooth-clothed tables, elegant china and glassware suggest a rather formal approach, but it feels entirely appropriate for the tasty cuisine, not to mention the truly comprehensive selection of fine wines – there can't be many roadside stops with a cellar list like this. A short drive takes you to Bodiam Castle.

Food serving times:
Tuesday-Saturday:
    12pm-2pm, 7pm-9pm
Monday: 12pm-2pm
Prices:
Meals: 16.95/21.95 (set price 2/3 course lunch/dinner) and a la carte 24.00/33.00

On B2244 Hawkhurst to Sedlescombe road, by the Bodiam Castle crossroads. Parking.

Typical Dishes

Lobster and salmon sausage, tandoori foam

Halibut steamed with lemongrass

Rhubarb and fig pudding

Danehill

030 **Coach & Horses**

School Lane, Danehill RH17 7JF

Tel.: (01825) 740369
e-mail: coachandhorses@danehill.biz

Harveys Best, 2 guest ales changing weekly

Rough-hewn stone gives this Sussex hostelry a solid presence, softened somewhat by the magical nearby presence of the Bluebell Railway. The locals love it here; they're still an important part of its character, despite its recent "conversion" into a destination dining pub, and can usually be found having an afternoon ale in the small bar as you enter, dogs at their side. There are two separate dining areas, a top one which enjoys the atmosphere created in the bar, and another in the converted stables, with well-spaced tables, beams adorned with dried hops, and walls decorated with modern art. Particularly welcoming service adds the final touch to seasonally changing modern menus that dance to a distinctly Gallic tune: dishes are robust, frill-free, and full of flavour.

Food serving times:
Monday-Saturday:
      12pm-2pm, 7pm-9pm
Sunday: 12pm-2pm
Closed 25 December (pm), 26 December and 1 January (pm)

Prices:
Meals: 12.50 (Monday-Thursday 2 course supper) and a la carte 24.00/25.00

Typical Dishes

Home cured bresaola

Blanquette of Danehill lamb

White chocolate and raspberry tart

0.75mi North East on Chelwood Common Rd. Parking.

East Chiltington

031 The Jolly Sportsman

Chapel Lane, East Chiltington BN7 3BA

Tel.: (01273) 890400 - Fax: (01273) 890400
e-mail: info@thejollysportsman.com - Website: www.thejollysportsman.com

 2-3 Regularly changing ales, mainly from micro breweries

Once you know the right sequence of narrow country lanes, the trip to the Jolly Sportsman is half the fun; set in the lee of the South Downs, it's just secluded enough for driver and map reader to feel they've earned that first drink. Not that everyone comes from far afield; the enthusiastic team here certainly know the locals, and regulars are as likely to head for the cheerfully painted dining room as prop up the bar. As well they might: dishes from an appetising menu, with a sensible balance and extra variety from the specials list, prove to be well-presented and, as a rule, their clean-cut, direct flavours come over well. Should any of the local artwork on the walls catch your eye over coffee, ask at the bar: if the price is right, it's yours! Pretty rear garden and terrace.

Food serving times:
Tuesday-Thursday:
12.30pm-2.15pm, 7pm-9pm
Friday-Saturday:
12.30pm-2.15, 7pm-10pm
Sunday: 12.30pm-3pm
Closed 24-28 December
Prices:
Meals: 15.75 and a la carte 21.50/29.00

5.5mi Northwest of Lewes by A275 and B2116 off Novington Lane. Parking.

Typical Dishes

Spiced mussel wontons

Rump of Ditchling lamb with Sicilian aubergine

Chocolate and Armagnac prune block, coffee sauce

Fletching

032 **The Griffin Inn**

Fletching TN22 3SS

Tel.: (01825) 722890 - Fax: (01825) 722810
e-mail: info@thegriffininn@.co.uk - Website: www.thegriffininn.co.uk

    VISA **AE**

Harveys Best Bitter, King of Horsham, Tanglefoot

P ubs are meant to lie at the heart of a community, and this one certainly fits the bill. Reassuringly situated in the middle of a smart village, and boasting huge views to Ashdown Forest, the Griffin dates back to the 16C, as witnessed by the open fires, beams and oak panelling. The feel of a local is enhanced by the pool table at the back and the informality when ordering food: no bookings taken, order directly from the bar. Go through to the restaurant and it's something else again: rafters, candlelight and linen-clad tables. Modern menus have pride of place here: European and local dishes are prominent, such as fish risottos and roasted wood pigeon. Up-to-the-minute bedrooms – shared between the main house and garden annexe – are comfortable.

Food serving times:
Monday-Sunday:
   12pm-2.30pm, 7pm-9.30pm
Closed 25 December,
1 January (dinner)
Fixed price Sunday lunch
Prices:
Meals: 25.00 (Sunday lunch only) and a la carte 20.25/28.32
13 rooms : 80.00/130.00

Typical Dishes

Smoked paprika-fried squid

Roast rump of lamb, spinach risotto cake

Vanilla pannacotta

Between Uckfield and Haywards Heath off A272. Parking.

Heathfield

033 Star Inn

Church St, Old Heathfield, Heathfield TN21 9AH

Tel.: (01435) 863570 - Fax: (01435) 862020
e-mail: heathfieldstar@aol.com - Website: www.thebestpubsinsussex.co.uk

 Harveys Best, Shepherd Neame Early Bird, Welton's Old Harry

Standing in the grounds of the village church, this ivy-clad 14C pub is particularly charming on fine afternoons, when drinkers and diners have the run of a lovely lawned garden with tree-trunk benches, but don't wait for the first summer sun. Two intimate and ultra-traditional bars, with silver tankards hanging from the beams, are made all the more cosy by a wood-burning stove and an open fire: a couple of tables are tucked into a big inglenook fireplace. One blackboard lists familiar pub meals alongside ploughmans and potatoes, others offer the season's specials; expect decent-sized helpings of robust cooking in either case. The Star is so well regarded in the neighbourhood that it's as well to book, even for a midweek lunch, but at busy times they open the upstairs restaurant; some tables to one side have views of the church.

Food serving times:
Monday-Sunday:
  12pm-2.15pm, 7pm-9.30pm
Closed dinner
25-26 December
Prices:
Meals: a la carte 18.50/28.50

South East 2 miles by A265, off B2096. Parking.

Typical Dishes

Devilled whitebait

Slow-cooked half saddle of lamb

Black pepper highlight with ice cream

Piltdown

034 **The Peacock Inn**

Shortbridge, Piltdown TN22 3XA

Tel.: (01825) 762463

e-mail: matthewarnold@aol.com - Website: www.peacock-inn.co.uk

Harveys Best, Abbot Ale, Fuller's London Pride

A quintessentially English pub in the heart of the Sussex countryside, its 16C black and white timbered exterior enhanced by two very neatly trimmed yew trees at the entrance. There are benches at the front, too, and a sign with a brightly painted peacock in full plumage. The rear has a children's play area and large paved terrace, where they sometimes host barbecues in summer. Inside are spacious bar rooms, full of character: log fire, dark beams, brass ornaments and an old framed peacock tapestry in pride of place. A variety of photos cover the walls: those of the owner with celebrity guests testify to the Peacock's enduring popularity and warm atmosphere. Menus are traditional and unpretentious, complemented by chef's blackboard specials, with fresh ingredients from mainly local suppliers. The home-made desserts are warmly recommended.

Food serving times:
Monday-Sunday:
   12pm-2.30pm, 6pm-9.30pm
Closed 25-26
and 31 December
Booking advisable
at weekends
Prices:
Meals: a la carte 17.50/30.00

8mi East of Haywards Heath by A272 and Shortbridge Lane. Parking.

Typical Dishes

Crayfish tails and smoked salmon

Peacock chicken topped with mozzarella

Fruit brûlée

Rushlake Green

035 The Horse and Groom

The Green, Rushlake Green TN21 9QE

Tel.: (01435) 830320
Website: www.thebestpubsinsussex.co.uk

  VISA AE MC

Master Brew, Spitfire, Kent's Best

One for the traditionalist in all of us: horsebrasses twinkle, copper kettles gleam and ostlers and riders pose proudly with their glossy steeplechasers in the old prints above the fire. The two cosy, beamed rooms, their candles lit even at lunchtime, are at either end; although the Gun Room, its three fearsome-looking shotguns kept safely in the rack, is set slightly apart from the bar, the same menu is available throughout the pub. Using seasonal produce and market-fresh meat and fish, it's generous country cooking through and through. Full-flavoured roast lamb and other classics are served in good-sized portions and with prompt and friendly staff into the bargain, it's no wonder they're busy.

Food serving times:
Monday-Sunday:
   12pm-2.15pm, 7pm-9.30pm
Prices:
Meals: a la carte 21.00/30.00

Typical Dishes

Wild duck on parsnip purée

English pork fillet, cider sauce

Squidgy chocolate meringue

3mi Southeast of Heathfield by B2096. Parking.

Wartling

036 **The Lamb Inn**

Wartling Rd, Wartling BN27 1RY

Tel.: (01323) 832116
Website: www.lambinnwartling.co.uk

 Harveys Sussex Ale, Gribble's Toffs, King & Co Amarillo

On the edge of the Pevensey Levels, this part 16C pub is personally run and proudly traditional. Little black-framed windows give it the look of a country cottage from the outside, as do the dark beams and pretty chintz patterns in the little front bar, while the more spacious restaurant is decorated in shades of terracotta and dusky pink. The menu – served throughout – changes weekly, with plenty of thought going into the choice of ingredients and new season's produce, be it Southdown lamb or additive-free beef from the farm right next door. The choice of sausages and pies varies every day, and there's a separate seafood menu. Chirpy and prompt staff serve their guests well.

Food serving times:
Monday-Sunday:
11.45am-2.15pm,
6.45pm-9pm

Prices:
Meals: a la carte 17.40/27.15

3.75miles Southeast of Herstmonceaux by A271 and Wartling Rd. Parking.

Typical Dishes

Tartlet of fresh crab

Breast of Suffolk farm chicken

Chocolate and praline bread and butter pudding

Baughurst

037 The Wellington Arms

Baughurst Rd, Baughurst RG26 5LP

Tel.: (0118) 982 0110

e-mail: simon@thewellingtonarms.com - Website: www.thewellingtonarms.com

VISA

 Wadworth 6X

Cluttered and characterful, this former hunting lodge of the Duke of Wellington is 'one to watch'. Remodelled as a dining pub, it's a very cosy, atmospheric place with original terracotta tile floors and lots of impressive wood décor and beams. The clutter is a pleasing amalgam of ornaments, books, rustic pictures and knickknacks, never quite enough of a diversion to keep punters away from the well-stocked bar and adjacent wine rack. Chickens are kept in a pen in the rear paddock; by way of contrast, teas are imported from Australia! There are only eight tables for dining, so booking is essential. Modern British cooking takes centre stage, but worldwide influences are always simmering near the surface. Lunches are simpler, and very good value; it's all backed up by polite but chatty service.

Food serving times:
Wednesday-Saturday:
    12pm-2.30pm,
    6.30pm-9.30pm
Sunday: 12pm-2.30pm
Tuesday: 6.30pm-9.30pm

Prices:
Meals: 15.00 (set price lunch) and a la carte 22.00/35.00

Typical Dishes

Scallops on sauteed samphire

Seared Orkney Island gold rib eye steak

Sherry trifle

8mi North of Basingstoke by A339 and minor road through Ramsdell and Pound Green; South of village on the Kingsclere / Newbury road.

Burghclere

038 Carnarvon Arms

Winchester Rd, Whitway, Burghclere RG20 9LE

Tel.: (01635) 278222 - Fax: (01635) 278222
e-mail: info@carnarvonarms.com - Website: www.carnarvonarms.com

 VISA **MC**

 Timothy Taylor Landlords bitter, Fuller's London Pride

The very smart looking exterior of this north Hampshire establishment gives no clue to its actual age: the 1850s. Refurbishment has gone on apace inside too: a particularly spacious main bar and lounge area is enhanced by temptingly comfortable low-back leather sofas. While away the time browsing through handily placed newspapers and magazines. A good selection of real ales is complemented with an admirably eclectic mix of wines by the glass. Dining takes place in two rooms: the open, L-shaped main restaurant, or the anteroom for private parties. Menus are the same wherever you may be. If you're feeling adventurous, try dishes with an interesting range of modern combinations; if your taste is more conventional, then the classics section includes fish and chips or sausage and mash. Don't miss out on a trip to Highclere House up the road. At day's end, The Carnarvon Arms boasts comfy modern bedrooms.

Food serving times:
Monday-Thursday:
    12pm-3pm, 6pm-11pm
Friday-Saturday:
        12pm-11pm
Sunday: 12pm-3.30pm,
        6pm-10.30pm

Prices:
Meals: 14.95 and a la carte 18.00/28.00
12 rooms : 79.95/89.95

Typical Dishes

Pressed ham hock terrine

Double cooked shoulder of lamb

Orange polenta cake

5mi South of Newbury by A34 and minor road East. Parking.

Easton

039 Chestnut Horse

Easton SO21 1EG
Tel.: (01962) 779257 - Fax: (01962) 779037

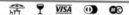 *VISA*

Archers Best, Courage Best, Chestnut Horse Bitter

Just a short drive from the centre of Winchester, The Chestnut Horse is a real find, with individuality and charm written right through it. For a start, there's the bar, showing its age in the best sense. A log fire, beams and rows of pint pots and jugs bring out the building's 16C character, while two more formal rooms introduce subtle changes of style: "Green" makes a natural setting for lunch, "Red", with dark tones offset by candlelight, is better for intimate dinners, but the pretty rear terrace, with an abundance of plants and flowers, trumps them both on a hot summer's day – friendly staff are happy to guide you round them all before you decide! An extensive menu runs from pub favourites to more modern dishes and a big line-up of specials.

Food serving times:
Monday-Saturday:
 12pm-2.30pm, 6pm-9.30pm
Sunday: 12pm-8pm (4pm in winter)
Closed Sunday evening in winter
Prices:
Meals: 10.00 (2 courses lunchtime & 6-7.30pm) and a la carte 16.00/30.00

Typical Dishes

Crab and crayfish tian

Oven roast chicken supreme

Warmed chocolate brownie

4mi North East of Winchester by A3090 off B3047. Parking

Hamble

040 The Bugle
High St, Hamble SO31 4HA

Tel.: (023) 8045 3000 - Fax: (023) 8045 3051
e-mail: manager@buglehamble.co.uk - Website: www.buglehamble.co.uk

Courage Best, Deuchars IPA and locally brewed beer in rotation

The chaps at the White Star have set their sights five miles down-water and come up with another winner. Nicely located amongst the craft on Southampton Water, The Bugle is a part 12C inn that's been carefully restored with much original charm remaining intact: to wit, a 15C footstep, exposed beams, wattle walls, stone and oak floors and an open fire stove with brick lining. On the ground floor the 16C dining room is intimately cosy and dotted with chunky wooden tables; upstairs, there's a lovely, snug private dining room with a tempting enticement: when you book, you get the key to the glass door of your own wine cellar. There's nothing fancy about the dishes on offer, just good, honest traditional favourites, all freshly prepared and ideal after messing about in a boat. Come along at lunchtime and you'll find some very good value menus up for grabs.

Food serving times:
Monday-Thursday:
　　　　12-2.30pm, 6pm-9.30pm
Friday:　　　12-3pm, 6-10pm
Saturday-Sunday:
　12pm-10pm (9.30pm Sunday)
Closed 25 December
Prices:
Meals: a la carte 14.95/24.95

7mi South East of Southampton by A3024 or A3025 and B3397. Public car park next to pub.

Typical Dishes

Pan fried mackerel, onion relish

Roast lamb chump

Pear and almond crumble

Highclere

041 The Yew Tree

Hollington Cross, Andover Road, Highclere RG20 9SE

Tel.: (01635) 253360 - Fax: (01635) 255035
e-mail: gareth.mcainsh@theyewtree.net

VISA *AE* *D* *MC*

Timothy Taylor Landlords Best, Fuller's London Pride

The rustic black and white pub outside Highclere looks the very picture of an English country inn, but it's carved out more than just a traditional role in village life. As well as its blackboard menus and dishes of the day, the well-restored part-17C bar still offers full measure to its drinkers, but the four classically elegant dining rooms at the back add candlelight and white linen to the same handsome period décor. Though a clear split between the two helps each keep their true atmosphere, the lunch and dinner menus are the same in both halves: a typical selection might take in lamb with champ and red onion marmalade, chicken en papillote and gravadlax - a taste of home for the amiable owner.

Food serving times:
Monday-Sunday:
        12pm-3pm, 6pm-10pm
Prices:
Meals: 14.50/16.50 (dinner (Sunday only)/lunch) and a la carte 22.00/48.00
6 rooms : 60.00

Typical Dishes

Salad of lobster à la Russe, sauce cocktail

Venison Pierre Koffmann au chocolat amer

Soufflé of raspberries

5mi South of Newbury by A343. Parking.

Littleton

042 The Running Horse 🛏

88 Main Road, Littleton SO22 6QS

Tel.: (01962) 880218 - Fax: (01962) 886596
e-mail: runninghorse@btconnect.com - Website: www.therunninghorsepubrestaurant.co.uk

Itchen Valley Winchester Ale, Palmers IPA

Delightful service from a considerate and well-drilled young team is just one element in a winning formula for the Running Horse, which has changed almost out of recognition from the run-down village pub that finally closed its doors. They re-opened on a radical rehaul – an attractive modern bar and a cleanly styled restaurant, smart wicker-backed chairs, delightful terrace with wrought iron furniture, even trendy new cutlery – and the gamble is paying off, with a good many takers for lighter bar lunches and the sophisticated but well-priced evening menu offering an enjoyable balance of full, fresh flavours.

Food serving times:
Tuesday-Saturday:
  12pm-2pm, 6.30pm-9.30pm
Sunday: 12pm-2pm
Closed 25 December
Prices:
Meals: a la carte 19.50/25.00
🛏 **9 rooms :** 65.00

Typical Dishes

Chicken parfait, pear chutney

Sauteed scallops, orange zest sauce

Apple tart

2.5mi North West from Winchester by B3049. Parking.

Ovington

043 Bush Inn

Ovington SO24 0RE

Tel.: (01962) 732764 - Fax: (01962) 735130
e-mail: thebushinn@wadworth.co.uk

 Wadworths 6X, IPA, JCB, Bishop's Tipple, Malt and Hops, Summersault and regular guest ales

Well-hidden down a winding country road, near the banks of the river Itchen, the 17C Bush Inn has all the understated friendliness you would hope to find in a family-run pub. Over the years it's accumulated an interesting collection of framed photographs and country memorabilia, and the feeling in the four little rooms, mostly for dining, is an easy and very natural one. Choose a table and pick from the blackboard: with a genuinely appetising range of wholesome, well-made dishes, including daily specials, this could be harder than you'd expect. Friendly service deserves a mention too, but the real bonus here is a lovely garden with plenty of seating: add some sun, and it's just perfect.

Food serving times:
Monday-Saturday:
   12pm-2.30pm, 6pm-9.30pm
Sunday: 12pm-2.30pm
Closed 25 December
Prices:
Meals: a la carte 19.50/31.50

Typical Dishes

Crab and leek tart

Beef Wellington

Baked fresh figs with balsamic and honey

5.75 mi East by B3404 and A31. Parking.

Romsey

044 The Three Tuns

58 Middlebridge St, Romsey SO51 8HL

Tel.: (01794) 512639

 VISA MC

Ringwood Best Bitter, Fuller's London Pride, Gales HSB, Ringwood Seasonal Bitter

Romsey town centre has seen various changes over the years, but The Three Tuns remains an engaging constant. It's been in Middlebridge Street for 300 years and the perennial log fire and timbers help it retain its period feel, much to the contentment of a large group of regulars. A facelift, though, is evident in the slate flooring and understated décor. The fairly large bar with vast wooden tables inhabits one side of the pub; a restaurant the other – this has a haphazard, rustic appeal with bare tables of various shapes and sizes alongside mismatched chairs. Relaxed but helpful service will ease you into a modern menu which you'll find characterised by capable, well-judged cooking using first-rate ingredients, not least game from the nearby Broadlands Estate, with lighter dishes available at lunchtime.

Food serving times:
Tuesday-Sunday:
12pm-2pm, 7pm-9pm
Prices:
Meals: a la carte 15.00/25.00

Typical Dishes

Seared scallops in garlic butter

Fillet steak with green peppercorn and brandy sauce

Crème brûlée

Towards the western end of the town, off the by-pass. Parking.

Southampton

045 **White Star Tavern and Dining Rooms**

28 Oxford Street, Southampton SO14 3DJ

Tel.: (023) 8082 1990 - Fax: (023) 8090 4982

e-mail: manager@whitestartavern.co.uk - Website: www.whitestartavern.co.uk

Fuller's London Pride

Naming their new venture after the Titanic's ill-fated shipping line was a brave move but, a few years on, it's full steam ahead for the team behind the White Star, who are making their London experience count in Southampton's wining and dining district. Neatly redesigned, the former chain pub is now split into an intimate lounge bar - complete with chill-out leather armchairs - and a comfortable dining room, spacious, understated and stylishly functional: all the old tables can be extended if a few more friends show up for dessert. A British/eclectic menu with a pleasantly familiar ring to it goes more free-form at lunch, with no distinction between "starters" and "mains".

Food serving times:
Monday-Thursday:
12pm-2.30pm,
6.30pm-9.30pm
Friday-Saturday:
12pm-3pm, 6.30pm-10pm
Sunday: 12pm-9pm
Closed 25-26 December and 1 January
Prices:
Meals: a la carte 20.00/29.95

Typical Dishes

Lobster ravioli with mint pea purée

Crisp fried shoulder of lamb

Bitter chocolate mousse

Southeast of West Quay shopping centre, off Bernard Street. Parking meters directly outside and public car park 2 mins away.

Sparsholt

046 Plough Inn

Main Road, Sparsholt SO21 2NW

Tel.: (01962) 776353 - Fax: (01962) 776400

Henry's IPA, Wadworth 6X, Wadworth JCB, Wadworth Summersault, St Austell Tribute

Proving that people really will go the extra mile for a good pub lunch, the friendly Plough Inn is often packed, even in midweek, so booking is a must. Even at its busiest, though, the atmosphere in the softly lit bars and lounges remains relaxed and warm, and in fine weather, a good-hearted crowd from the village and beyond are only too happy to spread out onto the front terrace and cottage garden, or take a seat on the benches in the field at the back, where the pub's donkeys crop the pasture with Eeyore-ish reserve. Back inside, big blackboard menus of wholesome country cooking offer some subtle variation: after a range of tasty starters, the mains diverge, with lighter pub fare on the one hand and more elaborate entrées on the other.

Food serving times:
Monday-Sunday:
12pm-2pm, 6pm-9pm
Closed 25 December
(booking essential)
Prices:
Meals: a la carte 18.00/28.00

Typical Dishes

Sauteed tiger prawns with chilli

Beef fillet, Madeira jus

White chocolate cheesecake

3.5mi Northwest of Winchester by B3049. Parking.

Stockbridge

047   The Greyhound

31 High St, Stockbridge SO20 6EY

Tel.: (01264) 810833 - Fax: (0870) 891 2897
e-mail: helenschoeman777@yahoo.co.uk - Website: www.thegreyhoundatstockbridge.co.uk

 VISA ⓜ©

> *Butcombe Traditional Bitter, Deuchars Caledonian IPA*

Standing snugly at one end of Stockbridge High Street since time immemorial, this honey-hued old stone pub now tends to attract a rather smartly casual set after a 21C clean-up in which its 18C features were carefully restored and brought to prominence. Country pursuits are a way of life around here, and locals tell tales at the bar of their fishing exploits along the nearby River Test. Bow your head if needs be to make progress through a characterful, low-beamed lounge, to arrive at the bare tables and wood flooring of two dining areas where 'shabby chic' is very chic indeed. It feels like a pub, but quite clearly has restaurant sensibilities reflected in the chef's metropolitan background and modern Anglo-French menus, which are prepared with skill and imagination and served by an enthusiastic brigade of young waiters.

Food serving times:
Monday-Saturday:
  12pm-2.30pm, 7pm-9.30pm
Sunday: 12pm-2.30pm
Closed 25-26 December,
1 January and dinner Bank Holidays
Prices:
Meals: a la carte 20.00/38.50
🛏 **8 rooms :** 65.00/100.00

Typical Dishes

Warm salad of ham hock

*Pan fried halibut,
Boulangere potatoes*

Cinnamon rice pudding

Stockbridge is on the A30 East of Salisbury. Parking.

Whitchurch

048 Red House Inn

21 London St, Whitchurch RG28 7LH
Tel.: (01256) 895558

Cheriton Pots Ale and weekly changing guest ales

To save any fruitless searches for red houses, what you're actually looking for is a row of 400 year-old whitewashed cottages: as you'll see inside, from the black and white photographs of the market town in bygone days, the conversion took place nearly a century ago. One door leads to the public bar, the other takes you into the restaurant: uncovered pine tables, a big mirror giving a pleasing sense of space and a large brick fireplace by the bar providing a homely atmosphere. Blackboard menus and the more formal printed menu have the same modern style. Weather permitting, tables are also available on the raised terrace outside.

Food serving times:
Monday-Sunday:
  12pm-2pm, 6pm-9.30pm
Closed 25 December
and 1 January
Prices:
Meals: a la carte 19.95/29.50

In the village. Parking. >>

Typical Dishes

Seared scallops with pea
veloute

Pan fried breast of duck,
saute potatoes

French lemon tart

Winchester

049 The Black Boy

1 Wharf Hill, Winchester SO23 9NQ

Tel.: (01962) 861754
e-mail: blackboypub@ntlworld.com

 VISA

Ringwood Best, Cheriton Pots Ale, Hopback Summer Lightning and 2 other guest ales

Fire buckets, reading glasses, door keys, books, corks and radiograms fill the gloriously quirky interior of this personally run pub. After a cordial greeting from the pub dog, settle down in one of the many relaxing corners with real fires and squashy sofas: one snug room is bathed in the gentle warmth of its own Aga. The lunchtime choice is not much more than sandwiches and a couple of hot dishes – tasty enough, and worth trying, but not in the same league as the evening menu, which offers fine seasonal and modern dishes with a touch of imagination. The Black Boy is not the kind of place you'd find by chance, but if you're after a casual, intimate dinner, that's yet another reason to go.

Food serving times:
Wednesday-Sunday:
12pm-2pm, Tuesday-Saturday: 7pm-9pm
Closed 2 weeks Christmas-New Year, 2 weeks September-October
Prices:
Meals: a la carte 24.25/29.40

Typical Dishes

Goat's cheese mousse

Loin of pork, black pudding, mustard mash

Chilled rhubarb soup

To the South of the city centre, near the junction of Chesil St and Quarry Rd. Parking off Chesil Street.

Winchester

050 **The Wykeham Arms**

75 Kingsgate St, Winchester SO23 9PE

Tel.: (01962) 853834 - Fax: (01962) 854411
e-mail: wykehamarms@accommodating-inns.co.uk

HSB, Butser and Fuller's London Pride

On a quiet street between the Cathedral and the College stands Winchester's third great institution, the Wykeham Arms. Founded back in the 1700s, it continues to draw a loyal local following but should be first on any visitor's itinerary too: intimate and charming, its comfortable snugs contain an intriguing collection of prints, flags, rackets, straw boaters and other sporting and school memorabilia, as well as old oak desks from the nearby classrooms. Well-informed young staff serve with enthusiasm and a good sense of timing; fresh, appetising cuisine – a modern-classic blend with nicely weighted flavours – puts the region's seasonal produce at the top of the list. Bedrooms are split between the main house – rich colour scheme and historical prints – and the annex across the road; the oak-panelled breakfast room is on the first floor.

Food serving times:
Monday-Saturday:
12pm-2.30pm,
6.30pm-8.45pm
Sunday: 12pm-2.30pm
Closed 25 December
Prices:
Meals: a la carte 14.50/28.50
14 rooms : 57.00/135.00

Near (St Mary's) Winchester College. Access to the car park via Canon Street only. Parking or street parking with permit.

Typical Dishes

Chicken liver parfait

Pan fried duck, stir-fried vegetables

Vanilla pannacotta

Freshwater

051 The Red Lion

Church Pl, Freshwater PO40 9BP
Tel.: (01983) 754925 - Fax: (01983) 754925

 Flowers Original, Fuller's London Pride, Goddards, Wadworth 6X

A handsome, part 14C building with little bay windows, this is as traditionally English a pub as any you might find on the slightly larger island across the water, and the characterful country style continues in its rustic interior. Run with a mix of enthusiastic quirkiness and good old fashioned hard work, it continues to do a thriving trade, with the focus squarely on a blackboard menu with daily variations – mostly traditional in its essentials, the pub's cuisine makes good use of its fresh ingredients, including newly-landed Channel fish. On busy days, your best chance of a seat may be in the garden or under the mini-marquee: a fixture since 2000, "the Dome" gets rather more use than the Greenwich version, but is generally reserved for private parties.

Food serving times:
Monday-Sunday:
    12pm-2pm, 6.30pm-9pm
Closed 25 December for food
Prices:
Meals: a la carte 20.00/25.00

Typical Dishes

Herring roes on toast

Braised lamb shank with mash and minted gravy

Chocolate pot with Cointreau

By the saltings of the River Yar. Parking.

Biddenden

052 The Three Chimneys

Hareplain Road, Biddenden TN27 8LW
Tel.: (01580) 291472

Adnams Best, Harveys Best, Directors'

H ere's a pub full of Kentish character: it's only down the road from Sissinghurst, so make a day of it and combine a visit to both. The Three Chimneys has been around since about 1420, and its lovely old exterior has a rough thick cream coat. The attractive terrace is packed in summer; at other times, don't miss the definitively rustic bar: yellowing walls, dried hops, absurdly characterful (and original) beams, little burner fire, lots of rough furniture. The restaurant, at the back, is smarter, in a palette of chocolate brown, with leather chairs, sealed wooden floors, painted wood-panelled walls and spacious tables; what's more, it faces the garden (where only Ploughman's are served). Dishes change regularly, from substantial salads to fish and steaks. Puddings are all homemade, in keeping with the warm, genuine feel that pervades here.

Food serving times:
Monday-Sunday:
  12pm-2pm, 6.30pm-9.45pm
Closed 25 December
and 31 December
Prices:
Meals: a la carte 20.00/31.00

West 1.5mi off A262. Parking. ❯❯

Typical Dishes

Baked field mushrooms

Roasted smoked haddock

Egg custard tart, strawberry
ice cream

Bodsham

053 Froggies at the Timber Batts

School Lane, Bodsham TN25 5JQ

Tel.: (01233) 750237 - Fax: (01233) 750176
e-mail: joel@thetimberbatts.co.uk - Website: www.thetimberbatts.co.uk

 Woodfordes Wherry, Fuller's London Pride, Adnams Southwold

A little piece of "la France profonde" in a lovely, creeper-clad, early Tudor pub. This unlikely success story is all down to the charming, French-born landlord who provides gentle bar-room bonhomie, superintends the spit-roast at the summer barbecues and teams up with his son in the kitchen to produce light bar lunches and unfussy and authentic Gallic classics from the regional cookbook. Fine fish and game are sourced locally, but the cheeseboard and the wine list – including a few vintages from a cousin's vineyard by the Loire – are proudly continental. Care and appreciation are obvious, and echoed in the service: staff are genuinely happy to recommend, explain, or provide enthusiastic translations. Frog ornaments decorate the brick pillars and window sills, and a welcoming, cosy feeling prevails.

Food serving times:
Tuesday (except after Bank Holidays) to Sunday:
12pm-2.30pm, 7pm-9.30pm
Closed 25 December,
1 January, first two weeks of March
-French-
Prices:
Meals: 22.00 (Sunday lunch only) and a la carte 25.00/32.00

Typical Dishes

Stuffed mussels
Confit of duck
Crème brûlée

Off B2068 between Canterbury and Hythe; close to Wye. Parking. ➤

Bridge

054 White Horse Inn

53 High St, Bridge CT4 5LA
Tel.: (01227) 832814 - Fax: (01227) 832814
Website: www.twhi-bridge.com

Y   *VISA*   AE   M©

Old Speckled Hen, Greene King etc

Particularly proud of their commitment to small local suppliers, not to mention their Kentish wines from Tenterden vineyards, the team at the White Horse have put together two menus with a common local and traditional theme. One, served in the classically styled dining room with more formal presentation and the little restaurant extras, has a touch more seasonality to it, while the bar menu combines long-standing pub favourites with more modern or original dishes. The British and Irish cheeseboard, with specialities from as close to home as Thanet and as far afield as Cork, deserves a menu in itself, and gets one, complete with tasting notes.

Food serving times:
Monday-Saturday:
    12pm-2pm, 7pm-9pm
Sunday: 12pm-2pm
Prices:
Meals: 25.00/25.00
and a la carte 25.00/25.00

Typical Dishes

Whitstable Bay scallops

Pan fried rib-eye steak with red wine jus

Local cheeses

5 miles from Canterbury, off A2.
Parking.

Dargate

055 The Dove

Plum Pudding Lane, Dargate ME13 9HB

Tel.: (01227) 751360

 ⚏ ♀ *VISA* ⏺

Shepherd Neame Master Brew and one seasonal beer

Unremarkable on the outside, this Victorian redbrick pub feels much friendlier once you walk up to the bar: the smiling landlady is only too pleased to sort out drinks, talk you through the menu and find you a table. Three little pine-fitted bar-rooms are warmed by open fires and decorated with black and white photos – a real visual history of village, pub and landlords down the years. A surprisingly extensive menu balances classic and modern influences to good effect: well-judged and richly flavourful dishes with solid French base. Even with one or two slightly pricier dishes, this is excellent value for money.

Food serving times:
Tuesday: 12pm-2pm
Wednesday-Saturday:
          12pm-2pm, 7pm-9pm
Sunday: 12pm-2pm
Closed Monday except Bank Holidays
(booking essential)
Prices:
Meals: a la carte 25.00/35.00

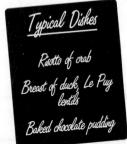

Typical Dishes

Risotto of crab

Breast of duck, Le Puy lentils

Baked chocolate pudding

Just off the A299 between Faversham and Whitstable; turn right at junction, 3/4mi on unmarked road to The Dove. Parking.

Igtham Common

056 Harrow Inn

Common Rd, Igtham Common TN15 9EB
Tel.: (01732) 885912 - Fax: (01732) 885912

 VISA

Greene King IPA, Abbot Ale

Don't be misled by the Harrow Inn's location, down a sleepy little lane in a Kentish hamlet – you'll have to get here pretty early to be sure of securing a seat in this pretty, part 17C stone and brick pub. An open fire divides the lovely, pleasingly traditional bar, although you might also find a free table in the back dining room and conservatory extension, where a printed menu replicates the list on the blackboard. With its share of more inventive recipes, there's a little more to this good, honest country cooking than you might expect: enjoy a tasty light lunch before a trip to nearby Knowle or the Tudor castle at Ightham Mote. Cheerful service.

Food serving times:
Tuesday-Saturday:
12pm-2pm, 6pm-9pm
Sunday: 12pm-2pm
Closed 26 December,
1 January, Bank Holiday
Mondays
Prices:
Meals: a la carte 18.00/30.00

5mi South East of Sevenoaks by A25 on Common Road. Parking.

Typical Dishes
Salmon and chive fishcake
Roast rack of lamb, red wine jus
Rhubarb crumble and custard

Lower Hardres

057 The Granville

Street End, Lower Hardres CT4 7AL
Tel.: (01227) 700402 - Fax: (01227) 700925

VISA **AE** **MC**

 Masterbrew and Shepherd Neames Seasonal Ale

Though big and open-plan in design, The Granville couldn't be more different from the chain-run drinking hangars of Britain's town centres. Light, well-kept and comfortable, its split into nicely airy sections which still share the good overall buzz of the place, and the service, though wonderfully laid-back, remains personal and helpful. The varied, interesting selection of dishes, frequently changing, is chalked up on the blackboard and delivers all the liveliness, piquancy and balance it promises. A serious regard for ingredients makes for distinct, resonant flavours: greens taste a fresh, chlorophyll green, and the excellent fish, much of it from the Kent coast, is always worth a try. Devotees of The Sportsman, Seasalter, will notice a strong family resemblance.

Food serving times:
Tuesday-Saturday:
12pm-2pm, 7pm-9pm
Sunday: 12pm-2.30pm
Closed 25 December
Prices:
Meals: a la carte 19.50/29.50

Typical Dishes

Scotch broth

Roast chicken, truffle cream sauce

Warm chocolate tart and blood orange ice-cream

3mi South of Canterbury on B2068. Parking.

Pluckley

058 The Dering Arms

Station Rd, Pluckley TN27 0RR

Tel.: (01233) 840371 - Fax: (01233) 840498
e-mail: jim@deringarms.com - Website: www.deringarms.com

Y *VISA* AE MC

Geachers, Dering Ale, Gold Star and Old Ale

Step through the heavy, original doors of this mid-19C Dutch-gabled former hunting lodge and experience the genuine feel of a 'local'. A pleasant rural atmosphere is evoked from blazing log fires, reclaimed tables and chairs, farming implements and bars festooned with hops. Emphasis is on the hefty seafood menus. You might find salmon fishcakes with sorrel sauce; monkfish with bacon, orange and cream; or skate wing with capers and black butter. If you're not in the mood for fish, then opt for the likes of confit of duck or the pie of the day. Afterwards, order a pint of real farm cider – the Dering specialises in them - and flop into a leather armchair in the cosy lounge.

Food serving times:
Tuesday-Saturday:
    12pm-2pm, 7pm-9.30pm
Sunday: 12pm-2pm
Closed 26-28 December
and 1 January
Prices:
Meals: a la carte 17.95/32.50
🛏 **3 rooms :** 35.00/45.00

Typical Dishes

Soft herring roes, smoked bacon

Fillet of sea bass, red wine sauce

Rich chocolate cake

1.5mi Southeast of Bethersden rd.
Beside the Railway Station. Parking.

Seasalter

059 The Sportsman

Faversham Rd, Seasalter CT5 4BP

Tel.: (01227) 273370

Seasonal ales - Early Bird, Goldings, Late Red and Porter; also Masterbrew, Whitstable Bay Organic Ale

Sheltering in the lee of the sea wall, this rather ramshackle pub doesn't promise much; inside, though, it's a different story. The simple, modern styling in pale pine looks a little stark at first, but as the log fires get going, the front and back bars fill up with a good mix of weekenders and regulars, sheep huddle on the marshes and circling gulls are blown past the window, it starts to feel quite cosy. A chatty, knowledgeable team, led by brothers Phil and Steve, runs the place with real enthusiasm, preparing a good-value blackboard menu centred on well-chosen seafood. Skillful combinations of flavours mean it's hard to put a foot wrong. Excellent quality and value.

Food serving times:
Tuesday-Saturday:
12pm-2pm, 7pm-9pm
Sunday: 12pm-2pm
Closed 25-26 December
Prices:
Meals: a la carte 25.00/35.00

2mi Southwest of Whitstable and then 2mi Southwest following coast road. Parking.

Typical Dishes

Rye Bay scallops, black pudding

Shoulder of Monkshill Farm lamb

Rhubarb sorbet and burnt cream

Speldhurst

060 **George & Dragon**

Speldhurst Hill, Speldhurst TN3 0NN

Tel.: (01892) 863125 - Fax: (01892) 863216

e-mail: julian@leefe-griffiths.freeserve.co.uk - Website: www.speldhurst.com

🏠 ☎ ♈ *VISA* Ⓜ©

Harvey's Best, Harvey Pale, Larkins Traditional, Westerns Summer Pearl

An ideal blend of North London pub style and deep-rooted Kentish loyalty, a sentiment fully returned by the regulars, who stop to read the parish news pinned up inside the door. Its interior is increasingly trendy but still fits perfectly and hasn't upset the welcomingly mellow but busy mood. Arty black-and-white shots of the owners' favourite pheasant shooters, chicken rearers and all-England cheesemakers – imagine Mario Testino and Lord Snowdon at the farmers' market – are a tribute to the primacy of fine ingredients. Here, "imported" food comes from the other side of the Medway and the chef regularly sends suppliers gleaning, foraging and rummaging round the county to unearth produce in the wild. Vigorously tasty dishes – combining culinary finesse with flavour in the raw – offers diners a real scope of seasonal originality.

Food serving times:

Monday-Saturday:
12pm-2.45pm, 7pm-10.30pm

Sunday: 12pm-5pm

Prices:
Meals: a la carte 25.00/35.00

Typical Dishes

Oxtail ragù, pumpkin and spinach gnocchi

Dexter beef chop

Marmalade brioche pudding

3,5 mi North of Royal Tunbridge Wells by A26. Parking.

West Peckham

061 The Swan on the Green

West Peckham ME18 5JW

Tel.: (01622) 812271 - Fax: (0870) 0560556
e-mail: info@swan-on-the-green.co.uk - Website: www.swan-on-the-green.co.uk

 On-site microbrewery - Trumpeter and others

Pub settings rarely come more attractively old English than this – the Swan's redbrick and ornate gabled exterior sits idyllically by the green, right next to the village's Saxon church. There's no pub garden, but benches perch along the terrace at the front. Inside, a framed history puts the inn's origins at 1526, but it's been given a pleasing modern makeover with pale wood throughout: the dried hops and real fire add a rustic twist. At the back is a micro-brewery, so a selection of unique ales are chalked up on the board behind the bar. There's a loyal local following and menus, featuring an interesting eclectic à la carte, change weekly. Try to visit in summer, when the owners provide blankets for you to eat on the green.

Food serving times:
Tuesday-Saturday:
12pm-2.30pm (2pm in winter),
7pm-9.30pm (9pm in winter)
Sunday-Monday:
12pm-2.30pm (2pm in winter)
Closed for meals 25 December
Prices:
Meals: a la carte 18.00/26.00

Typical Dishes

Wok fried tiger prawns
Char grilled rib eye steak
Walnut meringue roulade

7.75mi South West of Maidstone by A26 and B2016. Follow sign to church and green. Parking.

Aston Tirrold

062 The Sweet Olive at The Chequers Inn

Baker St, Aston Tirrold OX11 9DD

Tel.: (01235) 851 272
Website: www.sweet-olive.com

VISA **AE** **MC**

Hooky Bitter, Deuchars IPA

You can't get much more English than the ancient Ridgeway path or the rolling Chiltern Hills, both of which lie close to this solid, red-brick Victorian hostelry. French, though, is the prevailing culture here, with frequent cries of "Bonjour" and "Bon Apetit" renting the refined Oxfordshire air. That's because Stephane and Olivier, the owners, have brought their Gallic influence to bear and The Sweet Olive is reaping rich dividends. There's a drinkers' side to the pub, repaired to frequently by the locals, and a cosy, red tile floored dining room: you can lift knife and fork in either. Blackboard menus evolve constantly, and daily specials are verbally explained. French country cooking takes precedence, but classic British dishes are also available. Local produce is used in season, and cordial service is a byword. Incidentally, the French connection extends to décor, which includes wine box ends from renowned chateaux and growers.

Food serving times:
Monday-Tuesday and
Thursday-Saturday:
    12pm-2pm, 7pm-9pm
Sunday: 12pm-2pm
Closed February
Prices:
Meals: a la carte 10.00/25.00

4mi South West of Wallingford by minor road through South Moreton. Parking.

Typical Dishes

Tiger prawns in tempura

Escalope of venison, Port wine sauce

Treacle sponge

Barnard Gate

063 The Boot Inn

Barnard Gate OX29 6XE

Tel.: (01865) 881231 - Fax: (01865) 880762
e-mail: info@theboot-inn.com - Website: www.theboot-inn.com

Hook Norton Best Bitter, Brakspear Best Bitter, Wadsworth 6X, Fuller's London Pride

The Cotswold stone walls of this eclectic pub are covered with the footwear of the famous from Stanley Matthews to the Bee Gees, though it's not clear what drinks, if any, they ordered at the bar and whether a pint was paid for with a pair of old trainers. However, elsewhere at the Boot, tradition plays a stronger role: snug corners, welcoming fire, beams and flagstones. Tables are rustic to the core, and chairs clatter on bare boards. Eating at lunchtime can be a simple affair - thick cut sandwiches or a plate of gammon and chips - but things get a little more elaborate in the evenings, with a mixture of traditional and more inventive dishes to be enjoyed in the candlelight. Friendly, approachable service comes naturally here.

Food serving times:
Monday-Thursday:
  12pm-2.30pm, 7pm-9.30pm
Friday-Saturday:
  12pm-2.30pm, 7pm-10pm
Sunday: 12pm-3pm,
          7pm-10pm
(booking essential)
Prices:
Meals: a la carte 20.00/35.00

Typical Dishes

Salmon rillette

Roasted duck breast with lavender

White chocolate cheesecake

3.25mi East of Witney by B4022 off A40. Parking.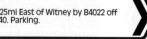

Bledington

064 The Kings Head Inn

The Green, Bledington OX7 6XQ

Tel.: (01608) 658365 - Fax: (01608) 658902
e-mail: kingshead@orr-ewing.com - Website: www.kingsheadinn.net

  room **VISA** **MC**

> *Hook Norton, 6X, Southern Bitter, Donnington's BB, Jouster,*
> *Golden Delicious, Cottage Whippet, Henry's - changing weekly*

A charming Cotswold setting and a warmly welcoming pub: what could be more idyllic on a perfect summer's day? The Kings Head traces its origins back to the 15C, and in all that time it can rarely have looked more inviting: it certainly entices the Morris dancers who happily congregate each summer on the green outside to perform the Bledington Dances. The place oozes style, with stone and wood floors, real fires and an archetypal modern country pub feel. Printed evening menus identify a solid traditional base, with good use of local produce: meat is bought from a renowned Cotswold butcher, fresh Cornish fish arrives daily, and vegetables are from nearby Evesham Vale. Bedrooms hold the promise of comfy country repose: a low-beamed stairway leads the way.

Food serving times:
Monday-Sunday:
  12pm-2pm, 7pm-9pm
  (9.30pm Friday & Saturday
  in summer)
Closed 25-26 December
Prices:
Meals: a la carte 23.25/30.00
12 rooms : 55.60/125.00

Typical Dishes

Devilled Lamb's kidneys

Smoked haddock and prawn pie

Banana pannacotta

4mi Southeast of Stow-on-the-Wold by A436 on B4450. Parking.

Buckland

065 The Lamb Inn

Lamb Lane, Buckland SN7 8QN

Tel.: (01367) 870484 - Fax: (01367) 870675
e-mail: enquiries@thelambatbuckland.co.uk - Website: www.thelambatbuckland.co.uk

 Hooky Bitter

This charming 18C pub luxuriates in a quiet village of Cotswold stone. Family owned for a number of years, it boasts a well-established local reputation and an extremely comfy atmosphere prevails, suitably enhanced by soft lighting, real log fire, and sheep motifs which show up in paintings, curios and even the capet. Choose to eat in a characterful beamed room or more formal linen clad dining area. Either way, the same blackboard menus are served; these consist of accomplished, traditional dishes, typified by locally smoked prawns and salad, loin of pork with wild mushrooms, and raspberry brulée with raspberry sorbet.

Food serving times:
Tuesday-Friday:
    12pm-2pm, 6.30pm-9.30pm
Saturday: 12pm-2pm,
                6.30pm-10pm
Sunday: 12pm-3pm
Closed 25 December - 8 January
Prices:
Meals: 15.00 (set price lunch and dinner) and a la carte 20.00/35.00
1 room : 50.00/95.00

Typical Dishes

Three cheese and red onion tart

Roast rack of English lamb, mint and sorrel

Junket

Between Faringdon and Kingston Bagpuize off A420. Parking.

Burford

066 **The Lamb Inn** 🛏

Sheep St, Burford OX18 4LR
Tel.: (01993) 823155 - Fax: (01993) 822228
e-mail: info@lambinnburford.co.uk - Website: www.cotswold-inns-hotel.co.uk/lamb

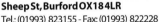

Brakspear, Hook Norton,

Weathered local stone announces this strikingly relaxed part 14C inn, set prominently in a picture-postcard market town. The interior is as quietly charming as you would expect: flagstone floors and open log fires in three antique furnished lounges. Go through a separate entrance to a cosy bar where a good selection of real ales is enjoyed by the regulars. A classically formal restaurant reflects the age of the inn: appealing menus mix traditional and modern dishes which range from roast best end of lamb with sweetbreads and bubble and squeak, to smoked cod with cauliflower cheese and mustard potatoes. Bedrooms underwent a refurbishment early in 2004: now you can tumble blissfully into beds clothed in fine Egyptian linen and quality fabrics.

Food serving times:
Monday-Sunday:
   12pm-2.30pm, 7pm-9.30pm
Prices:
Meals: 32.50 (set price dinner) and a la carte 21.90/32.95
🛏 **15 rooms :** 115.00/235.00

Typical Dishes

Grilled mackerel

Braised shoulder of lamb, parsnip purée

Frozen apple roulade

In town centre. Parking on the street or care of the Bay Tree Hotel.

Charlbury

067 **Bull Inn**

Sheep St, Charlbury OX7 3RR
Tel.: (01608) 810689
e-mail: info@bullinn-charlbury.com - Website: www.bullinn-charlbury.com

  VISA

Hook Norton, Brakspear and 1 changing guest ale

This charming hostelry has been delighting the locals of Charlbury since the 16C, and in 500 years it hasn't compromised one jot on its traditional appeal. Creeper-clad in summer, it's the quintessential country pub right down to its flagstone floors and inglenook fires. You can whet your appetite before visiting with a stroll along the banks of the River Evenlode, just five minutes' walk away. The rustic bar is divided into three booths with wicker and pine chairs; the restaurant continues the rural theme with more hardy stone floors and rugged pine tables. Concise, fresh menus have earned the Bull a fine local reputation for its cooking: you might find braised lamb shank with a mint and redcurrant gravy; smoked haddock Florentine; or chicken, smoked ham and leek casserole.

Food serving times:
Tuesday-Saturday:
    12pm-2pm, 7pm-9.30pm
Sunday: 12pm-2pm
Monday: 7pm-9pm
Closed 25 December.
Closed Mondays in winter.
Prices:
Meals: 18.75 (set price Sunday lunch) and a la carte 17.00/ 26.00
4 rooms : 65.00/85.00

Typical Dishes

Curried parsnip and apple soup

Minted lamb shank, redcurrant gravy

Sticky toffee pudding

Charlbury is 7mi North of Witney by B4022. Parking.

Chipping Norton

068 The Masons Arms

Banbury Rd, Swerford, Chipping Norton OX7 4AP

Tel.: (01608) 683212 - Fax: (01608) 683105
e-mail: themasonschef@hotmail.com - Website: www.masonsarms.co.nr

 Hook Norton Best, Brakspear Special

A roadside Cotswold inn, raised above the norm by the keenness of a husband and wife team, whose hospitable approach seems to have spread to the rest of the helpful young staff. Dating back to the 1800s, its origins are rather mysterious – quite appropriate for a former Freemason's lodge – but apart from a nod to its Masonic past near the entrance, the interior resonates with bright, 21C country style: more rattan chairs and polished floors than horse brasses and swirly carpets. In contrast, the owner is a great advocate of culinary tradition. For the most part, only local produce makes it into the kitchen, and many methods and recipes described on the blackboard owe as much to the Victorian cookbook as to contemporary cuisine. Robust, flavourful food might include braised oxtail or sea bass in gazpacho sauce. Lovely views from the garden.

Food serving times:
Monday-Sunday:
12pm-2.15pm, 7pm-9.15pm
Closed 25-26 December
Prices:
Meals: 10.95 (Monday-Thursday) and a la carte 18.00/27.00

Typical Dishes

Pan fried Scottish scallops

Chargrilled venison steak

Vanilla pannacotta

4mi North East of Chipping Norton by A361. Parking.

Christmas Common

069 The Fox and Hounds

Christmas Common OX49 5HL

Tel.: (01491) 612599
e-mail: kiran.daniels@btconnect.com

 Brakspear Ordinary, Brakspear Special, Seasonal Ale

Ideally set for walkers, with the Chilterns and the Ridgeway Path to hand, the pub's been here in the hills, in what's now rare red kite territory, since the 15C; recent years have seen a bit of updating, including the new restaurant, which has metamorphosed from the old barn. The pub proper retains its tiled and beamed interior, with minimal contemporary styling: the gentle crackle in the inglenook on all but the hottest days, a delightful, laid-back atmosphere and plenty of quirky appeal. The menu is concise and features fresh and strictly seasonal ingredients. Local suppliers stock the kitchen; eggs come from 'the man up the road'. The blend of contemporary and classic dishes rests on solid French roots and produces original combinations with individual flair.

Food serving times:
Monday-Saturday:
12pm-2.30pm, 7pm-9.30pm
Prices:
Meals: a la carte 23.00/31.00

South East of Watlington, near Shotridge Wood. Parking.

Typical Dishes

Spiced aubergine casserole

Confit belly pork, Asian broth

Warm apricot and almond tart

Church Enstone

070 The Crown Inn

Mill Lane, Church Enstone OX7 4NN

Tel.: (01608) 677262 - Fax: (01608) 677394
Website: www.crowninnenstone.co.uk

  VISA

 Hook Norton Best Bitter, Hobgoblin (Wychwood Brewery)

Close to the gurgling River Glyme, this 17C pub of Cotswold stone is one of the highlights of a charming little village. It's a well-kept establishment, personally run by a husband and wife team: she keeps things ticking over in the main bar while he does the cooking. Refurbishment has added a modish seagrass carpet across the floor, but other features have stayed reassuringly traditional: a cottagey bar, log fire in stone fireplace, beams and exposed stone. You can eat in two areas: a bright dining room with red hued walls and uncovered pine tables, or a conservatory extension. The lunchtime blackboard menu gives way to a more expansive repertoire in the evening, while charming, attentive service adds an extra dimension to the invariably pleasant atmosphere.

Food serving times:
Monday: 7pm-9pm
Tuesday-Saturday:
12pm-2pm, 7pm-9pm
Sunday: 12pm-2pm
Closed 25-26 December
and 1 January
Prices:
Meals: a la carte 18.00/25.00

Typical Dishes

Lightly battered squid with aïoli

Crisp roast duck leg, cider dressing

Chocolate pudding

3.5mi Southeast of Chipping Norton by A44. Parking.

Churchill

071 The Chequers

Church Rd, Churchill OX7 6NJ
Tel.: (01608) 659393

 Flowers, Marston's Pedigree, Hook Norton, Adnams, Old Speckled Hen, Edgar's, Hobgoblin

Set on the main road of a delightful Cotswold village, this charming hostelry is idyllically placed opposite All Saints Church. It's been creating quite a buzz since it opened its doors in the spring of 2004, after nine months of refurbishment, having lain idle for five years. An 18C inn lurks in there somewhere; the owners have added in a sympathetic and careful way using honey coloured Cotswold stone. The bustling atmosphere is testament to good local opinion. You can dine in two areas: downstairs – a combination of beams, high arched ceiling and exposed stone; or upstairs, where a cosy lounge is ideal for pre- or post-prandial drinks. Well-balanced menus might include pan fried swordfish with olive beurre blanc, or tenderloin of pork with grilled black pudding.

Food serving times:
Monday-Sunday:
12pm-2pm, 7pm-9.30pm
Closed 25 December for meals
Prices:
Meals: a la carte 18.50/20.00

South West of Chipping Norton by B4450. Parking.

Typical Dishes

Black pudding and bacon salad

Tenderloin of pork, red wine sauce

Sticky toffee pudding

Crays Pond

072 The White Lion

Goring Rd, Goring Heath, Crays Pond RG8 7SH

Tel.: (01491) 680471 - Fax: (01491) 681654
e-mail: reservations@whitelioncrayspond.com - Website: www.whitelioncrayspond.com

Greene King IPA, Abbot

A stylish mix of old and new has earned this village pub outside Goring a strong local reputation. Part built in 1756, its wooden window shutters and paved terrace give it a modern veneer, but old beams and low ceilings have been retained from a refurbishment in 2003, which now sees smart oak floors combined with burgundy and sage green walls. These are adorned by framed menus from Gordon Ramsay, Le Manoir and the like, some of which were obtained from patrons' visits, others from auction. Soft wall lighting enhances a couple of roaring log fires. Eclectic dishes and good British staples dominate menus which offer a robust, hearty choice and plentiful portions. Everything is cooked freshly to order, from the homemade chips to puddings. This is a busy, popular destination: it could be worth booking at weekends.

Food serving times:
Tuesday-Saturday:
12pm-2.30pm,
6.15pm-9.30pm
Sunday: 12pm-2.30pm
Closed 25 December
Prices:
Meals: a la carte 20.00/30.00

2mi East of Goring on B4526. Parking.

Typical Dishes

Warm smoked salmon salad

Confit pork belly, Boston beans

Sticky date pudding

Cuddesdon

073 The Bat & Ball Inn 🛏

28 High St, Cuddesdon OX44 9HJ

Tel.: (01865) 874379 - Fax: (01865) 873363

e-mail: bb@traditionalvillageinns.co.uk - Website: www.traditionalvillageinns.co.uk

🔭 🍷 ✎room *VISA* Ⓜ️Ⓒ

House LBW, Marston Pedigree and 1 guest ale - Adnams, Broadside etc

Cricket lovers will be in their element here, with enough conversation pieces to see them through lunch – and the tea interval. Scorebooks, trophies and old cigarette cards are proudly displayed and batting gloves hang above the window in the flag-floored bar, while the very rafters of the new dining room are braced with ancient stumps and well knocked-in bats: some, with a blackboard slab set into the willow, list the chef's daily specials. British cooking, hearty and plentiful, runs from venison in red wine to cod and chips, by way of salads and lunchtime baguettes or panini, all served at big pine tables by a young team who are casual, friendly and far too modest to mention Australia's defence of The Ashes. For the full Test Match Special experience, they also serve decent slabs of chocolate cake.

Food serving times:
Monday-Sunday:
12pm-2.45pm,
6.30pm-9.45pm

Prices:
Meals: a la carte 18.00/32.00
🛏 **7 rooms :** 56.00/68.00

Typical Dishes

Sharing Camembert fondue

Saute chicken Perigourdine

Strawberry pavlova

6mi East of Oxford city centre. Parking. ➤➤

Faringdon

074 ## The Trout at Tadpole Bridge

Buckland Marsh, Faringdon SN7 8RF

Tel.: (01367) 870382

e-mail: info@troutinn.co.uk - Website: www.troutinn.co.uk

 room *VISA*

3 in winter, 4 in summer

This attractive old inn stands next to a pretty bridge by the Thames and is locally renowned by the anglers who gather along the riverbanks. You can watch them in action - or inaction - from the Trout's relaxing terrace: on the menus, the eponymous fish itself is caught by a local fisherman. The rustic interior has a number of charmingly refurbished rooms, boasting a mix of old pine and polished tables, assorted chairs, and newspapers and magazines lying invitingly to one side. It's most certainly a pub to stretch out in. Cooking is satisfying and reliable: game and meat come from local estates and farms, with some vegetables picked fresh from the back garden. Tasty, accomplished dishes, including seafood specials on the blackboard, are the result. Smart bedrooms may entice weary rod danglers.

Food serving times:
Monday-Saturday:
    12pm-2pm, 7pm-9pm
Sunday: 12pm-2pm
Closed 25-26 December, 31 December, 1 January and last week in January

Prices:
Meals: a la carte 18.95/31.95
6 rooms : 55.00/110.00

Typical Dishes

King scallops, celeriac purée

Roast loin of venison, pear chutney

Lemon posset

4.5mi Northeast of Faringdon by A417, A420 on Brampton road. Parking.

Great Tew

075 ## Falkland Arms

Great Tew OX7 4DB

Tel.: (01608) 683653 - Fax: (01608) 683656
e-mail: sjcourage@btconnect.com - Website: www.falklandarms.org.uk

VISA **AE** **MC**

> *Wadworth IPA, 6X, 1 seasonal guest ale, up to 4 guest ales and a real cider*

A picture-perfect village inn without a scrap of preciousness or pretension. Its 17C Cotswold stone is wreathed in ivy and climbing roses; in the cosy, flag-floored bar, orderly rows of crocks and mugs hang from the beams and polished pint-pot tankards glint in the lamplight. Chalked up on the board are six classic dishes, tasty and fortifying, plus potatoes and baguettes, but plenty of the locals are happy enough with the friendly welcome, a seat on the old settles and benches, a well-kept beer and a bit of old-English aromatherapy: tins of snuff and clay pipes are sold behind the bar. The spiral staircase leads up to six charming, period styled rooms in country patterns.

Food serving times:
Monday-Saturday:
12pm-2pm, 7pm-8pm
Sunday: 12pm-2pm
(booking essential)
Prices:
Meals: a la carte 17.00/27.00
5 rooms : 115.00

6.5mi East of Chipping Norton by A361 and B4022. Parking in village car park.

Typical Dishes

Grilled goat's cheese salad

Slow cooked shank of lamb

Blueberry crème brûlée

Hanwell

076 Moon and Sixpence

Main Str, Hanwell OX17 1HW

Tel.: (01295) 730544 - Fax: (01295) 730147
e-mail: moonand.sixpence@virgin.net - Website: www.moonandsixpencehanwell.com

  VISA

Hook Norton 'Hooky Bitter', Charles Wells Bombardier

Interesting times at Hanwell's old village inn, owned and run by two brothers who were determined to give the Moon and Sixpence more than just a quick spit and polish. Even after the most well-meaning makeovers, a new lease of community spirit is never guaranteed, but Hanwell has really taken to its new-look pub. An appealing and wide-ranging menu certainly helps, offering everything from dependable pub classics to more contemporary recipes, all soundly prepared and fairly priced; a barbecue at the back, with a little terrace next to it, gets plenty of use in the summer if the weather plays its part. The real-ale enthusiasts have no complaints either, and its modern bar is as popular as ever.

Food serving times:
Tuesday-Sunday:
12pm-2pm
Monday: 6pm-9pm
Prices:
Meals: 7.50 (set price lunch and dinner) and a la carte 20.00/35.00

Typical Dishes

Tempura battered prawns

Braised lamb shank

Tarte Tatin with Calvados sorbet

3.5mi northwest of Banbury by A422 and B4100. Parking.

Henley-on-Thames

077 The Three Tuns Foodhouse

5 Market Pl, Henley-on-Thames RG9 2AA

Tel.: (01491) 573260
e-mail: thefoodhouse@btconnect.com

VISA **M**

Brakspear Bitter

Henley isn't all about the river and the regatta. There's a smart, buzzing town beyond the bridge, and right in the heart of the market place is this little pub sandwiched between the shops. It's an early 16C hostelry with a traditional appearance: 'foodhouse' has been added to the frontage to denote its recent change of tack. There's a distinct gastro-pub style here. The front bar is quirkily fashionable, while the back has been transformed into a cosy, dining area with rough ceiling beams, a mix of oak tables and old school style chairs and an offbeat clutch of collectables and curios: many of the furnishings are supplied by a local antiques shop. Menu ingredients are also locally sourced. Much market-fresh produce goes into the interesting British and Mediterranean dishes.

Food serving times:
Monday-Saturday:
12pm-2.30pm, 7-10pm
Prices:
Meals: a la carte 25.00/45.00

Typical Dishes

English asparagus, poached
gull's egg

Dorset skate, crab broth

Rhubarb and vanilla
cheesecake

In the town centre. Public parking off Greys Rd and at the Railway Station.

Kidmore End

078 **The New Inn** 🛏

Chalkhouse Green Rd, Kidmore End RG4 9AU

Tel.: (0118) 972 3115
Website: www.thenewinnrestaurant@4cinns.co.uk

Brakspear Original, Bee Sting, Henry on Thames, Dirty Tackle

The hustle and bustle of Reading is only five miles away but you wouldn't realise it from the sleepy charms of this Oxfordshire hamlet and the comfy enticements of its focal point, The New Inn, which, though smartened up outside, still proudly bears its 16C hallmarks within. The cosy, atmospheric bar's rough floorboards, beams and open fires are all you'd expect from a proper pub of the era, and this is a fine spot to lay your hat and sup a pint. Most diners, meanwhile, head to the snazzy restaurant, where a few original beams merge tastefully with the smart wood tables and crisp white walls. Here, there's a nicely balanced menu ranging from pub favourites to more adventurous fare; you can also eat in the bar or delightful canopied terrace. A treat awaits overnighters: six bedrooms, some with balconies, which are stylish, modern, very comfy and well equipped.

Food serving times:
Monday-Saturday:
    12pm-2.30pm, 6pm-10pm
Sunday: 12pm-2.30pm
Prices:
Meals: a la carte 20.00/25.00
🛏 **6 rooms :** 65.00/110.00

Typical Dishes

Chicken liver parfait

Panache of fresh fish

Sticky toffee pudding with toffee sauce

4mi North of Reading by A4074 and minor road east. Parking.

Kingham

079 The Tollgate Inn

Church St, Kingham OX7 6YA

Tel.: (01608) 658389

e-mail: info@thetollgate.com - Website: www.thetollgate.com

  Hook Norton Ales

At the northwest corner of Oxfordshire stands this 17C Grade II listed former farmhouse built of local stone. It's situated in a typically attractive Cotswold village within striking distance of Stow and Moreton-in-Marsh, and has been sympathetically modernised with oak floors and bright colours. Plenty of original charm remains in place courtesy of rafters and wood-burning stove, and the well-populated front bar is a buzzing mix of locals and tourists. You can choose to eat here, or repair to a rear dining area, where smartly laid tables and comfortable high-back chairs lend it a slightly more formal air. Lunch here is a simple affair of sandwiches or compact blackboard menu. Dinner takes on a more serious tone, with restaurant style dishes encompassing a global range, underpinned by good Cotswold ingredients. Pleasantly appointed bedrooms await the weary tourist.

Food serving times:
Tuesday-Saturday:
  12pm-2.30pm, 7pm-9.30pm
Sunday: 12pm-2.30pm
Closed 25 December
Prices:
Meals: a la carte 17.00/30.00
9 rooms : 60.00/100.00

Typical Dishes

Pan fried tiger prawns

Gloucester Old Spot belly pork

Pear and almond frangipane

3mi South West of Chipping Norton by B4450 to Churchill and minor road West. Parking.

Leafield

080 **The Navy Oak**

Lower End, Leafield OX29 9QQ

Tel.: (01993) 878496
e-mail: thenavyoak@aol.com - Website: www.thenavyoak.co.uk

   VISA **MC**

 Hook Norton, Brakspear, Windrush Ales - Cotswold Lager

For five years this solid stone pub lay barren in its leafy environs on the eastern edge of the Cotswolds, awaiting the kiss of life. Along came Alastair and Sarah with big ideas, a warm and personal style, and refurbishment ideas that would kick-start the Navy Oak into a stylish new existence. A glowing fire, cosy seating and warm, modern colours tick all the right boxes on a chilly day when the wind blows in from the hills. There are two main dining areas exuding a fine rustic air. Though not close to the sea, this is a pub with the bracing smell of seafood in its nostrils: Alastair worked for Rick Stein, and the menu reflects his time there. Good value, appealing, daily changing menus are supplemented by a more formal, linen clad dining experience on Fridays and Saturdays.

Food serving times:
Tuesday-Saturday:
    12.30pm-2pm, 7pm-9pm
Closed first 2 weeks
in January

Prices:
Meals: a la carte 20.00/30.00

Typical Dishes
Goat's cheese crostini
Char grilled local fillet steak
Banana tart Tatin, banana ice cream

5.75 miles Northwest of Witney by B 4022 (Charlbury Rd). Parking.

Littleworth

081 The Snooty Fox Inn

Littleworth SN7 8PW
Tel.: (01367) 240549

 Young's Best, Marstons Pedigree

To the south: the Vale of White Horse. To the north: the Thames Path. Slap bang in the middle: this yellow-painted roadside pub with gardens and a welcoming, if somewhat minimalist, ambience for visitors to this pleasant part of Oxfordshire. The spacious interior fans out into a coterie of private dining areas supported by oak beams, with wooden flooring and polished tables. Further in you can choose a nice, comfy sofa to loll around in as you peruse the huge wine rack beside a modern bar. A blazing, brick-built fireplace adorns the main dining room, where an extensive menu takes a bit of investigating. In the end, you might decide on slow-roasted half-shoulder of lamb glazed with honey, or lamb kidneys turbigo; an interesting range of fish and pasta dishes waits temptingly in the wings.

Food serving times:
Monday-Sunday:
12pm-12.45pm, 6pm-9.45pm
Prices:
Meals: 10.00 (set price 2 courses Monday-Wednesday) and a la carte 18.00/27.00

3mi Northeast of Faringdon by A417 off A420. Parking.

Typical Dishes

Duck liver and Madeira pate

King prawn and scallop thermidor

Bread and butter pudding

Maidensgrove

082 The Five Horseshoes

Maidensgrove RG9 6EX

Tel.: (01491) 641282 - Fax: (01491) 641086
e-mail: admin@thefivehorseshoes.co.uk - Website: www.thefivehorseshoes.co.uk

Brakspears Ordinary, Special and seasonal

Halfway between the Ridgeway and the upper Thames, this pleasantly down-to-earth pub in 17C redbrick looks out over wooded hills. In summer, you'll want to make straight for the tables in the conservatory, but the same menu is served in the cosy main bar; its low, black-beamed ceiling is papered with old banknotes, some in currencies which haven't aged nearly as well. Tasty dishes might include smoked trout and salmon salad, or pork with Stilton, mango and ginger or scampi and chips: it's substantial cooking on a traditional base and there's always a good turnout for summer barbecues in the garden. The Oxfordshire Way skirts the village, and there are plenty of shorter rambles around the woods, but walkers should make sure they have somewhere to stow their muddy boots. Stonor Park, a part-Tudor manor house, is a few minutes' drive away.

Food serving times:
Monday-Friday:
12pm-2.30pm, 6.30pm-10pm
Saturday: 12pm-3pm,
6.30pm-10pm
Sunday: 12pm-4pm
Closed Sunday dinner
Prices:
Meals: a la carte 16.50/23.50

Near Stonor Park. North of Henley by A4130 on B480, then 0.75mi West. Parking.

Typical Dishes

Potted shrimps

Five Horseshoes pork pie, piccalilli and cheese

Treacle tart

Sibford Gower

083 The Wykham Arms

Temple Mill Road, Sibford Gower OX15 5RX

Tel.: (01295) 788808 - Fax: (01295) 788806
e-mail: info@wykhamarms.co.uk - Website: www.wykhamarms.co.uk

 VISA MC

Hook Norton Bitter, Wadworth 6X

The pub in this pretty village opened its characterful doors in May 2004 and became an instant hit with Oxfordshire locals and Cotswold tourists. This was a farmhouse 400 years ago. Since then, it's been added to but the thatched roof and hanging baskets mean it's still very pretty and charming. There's a bright interior, accentuated by wood flooring, original inglenook fireplace in the bar, low beamed ceiling and dining areas spread between the bar and other rooms adjacent to it. A separate spacious garden or the terrace is an ideal spot to pop a champagne cork on a summer's day. Dine on inventive modern fare; reworked contemporary British classics with local ingredients a top priority.

Food serving times:
Tuesday-Saturday:
　12pm-2.30pm, 7pm-9.45pm
Sunday:　　　　12pm-2.30pm
Closed 25 and 26 December
Prices:
Meals: 20.00 (Sunday lunch)
and a la carte 21.90/35.00

8mi West of Banbury by B4035. Parking.

Typical Dishes

Saute of black pudding

Line-caught Brixham sea bass

Brioche and butter pudding

South Leigh

084 Mason Arms

South Leigh OX29 6XN

Tel.: (01993) 702485

No real ales offered

Sensitive vegetarians and critics beware: this may not be the place for you! It's run in highly 'individualistic' style by the owner who keeps a tight reign on what he serves, and whom he serves it to! The pub itself is a charming 15C thatched inn with pleasant gardens in a tranquil village. Inside, much of the interior is given over to the restaurant: antiques are set on both solid wood and linen-clad tables. Three fascinating rooms have dark walls enhanced by paintings, and cigar boxes mingling with old wine bottles: fine vintages and cigars are evidently a personal passion, and appreciation of both is encouraged. Food is quite classically based, on both menu and blackboard specials, and ranges from cottage pie to caviar. If you're staying overnight, two clean, functional bedrooms await.

Food serving times:
Tuesday-Saturday:
12pm-3pm, 7pm-10pm
Sunday: 12pm-3pm
Closed 1 week at Christmas, 1 week in Spring, 3 weeks in August

Prices:
Meals: a la carte 20.00/50.00
2 rooms : 35.00/65.00

3mi Southeast of Witney by B4022. Parking.

Typical Dishes

Smoked salmon

Roast duck

Treacle tart

Sprigg's Alley

085 Sir Charles Napier

Sprigg's Alley OX39 4BX
Tel.: (01494) 483011 - Fax: (01494) 485311
e-mail: info@sircharlesnapier.co.uk - Website: www.sircharlesnapier.co.uk

Wadworth IPA and 6X from the wood

The big draw of this attractive flint-built pub-restaurant regularly turns the sleepy Oxfordshire hamlet of Sprigg's Alley into a vibrant, buzzy location. Very much a dining destination, it nevertheless retains a pubby feel with beer from the wood and roaring fires in the low-beamed bar. Individuality is writ large, particularly the elegant restaurant – where most people head – which has commissioned marble sculptures, antique silver and smart linen napkins. It opens onto pleasant gardens, a further attraction for diners once summer's here. Interesting menus showcase game and local produce in a seasonal menu that's prepared with care to a most agreeable standard. Service is never less than engaging, which is one reason why those visitors keep coming back.

Food serving times:
Tuesday-Saturday:
12pm-2.30pm, 6.30pm-10pm
Sunday: 12pm-3.30pm
Closed 25-26 December and 1 other day over Christmas

Prices:
Meals: 15.50/16.50 (2 course set price lunch/dinner weekdays only) and a la carte 30.00/38.75

Typical Dishes

Jerusalem artichoke soup

Rack of lamb, herb crust

Apple and sultana mille feuille

2.5mi Southeast of Chinnor by Bledlow Ridge rd. Parking.

Stadhampton

086 Crazy Bear

Bear Lane, Stadhampton OX44 7UR

Tel.: (01865) 890714 - Fax: (01865) 400481

e-mail: enquiries@crazybeargroup.co.uk - Website: www.crazybeargroup.co.uk

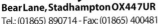

Ruddles County, Timothy Taylor Landlord, Old Speckled Hen

A traditional and rather understated pub appearance belies what's going on here. The Crazy Bear has a modern English restaurant upstairs, a Thai restaurant in the basement, a bar with a stuffed "crazy bear" where you can order cocktails, oysters and frozen vodkas (preferably not at the same time) on the ground floor, and bedrooms with zebra striped carpets and walls of peacock blue and purple, not to mention Philippe Starck inspired bathrooms. Of main interest for foodies is the Thai half of the eating equation: prawn in filo pastry with dipping sauce; duck with tamarind crust and Asian greens; and coconut parfait to round things off – good quality, accomplished and tasty dishes.

Food serving times:
Monday-Sunday:
12pm-3pm, 6pm-10pm

Prices:
Meals: 15.50 and a la carte 22.00/32.00

17 rooms : 80.00/325.00

Typical Dishes

Confit of duck leg terrine

Herb crusted rump of lamb

Salted butter caramel, chocolate sorbet

8mi South of Oxford by B480; off Wallingford rd. Parking.

Stoke Row

087 The Cherry Tree Inn 🛏

Stoke Row RG9 5QA

Tel.: (01491) 680430

e-mail: info@thecherrytreeinn.com - Website: www.thecherrytreeinn.com

    VISA

Brakspears Bitter and Special, and Brakspear Organic Bitter

A good dose of personality and enthusiasm from the owners has certainly helped in the renovation of this 17C inn, which has lost none of its relaxing, rural pub character in the process. Lovely polished wooden tables, low-beamed ceilings, scrubbed floors and fires lend an even charm to three main dining areas and two smaller non-smoking ones: there's also a pleasant garden terrace, its wooden benches shaded by broad standing parasols. An appealing blackboard selection of modern dishes changes by the day, typified by variety, good cooking and generous portions. Over in a nearby outbuilding, spacious but very cosy bedrooms, complete with smart fittings and excellent ensuite bathrooms, make this a good choice for an overnight stop.

Food serving times:
Monday-Sunday:
  12pm-3pm, 7pm-10.30pm
Closed 25-26 December
and 1 January
Prices:
Meals: a la carte 20.00/25.00
🛏 **4 rooms :** 65.00/85.00

Typical Dishes

Crab tartlet, vinaigrette

Roast belly of pork, cider jus

Steamed syrup & lemon sponge pudding

Between Henley on Thames and Goring off B481. Parking.

Toot Baldon

088 The Mole Inn

Toot Baldon OX44 9NG

Tel.: (01865) 340001 - Fax: (01865) 343011
e-mail: info@themoleinn.com - Website: www.themoleinn.com

VISA · AE · MC

Hook Norton, Spitfire, Fuller's London Pride

The sleepy hamlet of Toot Baldon, just outside Oxford, has had a serious wake-up call with the renaissance of this attractive old stalwart as a real top-notch dining pub heavyweight. Huge amounts have been invested in The Mole's stylish refurbishment and it shows. Impressive features include stone tiled flooring, beams galore, cosy lounge area with leather sofas leading into a series of four dining areas, roaring log fires, pine and oak tables, crisp napkins and fine glassware: it's no less than immaculate. Though virtually everything is angled towards eating, drinkers are nevertheless welcomed. Interesting, well-priced cuisine - running from rustic, earthy pub classics to more modern, globally influenced dishes – is prepared with assurance and care. Add light and personable service and the whole experience is positively charming.

Food serving times:
Monday-Saturday:
    12pm-2.30pm, 7pm-9.30pm
Sunday: 12pm-4pm,
                    6pm-9pm

Closed 25 December
and 1 January
Prices:
Meals: a la carte 20.00/30.00

6mi Southeast of Oxford; between B480 and A4074. Parking. ❯❯

Typical Dishes

Terrine of chicken, foie gras & ham hock

Scallops, crab cake and lobster cream

Chocolate mousse, walnut ice

Wantage

089 The Boar's Head

Church St, Ardington Wantage OX12 8QA

Tel.: (01235) 833254 - Fax: (01235) 833254

e-mail: info@boarsheadardington.co.uk - Website: www.boarsheadardington.co.uk

   room **VISA**

Butts Barbus Barbus, West Berkshire Brewery, Dr Hexter's Wedding Ale, Cotswold Premium

Stunning scenery, in the stirring shape of the Vale of White Horse and Lambourn Downs, is tantalisingly close to this pretty little pub in Ardington, an attractive downland village that's just outside Wantage. From the look of the interior, there's nowhere it would rather be: hunting curios and country magazines appear at every turn, pints of Berkshire ale sit on rough pine tables and a good mix of locals at the bar and chattering diners creates a warm, relaxed atmosphere. The menus come from a modern British direction, featuring some well-balanced combinations like entrecôte of Angus beef with corned beef hash, or stuffed fillet of sea bass with scallop mousse. One further recommendation remains: the bedrooms, which are particularly strong for a pub, in bright, breezy colours and no little style.

Food serving times:
Monday-Sunday:
    12pm-2pm, 7pm-9.30pm
Prices:
Meals: 14.50 (set price lunch) and a la carte 20.00/35.00
▭ **3 rooms :** 75.00/130.00

Typical Dishes

Seared scallops with crackling

Breast of duck, apple galette

Grand Marnier souffle, chocolate cream

2.25mi East of Wantage by A417. Next to the church. Parking.

Wootton

090 Kings Head 🛏

Chapel Hill, Wootton OX20 1DX

Tel.: (01993) 811340
e-mail: t.fay@kings-head.co.uk - Website: www.kings-head.co.uk

  VISA

Hooky Bitter, Old Hooky

Located in a pretty village just outside handsome Woodstock, this attractive 17C Cotswold stone house has a fair degree of charm. Whilst originally an inn, it cottoned on to the possibilities of pub dining in the 1980s and 90s, earning itself a headstart in the gastropub stakes. There's a delightful bar area at the front with roaring fire, where you can eat from a blackboard menu, which might include oriental dishes and fish specials. Cooking is tasty, wholesome and well executed with a smattering of the ambitious. To the rear is a rather stark but still comfortable restaurant with quality napkins. As in the bar, the cooking is impressive, and includes homemade breads and ice creams. The overall feeling of quality and freshness continues to the bedrooms, which are simple but spotless.

Food serving times:
Tuesday-Saturday:
12pm-2pm, 7pm-8.45pm
Sunday: 12pm-2pm
Closed 25-26 December and Monday except Bank Holiday Monday
Prices:
Meals: a la carte 18.00/28.00
🛏 **3 rooms :** 60.00/110.00

Typical Dishes

Home-cured salmon

Pork fillet, red onion marmalade and juniper sauce

Ginger pudding, vanilla ice cream

2.5mi North of Woodstock by A44. Parking; also on Chapel Hill.

Wytham

091 The White Hart

Wytham OX2 8QA
Tel.: (01865) 244372 - Fax: (01865) 248595
e-mail: whitehartwytham@aol.com

 VISA MC

 Hook Norton, Timothy Taylor's Landlord

Offering a perfect change of pace from Oxford, the White Hart is the pretty 18C village pub we would all love to have nearby: a relaxing atmosphere and an archetypal interior, right down to the fire in the hearth and the flagstone floor. Ask for a table in the front dining room, or a place on the attractive courtyard terrace warmed by heaters and tall clay ovens when the evening chill sets in. A laid-back but efficient young team provides attentive service of a carefully prepared menu, offsetting restyled classics with more inventive Modern British cooking: you might find a mustard-dressed salad of Stilton, bacon and black pudding, bream with tabbouleh and rocket pesto or fishcakes and mango salsa among the choices. Filled foccacias are a lighter lunchtime option.

Food serving times:
Monday-Friday:
12pm-3pm, 6.30pm-10pm
Saturday-Sunday:
12pm-4.30pm, 6.30pm-10pm
Closed dinner 25 December
Prices:
Meals: a la carte 18.00/30.00

Typical Dishes

Antipasti

Fillet steak and Dauphinoise potato, mustard veloute

Raspberry pannacotta

3.25mil North West of Oxford by A420 off A34 (northbound). Parking.

Abinger Common

092 The Stephan Langton Inn

Friday Street, Abinger Common RH5 6JR

Tel.: (01306) 730775

 Fuller's London Pride, Adnams, Hogs Back TEA

This bustling local favourite, set in a delightful woodland setting, owes its name to a 13C Archbishop of Canterbury and its popularity to a heartily satisfying style of country cooking; it's rightly regarded as one of the best eating destinations in the region. Regulars and walkers to picturesque local landmarks Leith Hill and Box Hill gather at the Langton, despite – or because of – its isolation and position at the end of a particularly elongated Surrey lane. Choose between two areas: a wood fitted pub that's capacious, rustic, and of admirable vintage; or a dining room where modern art peers down on equally creative gastronomic delights. Book in advance for the restaurant or get there early to sample and enjoy the fine cooking on daily changing menus at moderate prices. Good, efficient service from enthusiastic young staff is guaranteed.

Food serving times:
Tuesday-Saturday:
    12.30pm-3pm, 7pm-10pm
Sunday: 12.30pm-3pm
Prices:
Meals: a la carte 19.00/26.50

Typical Dishes

Chicken liver, pigeon & bacon terrine

Rump of lamb, boulangère potatoes

Buttermilk pudding, rhubarb

4.5mi Southwest of Dorking by A25. Parking.

Chiddingfold

093 ## The Swan Inn

Petworth Rd, Chiddingfold GU8 4TY

Tel.: (01428) 682073 - Fax: (01428) 683259
e-mail: enquiries@theswaninn.biz - Website: www.theswaninn.biz

 ⚞rest **VISA** **AE** **MC**

Fuller's London Pride, Hogback TEA, Bass

The handsomely mature exterior of this 14C Surrey redbrick village pub belies the extensive and stylish refurbishment which took place here in 2004. Despite the modern makeover, there remains a determinedly rustic atmosphere in most of the dining areas, with their bare wood tables. However, a formal dining room is available with white linen and elegant porcelain, while expansive terraced gardens beckon the summer visitor - dishes remain constant to all eating areas. Chic, understatedly-stylish bedrooms with air-conditioning and marble bathrooms await those staying overnight; their high-tech features, including plasma televisions, DVD players and broadband internet access will appeal to gadget-lovers.

Food serving times:
Monday-Sunday:
12pm-2.30pm, 6.30pm-10pm
Prices:
Meals: a la carte 18.00/28.00
🛏 **11 rooms :** 65.00/120.00
☕ 5.00

Typical Dishes

Seared scallop and asparagus salad

Calves liver and bacon

Cappuccino chocolate mousse

On the right hand side of the A283, approaching from the South. Parking opposite.

Mickleham

094 The King William IV

Byttom Hill, Mickleham RH5 6EL

Tel.: (01372) 372590

 🛖 🐾 **VISA** **MC**

Badger First Gold, Adnams, Hogsback TEA and 1 monthly changing guest ale

Overhung with trailing creepers, this very traditional, part-tiled pub stands a little way above the hamlet itself, its pretty terrace commanding views of the gentle hills. Where the workers from Lord Beaverbrook's estate once propped up the little taproom bar, you're now more likely to find weekend walkers and locals from round about, drawn by the promise of wholesome, dependable English cooking. Look for the list of modern seafood dishes up on a large blackboard. Personally run by a good-natured team, this is just the kind of unfussy place that would have got the approval of the bluff Sailor King, or his contemporary, the cleric and wit Sidney Smith, nicknamed "The Bishop of Mickleham" for his many visits of the village.

Food serving times:
Monday-Saturday:
12pm-2pm, 7pm-9.30pm
Sunday: 12pm-5pm
Closed 25 and 31 December
Prices:
Meals: a la carte 18.00/25.00

0.5mi North of Mickleham by A24. Difficult off-road parking nearby - allow time and patience! Public car park at the bottom of the hill.

Typical Dishes

Baked mushroom, ricotta and spinach

Calves liver with smoked bacon

Pecan and syrup tart

Ockley

095 Bryce's

The Old School House, Stane St, Ockley RH5 5TH

Tel.: (01306) 627430 - Fax: (01306) 628274
e-mail: bryces.fish@virgin.net - Website: www.bryces.co.uk

 VISA

 Fuller's London Pride, Hepworths, Sussex

Just a short walk from the lovely green stands the former village school, now a traditional, personally run pub with a sound reputation in this quietly well-to-do part of Surrey. The spacious if low-beamed bar is the place to go for fresh fish and chips, langoustines and lighter meals, though for something closer to restaurant dining, the more formal room to one side is the better bet. Besides a few meat dishes, it concentrates on fresh seafood, introducing some more adventurous choices on the specials board, like red mullet with spinach and pesto or a puff pastry galette of devilled crab, without dispensing with the classics: there would be an outcry if they tried, albeit a very polite one. As it is, a rather reserved regular clientele soon warm to the friendly and attentive service from a smartly dressed team.

Food serving times:
Monday-Sunday:
  12pm-2.30pm, 7pm-9.30pm
Closed 25-26 December,
1 January
- Seafood -
Prices:
Meals: 29.00 and a la carte
19.15/25.15

On A29. Parking.

Typical Dishes

Scallops and spinach,
Hollandaise

Black bream, crab and
coriander risotto

Orange and ginger pudding

West End

096 The Inn @ West End

42 Guildford Road, West End GU24 9PW

Tel.: (01276) 858652

e-mail: greatfood@the-inn.co.uk - Website: www.the-inn.co.uk

♓ *VISA* A≣

Fuller's London Pride, Courage Best

A busy roadside pub where the personable owners really lead from the front, energetically organising everything from themed suppers and wine tastings to just-for-fun boules tournaments in the pleasant garden out back. Even on an ordinary day you're likely to find the place busy, with a few knots of chatting regulars in the neatly overhauled modern bar and most of the diners in the conservatory or the dining room to the left; it's smarter than you might expect from the easy, informal tone of the place. A carefully prepared Modern British à la carte menu and their two or three-course lunch menus stand out as particularly good value: it's worth double-checking first, all the same.

Food serving times:
Monday-Sunday:
   12pm-2.30pm, 6pm-9.30pm
Prices:
Meals: 9.75/15.00 (2 course meal) and a la carte 19.90/32.15

Typical Dishes

Parsnip fritters, blue cheese dip

Rump of lamb, Dauphinoise potato

Carrot and cinnamon sponge

2.5mi from M3 on A322. Parking.

Windlesham

097 The Brickmakers

Chertsey Rd, Windlesham GU20 6HT

Tel.: (01276) 472267

e-mail: thebrickmakers@4cinns.co.uk - Website: www.4cinns.co.uk

 🍷 *VISA* AE M©

> Courage Best Bitter, Fuller's London Pride and seasonal ales - Hogs Back TEA

The very picture of a trim, Home Counties pub, built in Southern brick – naturally – and hung with baskets of flowers in summer. A simply styled room at the front, dominated by its big bar island, leads into a formal but still relaxed restaurant and adjoining conservatory. Sound, well-prepared cuisine weighs modern and traditional approaches to British cuisine and seems to have struck the right balance for its affluent clientele. A polite young team approach the job in hand with cheery enthusiasm. A short drive away is Chobham Common, a rolling heathland nature reserve; sometimes bleak, but a rare piece of quiet wilderness so close to the capital.

Food serving times:
Monday-Saturday:
12pm-2.30pm, 6.30pm-10pm
Sunday: 12pm-3pm,
7pm-9pm

Prices:
Meals: 25.95 (set price lunch and dinner) and a la carte 25.00/35.00

Typical Dishes

Thai crab cakes

Pork fillet, crushed new potatoes

Sticky toffee pudding, vanilla ice cream

East 1mi on B386. Parking.

Ashurst

098 The Fountain Inn

Ashurst BN44 3AP

Tel.: (01403) 710219
Website: www.aourinns.co.uk

 Harvey's Sussex Best, Fuller's London Pride; also seasonal ales and weekly local guest ale

This whitewashed, tiled former farmhouse, dating from 1572, draws in locals like flies to a trap: Paul McCartney's even been in. It's not hard to see what attracts so many here, apart from the obvious charms of the South Downs. An alluring garden and decked area by a pond is instantly relaxing, a skittle alley at the front fosters a bit of healthy local competition and the scents of the pleasant kitchen garden carry gently on the breeze. It's no less charming inside: the low-ceilinged bar has beams galore and leads into a series of characterful rooms where fires and flagged floors set the tone. Flavourful traditional cooking.

Food serving times:
Monday-Saturday:
    11.30-2pm, 6pm-9.30pm
Sunday: 12pm-3pm
Limited hours 25-26 December
Prices:
Meals: a la carte 14.00/25.00

Typical Dishes

Soup of the day

Homemade beefburger with onion relish, fries and salad

Bread and butter pudding

3.5mi North of Steyning on B2135. Parking.

Burpham

099 **George and Dragon**

Main St, Burpham BN18 9RR

Tel.: (01903) 883131 - Fax: (01903) 883341

 VISA **MC**

Arundel Castle, Kings Red River, Young's Special

This splendid old pub of mellow stone is set in a South Downs valley with sweeping views across to Arundel Castle on the skyline. Not surprisingly, it's prime walking country, so be prepared to share a pint with someone wearing big muddy boots. There's a large area at the front for outside dining in the sunny months, but at other times you'll want to get inside to sample the beamed bar, scrubbed pine tables and frothing real ale. It's where the regulars like to eat: steaks, pies and the like are on offer. To the left more diners settle into the small but irresistibly formed restaurant, which features an inglenook, full linen on antique tables and appealing mix of polished wood chairs. Menus are balanced, interesting and contemporary, using local produce and prepared with care and no little skill.

Food serving times:
Monday-Saturday:
12pm-2pm, 6.30pm-9pm
Sunday: 12pm-2pm
Closed 25 December
Prices:
Meals: a la carte 22.00/29.00

Typical Dishes

Confit of duck, crispy pancetta

Lamb shank, red wine sauce

Chocolate and raspberry tart

3mi Northeast of Arundel by A27. Parking.

Charlton

100 **The Fox Goes Free** 🛏

Charlton PO18 0HU
Tel.: (01243) 811461 - Fax: (01243) 811926
e-mail: thefoxgoesfree.always@virgin.net - Website: www.thefoxgoesfree.com

  VISA **MC**

Arundel Gauntlet, Arundel Mild, Ballards Best, Ringwood Forty-Niner

Arriving through the pretty village or off the hills, you can't miss this charming brick and flint pub, which is well-loved by its locals and gives them plenty back in return. Music nights, pub quizzes and themed dinners make it more than just a village meeting-place; fresh and hearty pub cooking, from sandwiches and bar favourites up to full meals, mixes contemporary and traditional ideas, and service is very warm and helpful. The dining room, cosy snug, big main bar and garden room have been carefully modernised but are still rich in originality and down-to-earth character, while the picnic tables, out in the sun or under the boughs of the trees, look far out over the start of the South Downs. Well-kept ensuite bedrooms, two reached from behind the bar, are well above pub average.

Food serving times:
Moday-Friday:
 12pm-2.30pm, 6.30pm-10pm
Saturday-Sunday:
                12pm-10pm
Closed 25 December
Prices:
Meals: a la carte 18.00/27.50
🛏 **5 rooms :** 55.00/100.00

6,75 mi North of Chichester by A286. Parking.

Typical Dishes

Baked goat's cheese, red pepper

Scallops with fresh herb risotto

Blueberry cheesecake

East Lavant

101 The Royal Oak Inn

Pook Lane, East Lavant PO18 0AX
Tel.: (01243) 527434 - Fax: (01243) 775062
e-mail: ro@thesussexpub.co.uk - Website: www.thesussexpub.co.uk

VISA AE MC

Sussex, Badger, Arundel

This elegant but relaxed Georgian pub, within a turbo blast of Goodwood Motor Circuit and close to the Channel and the South Downs, adds up to more than the sum of its parts. It contains not just an exceptionally busy inn with rustic walls of red brick and rafters, but also a barn and cottage – all with tastefully decorated and well-equipped bedrooms – set cosily round a charming courtyard. The pub cuisine is well-renowned in the Chichester area. There's an interesting à la carte choice with south European influence, and the specials board features perennial country pub favourites alongside modern dishes.

Food serving times:
Monday-Sunday:
12pm-3pm, 6.30pm-9.30pm
Closed 25 December and 1 January
Prices:
Meals: a la carte 22.00/40.00
6 rooms : 60.00/130.00

Typical Dishes

Crab cakes, fresh guacamole

Monkfish and king scallops, coconut cream sauce

White Russian pannacotta

Off A286 after the hump-back bridge.
Parking opposite the inn.

Elsted

102 Three Horseshoes

Elsted GU29 0JY

Tel.: (01730) 825746

 VISA **M©**

 Ballards Best, Horsham Best

From Uppark House to the Iron Age trails around Beacon Hill, the high, open downlands of East Sussex can make for exhilarating walking, and there are few more satisfying feelings than the stroll down from the scarp path to this welcoming 16C former drovers' inn, where you can enjoy more far-reaching countryside views from the garden or clink well-earned pints by the warmth of the wood burners. A delightful beamed bar where the beers are racked up in casks fills up quickly at the weekend, when it's as well to get your reservation in early; locals and even one or two escaping Londoners enjoy modern dishes from the blackboard or tuck into homemade pies, puddings and other hearty British favourites. Cordial and kindly service.

Food serving times:
Monday-Sunday:
  12pm-2pm, 6.30pm-9pm
Prices:
Meals: a la carte 20.00/25.00

Typical Dishes

Avocado and bacon, Stilton and mushroom sauce

Braised lamb, apricot and apple chutney

Treacle tart

5mi Southwest of Midhurst by A272 on Elsted rd. Parking.

Halfway Bridge

103 The Halfway Bridge Inn 🛏

Halfway Bridge GU28 9BP

Tel.: (01798) 861281

e-mail: hwb@thesussexpub.co.uk - Website: www.thesussexpub.co.uk

☒room VISA AE ① ⑩⑥

🍺 *Betty Stoggs Bitter, Youngs Bitter, Arundel Gold Bitter*

An easy-going, eat-where-you-like policy makes it all the more tempting to drop in and grab a table, but you may not always find your favourite corner free. A bustling crowd know a good thing when they see one, and come in numbers for seasonal cooking at a competitive price: winter dishes, for instance, could include black pudding salad with bacon and mushrooms or duck confit with honey and thyme, but tasty fish and game also make the specials board. To the back of the 17C pub itself – cosy and rustic with its stripped pine floors and log fires – you'll find the old barn, a reminder of the days when this was a coaching halt. Now smartly converted and facing a courtyard garden, it's split into thoughtfully appointed rooms, with vaulted ceilings, a few pieces of antique pine furniture and particularly impressive bathrooms.

Food serving times:
Monday-Sunday:
12pm-2.30pm, 6.30pm-9.30pm

Closed 25 December

Prices:
Meals: a la carte 22.00/35.00
🛏 **6 rooms :** 65.00/140.00

Typical Dishes

King scallops wrapped in bacon

Cannon of lamb on trio of potatoes in red wine jus

Chocolate fondant

Halfway between Midhurst and Petworth on the A272. Parking. ➤➤

Lickfold

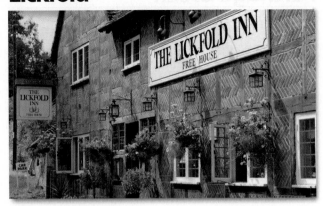

104 Lickfold Inn

Lickfold GU28 9EY

Tel.: (01798) 861285
e-mail: thelickfoldinn@aol.com - Website: www.thelickfoldinn.co.uk

    VISA ⓂⒸ

Hogsback Brewery TEA, Young's Best Bitter, Harvey's Sussex

Follow the narrow country road as it winds through the gentle Sussex countryside and eventually you'll catch a glimpse of the Lickfold Inn, a pretty, tile-hung pub dating back to the 1400s. The smart rear terrace, backing on to a mature garden, and the trimly kept bar, with its stone floor, open fires and scrubbed pine tables, are rather less formal than the dining room upstairs, but the same enjoyable modern cooking is available everywhere. Even on a weekday lunchtime you may find the place busy, but it doesn't dilute the informal charm and service is only a little stretched. Concise menu and specials board; ask about their popular summer barbecues.

Food serving times:
Tuesday-Saturday:
   12pm-2.30pm, 7pm-9.15pm
Sunday and Bank Holiday Monday:
   12pm-2.30pm
Closed 25-26 December
Prices:
Meals: a la carte 25.00/30.00

6mi Northwest of Petworth by A272. Parking.

Typical Dishes

Saffron cream moules
marinière,

Fillet of wild sea bass with
chilli herb crust

Lickfold Inn grand fromage

Partridge Green

105 The Green Man Inn

Church Rd, Jolesfield, Partridge Green RH13 8JT

Tel.: (01403) 710250 - Fax: (01403) 713212
e-mail: info@thegreenman.org - Website: www.thegreenman.org

 🍷 ✗ **VISA** **AE** **MC**

Harvey's Sussex Best

It's hard to imagine a more handsomely English-looking redbrick pub, but the winking earth-spirit on the pub sign should tip you off that there's a bit of a twist to this one. A stylish and polished interior is decorated with local prints and largely set for dining, though the busy atmosphere means there's still plenty of informal pub character to it. Locally sourced produce is at the hub of a mainly Modern British menu, but the surprise comes in the appealingly tasty selection of authentic Spanish tapas on offer alongside the lighter lunchtime bar classics. The whole place feels welcoming and well looked-after: charming service is the icing on the cake.

Food serving times:
Tuesday-Saturday and Bank Holiday Mondays:
    12pm-2.15pm, 7pm-9.30pm
Sunday: 12pm-2.15pm
Prices:
Meals: 14.95 (set price lunch) and a la carte 18.00/32.00

Typical Dishes

King scallops, cauliflower and red pepper purées

Confit of duck, sweet potato mash

Glazed lemon tart

Just out of the village on the B2135. Parking.

Petworth

106 Badgers

Coultershaw Bridge, Petworth GU28 0JF

Tel.: (01798) 342651

  VISA **MC**

 Badger's Best, Sussex Best

With its sash windows and River Rother location (it's just past the bridge), this smart white-painted former railway tavern is an ideal destination in pretty Petworth. Its eye-catching garden boasts weeping willows, and next door is the unique, Michelin Red Guide recommended Old Railway Station guesthouse. Badgers' interior is most pleasant: a beautiful oak-panelled bar has carvings with a 'badger and honey' theme, and lots of old photos depict its former Railway Inn-carnation. Jack Vettriano fans will find two of his sexy pictures, The Assessment and Game On, in a single-table alcove that gives a new twist to the word 'intimate'. Menus offer plenty of choice, a robust and wholesome mix of classic British dishes with global influences. There are fresh fish specials and homemade puddings too. South Downs ramblers staying on have the choice of three comfy, spacious rooms a cut above normal pub accommodation.

Food serving times:
Monday-Saturday:
12pm-2pm, 7pm-9pm
Sunday: 12pm-2pm, summer only 7pm-9-pm
Close 25 December and Bank Holidays
Prices:
Meals: a la carte 13.00/29.00
🛏 **3 rooms :** 80.00

2mi South of Petworth by A285 at Coultershaw Bridge. Parking.

Typical Dishes

Tiger tails in a Cajun spice

Lamb's kidneys with chillied Sherry and juniper

Four English cheeses

Stedham

107 Nava Thai at The Hamilton Arms

School Lane, Stedham GU29 0NZ

Tel.: (01730) 812555 - Fax: (01730) 817459
e-mail: hamiltonarms@hotmail.com - Website: www.thehamiltonarms.co.uk

 Ballard's Best, Fuller's London Pride, Horsham Best

Happily situated in the rolling South Downs, this whitewashed inn boasts an authentic Asian ambience barely a couple of miles from the attractive and quintessentially homespun appeals of Midhurst. The bar area at the front is brimming with Thai artefacts set around polished tables – during the week, this is where lunch is usually served. Adjacent: a homely, comfortable restaurant with a similar interior gets you in the mood for excellently prepared, tasty Thai dishes, monosodium glutamate and additive free. Enjoyment is enhanced by polite service from traditionally attired Thai waiters.

Food serving times:
Tuesday-Sunday:
12pm-2.30pm, 6pm-10.30pm
Bank Holiday Monday:
12pm-2.30pm
Closed 1 week January
- Thai -
Prices:
Meals: 19.50/21.50 (set price lunch/dinner) and a la carte 15.00/25.00

2mi West of Midhurst by A272. Parking.

Typical Dishes

Chicken satay

Chu Chgi Gung (curried prawns)

Thai egg custard

a. *Coteaux de Chiroubles vineyards (Beaujolais) ?*

b. *The vineyards around Les Riceys (Champagne) ?*

c. *Riquewihr and the surrounding vineyards (Alsace) ?*

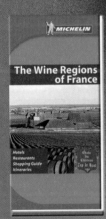

Can't decide ?

Then immerse yourself in the Michelin Green Guide !

- Everything to do and see
- The best driving tours
- Practical information
- Where to stay and eat
  The Michelin Green Guide:
  the spirit of discovery.

*A*s anyone west of the Avon will tell you, the historic West Country has been many countries in its time: the ancient land of Celtic saints and Arthurian legend, Drake's home port and the Old England of Hardy's Wessex are rediscovered every year by countless visitors, drawn by sun and surf and the West's astonishing variety. Where else can you find untamed moorland next to semi-tropical fantasy gardens? Which other region combines the magnificent Elizabethan Longleat House with the mysterious standing sarsens at Stonehenge, the genius of Brunel's grand designs and the exquisite style of Georgian Bath, not to mention the ultra-modern Eden Project? Add to this the seaside villages, sandy beaches and hundreds of miles of breathtaking clifftop trails and you have a glimpse of this amazing region, but for a real flavour of the place, get down to the dairy, the quay and the orchard. Come harvest time, Pippins, Dabinetts and Somerset Redstreaks are ripened for slow-matured dry ciders, "real" Cheddar and Blue Vinney cheeses are in every farmers' market and Brixham and Newlyn's fresh and cured seafood appear on the specials boards. But there's much more to West Country cooking than these three famous exports, as you'll soon discover…

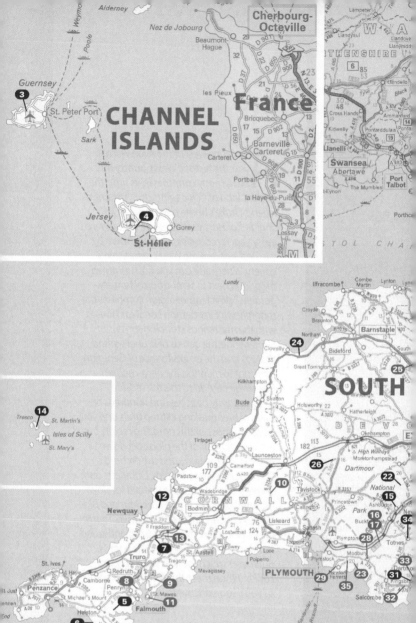

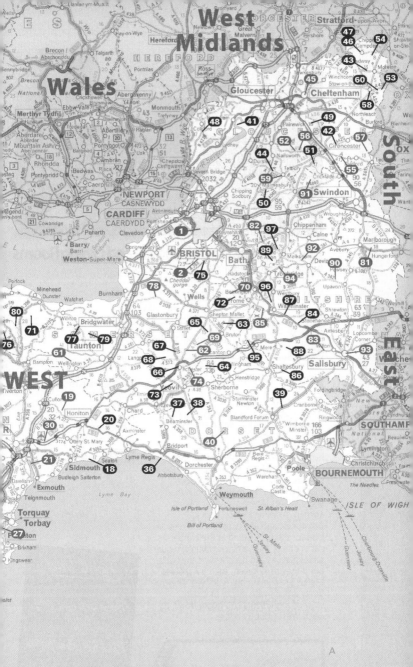

Bristol

001 The Albion Public House and Dining Rooms

Boyces Avenue, Clifton Village, Bristol BS8 4AA
Tel.: (0117) 9733522 - Fax: (0117) 9739768
e-mail: info@thealbionclifton.co.uk - Website: www.thealbionclifton.co.uk

   VISA

 Butcombe, Smiles, Sharp's Doombar

Charming Clifton is not all showy attractions like the bridge and the boutique shops; some treats take a little bit of finding, and to say The Albion was hidden away would be an understatement. Armed with a local map, search out this Grade II listed 17C inn hiding in a mews in the heart of the village. At the front is a terrace fronting a seemingly cosy little hostelry. Inside, though, things are more spacious than you'd expect. There's an open plan kitchen, reclaimed wood floors, flagstones, and plenty of space to relax in front of the fires, stand at the big bar or eat at one of the numerous chunky wood tables. Settles and benches line the walls, but if they're all taken, then try upstairs. Menus are concise but read well. They're firmly British, with plenty of locally sourced ingredients and good, down-to-earth West Country dishes.

Food serving times:
Tuesday-Sunday:
12pm-3pm, 7pm-10pm
Closed 25-26 December and 1 January
Booking essential.
Prices:
Meals: a la carte 30.00/40.00

In Clifton Village.

Typical Dishes

Baked duck eggs, spring truffle

Rib of beef, Anna potatoes

Toffee apple tarte Tatin

Chew Magna

002 **Bear & Swan**

South Parade, Chew Magna BS40 8SL

Tel.: (01275) 331100 - Fax: (01275) 332187
e-mail: enquire@bearandswan.co.uk - Website: www.bearandswan.co.uk

 VISA

Butcombe Bitter, Courage

A sturdy homage to Victoriana in the heart of a small, pretty but truly bustling village. The exterior is of sturdy stone and the 'proper' bar at one end has the same sterling qualities. Here you can enjoy a pint or a tasty snack at chunky rustic tables- mind you- only at lunchtime. In the evenings, the main blackboard menu takes centre stage. This can also be enjoyed in the main dining area at the other end of the bar where a hotchpotch of antique tables and chairs, reclaimed floor boards, and exposed stone work give a pleasant feel. You can watch the chefs at work in their open-plan kitchen as they prepare an ample, modern, eclectic range of dishes that draw diners from far and wide, attracted by locally renowned menus full of tasty West Country produce on daily changing menus.

Food serving times:
Monday-Saturday:
12pm-2pm, 7pm-9.45pm
Sunday: 12pm-2pm
Prices:
Meals: a la carte 17.00/30.00

Typical Dishes

Grilled asparagus on herb risotto

Herb crusted rack of lamb with aubergine pesto

Double chocolate mousse

In the centre of the village. Parking.

Kings Mills (Guernsey)

003 ## Fleur du Jardin

Castel, Kings Mills (Guernsey) GY5 7JT

Tel.: (01481) 257996 - Fax: (01481) 256874
e-mail: info@fleurdujardin.guernsey.net - Website: www.fleurdujardin.guernsey.net

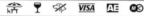

 Fuller's London Pride, Guernsey Sunbeam

Couldn't be more aptly named: this welcoming old inn has good-sized gardens, colourful borders, shrubs, bright hanging baskets and flower barrels. Inside, the laid-back bar and adjacent alcoves sport low beams and thick granite walls confirming their 15C origins: there's well tended Guernsey real ale on draught. But it's the daily menus of local seafood which give the Fleur its standing of quiet renown among tourists as well as locals. The beamed restaurant, with its reassuringly ancient granite fireplace, mixes these with a more eclectic, traditional range of dishes, or you can dine more informally at the bar. After eating, swim off delightful, nearby beaches, and sleep deeply in one of the pub's smart but cottagey bedrooms.

Food serving times:
Monday-Saturday:
  12pm-2pm, 6.30pm-9.30pm
      (9pm Sunday)
Closed 25-26 December
(dinner)
Prices:
Meals: a la carte 20.00/26.00
🛏 **17 rooms :** 47.50/116.00

3mi West of St Peter Port. Parking.

Typical Dishes

Scallops, mango and coconut relish

Noisette of lamb, redcurrant jus

Apricot and rosemary tart Tatin

Saint Aubin (Jersey)

004 Old Court House Inn

St Aubin's Harbour, Saint Aubin (Jersey) JE3 8AB

Tel.: (01534) 746433 - Fax: (01534) 745103
e-mail: ochstaubins@jerseymail.co.uk - Website: oldcourthousejersey.com

Pedigree and guest ales - Skinners, Ringway

This atmospheric 15C quayside inn has had a colourful history as a courthouse, merchant's house, and, more recently, bit-part player in the TV series Bergerac. Its traditional whitewashed façade looks beyond the harbour to St Helier. The main hub of activity is the Westward bar, built from the gig of a schooner scuttled off the Hurd Deep. Two areas are kept for dining: a characterful, Georgian glass-paned front room, or a courtyard restaurant at the back. Menus are the same throughout, and are rooted in the popular, tried-and-tested category: the highlight is the local seafood, in simple platters or elaborate specials, but the Old Court House is also good for the likes of vegetable lasagne or wild mushroom and asparagus risotto. Individually decorated bedrooms are colourful, countrified and most have harbour views.

Food serving times:
Monday-Sunday:
12.30pm-2.30pm, 7pm-10pm
Prices:
Meals: 10.00 (set price lunch and dinner) and a la carte 25.00/50.00
9 rooms : 40.00/120.00

Typical Dishes

Sauteed wild mushrooms and black pudding

Fresh Jersey lobster

Warm chocolate brownies with vanilla ice cream

4mi West of St Helier. Parking opposite.

Constantine

005 **Trengilly Wartha Inn** 🛏

Nancenoy, Constantine TR11 5RP

Tel.: (01326) 340332 - Fax: (01326) 340332
e-mail: reception@trengilly.co.uk - Website: www.trengilly.co.uk

🍷 ✕← **VISA** **AE** **①** **MC**

Sharps Cornish Coaster and guest beers - Skinners Knocker and Keel Over, Sharps Eden, Doom Bar, Lizard Point

A good place to learn Cornish – that's the Trengilly Wartha (translation: settlement above the trees), because the locals throng here. It's not the easiest place to get to, being at the tail end of some notorious near vertical lanes, but the end product's worth it. This former crofter's abode has been enlarged over the years, but everyone spills out into the garden in summer. The interior is dominated by the airy main bar, which, apart from serving fine ales, also boasts a terrific selection of wines. The scrubbed wood tables and old Cornish settles almost invite you to sit, sup and relax. Dine in a formal restaurant or conservatory where the hearty pub grub is enlivened by daily changing specials boards. Menus are richly influenced by the seasons, and cooking is well honed and solidly skilful.

Food serving times:
Monday-Saturday:
12pm-2.15pm, 6.30pm-9.30pm
Sunday: 12pm-2pm,
                          7pm-9.30pm
Restaurant:
Monday-Sunday:
                          7.30pm-9.30pm
Closed 25 December
Prices:
Meals: 29.00 (fixed price dinner) and a la carte 23.00/29.00
🛏 **8 rooms :** 50.00/96.00

Typical Dishes

Baked crab with herb cream

Chicken breast, chilli & cranberry butter

Chocolate truffle cake

1.5mi South by Fore St off Port Navas rd. Parking. ▶▶

Gunwalloe

006 The Halzephron Inn

Gunwalloe TR12 7QB
Tel.: (01326) 240406 - Fax: (01326) 241442
e-mail: halzephroninn@gunwalloe1.fsnet.co.uk

     VISA **AE** **MC**

Sharps Doom Bar, Wills Resolve, Special, St Austell Tribute, Halzephron Gold (organic ale brewed especially for us)

A visit to this extreme south-westerly corner of Cornwall wouldn't be complete without a visit to the Halzephron, staring out imperturbably across Mount's Bay. It knows its place: it's been here 500 years, and is wonderfully snug and rustic. The low ceiling boasts fine old timbers; gleaming copper and original paintings adorn the walls. Knick-knacks, curios and higgledy-piggledy décor enrich four adjoining dining rooms: food's a serious business here, and wide-ranging menus are fiercely Cornish in produce and style. Portions are of the hearty variety; an impressive selection of local real ales is an ideal way to wash down lunch or dinner, followed by a walk on the nearby South West Coast Path. Two neat, cosy bedrooms await.

Food serving times:
Monday-Sunday:
    12pm-2pm, 7pm-9pm
Closed 25 December
Prices:
Meals: a la carte 17.00/28.00
🛏 **2 rooms :** 48.00/84.00

Typical Dishes

Crab and chilli risotto

Beef fillet with goat's cheese, madeira sauce

Baked white chocolate cheesecake

3.5mi South of Helston by A3083. Parking.

Mitchell

007 The Plume of Feathers

Mitchell TR8 5AX

Tel.: (01872) 510387 - Fax: (01637) 83940
e-mail: lewinnich@btconnect.com - Website: www.theplume.info

 VISA ⓂⒸ

Sharp's Doom Bar, St Piran's, Directors, Eden Ale, Ruddles County

As good a break as you'll find from the drone of the A30, this smartly refurbished part 16C dining pub, away from the visitors' hotspots, comes into its own as an escape from the tourist influx of a Cornish summer, but you'll find a reassuringly good turnout - families and couples, groups of friends - on most days of the year. Set aside from an airy, sympathetically restored bar, several connecting lounges serve as the restaurant, although service is just as alert and organised at the bar. The cooking itself is steady as she goes - there is a sound, classic menu with blackboard specials - but the real draw is the relaxed, everyday atmosphere of the place: they have plenty of regulars, but are always happy to take on a few more. Large, bright bedrooms in the restored barns and stable. A well provides ample pure drinking water and water for the baths and showers.

Food serving times:
Monday-Sunday:
    12pm-5pm, 6pm-10pm
Prices:
Meals: a la carte 16.00/30.00
🛏 **5 rooms :** 41.25/75.00

Near the junction of A30 and A3076. Parking. ▶▶

Typical Dishes

Chicken liver parfait, pear chutney

Angus beefburger in foccacia, fries

Raspberry crème brûlée

Mylor Bridge

008 Pandora Inn

Restronguet Creek, Mylor Bridge TR11 5ST

Tel.: (01326) 372678 - Fax: (01326) 378958
Website: www.pandorainn.co.uk

 VISA Ⓜ©

Duchy Tribute, Tinners, Tribute and St Austell HSD

Sail up Mylor Creek, moor at the pontoon, and you'll have taken the scenic route to this stunningly located pub, which dates back to the 13C. Its charming interior comes courtesy of timbered ceilings for the vertically challenged, shiny stone floors, cosy corners, open fire and seaside pot pourri. Food can be eaten at the bar or at the slightly more formal Andrew Miller restaurant upstairs: hearty pub menus take in a wide range of favourites, but are quite rightly dominated by fresh seafood off the blackboard, so be patient with service. Crab bucket and bait are available at the bar or work off your meal with a relaxed walk along the creekside paths.

Food serving times:
Monday-Thursday:
   12pm-3pm, 6.30pm-9pm
Friday-Saturday:
  12pm-3pm, 6.30pm-9.30pm
Closed 25 December for food
Prices:
Meals: a la carte 18.95/26.95

Typical Dishes

Scallops with belly of pork and white onion sauce

Cornish cod with pea and mint purée, sauté potatoes

Crème brûlée

3.5mi North of Falmouth by A39 and B3292; fork left via Restronguet and Weir rd for 1mi. Parking.

Philleigh

009 **Roseland Inn**

Philleigh TR2 5NB

Tel.: (01872) 580254

e-mail: stallardsimon@yahoo.co.uk - Website: www.roselandinn.co.uk

 Cornish Doom Bar, Adnams

You know you're edging into rural heaven when you come by ferry to this out-of-the-way family-run Cornish pub – the chuch's next-door neighbour for the last 500 years – and step inside from the rose-covered courtyard. Just look around and admire the charming rustic surrounds: exposed black beams, open fires, rugged stone floors and scattered knick-knacks. A fine selection of real ales is on hand – a pint or two will go down exceptionally well with a dish or two from the traditional and unpretentious menus, which owe much of their hearty character to Cornish produce.

Food serving times:
Monday-Sunday:
12pm-2.30pm,
6.30pm-9.30pm
Closed 25 December
Prices:
Meals: a la carte 14.00/25.00

Situated between King Harry ferry and Ruan High Lanes. Parking.

Typical Dishes

Scallops and Parma ham, basil dressing

Shoulder of lamb, redcurrant and Port gravy

Baked plums and meringue

Rilla Mill

010 **The Manor House Inn**

Rilla Mill PL17 7NT

Tel.: (01579) 362354

Sharp's Ale, Marston's Pedigree, Old Speckled Hen - Skinner's Ale in summer

Chancing upon the somnolent village of Rilla Mill near the grand bleakness of Bodmin Moor, you'd be forgiven for not expecting anything too special down at the local. Wrong. An eye-catching makeover of the 360 year-old Manor House hits you as soon as you walk in. Homely touches light up all corners, from the very pleasant bar to the neat curtains, perfectly shelved books and colourful stack of board games. "No cheap peanuts here," says the landlord. He's good to his word: proper handmade crisps are for sale, and fresh walnuts with nut-crackers adorn each table. Exotic cocktails (you read it right) are also prominent here, courtesy of a blackboard selection called 'The Inn Thing'. Dining areas are neat and thoughtfully decorated, with local artwork for sale. Dinner itself is not to be taken lightly, with very seasonal, local produce to the fore, exemplified by suppliers taking pride of place on the blackboard.

Food serving times:
Tuesday-Sunday:
12pm-2pm, 7pm-9pm
Closed for food 25-26 December and 1 January
Restaurant closed Tuesday evening
Prices:
Meals: a la carte 20.00/31.50

5mi North of Liskeard by B3254 to Upoton Cross and side road East. Parking.

Typical Dishes

Cornish Blue and wild mushroom fritters

Wild boar, red cabbage

Jaffa cake with clotted cream

St Mawes

011 **The Victory Inn**

Victory Hill, St Mawes TR2 5DQ

Tel.: (01326) 270324 - Fax: (01326) 270238
Website: www.victory-stmawes.co.uk

 🍷 *VISA* ⓂⒸ

Sharp's Doom Bar, Bass, Black Sheep

There are various splendid ways of getting to the Victory Inn. You can reach it by ferry, road or on foot along the harbour; whichever alternative presents itself, the delights of the Roseland and Falmouth Bay are ever-present. This professionally run pub delights in a cosy interior with some charm, not a little enhanced by its enviable position on the Victory Steps next to the harbour. The real ale selection is broad; wander across to the open fire and mingle with the locals over a pint. The dining room is upstairs, a spacious area, with a more formal, contemporary feel and mainly used in the evening. As you might expect, seafood figures strongly on the menu, aided and abetted by Cornish ingredients, all very simple, fresh and unfussy. Tuck into moules marinière, perhaps on one of the few benches outside.

Food serving times:
Monday-Sunday:
    12pm-3pm, 6pm-9pm
- Seafood specialities -
Prices:
Meals: a la carte 22.50/30.00

Typical Dishes

Mussel pasta, garlic and tomatoes

Sea bream with Le Puy lentils

Lemon posset

Next to St Mawes harbour. Parking at the harbour car park. ➤

St Mawgan

012　The Falcon Inn 🛏

St Mawgan TR8 4EP

Tel.: (01637) 860225 - Fax: (01637) 860884
e-mail: enquiries@thefalconinn-newquay.co.uk - Website: www.thefalconinn-newquay.co.uk

  VISA **MC**

 Tribute, HSD, Tinners

Set just inland from the delights of Newquay, in the splendid Vale of Mawgan, this 16C wisteria-clad hostelry rejoices in a totally unspoilt character and a quaint surrounding of antique shops. The bar is cosiness itself: roaring log fire, comfy settles, large antique prints and, naturally enough, pictures of falcons on the walls; you can sit at homely farmhouse tables and chairs. Eat either here, in the French-windowed restaurant, or at a delicious cobbled courtyard in the front. Dishes are based around freshly-caught seafood which arrives on the plate from the nearby beaches at Newlyn; classic dishes also make a solid appearance.

Food serving times:
Monday-Sunday:
　　　12pm-2pm (2.30pm in summer), 6pm-9pm (9.30pm in summer)

Prices:
Meals: a la carte 14.00/20.00
🛏 **3 rooms :** 37.00/37.00

Typical Dishes

Smoked salmon and prawns

Sausages, mash & mustard gravy

Bread & butter pudding

Follow signs for the airport on A3059 between Newquay and St Colomb Major; the pub is down the hill. Parking.

Summercourt

013 Viners

Carvynick, Summercourt TR8 5AF

Tel.: (01872) 510544 - Fax: (01872) 510468
Website: www.vinersrestaurant.co.uk

Sharp's Doom Bar

This charming stone-built cottage, with origins stretching back to the 17C, can claim to have been here long before the landscaped encampments of mobile homes or the golf course next door, but it's a much more recent change which has really captured the local imagination. The bar near the entrance remains a good place for beer, nuts and pub chat, and drinkers are positively encouraged, though most will stay for one and head straight for the elegant new restaurant. Pale-toned walls, slate floors and high-backed velvet chairs strike a sophisticated note, taken up in a creative but affordable menu that shows sound culinary understanding: for an example of this generosity and balance, try grilled oysters in lime and chilli or sole in parsley butter with bean salad.

Food serving times:

Sunday: 12.30pm-3pm, 6.30pm-9.30pm

Closed 4 weeks in winter

Closed dinner Sunday end October to Whitsun - also dinner Monday mid September to mid July

Prices:

Meals: 16.95 (set price lunch Sunday only) and a la carte 26.85/33.75

At Carvynick Golf and Country Club, 1.5mi North West of the junction of A30 and A3058. Parking.

Typical Dishes

Terrine of foie gras

Turbot roasted in thyme and olive oil

Vanilla shortbread, lemon curd ice cream

Tresco (Scilly Isles)

014 New Inn

Tresco (Scilly Isles) TR24 0QQ

Tel.: (01720) 422844 - Fax: (01720) 423200
e-mail: newinn@tresco.co.uk - Website: www.newinn.tresco.co.uk

 rest **VISA**

Skinners Tresco Tipple, Betty Stogs, Tribute and Natural Beauty

An hospitable stopping off point on your way, perhaps, to the Old Blockhouse or Tresco Abbey Gardens, this stone built former inn may prove difficult to leave. It has a charming terrace garden - with plenty of seating - and views that extend across the beautiful island. In keeping with its surroundings, the traditional bar is packed with nautical memorabilia; other lounges have a friendly, bustling ambience – it's where the locals congregate. Back outside, a large semi-decked sun lounge is a good place to tuck into an extensive "snacky" menu or indulge in blackboard seafood specials. The dining room (remember to book first) is a striking bistro-style restaurant serving traditional favourites. If, indeed, you haven't moved on, bedrooms are simple, well-kept and comfortable.

Food serving times:
Monday-Sunday:
12pm-2.30pm, 7pm-8.30pm
(booking essential to non-residents) Accommodation rates include dinner

Prices:
Meals: 35.00 (fixed price dinner) and a la carte 20.00/30.00
16 rooms : 135.00/228.00

Near Tresco Stores >>

Typical Dishes

Chicken livers, champ and Madeira sauce

Shoulder of lamb, couscous

Sticky toffee pudding

Ashburton

015 ## Rising Sun

Woodland, Ashburton TQ13 7JT

Tel.: (01364) 652544 - Fax: (01364) 653628

e-mail: rising sun-hazel@btconnect.com - Website: www.risingsunwoodland.co.uk

  room **VISA**

Princetown Jail Ale and regularly changing guests ales - IPA, Dobs, Old Moggy

In the depths of the rolling countryside, this old drovers' inn is one to remember for hot summer afternoons, when families can enjoy some fresh Devon air at one of the terrace picnic tables in the garden, but the cosy and very traditional bar comes into its own at the turn of the year. The blackboard menu gives credit where it's due to a huge supporting cast of Wessex farmers, brewers and other suppliers, and approachable bar staff will happily talk you through the choices. Fresh and appetising dishes could include pigeon or smoked trout salads and sea bass with balsamic sauce – it depends on the season, of course – but their hearty pies are perennially popular; beef and Devon blue cheese and venison with stout and juniper head a short list of favourites.

Food serving times:
Monday-Saturday:
   12pm-2.15pm, 6pm-9.15pm
Sunday: 12pm-3pm, 7pm-9.15pm

Prices:
Meals: a la carte 18.00/24.00
4 rooms : 38.00/65.00

Typical Dishes

Brixham crab and avocado salad

Devon lamb with mint, redcurrant and red wine

Crème brûlee

Village signposted off A38. Parking.

Avonwick

016 The Avon Inn

Avonwick TQ10 9NB

Tel.: (01364) 73475
e-mail: rosec@beeb.net - Website: www.avoninn.co.uk

Sharps Doombar, Teignworthy Reel

If you're in this area of South Devon, there's a good chance you've been wandering on Dartmoor, in which case, thoughts turning to sustenance, the Avon Inn is a sure-fire bet. There's nothing too fancy about the pub itself: hanging floral baskets and a small side garden without, a few exposed beams and hop bines within. It's the food that takes centre stage here. The pleasant owners make everyone feel at home, and they take a great pride in the menus on offer. These are wide-ranging with a classical Gallic base (husband Dominique is French). A daily changing blackboard menu incorporates everything from light lunches to full-on dishes featuring plenty of local seafood and fish. The mats are local too, made of the local slate.

Food serving times:
Tuesday-Saturday:
　12pm-2pm, 6pm-19pm
Sunday: 　　　　12pm-2pm
Monday: 　6pm-9pm (buffet
　　　　　　　　only)
Closed Sunday dinner and
Monday lunch
Prices:
Meals: a la carte 18.00/26.75

Village signposted off A38. Parking.

Typical Dishes

Pate de campagne, chutney

Red mullet with saffron rice, shellfish bisque

Meringue, strawberries and cream

Avonwick

017 The Turtley Corn Mill

Avonwick TQ10 9ES

Tel.: (01364) 646100 - Fax: (01364) 646100
e-mail: mill@avonwick.net - Website: www.avonwick.net

 VISA MC

Tamar, Jail Ale, Dartmoor IPA, Tribute, Butcombe Blonde

Driving down to Cornwall? You could do a lot worse than take a minute's detour off the A38 to locate this refurbished 18C establishment named after one of its former owners. Smart oak and slate floors, local prints and slender bookcases, thoughtfully allied to beams and pillars from the original structure, give the place a clean, light and airy style, spacious enough to seat about 120. It's in an enviable setting, with a duck pond (including info on different breeds) and six acres of grounds bordered by the river Glazebrook. The wheel's been renovated too, though if you think you see it turning you've had too much to drink. There's a good selection of local ales, and the menu offers an ample selection for tired drivers, everything from pub classics to more up-to-date concoctions.

Food serving times:
Monday-Sunday:
12pm-9.30pm
Closed 25 December
(except drinks 12pm-2pm)
Prices:
Meals: a la carte 18.50/25.00

Village signposted off A38. Parking.

Typical Dishes

Chicken liver pate, red onion marmalade

Sea bass fillets on chorizo mash

Sticky toffee pudding

Branscombe

018 Masons Arms

Branscombe EX12 3DJ

Tel.: (01297) 680300 - Fax: (01297) 680500
e-mail: reception@masonsarms.co.uk - Website: www.masonsarms.co.uk

  ⁺×⁼rest **VISA**

 Otter Bitter, Masons Ale, Branoc, Tribute, Timothy Taylor Landlord

The picturesque village of Branscombe is one of the joys of the East Devon coast, nestling piecemeal in a deep valley right next to the sea. At its heart lies this 14C creeper-clad inn, visible to anyone up in the hills. It has a wonderfully bustling atmosphere, built around the unspoilt bar where hotel guests and locals mingle with a pint. The hearty ambience is enhanced with the surrounding ancient ships' beams, slate floors, and stone walls; a huge central fireplace is regularly used to spit-roast joints of meat at lunchtime and in the evening: modern British menus are highlighted by crab and lobster landed on Branscombe's beach. Bedrooms are divided between inn and cottages opposite.

Food serving times:
Monday-Sunday:
        11am-2pm, 7pm-9pm
(bar lunch)
Prices:
Meals: 25.00 (fixed price dinner) and a la carte 15.20/27.50
19 rooms : 40.00/160.00

In the village centre. Parking.

Typical Dishes
Terrine of chicken and foie gras
Beef Wellington, Marsala sauce
Iced chocolate and Amaretti biscuit terrine

Broadhembury

019 The Drewe Arms

Broadhembury EX14 3NF
Tel.: (01404) 841267 - Fax: (01404) 841267

  🍷   *VISA*   AE   M©

Otter Bitter, Ale, O'Hanlon's Yellowhammer

A delightful village deserves a delightful pub, and in this village tucked away in East Devon they've struck gold. A quintessentially English setting places the 13C Drewe Arms next to a church and opposite a row of cottages the colour of clotted cream. Gloriously unimproved, the interior seems not to have changed for centuries. Unusually, the walls are covered with carved walking sticks, while farming implements and even an eel-catcher's basket hang from the ceiling. The quiet is broken only by the satisfied murmurs of those drinking at the neat little bar or eating in the two dining areas. Fish is the focus of the menus. Typically, you might find marinated herrings, roasted cod with anchovies or salmon fishcakes with tomato and dill sauce; dishes are reassuringly well executed and very tasty.

Food serving times:
Monday-Saturday:
    12pm-2pm, 7pm-9pm
Sunday: 12pm-2pm
Closed 25 December
(booking essential) -
Seafood -
Prices:
Meals: a la carte 12.00/40.00

Typical Dishes

Crab thermidor

Turbot with Hollandaise sauce

Prune and Armagnac tart

Signposted off A373 north of Honiton. Parking.

Dalwood

020 **The Tuckers Arms** 🛏

Dalwood EX13 7EG

Tel.: (01404) 881342

e-mail: davidbeck@tuckersarms.freeserve.co.uk - Website: www.tuckersarms.co.uk

Otter Bitter, Courage Best, Palmers IPA, Old Speckled Hen

With its neatly trimmed thatch and little low windows, this medieval longhouse looks promising from outside, but it's a particular pleasure to find its style and history still so well reflected in the interior, both in the cosy lounge bar and the dining rooms. Plates and brasses decorate the beams and the venerable old stonework of the fireplace has been preserved. The cooking remains the big draw, though: a very affordable menu with a set-price option doesn't overlook local meat or seasonal game and has a good local reputation for its catch of the day: try smoked salmon cakes or John Dory in a delicate Devon cream sauce with asparagus, and follow it up with a tasty, traditional pudding like date and banana sponge, served with rum and toffee sauce.

Food serving times:
Monday-Saturday:
7pm-9pm
Sunday: 12pm-7pm
Prices:
Meals: 19.95 (fixed price dinner) and a la carte 12.95/19.95
🛏 **5 rooms :** 42.50/69.50

3.5mi West of Axminster by B3261, off A35. Parking.

Typical Dishes

Smoked haddock, Cheddar glaze

Lamb chop with liver and kidney

Lemon meringue pie

Exton

021 The Puffing Billy

Station Rd, Exton EX3 0PR
Tel.: (01392) 877888

Otter Ale, Bass

I f only all railway pubs were so inviting. Round the corner from Exton station and along the path beside the water, you come upon this smart, white pub. The open plan interior is decorated with original artwork: wood burner and leather sofas in the bar, banquettes in the dining room or halogen lights and exposed beams in the big airey extension. Wherever you decide to eat, the menu is a broad one, covering lunchtime sandwiches, traditional pub dishes on the blackboard, fine-dining classics and more 'informal' dishes, many of which are available in either starter or main size. If you're interested in seeing how it all happens, a few tables face the open kitchen. Your meal may even be spiced up by gunfire from the Royal Marines' barracks next door.

Food serving times:
Sunday-Thursday:
  12pm-2pm, 6.30pm-9.15pm
Friday-Saturday:
  12pm-2pm, 6.30pm-10pm
Closed Christmas to New Year
Prices:
Meals: a la carte 16.65/30.85

Typical Dishes

Butternut squash & herb risotto

Angus beef fillet, oxtail mash

Blackberry pannacotta, caramelised apples

Brown tourist sign off A376 to Exmouth, 3mi from junction 30 M5. Parking.

Haytor Vale

022 **The Rock Inn** 🛏

Haytor Vale TQ13 9XP

Tel.: (01364) 661305 - Fax: (01364) 661242
e-mail: inn@rock-inn.co.uk - Website: www.rock-inn.co.uk

  ⚥room **VISA**

Dartmoor Best, Old Speckled Hen

I n a pleasant little village near the eastern tip of Dartmoor stands this characterful looking pub with a long-standing owner. It was originally a coaching inn dating back to the mid-18C, and this is evidenced by the covered entrance and stone trough beside old stables. There are nooks and crannies a-plenty; the warren of rooms adds to the gloriously rural appeal of the place. Horse-brasses, unsurprisingly, are ubiquitous. Food orders are taken at the bar by a very pleasant team. Cooking is sound and satisfactory with an interesting meat menu, which might include pan-fried local pheasant breast on cider and fennel seed cabbage with a Merlot jus, shallots and roast walnuts, or suprême of Devon chicken on coconut risotto.
Accommodation is provided in the shape of surprisingly spacious and well-kept bedrooms.

Food serving times:
Monday-Sunday:
    12pm-2pm, 7pm-9.30pm
Closed 25 and 26 December
Prices:
Meals: 19.95/19.95 and a la carte 23.95/27.95
🛏 **9 rooms :** 65.95/106.95

Typical Dishes

Scallops, crispy bacon, roast garlic

Sea bass, mussel sauce

Brandy snap, mango sorbet

3.5mi West of Bovey Tracey by B3387. Parking. ▶▶

Holbeton

023 The Dartmoor Union

Fore St, Holbeton PL8 1NE

Tel.: (01752) 830288 - Fax: (01752) 830296
e-mail: info@dartmoorunioninn.co.uk - Website: www.dartmoorunion.co.uk

Dartmoor IPA and Otter Bitter

Once a Victorian workhouse and later a cider press-house, the Dartmoor Union seems to have found its true vocation at last - maintaining the tradition of pulling pints brewed in its own microbrewery. For all the activity inside, the pub can be hard to spot, as there's only a discreet brass plaque on its stone façade. Its bar is spacious and smartly furnished, hung with pictures of old Holbeton: gold inscriptions on the walls – including "manners maketh man" – may or may not inspire a more philosophical tone of pub debate. The dining room to one side offers a large, seasonal selection of modern and traditional dishes including a good value set lunch. The flower-filled terrace is lovely in summer, and so are Coastguards beach and its cliff walks, a short drive away.

Food serving times:
Monday-Sunday:
  12pm-2pm, 6.30pm-9.30pm
Prices:
Meals: 12.95 (fixed price lunch) and a la carte 18.85/27.95

Signposted off A379 southeast of Plymouth. Parking.

Typical Dishes

Twice baked goat's cheese soufflé

Best end of lamb, Madeira jus

Iced rhubarb parfait, crumble

Horn's Cross

024 The Hoops Inn

Horn's Cross EX39 5DL
Tel.: (01237) 451222 - Fax: (01237) 451247
e-mail: sales@hoopsinn.co.uk - Website: www.hoopsinn.co.uk

 Hoops Old and Special Ales, Sharpes Doom Bar, Sharps Atlantic IPA

An old wayside inn since the Middle Ages, this sizeable thatched pub still has plenty to offer the passer-by, including those who need a bed for the night – four rooms in the main house are particularly comfortable, but there are a further eight "standard" ones at the back. Its handsome bar preserves its wooden settles, bowed ceiling beams, cups, tankards and porcelains, not to mention traces of the well which once supplied water for home-brewed ales. A wide-ranging menu covers everything from lunchtime ploughmans and bar favourites, through afternoon teas to tasty dishes like seafood pie, lamb with rhubarb jus and sticky toffee pudding. A pretty terrace looks out over the water garden where birds of prey can occasionally be seen.

Food serving times:
Monday-Sunday:
7pm-9.30pm
10am-9pm for bar snacks

Prices:
Meals: 25.00/25.00 and a la carte 15.00/35.00
13 rooms : 55.00/95.00

On A39 east of Clovelly. Parking.

Typical Dishes

Game terrine, homemade piccalilli

Hoops fish stew, garlic bread

Traditional treacle tart, clotted cream

Knowstone

025 **The Masons Arms Inn**

Knowstone EX36 4RY

Tel.: (01398) 341231

e-mail: dodsonmasonsarms@aol.com - Website: www.masonsarmsdevon.co.uk

Cotleigh 'Tawny' Bitter

Nestled most serenely in a tiny hamlet just off the southern tip of Exmoor is this very attractive, yellow painted, part 13C little thatched inn. It's tremendously characterful inside, heavily beamed with flagged floors and a cosy front snug bar where locals gather to sup Exmoor ale drawn from the barrel. Go down some ruggedly ancient stone steps to find yourself in a candlelit dining room and admire the mural ceiling: you could be feasting 700 years ago! Rickety wood tables, benches and chairs are haphazardly set about the place; however, there's nothing haphazard about the food, as the new owner comes from a haute cuisine background including 12 years as head chef of the celebrated Waterside Inn at Bray-on-Thames.

Food serving times:
Tuesday-Saturday:
12pm-2pm, 7pm-9.30pm
Sunday: 12pm-2pm
Closed first 2 weeks in January
Prices:
Meals: 29.50 (set price lunch Sunday only) and a la carte 28.50/36.00

Village signposted off A361. Opposite the village church. Parking.

Typical Dishes

Ham hock and mushroom terrine

Devon beef fillet, Madeira sauce

Chocolate & hazelnut mousse

Lydford

026 **The Dartmoor Inn**

Moorside, Lydford EX20 4AY

Tel.: (01822) 820221 - Fax: (01822) 820494
e-mail: info@dartmoorinn.co.uk - Website: www.dartmoorinn.com

    VISA

Dartmoor Best, Otter

A bracing walk round Lydford Gorge can build a serious appetite and there's no better way of satisfying it than a visit to this locally renowned inn on the edges of Dartmoor. As befits its location, it boasts a pleasing rustic character, and enough dining areas to satisfy a coachload of gourmands. Open fires and arty prints on the walls create just the right feeling of relaxation. Good value set lunch menus where local produce is much in evidence in modern cuisine influenced by Mediterranean and local styles. If you stay overnight in one of the large and stylish bedrooms, you are sure of an excellent, even unconventional, breakfast in the morning.

Food serving times:
Tuesday-Saturday:
12pm-2.30pm, 7pm-10pm
Sunday: 12pm-2.30pm
Prices:
Meals: 16.95 (set price lunch and dinner (except Friday-Saturday)) and a la carte 26.50/35.00

3 rooms : 75.00/120.00

Typical Dishes
Goat's cheese, hazelnut dressing
Casserole of sea fish
Honey custard tart, glazed bananas

1mi East on A386. Parking.

Marldon

027 Church House Inn

Village Rd, Marldon TQ3 1SL

Tel.: (01803) 558279 - Fax: (01803) 664865

 Dartmoor Best, Otter Ale, Fuller's London Pride, Bass and Bombardier

Visitors to Torbay might like to make an excursion from the delights of Torquay and Paignton to this nearby, attractive inn by the church in Marldon: the pub itself is well signposted. It's a listed, whitewashed Georgian structure of 14C origins, and its characterful aspect continues inside with beams, rough stone walls and flagstone floors. There's a large central bar with adjoining rooms which tend to be used for dining but you can eat anywhere: you'll find plenty of drinkers mingling with diners. The bustling atmosphere doesn't faze the waiting staff: there's an invariably friendly service. Blackboard menus offer plenty of choice from the traditional to the more modern, with a guarantee that the vegetables have come from the village's allotment!

Food serving times:
Monday-Sunday:
12pm-2pm, 6.30pm-9.30pm
Prices:
Meals: a la carte 26.00/30.00

Off A380 between Torquay and Paignton - well signposted. Parking. ⟩

Typical Dishes

Ham hock terrine, caramelised apple

Gilt head bream, fennel and lemon

Butterscotch and pecan

Modbury

028 White Hart

Church St, Modbury PL21 0QW
Tel.: (01548) 831561

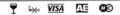

Tribute, Spitfire

This traditional black-and-white fronted pub leaves behind all traces of its coaching inn heritage once you step through the front door. This is most definitely a modern dining pub, but one where the locals happily fit in clutching a pint at the bar, especially in winter with the log fire burning brightly and ladies relaxing in the deep leather Chesterfields. The rest of the pub is given over to the enjoyment of food. Smart linen napkins on large wooden tables herald innovative dishes listed on a vast A3 sheet. The wide choice has a modern bistro/brasserie feel – particularly impressive is the great value fixed price lunch and early evening menu. Parties are catered for in the first floor Assembly Rooms. Word of warning: watch out for the well if you've had a bit too much to drink. It's covered with glass but might still surprise the unwary!

Food serving times:
Tuesday-Saturday:
    12pm-2.30pm, 6pm-9pm
Sunday: 12pm-2.30pm
Closed 25 December
and 1 January

Prices:
Meals: 15.45 (set price lunch/dinner) and a la carte 23.50/30.00

On A379 between Kingsbridge and Yealmpton.

Typical Dishes

Medley of fish, sorrel sauce

Braised rib of beef, horseradish sauce

Apple tart, clotted cream

Noss Mayo

029 The Ship Inn

Noss Mayo PL8 1EW

Tel.: (01752) 872387

e-mail: ship@nossmayo.com - Website: www.nossmayo.com

 Tamar Best Bitter, Princetown Jail Ale, St Austell Tribute, Butcombe Blonde, and a guest beer in summer

Go down a winding South Hams road to get to this idyllically located pub, a exciting dash of white in a delightful inlet surrounded by hills. At low tide you can approach the front entrance from the hard but at high tide, entry is via a back door at first-floor level; when there's a very high tide do not park on the 'hard'. The lovely outdoor terrace is overlooked by a delightful canopied upper deck. The oldest part of the Ship dates from the 1700s but the interior is up to date with lovely local prints, glossy wood furniture, piles of books and newspapers and games to play, like Scrabble and chess. Friendly staff serve up an extensive menu, ranging from the simple to the adventurous including local seafood. Afterwards, take a stroll in the village, cross the inlet to visit equally attractive Newton Ferrers, or embark on a salty walk on the South West Coast Path.

Food serving times:
Monday-Sunday:
12pm-9.30pm
Prices:
Meals: a la carte 10.00/25.00

Signed off A379 10.5mi Southeast of Plymouth; turn right into B3186. Restricted parking, particularly at high tide.

Typical Dishes

Blue cheese and apple pate, brioche

Fish pie, green vegetables

White chocolate cheesecake

Rockbeare

030 **Jack in the Green Inn**

London Rd, Rockbeare EX5 2EE

Tel.: (01404) 822240 - Fax: (01404) 823445
e-mail: info@jackinthegreen.uk.com - Website: www.jackinthegreen.uk.com

Otter Ale, Ruddles Best Bitter

This whitewashed pub is not just another roadside pub near Exeter airport. Although much extended, it retains an air of the traditional with its carpets and beams. The lounge bar has banquette seating and dark wood tables, but the more characterful – and more sophisticated – place to eat is the restaurant, which spans three rooms in the oldest part of the premises. You can select from the range of dishes listed on the blackboard or from a regularly changing à la carte menu. Cooking in the modern British style is accomplished and well presented. The pub can get busy with its regular customers as well as corporate parties from the business park.

Food serving times:
Monday-Saturday:
 12pm-2pm, 6pm-9.30pm
Sunday: 12pm-9.30pm
Closed 25 December-
5/6 January
Prices:
Meals: 22.95/24.25 (Sunday lunch) and a la carte 18.00/ 30.00

6.25mi East of Exeter by A30. Parking at the back.

Typical Dishes

Ham hock and foie gras terrine

Steak and kidney pie and mash

Coconut and lemongrass pannacotta

375

Slapton

031 The Tower Inn

Church Rd, Slapton TQ7 2PN

Tel.: (01548) 580216

e-mail: towerinn@slapton.org - Website: www.thetowerinn.com

  room **VISA** **AE** **MC**

Butcombe Bitter, St Austell Tribute, Badger Tanglefoot

Follow the signs to discover this hidden gem, a remarkably preserved inn, built in 1347, which once belonged to the Collegiate Chantry of St Mary; the old church tower still keeps watch over a charming walled garden. Inside, inviting flagged and beamed bar-parlours – one with a fireplace stripped back to the old stone – connect with a slightly smarter dining room strung with hop bines. In such characterful old surroundings, it comes as quite a surprise to see a number of more contemporary dishes among the classics: generous, well-prepared platters of piquant antipasti are something of a speciality. Three simple little bedrooms are designed with stopovers in mind.

Food serving times:
Monday-Sunday:
12pm-2pm, 7pm-9pm
Closed 25 December,
Sunday dinner and Monday
November-March
Prices:
Meals: a la carte 18.00/25.00
3 rooms : 40.00/60.00

Typical Dishes

Smoked prawns, mackerel, trout and salmon

Venison Bourguignon, blue cheese dumplings

West Country cheeses

6mi Southwest of Dartmouth by A379; signed between Dartmouth and Kingsbridge. Parking with exceptionally narrow access.

Stokenham

032 The Tradesman's Arms

Stokenham TQ7 2SZ

Tel.: (01548) 580313 - Fax: (01548) 580657
e-mail: nick@thetradesmansarms.com - Website: www.thetradesmansarms.com

   VISA Ⓜ

 Brakspear Bitter, Devon Pride, Bass, Eddystone and 1 guest ale

A glistening seven-mile finger of golden coastline runs along this part of South Hams, and the nearby Tradesman's Arms has the kind of charm which fits in unobtrusively with such enviable surroundings. It's a part-thatched, 14C building that used to serve as workmen's cottages. There is a pleasant garden with benches overlooking the village' field or a choice of rooms in which to idle away time looking across a green and pleasant South Devon valley, a pint of real ale at your side - the main bar with its stone fireplace and beamed ceiling or a second room with wood burner and linen-clad tables. Both rooms serve the same menu, based around fish and game which, naturally enough, are fresh from the most local of sources: typically, Brixham fish or scallops from Start Bay.

Food serving times:
Monday-Sunday:
12pm-2.30pm,
6.45pm-9.30pm
(booking essential)
Prices:
Meals: a la carte 17.95/25.00

Typical Dishes

Crab and prawn tower

Sauteed scallops, carrot and leek ragout

Sticky toffee pudding

On A379 between Kingsbridge and Dartmouth. Parking. ❯

Strete

033 The Kings Arms

Dartmouth Rd, Strete TQ6 0RW

Tel.: (01803) 770377 - Fax: (01803) 771008
e-mail: kingsarms-devon-fish@hotmail.com - Website: www.kingsarms-dartmouth.co.uk

  rest **VISA**

 Adnams, Otter Ale, Fuller's London Pride

From being slightly rundown – to put it kindly – The Kings Arms has picked itself up in fine style. A white-painted roadside pub with a distinctive balcony, it's easy to spot as you drive up, but this is not its best side, and anyone who has spent a slow, sunny lunchtime in the garden or the pleasant rear terrace is sure to agree. The bar itself, decorated with old local pictures, is fine but small; it's worth going for the extra comforts of the dining room. Two window tables are the prime spots, but bare beams and seats in nautical blue give the whole place a nice, fresh feel. Lunches are slightly lighter but, even here, fish and chips with mushy peas is the odd one out in a menu of modern classics. Dinners make even more use of local, seasonal ingredients, including Devon seafood, meats and cheeses. Fresh, unfussy flavours.

Food serving times:
Monday-Sunday:
12pm-2pm, 7pm-9pm
Closed dinner Sunday and all day Monday November to Easter
Prices:
Meals: a la carte 23.00/34.00

4mi Southwest of Dartmouth by A379. Private parking 100 yds away on main street.

Typical Dishes

Tempura of king prawns, carpaccio of tuna

Fillet of sea bream, spiced couscous

Hot chocolate fondant

Totnes

034 The Steam Packet Inn 🛏

St Peter's Quay, Totnes TQ9 5EW
Tel.: (01803) 863880 - Fax: (01803) 862754
e-mail: steampacket@buccaneer.co.uk - Website: www.thesteampacketinn-totnes.co.uk

Otter Bright, Butcombe and guest ale

There's been a pub here since the turn of the 19th Century, delightfully sited on the quay in the centre of Totnes, where boats still tie up and bobble on the gentle tides. Much original charm is retained in the cosy, rustic bar with its rafters and wood floors; peer deep and you'll find locals hidden away in the nooks and crannies. But it's the large conservatory overlooking the River Dart and its huge terrace that people come for. This is an idyllic spot to tuck into something off the versatile menu that offers simple pub dishes as well as more adventurous and interesting modern alternatives. Ingredients are as local as the herbs from chef's kitchen garden. There are four bedrooms where relaxing river views go hand-in-hand with clean, fresh designs.

Food serving times:
Monday-Sunday:
  12pm-2.30pm, 6pm-9.30pm
Prices:
Meals: a la carte 23.00/25.50
🛏 **4 rooms :** 55.00/79.50

Typical Dishes

Mackerel, new potatoes and rocket salad

Tuna, red pepper and coriander salsa

Lemon and wine posset

At the bottom of the hill by the river. Parking.

Yealmpton

035 Rose & Crown

Market St, Yealmpton PL8 2EB

Tel.: (01752) 880223 - Fax: (01752) 881058
e-mail: info@theroseandcrown.co.uk - Website: www.theroseandcrown.co.uk

 no real ales offered

It's easy to whiz through South Hams villages on your way to the delights of Noss Mayo, Newton Ferrers or Burgh Island. But put the brakes on in Yealmpton, and check out this neat, modernised pub on a corner, not least for its attractive rear walled terrace with canopies and water feature. Inside, enclosed by rough stone walls, is a big central bar and a spacious, open plan design that allows for casual seating areas with family-sized leather sofas, and places to eat with large benches and tables or a more formal dining space. Here you can tuck into modern 'restaurant' dishes with a Pacific Rim edge, along with a good value fixed priced lunch menu, washed down by Devon ales or something off the accessible wine list. If your taste is for something a bit more fishy, then you can step outside the pub to the Seafood Restaurant where a good range of shellfish is on offer.

Food serving times:
Monday-Sunday:
12pm-2.30pm, 6.30pm-9.30pm

Closed 25 December
Prices:
Meals: 12.95 (set price lunch) and a la carte 19.50/28.00

7mi Southeast of Plymouth by A379. Parking.

Typical Dishes

Confit duck, caramelised apple

Roast duck, bok choi, Armagnac jus

Dark chocolate mousse

Bridport

036 The West Bay

Station Road, West Bay, Bridport DT6 4EW

Tel.: (01308) 422157 - Fax: (01308) 459717
e-mail: info@thewestbay.co.uk - Website: www.thewestbay.co.uk

 room *VISA* **AE** **MC**

 Palmers 200, Palmers IPA, Palmers Copper ale on draught

S itting just yards from the harbour, there's been a pub on this spot since 1739 and you can still imagine the smugglers and crusty seafarers planning their moonlit jaunts. The front of the bar is still popular with the locals, and the low-beamed ceiling adds to the intimate atmosphere. Behind the bar is the slightly more formal restaurant with its neat arrangement of pine tables and chairs. A blackboard menu offers an extensive range of refreshingly local seafood, which is delivered twice a day. Lunchtime offers a lighter option. In this part of the world, eating al fresco comes naturally, and a summer terrace gives an opportunity to catch up with news from Lyme Bay's fossil gatherers. It's a busy place, so make sure you book first. Four simple bedrooms await upstairs.

Food serving times:
Monday-Saturday:
   12pm-2pm, 6.30pm-9.15pm
Sunday: 12pm-2pm
booking essential
Prices:
Meals: a la carte 20.00/30.00
🛏 **4 rooms :** 70.00/85.00

Typical Dishes

Baked scallops, garlic butter

Roasted monkfish, red pepper sauce

Chocolate mocha tart

1.75mi South of Bridport by B3157. Near the harbour. Parking.

Corscombe

037 **The Fox Inn**

Corscombe DT2 0NS
Tel.: (01935) 891330 - Fax: (01935) 891330

⊱room **VISA** **MC**

Butcombe Bitter and Exmoor Ale

S ticky soot, built up over time, lies ingrained on the walls above the fireplaces here. It's one of many endearing features of this mightily charming thatched 17C pub, which boasts several fascinating areas. Two stone floored main bar rooms are intimate and dripping with rural ambience, typified by pews, slate-clad bar and scrubbed pine furniture. Country style imbues the extremely characterful breakfast room, where the first meal of the day is cooked on the Aga; look out for the dog that rests there. A mellow old conservatory has a large table constructed from one strip of oak felled in the 1987 storms. And the food? Dine on well-judged traditional dishes using the best seasonal produce, including well-renowned blackboard fish specials, washed down with something from the reasonably-priced wine list. There are cosy bedrooms, too, endowed with homely charm.

Food serving times:
Monday-Sunday:
    12pm-2pm, 7pm-9pm
Closed 25 December
Prices:
Meals: a la carte 19.00/32.00
🛏 **4 rooms :** 55.00/100.00

3.5mi Northeast of Beaminster. Parking.

Typical Dishes

Pan-fried wood pigeon, red onion confit

Roast medallion of wild boar with ham hock mash

Treacle tart

Evershot

038 Acorn Inn

28 Fore St, Evershot DT2 0JW

Tel.: (01935) 83228 - Fax: (01935) 83707
e-mail: stay@acorn-inn.co.uk - Website: www.acorn-inn.co.uk

  ⅙room **VISA** **AE** **MC**

Draymens, Greene King, Abbot Ale

This neat 16C inn in sleepy Evershot still feels like a proper village local, with friendly neighbourhood rivalries kindled at the skittle alley and cooled off with pints of Devon guest ales and ciders, but the oak-panelled main bar, warmed by an open fire in winter, also attracts diners from further afield. Two further rooms in pale wood are just for dining. British pub favourites appear alongside classic dishes with a light modern touch and plenty of local produce; a blackboard menu lists daily changing seafood specials. Recently refurbished bedrooms with designer touches including plasma televisions and separate breakfast room with country style feel.

Food serving times:
Monday-Sunday:
    12pm-2pm, 7pm-9pm
Prices:
Meals: a la carte 20.00/32.50
🛏 **10 rooms :** 75.00/140.00

Typical Dishes

Smoked salmon tempura

Rack of lamb, Puy lentils, red wine jus

Apple and apricot rice pudding

7mi Northeast of Beaminster by B3163. Parking.

Farnham

039 The Museum Inn

Farnham DT11 8DE

Tel.: (01725) 516261 - Fax: (01725) 516988
e-mail: enquiries@museuminn.co.uk - Website: www.museuminn.co.uk

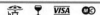

 Ringwood Best, Timothy Taylor, Hop Back, Summer Lightening

Standing at the main crossroads of the village, the original, part-thatched Museum Inn has long since received an addition here and an extension there, but the pub as it stands today seems not only smart, bright and well-tended, but seamlessly characterful too. Diners have the choice of four dining rooms, furnished with antique dressers and scrubbed tables and decorated with curiosities from old paintings to stags heads, but as they don't take bookings here, you may be asked to take a seat in the bar first before heading through for classic-contemporary dishes like chicken parfait, duck confit and haddock and mustard risotto. Spacious, quite luxuriously styled bedrooms really are a cut above the average inn; if you don't feel quite ready for bed, the residents lounge might tempt you with a cosy fire and plenty of reading matter.

Food serving times:
Monday-Sunday:
   12pm-2pm, 7pm-9.30pm
Closed 25 December,
dinner 31 December
Prices:
Meals: a la carte 25.50/31.00
🛏 **8 rooms :** 85.00/150.00

Typical Dishes

Venison carpaccio

Osso buco, glazed vegetables

Warm vanilla rice pudding

7.5mi Northeast of Blandford Forum by A354. Parking.

Plush

040 Brace of Pheasants

Plush DT2 7RQ

Tel.: (01300) 348357
e-mail: info@braceofpheasants.co.uk - Website: www.braceofpheasants.co.uk

Butcombe Traditional, Ringwood Best, Otter Bitter, Sharp's Doombar and Eden Ale, Palmers Copper Ale, Weymouth Bitter

The Giant of Cerne Abbas is not much more than a (giant's) stone-throw from this gloriously secluded 16C thatched inn, which revels in a pleasant rural setting midway between Dorchester and Blandford Forum. In keeping with the surroundings and exterior, the pub – formerly two thatched cottages and a smithy - has a cosy, characterful interior, dominated by the large bar where locals gather to sup pints or partake of the robust, tasty cooking, which has earned a solid local reputation. The same is served in a slightly more formal parlour, or non-smoking dining area for families. There's a pretty rear garden for summer use, with the woods and bridleways of the Piddle valley beyond.

Food serving times:
Tuesday-Sunday and Bank Holidays Monday:
12.15pm-2.30pm,
7.15pm-9.30pm
Closed 25 December
Closed for dinner Sunday in winter
Prices:
Meals: a la carte 18.00/31.00

Typical Dishes
Chicken and bacon terrine
Woodpigeon, Marsala cream sauce
Chocolate pudding, chocolate sauce

7mi North of Dorchester by B3143 and minor road East. Parking.

Arlingham

041 The Old Passage Inn

Passage Rd, Arlingham GL2 7JR
Tel.: (01452) 740547 - Fax: (01452) 741871
e-mail: oldpassageinn@ukonline.co.uk - Website: www.fishattheoldpassageinn.co.uk

Moles

Originality is the keyword to this bright green painted family-run establishment, perched in an isolated spot where the Severn starts to twist and turn. Any resemblance to a cosy, small-town country inn ends at the dining room, where gastronomic ambitions spiral off on a modern tangent. All efforts go into an accomplished seafood menu; cooking is bold, generous and suitably rustic. A small private dining area at the front can be booked for special occasions. The three bedrooms are funky. They're called Red Mullet, Yellow Finned Tuna and Green Lipped Mussel, and they're all strikingly modern, bright, hi-tec and highly individual and with a kingsize bed. Views of the Severn from the restaurant and rooms.

Food serving times:
Tuesday-Saturday:
      12pm-2pm, 7pm-9pm
Sunday: 12pm-2pm
Closed 24-30 December
Prices:
Meals: a la carte 23.50/33.50
3 rooms : 55.00/95.00

Typical Dishes

Scallops thermidor

Baked hake, dill and white wine sauce

Warm pear and almond tart

On the banks of the River Severn, 2.5mi Northwest of Frampton on Severn. Parking.

Barnsley

042 **Village Pub**

Barnsley GL7 5EF

Tel.: (01285) 740421

e-mail: reservations@thevillagepub.co.uk - Website: www.thevillagepub.co.uk

  ⚐-room **VISA**

Wadworth 6X and Hook Norton Best

A really special place – too good and too affordable to save for special occasions. Renovated with impeccable taste, five connecting rooms of this part-17C inn lead from gleaming oak floors to spotless flagstones, bright botanical prints and Regency colours to Persian carpets and wingback chairs; the elegant, beamed bedrooms in French country style are every bit as inviting. The real highlight, though, is the daily-changing menu. Dilligently sourced produce, local and organic where possible, and a dash of originality raise appetising modern dishes well above the norm: try tagliatelle with a rich, dark venison and chicken liver sauce, haddock with potato and bacon salad and a deliciously buttery banana cheesecake. Keen and accommodating staff who make sure you're well looked-after.

Food serving times:

Monday-Thursday:
12pm-2.30pm, 7pm-9.30pm

Friday: 12pm-2.30pm, 7pm-10pm

Saturday: 12pm-3pm, 7pm-10pm; Sunday: 12pm-3pm

Prices:

Meals: a la carte 24.50/28.50

🛏 **6 rooms :** 75.00/90.00

4mi North East of Cirencester, on the B4425. Parking.

Typical Dishes

Gravadlax of sea trout

Veal escalope, wild rocket salad

Blood orange and almond tart

Bourton-on-the-Hill

043 Horse & Groom 🛏

Bourton-on-the-Hill GL5 9AQ

Tel.: (01386) 700413 - Fax: (01386) 700413
e-mail: greenstocks@horseandgroom.info - Website: www.horseandgroom.info

VISA ⓜ⊚

Everard's Tiger, Hooky, Purity Brewing UB4, Wye Valley Dorothy Goodbody, Cotswold Brewing Company Premium Cotswold

Be careful getting to the Horse and Groom. It's on a busy main road (especially in the summer) adjacent to a dangerous corner. That said, and precautions taken, this is a lovely 18C former coaching inn built of attractively yellowing Cotswold stone, with a neat little terraced garden to the rear that has a veg and fruit patch on view. Inside, you'll feel instantly at home in a big, welcoming bar that shows its age with pride in the form of weathered beams and exposed stone. Tables are scattered hither and thither, and a friendly team is on hand to take care of your order: the owners know all about what makes a good pub – their parents run the delightful Howard Arms in Ilmington. Blackboard menus at the Horse and Groom change constantly, sometimes twice a day. Expect to see proper English cooking with good Cotswold produce setting the pace. It's a busy place, so book in advance. Evolving bedrooms are being upgraded and modernised.

Food serving times:
Monday: 7pm-9pm
Tuesday-Saturday:
 12pm-2pm, 7pm-9pm
 (9.30pm Friday & Saturday)
Sunday: 12pm-2pm
Closed 25 and 31 December
Prices:
Meals: a la carte 18.00/25.00
🛏 **5 rooms :** 65.00/115.00

Typical Dishes

Homemade Scotch quail eggs

Beef burger, onion marmalade, aïoli

Vanilla pannacotta, rhubarb

1mi West of Moreton in the Marsh by A44. Parking.

Calcot

044 The Gumstool Inn

Calcot GL8 8YJ

Tel.: (01666) 890391 - Fax: (01666) 890394
e-mail: reception@calcotmanor.com - Website: www.calcotmanor.co.uk

Uley Best Bitter, Butcombe Blonde, Nailsworth Mayor's Bitter,
Wickwar, Cotswold Way

The cheerful, civilised Gumstool proudly nurtures its own identity beside an impressive neighbour – Calcot Manor - in one of Gloucestershire's most pleasing locations. It boasts a bustling intimacy, as locals and hotel guests mingle. Gingham curtains, hop bines and a leather armchair by the open fire lend traditional flavours to a generally modern ambience. Rustic but comfy about sums it up. You'll eat well here: bold, imaginative cooking is invariably flavoursome, with influences drawn from the Mediterranean. Dishes can be taken in ample (starter), or generous, portions. Staff create a very relaxed style, but you'll always feel you're being well looked after.

Food serving times:
Monday-Sunday:
12pm-2pm, 7pm-9pm
(booking essential)
Prices:
Meals: a la carte 20.00/50.00
30 rooms : 170.00/210.00

Typical Dishes

Wild mushroom and spinach pancake

Rabbit and root vegetable pie

Baked chocolate fondant, crème fraîche sorbet

3.5mi West of Tetbury on A4135, in grounds of Calcot Manor Hotel. Parking.

Cheltenham

045 **The Beehive**

1-3 Montpellier Villas, Cheltenham GL50 2XE

Tel.: (01242) 702270 - Fax: (01242) 269330
e-mail: beehive@slak.co.uk - Website: www.slak.co.uk

 VISA AE MC

 Jouster, 6X and Pedigree

The quiet, residential Georgian Montpelier area of Cheltenham may not be the first place you'd think of for locating a down-to-earth pub, especially one tucked away on a corner, but it's worth going that extra mile to check out the Beehive. Though expanded, its original cosy green and frosted glass façade is still present. Not a lot has changed inside, either: rough wooden floorboards, a bar and various settles, benches and large wood tables, along with a wood burner and even a slot machine, give it a genuine unaffected 'proper' pub feel. There's a separate snug, above which is a former Masonic lodge hall, where more dining tables are set. Locally renowned, the cooking here is good and honest, not really traditional pub fare, but in the up-to-date restaurant league.

Food serving times:
Monday-Tuesday:
12pm-2.30pm, 6pm-9pm
Wednesday-Saturday:
12pm-2.30pm, 6pm-10pm
Sunday: 12pm-3.30pm
Closed 25 December
Prices:
Meals: 15.00 (set price Sunday lunch) and a la carte 20.00/27.50

South of town centre; off southside of Montpellier Terrace. Some on road parking or the Bath Road car park.

Typical Dishes

Lamb's sweetbread with sauce Tartare

Chicken, truffle mash and asparagus

Lemon tart, pear sorbet

Chipping Campden

046 **Eight Bells Inn**

Church St, Chipping Campden GL55 6JG

Tel.: (01386) 840371 - Fax: (01386) 841669
e-mail: neilhargreaves@bellinn.fsnet.co.uk - Website: www.eightbellsinn.co.uk

    VISA ⓜⓒ

Hook Norton Hooky Bitter, Old Hooky, Purity Brewery Co, Ubu, Goffs Jouster

With its typical gables, little leaded windows and steep-pitched roof, the charming 14C Eight Bell Inn stands out even in well-preserved Chipping Campden. It once housed the stonemasons working on the nearby bell-tower, and history is still writ large on the rustic interior. The ancient beams over the bar are now studded with brasses and hung with mugs, and a glass plate set into the floor reveals an old passage running from St. James' Church, thought to have been used for escaping the persecutions of the Reformation or the dangers of the Civil War rather than for discreet exits after last orders. A succinct modern menu and specials board balances the eclectic and the traditional: chunky baguettes are a popular choice at lunch. Pine-fitted bedrooms in bright blues and yellows provide the essentials.

Food serving times:
Monday-Sunday:
   12pm-2.30pm, 6.30pm-9pm
Closed 25 December
Prices:
Meals: a la carte 22.00/28.50
🛏 **7 rooms :** 50.00/115.00

In centre of town. Unlimited parking on road.

Typical Dishes

Smoked salmon parcel

Chicken, spiced Catalan bean cassoulet

Sticky toffee pudding, vanilla ice cream

Chipping Campden

047 The Kings

The Square, Chipping Campden GL55 6AW
Tel.: (01386) 840256 - Fax: (01386) 841598
e-mail: info@kingscampden.co.uk - Website: www.kingscampden.co.uk

 Hooky Hook Norton Best Bitter

This archetypal Cotswold inn is a real treat. Behind the handsome 17C façade, two surprisingly spacious, antique-furnished rooms, decorated with pictures on a culinary theme, are the perfect place to enjoy a well-balanced menu with a hint of brasserie style – dishes like pork with apple and Calvados, or asparagus salad, make the most of local produce in all its seasonal variety. Countless delightful details raise the bedrooms well above the usual pub standard: impeccably tasteful and never fussy, some even have oak four-poster beds. The pretty rear courtyard, bordered with lavender, is blissfully quiet after the bustle of the town in summer.

Food serving times:
Monday-Sunday:
12pm-2.30pm, 6.30pm-9.30pm
Prices:
Meals: a la carte 20.00/35.00
12 rooms : 72.50/165.00

Typical Dishes
Smoked salmon, caper and lemon dressing
Fillet steak, home cut chips
Sticky toffee pudding, ice cream

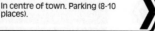 In centre of town. Parking (8-10 places).

Clearwell

048 **The Wyndham Arms**

ClearwellGL168JT

Tel.: (01594) 833666 - Fax: (01594) 836450
e-mail: res@thewyndhamhotel.co.uk - Website: www.thewyndhamhotel.co.uk

  VISA

Wyndham Brew and Freeminer

Visitors are spoiled for choice in this part of the Forest of Dean: the Clearwell Caves and medieval Castle are close at hand, while the Perrygrove Railway is just up the road. Paying a visit to this attractive village inn with 13C origins fits in seamlessly on the tourist trail. A pleasant outside terrace is a good spot for summer relaxing; inside, there's much character to admire, particularly in the bar, which proudly boasts flagstones, bare white walls, rafters, chimney, old bread baking oven in a corner, and paintings for sale on the walls. Hearty, well-cooked, keenly priced dishes keep locals and tourists alike happy. Six bedrooms in the original inn provide characterful accommodation and there are twelve further rooms in the nearby annexe.

Food serving times:
Monday-Saturday:
 12pm-2pm, 6.30pm-9pm
Sunday: 12pm-2.30pm,
 7pm-9pm

**26 and 31 December
and 1 January**
Prices:
Meals: a la carte 19.50/29.50
18 rooms : 45.00/115.00

By the Cross in the village. Parking.

Typical Dishes

Chicken liver parfait, gherkin salsa

Stuffed loin of pork, apple mash

Sticky toffee pudding

Cockleford

049 The Green Dragon Inn

Cockleford GL53 9NW

Tel.: (01242) 870271 - Fax: (01242) 870171
e-mail: green-dragon@buccaneer.co.uk - Website: www.green-dragon-inn.co.uk

 VISA AE MC

 Hook Norton, Butcombe, Courage Directors

The classic direction "in the middle of nowhere" is a pinpoint indication for this authentic old Cotswold pub in a delightfully remote setting along a country road. A typical honey-gold stone façade serves notice of the warm ambience within: beams, log fire and an authentic rustic style dating back to the 17C. Take your pick of three rooms around the double bar – one is particularly devoted to dining. There's an elaborate choice of menu with a touch of Italian inspiration, so you might find roast fig, taleggio and Parma ham bruschetta for starters, followed by fried gnocchi with white truffle oil, Parmesan and oyster mushrooms for main course. Visitors to the area may wish to stay overnight in plain, simple yet well-equipped bedrooms.

Food serving times:

Monday-Friday:
12pm-2.30pm, 6pm-10pm
Saturday: 12pm-3pm, 6pm-10-pm
Sunday: 12pm-3.30pm, 6pm-10pm

Prices:
Meals: a la carte 20.00/35.00
9 rooms : 57.00/75.00

Typical Dishes

Brie filo parcels, cranberry sauce

Sea bass, prawn and mango salsa

Banoffee pie

5mi South of Cheltenham by A435. Parking.

Didmarton

050 The Kings Arms

The Street, Didmarton GL9 1DT
Tel.: (01454) 238245 - Fax: (01454) 238249

 VISA MC

Uley Bitter, Sharps Eden, Rucking Mole, Butcombe Bitter, Hop Back Brewery

This 17C former coaching inn looks most resplendent in its honey coloured overcoat - fitting apparel for a trusted Cotswold family member. Inside is just as good. Hops clamber over beams and local stone merges seamlessly with terracotta walls. A bright and cheerful fire-lit bar with oak settles is perfect for a winter's evening. During the summer months, there's an ideal garden setting for drinks and gentle slumbers. The bright dining room offers a reassuringly hearty menu of tried-and-tested dishes which might include local sausages with buttered mash and onion gravy, or fresh Cornish crab. Pine-fitted bedrooms are simple - wake refreshed for trips into nearby Malmesbury or Tetbury.

Food serving times:
Monday-Sunday:
 12pm-2pm, 7pm-9.30pm
Prices:
Meals: a la carte 17.95/22.95
4 rooms : 55.00/80.00

Typical Dishes

Pigeon breast, cherry tomato compote

Rack of lamb, red wine cassoulette

Sticky toffee pudding

5.5mi Southwest of Tetbury on A433. Parking.

Ewen

051 **The Wild Duck Inn** 🛏

Drake's Island, Ewen GL7 6BY

Tel.: (01285) 770310 - Fax: (01285) 770924
e-mail: wduckinn@aol.com - Website: www.thewildduckinn.co.uk

☂ 🍷 *VISA* 🅰🄴 🟠🄒

Theakston Best and Old Peculiar, Duck Pond, Archers Golden, Young's St George, Bombardier and guest ale

Equally remarkable on the inside and the outside, this privately owned Elizabethan house seems almost too imposing to have started life as a mill, but though the ancient oil paintings do have a hint of stateliness about them, there's an unmistakeable pub atmosphere to the place: intriguing artefacts and bushy swags of hops decorate a series of intimate bar-rooms. Upstairs and in the modern wing, imaginatively styled bedrooms, two with four-poster beds, all share the same richly comfortable ambience. An extensive daily menu, supplemented by blackboard specials, combines modern and traditional dishes and includes a good choice of fresh fish landed at Brixham. Weather permitting, the giant chess set on the terrace offers a more intellectual way to decide who picks up the bill for lunch..

Food serving times:
Monday-Saturday:
　　12pm-2pm, 6.30pm-10pm
Sunday:　　　　　　12pm-2pm,
　　　　　　　　6.30pm-9.30pm
Closed 25 December
Prices:
Meals: a la carte 18.00/26.00
🛏 **12 rooms :** 70.00/120.00

3.25mi Southwest of Cirencester by A429. Parking.

Typical Dishes

Selection of meats, cheese and vegetables

Tuna steak, Parma ham and tomato salad

Warm hazelnut tart

Frampton Mansell

052 The White Horse

Cirencester Rd, Frampton Mansell GL6 8HZ

Tel.: (01285) 760920

e-mail: emmawhitehorse@aol.com - Website: www.cotswoldwhitehorse.com

 Hook Norton Best Bitter, Uley Best Bitter, Arkell's Summer Ale (in season)

From dismal nonentity to bright, modern gastropub, it's been a busy few years for The White Horse, and the friendly, responsive service suggests a team enjoying their success. More cheerful-looking than you would ever guess from the outside, the interior divides into a cosy and very relaxed bar, where they serve snacks and baguettes at lunchtime, and a colourful dining room offering a more ambitious menu. Fairly priced dishes, typically including grilled sardine fillets and roasted tomato, rich chicken liver parfait and sea bass on warm baby vegetables, blend bold, contemporary flavours with a streak of originality. An ever-growing local reputation means it's worth getting there early at weekends.

Food serving times:

Monday-Saturday:
  12pm-2.30pm, 7pm-9.45pm
Sunday: 12pm-3pm

Closed first 4 days of January

Prices:
Meals: a la carte 20.00/30.00

Typical Dishes

Scallops, apple & horseradish mash

Pork fillet with dates

Champagne, raspberry & elderflower jelly

7mi West of Cirencester by A419. Parking.

Lower Oddington

053 The Fox Inn

Lower Oddington GL56 0UR

Tel.: (01451) 870555 - Fax: (01451) 870669
e-mail: info@foxinn.net - Website: www.foxinn.net

 &⇔room **VISA**

Hook Norton, Abbott, Wickwars Cotswold Ale

A charming village deserves a charming pub, and Lower Oddington has one, an ivy-covered inn not far from the 11C church. 2005's Pub of the Year goes from strength to strength: there's a well cared-for atmosphere in the smartly cosy dining rooms – beams and fireplaces, nooks and crannies, books and candlelight – although the first impression, on most nights of the week, is of friendly chat and activity. Imperturbable young staff have it all under control, even during the busiest lunchtimes, serving enjoyable, flavoursome cooking with its share of British classics like steak and kidney pudding and Bakewell tart. Seafood fans will want to try the potted shrimps, or even ask in advance about their special fish days. Three delightful bedrooms, sumptuously furnished with antiques, are always in immaculate order.

Food serving times:
Monday-Sunday:
    12pm-2pm, 6.30pm-10pm
Closed 25 December
Prices:
Meals: a la carte 17.95/27.65
⇔ **3 rooms :** 68.00/95.00

Typical Dishes

*Wild mushroom and
Parmesan tart*

*Rabbit fricassée, Dijon
mustard cream*

Rice pudding with fruit jam

3mi East of Stow-on-the-Wold by A436. Parking.

Paxford

054 Churchill Arms

Paxford GL55 6XH
Tel.: (01386) 594000 - Fax: (01386) 594005
e-mail: mail@thechurchillarms.com - Website: www.thechurchillarms.com

     ←room **VISA**

 Hook Norton Best, Ansells Moonlight and 1 guest ale often from Wye Valley or North Cotswold Brewery

This well-kept, instantly likeable pub is a confirmed local favourite and even at its busiest – when service can start to fray a little at the edges – a laid-back atmosphere still prevails: it's usual to see locals, walkers and visitors to nearby Hidcote Manor propping up the bar and chatting as they patiently bide their time for a table. Bookings are not accepted but it's worth the wait; fresh, contemporary, seasonal cooking, using fine ingredients from trusted regional suppliers, is served up at prices which are generous going on philanthropic. Recent successes, typically robust and enjoyable, include asparagus with shallot dressing and smoked goose, crisp, full-flavoured duck confit with cauliflower purée, and a rich chocolate torte. Simple, stylish rooms, half in the modern extension, make a good base for a weekend in the Cotswolds.

Food serving times:
Monday-Sunday:
12pm-2pm, 7pm-9pm
Prices:
Meals: a la carte 17.50/26.00
4 rooms : 40.00/70.00

3mi East of Chipping Campden by B4035. On street parking.

Typical Dishes

Smoked haddock pancake

Pheasant, aubergine caponata & Pont-neuf potatoes

Almond meringue, baked figs

Poulton

055 The Falcon Inn

London Rd, Poulton GL7 5HN

Tel.: (01285) 850844

e-mail: info@thefalconpoulton.co.uk · Website: www.thefalconpoulton.co.uk

Hook Norton Best, Hooky Bitter and guest ales · Good Old Boy, Hopback Brewery Odyssey, White Horse Bitter, Ramsbury Bitter

More contemporary inside than the exterior suggests, the thoroughly refitted Falcon has, if anything, gained in neighbourly good nature since its conversion to a dining pub. Relaxed and friendly in atmosphere, there's a main room with a log fire, seagrass carpets, scrubbed pine tables and mix-and-match chairs and pews, and more dining space in the converted skittle alley, from where you can peek into the kitchen and see how lunch is coming on. The young owner with enthusiasm to burn does the cooking and puts faith in local suppliers; hearty Modern British dishes, never over-elaborate, with a well-balanced wine list.

Food serving times:
Monday-Saturday:
12pm-2.m, 7pm-9pm
Closed for food 25-26 December and 1 January
Prices:
Meals: a la carte 20.00/30.00

Typical Dishes

Fillet of beef, Parmesan and rocket

Belly of pork, sage and cider gravy

Chocolate brownie

Village on A417 between Cirencester and Fairford. Parking.

Sapperton

056 The Bell

Sapperton GL7 6LE
Tel.: (01285) 760298 - Fax: (01285) 760761
e-mail: thebell@sapperton66.freeserve.co.uk - Website: www.foodatthebell.co.uk

 VISA 🅜🅒

> *Uley Old Spot, Bath Ales Spa, Butcombe Bitter, Wickwar Cotswold Way*

Over the past few years, a dedicated young team have really seen their efforts pay off. The Bell is a much-loved local institution: spotless, smart, uncluttered and wonderfully comfortable, with the warm glow of Cotswold stone inside and out. A well thought-out repertoire, plus daily specials, finds room for pub favourites and appetising modern dishes which make the most of whatever's in season: fortifying midwinter fare includes local pheasant and wild mushrooms braised in wine – tender, earthy and rich – and a moist, dark date and toffee pudding. There are some invigorating walks through woods and meadows, and a log fire and a big wood-burning range to welcome you back, or tables in the courtyard if the sun is shining.

Food serving times:
Monday-Sunday:
 12pm-2pm, 7pm-9.30pm
Closed 25 December
and 3-10 January
Prices:
Meals: a la carte 21.00/35.00

Typical Dishes

Cheese fritters, aubergine chutney

Beef burger, tomato relish, fries

Trio of homemade ice creams

5mi West of Cirencester by A419. Parking.

Southrop

057 The Swan

Southrop GL7 2NU

Tel.: (01367) 850205 - Fax: (01367) 850517
e-mail: grazzer@gmail.com - Website: www.theswanatsouthrop.co.uk

 Wadworth 6X, Doombar, Hook Norton, Timothy Taylor's Landlord

Looking little changed by the centuries, the ivy-covered inn has kept its characterful beamed ceiling, its log fire and its busy public bar. The main dining room is laid for informal eating, and features modern art which is available for sale. Here, the manager and chef bring their experience from Terence Conran's Bibendum to a contemporary menu with a subtle Mediterranean flavour and a touch of West End sophistication - there's a very good-value fixed price set menu. To round off the evening with some healthy competition, they even have a skittle alley for hire: try finding one of those in Kensington!

Food serving times:
Monday-Sunday:
    12pm-2.30pm, 7pm-10pm
Closed 25 December
Prices:
Meals: 16.50 (set price lunch) and a la carte 21.00/32.00

Village signed off A417 to the North of Lechlade. Parking on road and at village hall.

Typical Dishes

Crab vinaigrette with herbs

Roast cod with rainbow chard, sauce verte

Rhubarb and orange crumble

Stow-on-the-Wold

058 Eagle & Child

Digbeth St, Stow-on-the-Wold GL54 1BN

Tel.: (01451) 830670 - Fax: (01451) 870048

e-mail: enquiries@theroyalisthotel.co.uk - Website: www.theroyalisthotel.co.uk

Hook Norton, Bass

Not many pubs can boast a leper hole in their armoury (well, in the cellar, to be precise). But that's the case here, in a building that, over a thousand years ago, was a hospice sheltering lepers. It claims to be England's oldest inn, and can certainly boast some impressive history: the discovery of a Civil War Royalist commander's letter, a tunnel leading from the bar to the church opposite, and an ancient frieze. The rooms themselves have thousand year-old timbers. To get to them, go through the reception of the Royalist Hotel and cross the threshold of a pub where you'd feel cheated if there wasn't the tangible whiff of history and rustic charm (don't worry, there is). There's also a sunny, bright conservatory and a restaurant with soft lighting and beams serving well-priced modern menus with a distinct French influence.

Food serving times:
Monday-Sunday:
   12pm-2.30pm, 7pm-9.30pm
Prices:
Meals: a la carte 20.00/35.00
14 rooms : 50.00/130.00

At the Royalist Hotel. Parking.

Typical Dishes

Sautéed veal sweetbreads

Sea bass, new potatoes, sauce Niçoise

Glazed lemon tart, raspberry sorbet

Tetbury

059 The Trouble House

Cirencester Rd, Tetbury GL8 8SG

Tel.: (01666) 502206 - Fax: (01666) 504508

e-mail: enquiries@troublehouse.co.uk - Website: www.troublehouse.co.uk

  🍷 **VISA** **AE** **MC**

	Wadworth 6X, Wadworth Henrys IPA

You might easily speed past this nondescript roadside inn, but you'd be missing some of the best pub food in England, known far and wide. Imagination and quiet finesse bring out some great natural combinations of flavours in classic and modern British recipes. These can be deliciously simple and satisfying, but more refined dishes lose none of their robust and moreish appeal. Grab a seat at one of the modest, chunky wooden tables in one of three low-beamed bars, with roaring fires and hop-trimmed beams: neat, down-to-earth and very welcoming, friendly service.

Food serving times:
Tuesday-Saturday:
12pm-2pm, 7pm-9.30pm
Sunday: 12pm-2pm
Closed 25 December
to 5 January
Prices:
Meals: a la carte 28.00/35.00

Typical Dishes

Roasted scallops with crayfish

Oxtail Bourguinon, creamy mash

Trouble House dessert plate

2mi Northeast on the A433. Parking.

Upper Oddington

060 Horse and Groom

Upper Oddington GL56 0XH

Tel.: (01451) 830584
e-mail: info@horseandgroom.uk.com · Website: www.horseandgroom.uk.com

 room   VISA

 Wye Valley Best, Hereford Pale Ale, Wickwar Cotswolds Way, Arkells 3B, Wye Valley Butty Bach, Barley Mole

More "well-kept" than "well-kept secret", this busy, part 16C former coaching inn loses nothing by its rural hamlet location. The interior is charming, its timbers and crackling fires distributed over a spacious three rooms; they're invariably buzzing as the staff weave from kitchen to table with honest, tasty home-made dishes. Service, mostly from efficient young travellers, is never less than warm and cordial. Those wanting to steer clear of Stow's heaving guesthouses can stay here – the single rooms have plenty of character, but their sloped ceilings and beams may prove a nuisance after a healthy intake of the inn's wet stuff!

Food serving times:
Monday-Sunday:
12pm-2pm, 6.30pm-9.30pm
Prices:
Meals: a la carte 18.00/25.00
7 rooms : 60.00/89.00

Typical Dishes

Crab beignets, mango & chilli salsa

Belly of pork, black pudding and apple jus

White chocolate tart

2mi East of Stow-on-the-Wold by A436. Parking.

Appley

061 **The Globe Inn**

Appley TA21 0HJ

Tel.: (01823) 672327

Website: www.theglobeinnappley.co.uk

Palmers Copper Ale and other guest ales - Butcombe Brunel, Butcombe Blond, Sharps Doom Bar, Cotleigh 25, Wadworth 6X

Cosy and traditional, even pleasantly old-fashioned in some ways, the inn's welcoming interior shows the influence of a genial man who clearly sees himself as custodian of the Globe as well as its chef and long-standing landlord. The building itself has origins in the 1400s, but there's nautical history too, in the pictures, prints and photos of the Titanic decorating one wall, and a touch of nostalgia in the display case of die-cast Dinky and Corgi cars and vans. Hard to fault for generosity, the tasty, substantial pub cooking often has a subtle international touch; service is well-organised and invariably polite. If the sun's out, lounge with lunch and beers in the garden before setting off on a walk near the Devon border; if it's not, you could always ask to book the skittle alley.

Food serving times:

Tuesday-Saturday and Bank Holiday Monday:
12pm-2pm, 7pm-9.30pm

Sunday: 12pm-2pm

Closed 25-26 December

Prices:

Meals: a la carte 16.00/25.00

6mi West of Wellington on A38 (Appley is signed). Parking.

Typical Dishes

Smoked haddock and bacon chowder

Monkfish and salmon, cream sauce

Banana pancake

Babcary

062 The Red Lion Inn

Babcary TA11 7ED
Tel.: (01458) 223230 - Fax: (01458) 224510

Teignworthy, Otter Ales, Yellow Hammer

Set to one side, the bar of the Red Lion Inn- complete with bar skittles- cedes pride of place to two spacious, airy lounges. One's more particularly given over to eating, but they share a contemporary country style: oriental rugs, neatly set, rustic wooden tables and framed paintings and Red Lion posters on the walls. It's not over-formal, and this clearly suits a lively crowd of lunchers, from local families to passers-by who were lucky enough to drop in on spec.; service might slow a fraction on the busiest days, but a young team stays positive and polite. Exciting menus and regularly changing blackboard feature contemporary combinations and locally reared Somerset beef.

Food serving times:
Monday-Saturday:
   12pm-2.30pm, 7pm-9.30pm
Sunday: 12pm-2.30pm
Closed 25 December
Prices:
Meals: a la carte 21.75/27.50

Typical Dishes

Fishcake, Hollandaise sauce

Herb crusted rack of lamb

Raspberry crème brûlée, almond shortcrust biscuit

4.5mi Northeast of Ilchester by A37. Parking.

407

Batcombe

063 The Three Horseshoes Inn 🛏

Batcombe BA4 6HE

Tel.: (01749) 850359 - Fax: (01749) 850615
e-mail: shirley@thethreehorseshoesinn.co.uk

  VISA

 Butcombe Bitter, Wadworth 6X, Bats in the Belfry (Blind Man's Brewery)

This delightfully set rural pub is reached in true country fashion: down twisty country lanes until you get to the village church. The long, low bar which gives The Three Horseshoes its internal character is distinguished by its beams and painted stone walls; an inglenook boasts a wood-burning stove, there are cosy, cushioned window seats and a wonderfully characterful snug. The menus are of the modern variety, and come with some interesting combinations. You can indulge in a pretty, converted barn dining room with exposed stone, while a back terrace is an ideal place to sit on the grass in summer and inhale the sweet Somerset air.

Food serving times:
Tuesday-Sunday:
    12pm-2pm, 7pm-9pm
Prices:
Meals: a la carte 20.00/30.00
🛏 **3 rooms :** 50.00/70.00

Signposted off the A359, midway between Castle Carey and Frome. Tucked away behind the church. Parking.

Typical Dishes

Moules marinières

Ham hock casserole, herb dumplings

3 mini traditionals

Corton Denham

064 The Queen's Arms 🛏️

Corton Denham DT9 4LR

Tel.: (01963) 220317
e-mail: relax@thequeens-arms.com · Website: www.thequeens-arms.com

 🍽 ▼ ✂ **VISA** **AE** **MC**

  Otter Bitter, Butcombe, Timothy Taylors Landlord and guest ales

Tucked away in a quiet village between the lovely town of Sherborne and the roaring A303 stands this pleasant 18th century stone built pub, personally run by young owners. Appearances can deceive: the traditional façade here hides an interior where the 'usual' rustic pubby staples have been pretty much jettisoned for a relaxed, contemporary, informal feel, typified by armchairs and sofas you can sink into while sipping your real ale or bottled beer, of which there is a fine worldwide range. British dishes using fine local produce form the backbone of the menus: you can eat in the bar or book for the smart adjacent dining room. There's a delightful rear terrace, too. Bedrooms are more than a cut above the pub norm, offering individually styled luxury with superb bathrooms.

Food serving times:
Monday-Sunday:
    12pm-3pm, 6pm-10pm
Prices:
Meals: a la carte 16.00/20.00
🛏️ **5 rooms :** 60.00/120.00

Typical Dishes

Pigeon breast, Puy lentils & parsnip crisps

Beer braised pheasant, crushed potatoes

Lemon curd pavlova

Parking. ⟩

Ditcheat

065 ## Manor House Inn

Ditcheat BA4 6RB
Tel.: (01749) 860276
Website: wwww.themanorhouseinn.co.uk

Butcombe, Bath Ales, Cottage Brewery, Sharp's

F ans of the turf are well catered for –
in both senses - at this characterful
part 17C ex-coaching inn near
Glastonbury. Not only can they tuck into
the Manor House's locally renowned
rustic fare, they can also sit by the
windows of the bar or restaurant and
watch a regular procession of horses and
jockeys making its way to the local
gallops. In the recently opened Sports Bar,
framed silks hang proudly: Ditcheat is
home to one of racing's top trainers Paul
Nichols. Diners can take their pick of
places to eat: apart from the flagged bar
with hatch and similarly traditional dining
room, there's a lawned garden for fine
weather. Food covers a pretty eclectic
range, from classic British staples to more
modern European influenced offerings.
There are pleasantly refurbished
bedrooms, and an enviable setting next to
the village's pretty St.Mary's church.

Food serving times:
Monday-Saturday:
12pm-2pm, 7pm-9.30pm
Sunday: 12pm-2pm
Closed meals 25 December
Prices:
Meals: a la carte 16.00/30.00
3 rooms : 50.00/80.00

Typical Dishes

Pan-fried breast of pigeon

Roast rack of lamb, parsnip
purée, red wine sauce

Local cheeses

4mi South of Shepton Mallet by A37
and minor road left. Parking.

Ilchester

066 Ilchester Arms

The Square, Ilchester BA22 8LN
Tel.: (01935) 840220 - Fax: (01935) 841353
Website: www.the-ilchester-arms-hotel.co.uk

Fuller's London Pride, Spitfire

First licensed in 1686, this impressive looking Somerset pub shows its age with appropriate dignity, the profusion of ivy on its exterior just adds a little more rural charm. It stands proudly in the village centre, a relaxing oasis from the hustle and bustle of nearby Yeovil. Public areas are relaxing and intimate, typified by two small lounges and an airy, wood decorated bar - like being down at the local, which many of the customers are. A bistro continues this informal theme, its daily changing blackboard menus have a hearty and familiar ring. At any given time you might try rich, rosemary scented lamb casserole with spring vegetables, confit of duck with garlic crust and cassoulet beans or seared calves liver with onions, bacon and mash. Sizable bedrooms have a good range of facilities.

Food serving times:
Monday-Saturday:
   12pm-2.30pm, 7pm-9.30pm
Sunday: 12pm-2.30pm
Closed 26 December
(bar lunch)
Prices:
Meals: a la carte 17.50/26.50
7 rooms : 60.00/75.00

Parking.

Typical Dishes
Smoked haddock and asparagus ravioli
Medallions of Venison, Port jus
Steamed chocolate, orange & walnut pudding

Kingsdon

067 Kingsdon Inn

Kingsdon TA11 7LG

Tel.: (01935) 840543

e-mail: robert@rhorler.freeserve.co.uk - Website: www.kingsdoninn.co.uk

 VISA M©

3 real ales from local breweries such as Otter, Bath Ales and Butcombe

This part 17C thatched inn knows how to pack 'em in. The best advice is: "Get here early!" Punters are drawn by the unadulterated charm of the place, as well as its rather handy position just off the A303 in a picturesque village near the attractive town of Somerton. It possesses bags of character: low bowed ceiling, wood burning stove, stripped pine built-in wall seat, scatter cushions and stone floors. Four snug, adjoining rooms provide dining options; there's a pleasant garden too. Traditional, popular dishes – and lots of them – show up on a busy looking blackboard menu: everything from whitebait to lambs liver to goats' cheese salad.

Food serving times:
Monday-Sunday:
   12pm-2pm, 7pm-9.30pm

Prices:
Meals: 12.20 (Sunday set lunch) and a la carte 14.00/ 26.00

2 rooms : 45.00/70.00

2.5 mi South East of Somerton on B3151. Parking.

Typical Dishes

Crab and crayfish Mornay

Roast duck, Somerset scrumpy sauce

Sticky ginger pudding, ginger ice cream

Long Sutton

068 The Devonshire Arms

Long Sutton TA10 9LP

Tel.: (01458) 241271 - Fax: (01458) 241037
e-mail: mail@thedevonshirearms.com - Website: www.thedevonshirearms.com

Teignmouth Reel Ale, Hopback Crop Circle, Bath Ales Spa

Rather prettily sited overlooking the green in an attractive village, The Devonshire Arms is a smart, creeper-clad 17C former hunting lodge. If the weather's in a clement mood, it's a toss-up whether to go inside or out, as to the rear there's a large come-hither walled garden as well as a suntrap of a terrace. Inside, all vestiges of period character have been usurped by modernity, in the shape of cavernous deep brown leather sofas which vie for space with tubby wood tables. At lunchtime you can choose between tapas menus or other light dishes. A more refined a la carte prevails at dinner. Fine ingredients are used to good effect on accomplished dishes employing precise cooking skills. Two of the bedrooms are over the courtyard: all are lovely and comfortable, with bold colour schemes, coir flooring, futon style beds and wicker loungers. Oh, smart digital TVs, too.

Food serving times:
Monday-Saturday:
  12pm-2.30pm, 7pm-9.30pm
Sunday: 12pm-2.30pm,
              7-9pm

Closed dinner Sunday
October-May
Prices:
Meals: a la carte 20.00/30.00
9 rooms : 60.00/120.00

4mi East of Langport by A372.
Parking.

Typical Dishes

Squid with red pepper, chilli and Puy lentils

Duck confit and rice noodles

Crème brûlée with passion fruit

Lovington

069 The Pilgrims at Lovington

Lovington BA7 7PT

Tel.: (01963) 240600

e-mail: thejools@btinternet.com - Website: www.thepilgrimsatlovington.co.uk

Cottage Champflower Ale

Y ou'd probably not stop here at first sight: Pilgrims doesn't look anything special from the outside. But its slogan – 'the pub that thinks it's a restaurant' – gives a hint of what to expect inside. Beyond the front door, there's a transformation. It does, indeed, have a smart, pleasant restaurant style: deep burgundy and exposed stone walls, coir mat flooring and bright, cheerful watercolours mostly by a local village artist. The bar isn't forgotten; it's traditional in character, with flag floors and low beams. Cookery books are piled on a piano and matchboxes from around the world decorate the walls. Menus, in the modern style, revel in interesting variations.

Food serving times:
Wednesday-Saturday:
    12pm-2.30pm, 7pm-9pm
Sunday: 12pm-2.30pm
Closed first week in May and
first 2 weeks in October

Prices:
Meals: a la carte 17.00/36.00

Typical Dishes

Mushroom tart

Monkfish and scallops with smoked bacon

West Country cheeses

4mi South West of Castle Cary by B3153 signposted Somerton and A371 on B3153. Parking.

Lower Vobster

070 The Vobster Inn

Lower Vobster BA3 5RJ

Tel.: (01373) 812920 - Fax: (01373) 812920
e-mail: rafael.davila@btopenworld.com

Butcombe Bitter, Butcombe Blonde and various guests ales

Very much the centre of its tiny Somerset village, the Vobster Inn, run by a husband and wife team, takes its duty seriously and does its best to keep everyone happy, from young families and older couples, out enjoying the sun at the terrace tables, to the unhurried neighbours enjoying a slow pint inside. Adjoining the bar, a long lounge serves as the restaurant, its walls painted with grapes and lined with posters, labels, wine racks and even old wine cases. Sensibly allowing room for market-fresh specials, fish and seafood are always on the menu and there's always a good selection of hand-crafted West Country cheeses on offer.

Food serving times:
Monday-Saturday:
     12pm-3pm, 7pm-11pm
Sunday: 12pm-4pm
Closed 25-26 December, also Sunday (dinner) and Monday (except bank holidays)
- Seafood -
Prices:
Meals: a la carte 18.00/28.00

Typical Dishes

Rabbit and pistachio terrine

Sea bass with saffron rissotto

Cinnamon sugar dusted banana fritter

From Frome head northwest to Radstock on the A362. Vobster is signposted approx 5.5mi off the A362. Parking.

Luxborough

071 The Royal Oak Inn of Luxborough

Exmoor National Park, Luxborough TA23 0SH

Tel.: (01984) 640319 - Fax: (01984) 641561
e-mail: info@theroyaloakinnluxborough.co.uk - Website: www.theroyaloakinnluxborough.co.uk

 VISA **M©**

Cotleigh Tawny, Palmers IPA and 200, Exmoor Gold, Exmoor
Wildcat

I n a fold of the rolling Brendon Hills, surrounded by picture postcard cottages, the Royal Oak is in the most idyllic position possible. Once you've located the pub among the many lanes of the area, step into a low beamed and log fired bar featuring an impishly accurate cartoon of one of the regulars (who may well be sitting there with pipe and pint). Invitingly furnished dining rooms in deep olive tones lead off from here; another rustic bar keeps them company and the atmosphere carries over from here. Suppliers knock at the front door with their produce, so there's no shortage of local inspiration: chicken with bacon lardons, cider, cream and local apple brandy is a satisfying blend of West Country flavours. There are a dozen en-suite bedrooms for those wishing to stay on.

Food serving times:
Monday-Sunday:
12pm-2pm, 7pm-9pm
Closed 25 December
Prices:
Meals: a la carte 15.00/25.00
10 rooms : 55.00/85.00

Typical Dishes

Filo basket of mussels

Roast rack of Exmoor lamb

Mango cheesecake

Luxborough is signed off A39 East of Minehead or off B3224 Exford to Taunton road. Parking

Mells

072 The Talbot Inn

Selwood St, Mells BA11 3PN

Tel.: (01373) 812254 - Fax: (01373) 813599
e-mail: roger@talbotinn.com - Website: www.talbotinn.com

Butcombe Bitter Plus, Fullers London Pride

This utterly charming 15C stone-built coaching inn boasts an immediate impact with its cobbled courtyard and walled garden with pétanque piste and vine-covered pergola. The effect continues in a pleasant, intimate main bar, where dried hops cling to the beams and green candles flicker in old wine bottles. Here, indulge in hearty, traditional bar meals with daily changing blackboard dishes or a more serious dinner menu with fish specials from Brixham. You can also drink in a large tythe barn, its ancient character recently enhanced by a mural depicting life in Mells through the ages. Bright, pretty, individually appointed bedrooms make a night's stopover worthwhile.

Food serving times:
Monday-Sunday:
    12pm-2pm, 6.45pm-11pm
Prices:
Meals: a la carte 23.00/30.00
8 rooms : 65.00/145.00

Typical Dishes

Pate with spiced apple chutney

Gressingham duck, chilli plum sauce and celeriac mash

Lemon meringue pie

4mi West of Frome. Parking. 〉〉

Montacute

073 Phelips Arms

The Borough, Montacute TA15 6XB

Tel.: (01935) 822557 - Fax: (01935) 822557
e-mail: info@phelips.co.uk - Website: www.phelipsarms.co.uk

Palmers IPA, Palmers Zoo and Palmers Copper Ales

Montacute derives most of its fame from historic Montacute House, owned by the National Trust (100 yards down the road), but this attractive part-17C sand coloured inn provides another reason to turn off the A303. It's a good, traditional pub but very small - there are only 11 tables. Bright lights and swirly carpet are offset with dark wood tables and chairs given a modern lift by bright red and blue curtains and cushions with the owner's own photos and paintings displayed on the walls. The contemporary touches carry over to the cooking, which boasts some interesting, eclectic choices which are cooked to perfection and well presented. Long back garden with benches.

Food serving times:
Tuesday-Thursday:
   12pm-2pm, 6.30pm-9pm
Sunday: 12pm-2.30pm
Closed 1 week in January
Prices:
Meals: a la carte 15.00/25.00
🛏 **3 rooms :** 55.00/75.00

Typical Dishes

Jerusalem artichoke and scallop soup

Braised Seville orange beef, horseradish dumplings

Profiteroles

5mi Northwest of Yeovil by A3088 (Montacute is signposted). Public parking in the square in front of the pub.

South Cadbury

 074 **The Camelot**

Chapel Rd, South Cadbury BU22 7EX

Tel.: (01963) 440448 - Fax: (01963) 441462

e-mail: enquiries@thecamelot.co.uk - Website: www.thecamelot.co.uk

 🕇🕇 🍷 ⇔ **VISA** **MC**

Sharp's Doombar and 2 guest beers

So named because (allegedly) a hill in Cadbury is the original site of King Arthur's Camelot. True or not, one thing's for sure…good food here is no myth. Owned by the Montgomery family – well known in these parts for producing award-winning cheeses for nearly 100 years – this little pub was modernised in 2004 to give it a light, airy, uncluttered ambience, enhanced by stylish local artwork on the walls. Modish wood tables are dotted about and laid for eating, but there's still plenty of space for locals to enjoy a pint; in fact, they've restored the skittle alley here. Lunch features home-made pies and sandwiches, whereas at night a distinctly more modern selection, precisely cooked with local produce and offering great value, tempts the palate: there's a large first-floor area resembling a restaurant catering for the influx of weekend diners.

Food serving times:
Monday-Sunday:
    12pm-2.30pm, 7pm-9pm
Prices:
Meals: a la carte 22.50/35.90

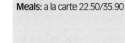

4.5mi South of Castle Cary by B3152 off A359. Parking.

Typical Dishes

Camelot smoked garlic

Rack of lamb, cranberry jus

Montgomery cheese plate

Stanton Wick

075 ## Carpenters Arms 🛏

Stanton Wick BS39 4BX

Tel.: (01761) 490202 - Fax: (01761) 490763
e-mail: carpenters@buccaneer.co.uk - Website: www.the-carpenters-arms.co.uk

 🕸 🍷 ⚭room 🚫 **VISA** **AE** **①** **⑩⑨**

🍺 *Butcombe, Wadworth 6X, Courage Best*

The Carpenters Arms is actually a group of 300-year old converted miners' cottages. Now it glows with a pubby contentment, typified by dark wooden furniture, candles in wine bottles, built-in wall seats and, of course, the original exposed stone walls. A big log fire roars in winter. Its long, low exterior is offset with hanging baskets, bright flowers and the tranquility of the surrounding countryside. For diners, a snug inner "parlour" awaits with fresh flowers on the tables and beams above. Modern cooking prevails, proof of popularity confirmed by the number of tables taken. Upstairs: sizable, pine furnished bedrooms in subtle floral patterns and modern bathrooms.

Food serving times:
Monday-Saturday:
12pm-2pm, 7pm-10pm
Sunday:
12pm-2.30pm, 7pm-9pm
Closed dinner 25-26 December
Prices:
Meals: a la carte 19.00/27.00
🛏 **12 rooms :** 67.00/95.00

Typical Dishes

Fried squid, cucumber and tomato salad

Steak, mushroom and Butcombe Ale pie

Bread and butter pudding

9mi South of Bristol (just off the A37) signposted off A368. Parking.

Tarr Steps

076 **Tarr Farm Inn**

Tarr Steps TA22 9PY
Tel.: (01643) 851507 - Fax: (01643) 851111
e-mail: enquiries@tarrfarm.co.uk - Website: www.tarrfarm.co.uk

 🍷 VISA ⓜ©

 Exmoor Ale, Fullers London Pride.

The old clapper bridge at Tarr Steps has crossed the River Barle since time immemorial, and Tarr Farm has had privileged access to this unchanging tranquillity since the Elizabethan age. In the heart of Exmoor, it's one of the more gloriously remote inns of the West Country, and its neat garden is a fine spot to absorb the peaceful surroundings. Your rapture may well continue when you step inside…there's a hugely characterful and cosy beamed bar serving Exmoor ales. Typical pubby lunchtime dishes give way to a comprehensive evening menu of accomplished, interesting dishes featuring a wealth of fine local produce, served in the bar or intimate restaurant. Bedrooms here are special, too. Comfy, spacious and furnished in an eye-catching way, they offer every conceivable luxury, while, for the more adventurous, a host of Exmoor outdoor pursuits are on the doorstep, and can be arranged by the hosts.

Food serving times:
Monday-Sunday:
   12pm-3pm, 6.30pm-9.30pm
Closed first 10 days in February
Prices:
Meals: a la carte 18.00/27.00
🛏 **9 rooms :** 80.00/130.00

Signed off B3223 Dulverton to Exford road. Parking.

Typical Dishes

Seared scallops, cauliflower purée

Fillet of Exmoor beef with tomato tart Tatin

Lemongrass pannacotta

Triscombe

077   **The Blue Ball Inn** 🛏

Triscombe TA4 3HE

Tel.: (01984) 618242 - Fax: (01984) 618371
e-mail: info@blueballinn.co.uk - Website: www.blueballinn.co.uk

 🍷 **VISA** 💳

Cotleigh's Tawny and 2 other beers including Cotleigh, Exmoor, Otter, Butcombe, St Austell

A walk in the gorgeous Quantocks requires sustenance along the way, so arm yourself with a map and pitch up at the Blue Ball in good time for lunch. It's a wonderfully inviting place: you can't go far wrong with a 15C thatched and stone-built former stables. There are exposed roof timbers, wooden floors and a large picture window with beautiful views over the surrounding countryside. The menus are imaginative, wide ranging and full of local ingredients. Hungry ramblers can get chunky baguettes at lunchtime; more serious diners can feast on modern and traditional British pub classics. Two modern, stylish and open-plan bedrooms with luxury bathrooms are set in what was the original pub next door.

Food serving times:
Monday-Sunday:
    12pm-2pm, 7pm-9pm
Closed 25 December
(booking essential)
Prices:
Meals: a la carte 20.00/30.00
🛏 **2 rooms :** 40.00/85.00

Typical Dishes

Cornish crab gazpacho
Old Castle saddleback pork
Dark chocolate pudding

4.5mi North of Bishops Lydeard by A358. Parking.

Wedmore

078 The Sexey's Arms

Sexey's Road, Wedmore BS28 4NT

Tel.: (01934) 712487 - Fax: (01934) 712447
e-mail: enquiries@thesexeysarms.co.uk - Website: www.thesexeysarms.co.uk

 VISA AE MC

Butcombe and guest ale - changing regularly

First of all, let's clear up the name. Hugh Sexey was a Chancellor of the Exchequer to Queen Elizabeth I who gave the hamlet of Blackford to him in lieu of his services: local schools are also named after him. So that's sorted. The pub was originally a group of 16C cottages that evolved into a cider house, then a hostelry. Exuding much typical pubby character, the bar's split between a locals snug with dartboard and the dining section where you can either eat at the bar or in an informal restaurant with its tiled floor, beams, inglenook fireplaces and exposed stone walls. Whichever you decide upon, the menu's the same: modern classics as well as simpler pub fare with a blackboard listing the daily and fish specials. Thierry, the keen French owner/chef, cooks with precision and skill.

Food serving times:
Tuesday-Thursday:
12-2pm, 7-9pm,
Friday-Saturday:
12-2pm, 7-9.30pm
Sunday: 12-2pm
Prices:
Meals: a la carte 19.00/30.00

Typical Dishes

Tartlet of sweet potato and goat's cheese

Fillet of Exmoor venison

Molten chocolate & rum pudding

1.75mi West on B3139. Parking.

West Bagborough

079 The Rising Sun Inn

West Bagborough TA4 3EF

Tel.: (01823) 432575

e-mail: rob@theriser.co.uk - Website: www.theriser.co.uk

VISA

Cotleigh Tawny, Cotleigh 25, Butcombe Gold, Exmoor Fox, Fuller's London Pride

G rab a pint, sit for a while on one of the outside benches hard up against the front of this pretty stone pub, and take in the invigorating air of one of Somerset's most elevated and delightfully located pubs: indeed, it feels like the whole village is on the verge of dropping off the side of the Quantocks. The Rising Sun has 16th century origins, but was rebuilt a few years ago after a fire that lit up the surrounding hillside. There's oak in the beams and slate on the floors, but a modern feel prevails. It's not a big place, and you'll find locals at the bar in close proximity to diners from far afield. A smart upstairs room has exposed trusses, local artwork and a wonderful rural view from big windows. Light, traditional pub lunches give way in the evening to more interesting modern dishes with fresh Somerset ingredients. Wake up to a stylish bedroom with exposed beams.

Food serving times:
Tuesday-Saturday:
    12pm-2pm, 7pm-9pm
Sunday: 12pm-2pm
Bank Holiday Monday:
    12pm-2pm, 7pm-9pm
Prices:
Meals: a la carte 21.00/26.00
🛏 **2 rooms :** 75.00/85.00

Typical Dishes

Game terrine, piccalilli

Quantock duck breast and roasted plums

Meringue, Whisky cream and raspberries

10.5mi North West of Taunton off A358. Parking in the road.

Winsford

080 The Royal Oak Inn

Exmoor National Park, Winsford TA24 7JE

Tel.: (01643) 851455 - Fax: (01643) 851009
e-mail: enquiries@royaloak-somerset.co.uk - Website: www.royaloak-somerset.co.uk

VISA AE MC

Exmoor Ale, Exmoor Stag, Exmoor Beast, Butcombe, Spitfire and 2 guest ales

Facing the shaded green and its trim cottages, the old Royal Oak, its thatched roof turned and folded, stands at the heart of Winsford, a charming village best known for its little interlacing streams and its old packhorse bridge across the River Exe. Inside the pub, one cosy lounge leads into another, their original rural style proudly preserved, to the delight of visitors from out of town; cushioned benches are grouped to form intimate little booths. Out-and-out English cooking seems right at home here, and a no-nonsense menu sticks to the classics, from lunchtime pies and sandwiches in the bar to generous plates of steak and kidney pudding with tasty rhubarb crumble and cream to follow. After lunch, Exmoor beckons, with mile upon mile of heather upland and wooded valleys to be explored.

Food serving times:
Monday-Sunday:
12pm-8pm, 8.30pm-11pm
Prices:
Meals: a la carte 15.00/75.00
12 rooms : 75.00/136.00

Typical Dishes

Parma ham with balsamic chocolate

Halibut, crayfish tails and glazed apple

Poached pears and vanilla ice

5mi North of Dulverston by B3223. Opposite the village green. Parking.

Axford

081 The Red Lion Inn

Axford SN8 2HA

Tel.: (01672) 520271

e-mail: info@redlionaxford.com - Website: www.redlionaxford.com

🍷 🥄 **VISA** Ⓜ️Ⓒ

Ramsbury Gold, Hook Norton Best and guest ales from Cottage Brewing Company and Hopback Brewery

This brick-and-flint inn of 17C pedigree immediately impresses as a warm and welcoming place. The top area is a lovely lounge bar with roaring fire and a gaggle of contented smokers, and there are fresh flowers on the main bar. Throughout the remainder of the inn a wide range of pictures by local artists is on sale. The blackboard choice of dishes is split into starters, mains and fish and are, largely speaking, from a traditional base. They're served in either the neatly kept dining room, full of old and new silver and china jostling for attention, or conservatory, where tankards and water jugs hang beseechingly from the ceiling. There's one more blackboard, announcing wines by the glass, and when the scoffing and quaffing are done, diners are invited to fill in a card and be kept informed on future menus and events.

Food serving times:
Monday-Sunday:
12pm-2pm, 7pm-9pm
Closed 25 December
Prices:
Meals: a la carte 18.50/28.50

4mi East of Marlborough; follow signs for Axford. Parking. ➤➤

Typical Dishes

Crab and prawn fishcakes

Rack of lamb,
blackcurrant and rosemary

Strawberry and balsamic
semi-freddo

Box

082 **The Northey**

Bath Rd, Box SN13 8AE

Tel.: (01225) 742333 - Fax: (01225) 742333
e-mail: ohhcompany@aol.com - Website: www.ohh.org.uk

Wadworth 6X, IPA

There's not really anything remarkable about this roadside pub, at least, not from the outside. It's worth pulling over all the same, though. A thorough makeover has worked wonders on the old, slightly charmless interior and, while the bar remains, with a few sofas, much of the space is given over to simply set dining tables. It's less of a drinking "local" than it was before, but you can hardly blame the friendly team at The Northey for sticking to what they do best: well-weighed flavours are a constant theme in their appetising, well-judged dishes, which are served with tidy efficiency, and all for a very fair price. You could just have a sandwich but, with good modern cooking for the asking, you might feel you were missing out.

Food serving times:
Sunday-Thursday:
7pm-9.30pm
Friday-Saturday:
7pm-10pm
Closed 25-26 December,
31 December (dinner)
and 1 January (dinner)
Prices:
Meals: a la carte 20.00/30.00

Typical Dishes

Peppered duck breast, mango salad

Sea bass & mussels, rocket mash

Fig and frangipane tart

4,75 mi from Bath on A4. Parking.

427

Burcombe

083 The Ship Inn

Burcombe Lane, Burcombe SP2 0EJ

Tel.: (01722) 743182

e-mail: theshipburcombe@mail.com - Website: www.theshipburcombe.co.uk

Wadworth 6X, Courage Best, Flowers IPA

Looking traditional and well cared-for, the trim, part 17C Ship Inn lives up to expectations on the inside. Pass under the model of a man o' war in full sail, fixed in a gabled niche above the door, and into a nicely modernised open-plan bar: old exposed timbers and open fires are still in place, and so too is the rural atmosphere you'd expect. Diners and drinkers take their seats where they like and a fresh and tasty seasonal menu with a modern touch, together with traditional classics and a blackboard full of specials, offers plenty of choice: regular themed dinners and summer barbecues lend further variety. But one of the nicest things about the Ship is its lovely rear garden which runs down to a tributary of the river Nadder – find a table in the sun and make yourself comfortable.

Food serving times:
Monday-Thursday:
  12pm-2.30pm, 6.30pm-9pm
Friday-Saturday:
  12pm-2.30pm,
  6.30pm-9.30pm
Sunday: 12pm-2.30pm,
  7pm-9pm
Closed 2 weeks in January
Prices:
Meals: a la carte 17.95/29.40

Typical Dishes

Apple, crab and avocado remoulade

Pan fried pork cutlet with ginger sweet potato mash

Trio of chocolate desserts

5,25 mi West of Salisbury by the A36 off A30. Parking.

Codford St Mary

084 George

High St, Codford St Mary BA12 0NG

Tel.: (01985) 850270

Website: www.thegeorgecodford.co.uk

 room **VISA**

Timothy Taylor's Landlord, Hook Norton Hooky and 1 guest ale - Ringwood Best

The wild expanse of Salisbury Plain stretches away from this whitewashed 18C pub-hotel in a pretty village. Culture prevails in the Woolstone Theatre opposite; The George, meanwhile, makes a successful appeal to other senses. Although not the place for a cosy meal à deux - there are no beams or cosy decor - the strength of this place lies in the food. The experienced chef-patron uses seasonally changing, locally-sourced ingredients with daily specials appearing on a blackboard. Lunch menus are simpler in style and give way to a concise, regularly changing evening menu. Whet the appetite first by relaxing with a drink and a magazine in the comfortable lounge. If thoughts of the dark Plain are too much to contemplate at night, stay in one of their clean, simple bedrooms.

Food serving times:

Wednesday-Saturday and Monday:
12pm-2pm, 7pm-9pm

Sunday: 7pm-9pm

Closed Sunday dinner and Tuesday

Prices:

Meals: a la carte 18.00/35.00

3 rooms : 45.00/70.00

Typical Dishes

Brixham scallops, Bloody Mary dressing

Salmon, basil mash and red pepper fondant

Vanilla poached pear

Village signposted off the A36, southeast of Warminster, or use the A303 which is close by. Parking.

Corsley

085 The Cross Keys

Lyes Green, Corsley BA12 7PB
Tel.: (01373) 832406 - Fax: (01373) 832934
Website: www.crosskeysatcorsley.com

 VISA AE MC

Henry's IPA, Wadworth 6X, JCB, Archers and guest beers

A typically rural pub in a typically rural area: all the credentials for a satisfying experience in deepest Wiltshire. The owners of this charming 14th century pub go out of their way to create a warm, relaxed feel, with the bright, colourful walls filled with local photos and prints of outdoor pursuits, the open fires and the friendly, even lightly jokey service. Choose between dining areas either embellished by fresh flowers or tubby candles. Either way you'll eat at scrubbed tables from an extensive menu featured on three blackboards. Dishes are keenly priced, freshly prepared, and very tasty, carefully utilising local supplies and suppliers. Try something from the notable fish range.

Food serving times:
Monday-Saturday:
    12pm-2pm, 7pm-9.30pm
Sunday: 7.15pm-9pm
Closed 25, 26 December (evening) and 1 January (evening)
Prices:
Meals: a la carte 15.25/25.75

Typical Dishes

King scallops with smoked bacon

Wild venison, redcurrant jus

White chocolate and Cointreau cheesecake

Midway between Frome and Warminster on A362; pub is signed. Parking.

Donhead St Andrew

086 Forester Inn

Lower St, Donhead St Andrew SP7 9EE

Tel.: (01747) 828038 - Fax: (01747) 828050

e-mail: enquiries@foresterinndonheadstandrew.co.uk - Website: www.foresterinndonheadstandrew.co.uk

   VISA

 Ringwood, Sharp's Doombar, Wadsworth 6X, Donhead Bitter

I f you've a penchant for stone-built, thatched pubs with 13th century origins, then this most definitely is the place for you. The Forester is tucked away in a quaint village on the Dorset/Wiltshire border, and its beguiling exterior is enhanced by a small garden and lovely terraced area that surrounds one of its sides. All that's missing is the sea… The main bar is just like you'd expect: beamed, exposed stone walls, large inglenooks; with an attractive extension which resembles the interior of a barn: a big space with exposed roof trusses and doors and windows out onto the terrace. Menus here offer ample choice, and locally sourced ingredients make a plentiful showing; cooking is firmly in the modern bracket. Upstairs, the spacious bedrooms are done out in a pleasant contemporary style – a surprising juxtaposition to the pub's more rustic charms.

Food serving times:

Monday-Saturday:
12pm-2pm, 6.30pm-9pm

Sunday: 12pm-2pm, 7pm-9pm

Prices:

Meals: a la carte 20.00/30.00

2 rooms : 57.50/110.00

5 mi East of Shaftesbury by A30. Parking.

Typical Dishes

Foie gras terrine

Roast saddle of venison, loganberry and sloe jus

Blackberry and white chocolate soufflé

Heytesbury

087 The Angel Inn

High St, Heytesbury BA12 0ED

Tel.: (01985) 840330 - Fax: (01985) 840930

e-mail: admin@theangelheytesbury.co.uk - Website: www.theangelheytesbury.co.uk

VISA **MC**

Moorlands, Greene King IPA, Smiles, 6X

In a pretty village on the edge of Salisbury Plain stands this attractive roadside 17C inn. There's a delightful courtyard terrace and stylish, refurbished ground floor, boasting a cosy lounge with soft leather tub seats, roaring fire, and, further along, a snug though spacious bar. To one side, an elegant, contemporary restaurant completes the picture. Modern pub classics go down well at lunch, as you would expect but, in the evening, things move on with a particularly interesting à la carte that's well prepared and cooked with precision with steak a speciality. Staying overnight is a wise move here. Cosy, well-appointed bedrooms have been undergoing refurbishment.

Food serving times:
Monday-Saturday:
  12pm-2.30pm, 7pm-9.30pm
Sunday: 12pm-3pm,
          7pm-9.30pm
Closed meals 25 December
Prices:
Meals: 16.95 (set price lunch) and a la carte 25.00/35.00
8 rooms : 60.00/75.00

Typical Dishes

Peppered beef carpaccio

Fillet of local venison, roast salsify and pepper sauce

Lemon posset

On A36 4 mi Southwest of Warminster by B3414, or off A303. Parking.

Hindon

088 The Lamb Inn

High St, Hindon SP3 6DP

Tel.: (01747) 820573 - Fax: (01747) 820605
e-mail: info@lambathindon.co.uk - Website: www.lambathindon.co.uk

Young's Bitter, Young's Special and 2 guest ales

The Lamb has a substantial reputation for feeding travellers as it used to be a much-frequented coaching inn. The 21st century sees it adequately keeping up the tradition: its attractive creeper-clad façade is the destination for a steady stream of hungry diners, many of them passing nearby on their way to the West Country. Conveniently set just off the A303, it has a most beguiling interior of deep burgundy walls, wood and flagged floors, rafters, a gallery's worth of pictures, and higgledy-piggledy tables and chairs filling every conceivable space. A large blackboard menu forms the core of the dishes offered: expect game and traditional English fare, peppered with lighter and more traditional pub favourites. As befits an inn, there are 14 bedrooms pleasantly furnished and not without some character…especially their tartan carpets.

Food serving times:
Monday-Saturday:
12pm-2.30pm,
6.30pm-9.30pm

Prices:
Meals: a la carte 25.00/35.00
14 rooms : 70.00/99.00

12mi West of Wilton by A30 and B3089. Parking.

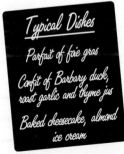

Typical Dishes

Parfait of foie gras

Confit of Barbary duck, roast garlic and thyme jus

Baked cheesecake, almond ice cream

Holt

089 The Tollgate Inn 🛏

Ham Green, Holt BA14 6PX

Tel.: (01225) 782326 · Fax: (01225) 782805
e-mail: alison@tollgateholt.co.uk · Website: www.tollgateholt.co.uk

 🍷 ⇥✕ **VISA** Ⓜ②

> *Tunnel Vision (Box Brewery), Pitchfork (RCG Brewery), Blind House (Box Brewery), Godfather (Itchen Valley Brewery)*

Despite its rather noisy location at a busy road junction, the locals of Holt have made this hearty old pub of Bath stone a wonderfully friendly place to be. Conviviality stretches across all areas, aided and abetted by strategically placed sofas and a log-burning stove. No one seems in a rush as they linger over newspapers and magazines. If and when you decide to eat you have a choice of two venues. A cosy room adjacent to the bar offers a traditional feel, while upstairs, in a former chapel, is a more formal restaurant with original chapel windows and lofty timbers. Local ingredients are proudly advertised on the menus, and dishes exhibit distinctly modern overtures. Bedrooms have a more traditional outlook, but are cosy and comfortable.

Food serving times:
Tuesday-Saturday:
  12pm-2pm, 7pm-9pm
Sunday: 12pm-2pm
Closed 25-26 December and 1 January

Prices:
Meals: 12.95 (fixed price lunch) and a la carte 22.00/32.00
🛏 **4 rooms :** 50.00/95.00

Typical Dishes

Foie gras terrine

Venison with red cabbage, Madeira jus

Trio of vanilla

On B3107 midway between Bradford-on-Avon and Melksham. Parking.

Marden

090 The Millstream

Marden SN10 3RH

Tel.: (01380) 848308 - Fax: (01380) 848337
e-mail: mail@the-millstream.co.uk - Website: www.the-millstream.co.uk

  VISA

Wadworths JCB, Bishop's Tipple, 6X, Henry's IPA, Summersault

Look across the delightful garden with its unusual peacock sculpture to the river Avon from this recently enlarged, Vale of Pewsey pub. The pastoral delights to be enjoyed here are timeless; inside an appealing refurbishment has taken place: champagne is served by the glass in a bar that stays open all day. This old pub's recent makeover has nevertheless left it with much original character: pale beams, thick wattle walls in a mustard palette, log burners and antiques enliven the open-plan section. There are several dining areas, with vertical beams acting as dividers. Tables are in antique wood but the menus are of more recent vintage: if you need help, the bubbly owner is only too keen to please. Much of the local produce is organic and fish is fresh from Looe.

Food serving times:
Tuesday-Sunday and Bank Holiday Monday:
   12pm-3pm, 7pm-9.30pm
Closed 25 December

Prices:
Meals: 18.00 (set price lunch (Tuesday-Friday)) and a la carte 22.00/28.00

6.5mi Southeast of Devizes by A342 and minor road North. Parking.

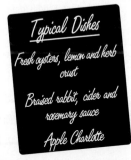

Typical Dishes

Fresh oysters, lemon and herb crust

Braised rabbit, cider and rosemary sauce

Apple Charlotte

Oaksey

091 ## The Wheatsheaf at Oaksey

Wheatsheaf Lane, Oaksey SN16 9TB
Tel.: (01666) 577348

 Hook Norton Best Bitter, Bath Gem, Courage Best, Deuchars

Neatly flanked by the attractive trio of Malmesbury, Tetbury and Cirencester, this charming little inn reflects the minimalist appeal of the gloriously rural village from which it takes its name. There's lots of pubby character here: the original bar in situ, solid beams, wood floor, and exposed walls of stone decorated with farming implements above an inglenook fire. Rubbing shoulders with locals having a pint, you can eat at the simple tables or repair for a touch more comfort to the rear of the bar where a hint of modernisation has taken place. A tiny front terrace is popular in clement weather. Food is important here. Menus offer a concise choice of simple lunch fare to far more ambitious modern British dishes cooked with care and accomplished assurance. For the athletic, there's a skittle alley across the road!

Food serving times:
Tuesday-Saturday:
 12pm-2pm, 6.30pm-9.30pm
Sunday: 12pm-3pm
Prices:
Meals: 15.95 (fixed price lunch or dinner) and a la carte 21.00/27.00

5.5mi North of Malmesbury; signed off A429. Parking.

Typical Dishes

Cornish crab cake

Duck breast, Parmesan mash

Cinnamon pannacotta, apple spring roll

Rowde

092 The George & Dragon

High Street, Rowde SN10 2PN

Tel.: (01380) 723053
e-mail: thegandd@tiscali.co.uk

 VISA ⓜ©

Butcombe Bitter, Ringwood 49er, Nicks, Holymoly, Fuller's London Pride

The lazy waters of the nearby Kennet and Avon Canal create the ideal mood for a visit to this divinely characterful pub in the Vale of Pewsey. Its epicentre is a gorgeous stone fireplace crackling heartily in the darker months. The low timbered ceiling just adds to the feeling of rich warmth; outside, summer sunshine can be enjoyed in a smart little garden. There are two small areas in which to dine - adjacent to the fire or in the dining room - but either way, you can't go wrong, but be sure to book as it gets very busy. Keenly-priced menus place the emphasis on plenty of daily changing specials, and the cooking is simple, robust and classic, with the emphasis on seafood specialities. As well as good value menus, you can also rely on polite, friendly service from the young owners.

Food serving times:
Tuesday-Friay:
    12pm-3pm, 7pm-11pm
Saturday: 12pm-4pm,
    7-11pm
Sunday: 12pm-4pm
Closed 1-8 January
(booking essential)
Prices:
Meals: 15.50 (fixed price lunch) and a la carte 20.00/33.50

Typical Dishes

Scallop and black pudding brochette

Wild sea bass, soy and ginger

Apple and rhubarb crumble, clotted cream

Just North of Devizes on A342. Parking.

Salisbury

093 The Haunch of Venison

1 Minster St, Salisbury SP1 1TB

Tel.: (01772) 411313 - Fax: (01772) 341774
e-mail: oneminsterst@aol.com - Website: www.oneminsterstreet.co.uk

 VISA Ⓜⓒ

6X, Best Courage

Most people come to Salisbury to visit the Cathedral; locals stay in the city to frequent The Haunch – they've been doing it since the 14th century when its first recorded use was to house craftsmen working on the spire. It's an immensely charming and characterful place. Its huge oak beams pre-date even the building itself and are believed to originate from early sailing vessels. Half way up the stairs is 'The House of Lords', once used to accommodate higher clergy, now a snug for private parties, where an old bread oven, with iron gate, keeps guard of a mummified hand! The ground floor bar has its own charms: unique floor with former Choristers tiles and bar top completely made of pewter. The main dining room, 'One Minster Street', on the first floor, has bags of individuality including original wobbly ceilings. Menus are eclectic, drawn from past and modern eras, served on lovely polished wooden tables.

Food serving times:
Monday-Thursday:
   12pm-2.30pm, 6pm-9.30pm
Friday-Saturday:
   12pm-2.30pm, 6pm-10pm
Prices:
Meals: 9.90/9.90 and a la carte 15.00/40.00

Typical Dishes

Haddock fishcake

Venison sausage with mash, red onion marmalade

Rhubarb, apple and lingonberry crumble

In the city centre; south of the bus station.

Semington

094 The Lamb on the Strand

99 The Strand, Semington BA14 6LL

Tel.: (01380) 870263 - Fax: (01380) 871203
e-mail: philip@cbcc.fsworld.co.uk

🍷 VISA AE M©

Butcombe Bitter, Ringwood Best, C Wells Bombardier, Shepherd Neame Spitfire, Otter Ale, Hidden Brewery, Palmers IPA

This ivy clad, red brick inn is a rather diverting attraction on the busy road out of Trowbridge. It has a characterful feel, its 18C origins typified by the low beams; a woodburner and log fire adds to the pleasing ambience. A series of pleasantly furnished rooms affords lots of space to relax with a pint of real ale or a glass of wine from the landlord's carefully selected list. If the weather's good, eat outside in the attractive walled garden. Menus are traditional and extensive; consistently fresh food is served with abundant use of local produce: the mouth-watering cheese pudding is a sure-fire hit. Service at this family-run establishment is invariably efficient, friendly and helpful.

Food serving times:
Monday-Saturday:
   12pm-2pm, 6.30pm-9pm
Sunday: 12pm-2pm
Closed 25 December and 1 January
(booking essential)
Prices:
Meals: a la carte 18.00/22.00

Typical Dishes

Roast tomato, red onion and Mozzarella tartlet

Game casserole, vegetables and new potatoes

Pear and almond tart

Between Trowbridge and Devizes on A361 near Semington village. Parking.

Stourton

095 ## The Spread Eagle Inn
Church Lawn, Stourton BA12 6QE
Tel.: (01747) 840954
Website: www.spreadeagleinn.com

Kilmington (local)

Stourhead House is a superb National Trust property and its gardens are rightly acknowledged as amongst the best in England. Not so well known is this attractive 18C inn tucked away in a charming courtyard at the end of the invigorating circular walk round the grounds. There are three rooms to settle into: one at the front with a bar, and two to the rear, larger and pleasantly appointed with rough wooden tables and chairs and typical 18C styling, set off by deep burgundy coir floor coverings and even a few sofas. It all gets very busy at lunchtimes as visitors to the gardens arrive for sustenance, and simple menus reflect this; evenings take on a more serious aspect, with a la carte menus of locally sourced ingredients. The five bedrooms offer simple comforts – they're a great idea for those who want to enjoy the estate at a less hurried pace!

Food serving times:
Monday-Sunday:
   12pm-3pm, 7pm-9pm
Prices:
Meals: 22.00 (set price dinner) and a la carte 19.20/22.00
5 rooms : 60.00/98.00

Typical Dishes

Goat's cheese mousse, pear & walnut salad

Loin of Old Spot pork, parsnip purée

Treacle tart and clotted cream

4mi North East of Wincanton by A303 and B3092 North. Parking.

Upton Scudamore

096 The Angel Inn 🛏

Upton Scudamore BA12 0AG

Tel.: (01985) 213225 - Fax: (01985) 218182
e-mail: mail@theangelinn.co.uk - Website: www.theangelinn.co.uk

Wadworth 6X, Butcombe and guest ales

To the east the vast expanses of Salisbury Plain offer a rather forbidding prospect, but in this cosy 16C inn all is relaxed and cheerful. The patrons see to that, running the Angel in their own personalised and dedicated way; the warm character of the establishment all adds to the experience. There's a lovely, sunny rear terrace with barbeque for summer days, but the interior's no less inviting, rustic charm seamlessly linked to rural setting. Scrubbed wooden floors, original artwork and candlelight will make you want to linger. Fine cooking will have much the same effect. Appealing, modern dishes are supplemented by blackboard fish specials: try, perhaps, roast scallops with chilli jam followed by roast monkfish with spinach and new potatoes. The comfortable rooms are invariably spotless.

Food serving times:
Monday-Sunday:
12pm-2pm, 7pm-9.30pm
Closed 25-26 December and 1 January
Prices:
Meals: a la carte 20.00/30.00
🛏 **10 rooms :** 72.00/85.00

Village signed off A350 to the north of Warminster. Parking.

Typical Dishes

Tiger prawns with chorizo sausage

Roast rump of lamb, sweet onion jus

Sticky toffee pudding

Whitley

097 The Pear Tree Inn

Top Lane, Whitley SN12 8QX
Tel.: (01225) 709131 - Fax: (01225) 702276
e-mail: enquiries@thepeartreeinn.com - Website: www.thepeartreeinn.com

Stonehenge Pigswill, Bath Gem, Moles Best, The Hidden Quest

Though not far from Bath, visitors to this attractive Cotswold stone inn may be tempted to stay put once they've indulged in what's on offer here. A pleasant front garden leads in to what can best be described as a stylish country dining pub and restaurant. Owners are keen to stress the amount of home produced food that goes into their menus: soups, sausages, bread, sorbets and ice cream are all made on the premises and Wiltshire suppliers provide game and meat. End results are a pleasing amalgam of traditional and modern dishes with a European accent. Staying overnight is a pleasure: bedrooms drip with contemporary style. There's impressive use of beautiful local oak and re-claimed barn doors; you'll also find top quality linen, the very best toiletries, and super-smart chrome fittings.

Food serving times:
Monday-Sunday:
12pm-2.30pm,
6.30pm-9.30pm
Closed 25-26 December and 1 January
Prices:
Meals: 16.00 (set price lunch) and a la carte 21.50/32.50
8 rooms : 75.00/105.00

Northwest of Melksham; Whitley is signed off A365. Parking.

Typical Dishes

Ravioli of braised beef
Monkfish with borlotti beans
Blood orange jelly, chocolate ice cream

NEW Michelin tourist guides: expand your holiday horizons

MICHELIN

Provence

Plan
Discover
Explore

French Rivie... Dordog... Berry Limous... Châteaux ... the Loi... Great Britain

- *New cover*
- *New layout*
- *New information*
- *New destinations*

*I*n recent years, the restored Jewellery Quarter, Brindleyplace and Centenary Square, not to mention the shops and bars of Mailbox and the new Bullring, have brought revival and recognition to ever-evolving Birmingham. But not far from Britain's hard-wrought second city, Coalbrookdale, picturesque Ironbridge and the towns of The Potteries and The Black Country offer poignant reminders of the industries that made them and shaped their working way of life. Further afield, and further back in time, Warwick and world-famous Stratford span the centuries, while the reflections of Viking and Celtic art at Kilpeck Church look back to a more ancient past. Explore prosperous period towns like Ludlow and Lichfield, visit the cathedral cities of Hereford and Worcester or take in some of England's most captivating countryside, from the upper Wye to the lower Peaks, by way of Elgar's beloved Malverns and Housman's "blue remembered hills". The discoveries continue in the region's pubs and inns, with cider and orchard fruits from the Vale of Evesham, Herefordshire beef, Gloucester's well-known cheeses and, most famously of all, the Burton beers which transformed the great British pint over 200 years ago.

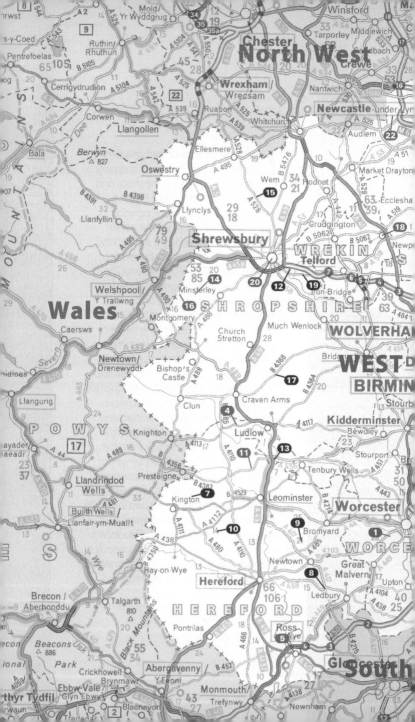

Bransford

001 ## Bear and Ragged Staff

Station Rd, Bransford WR6 5JH

Tel.: (01886) 833399 - Fax: (01886) 833106
e-mail: enquiries@bear.uk.com - Website: www.bear.uk.com

 VISA **AE** **⓪** **⓪⓪**

St. George's Best Bitter, Draught Bass

Satisfyingly familiar pub classics and more formal restaurant recipes run side by side on the Bear and Ragged Staff's huge blackboards; add to this the occasional fish specials and there's sure to be something that appeals. What's more, even with such a big choice, it's safe to assume the cooking will be tasty and prepared with sound culinary know-how. In fact, it would be easy to take this country pub for granted: unremarkable on the outside, comfortable and traditional within, it seems almost too pleasant and unassuming for its own good, but fortunately the locals know a good thing when they see it. Service is friendly with no standing on ceremony: though the pub is divided into a classically styled dining room and bar, you can order what you like and eat it where you choose.

Food serving times:
Monday-Saturday:
12pm-2pm, 6.30pm-9pm
Sunday: 12pm-2pm,
7pm-9pm

Closed dinner 25-26 December and dinner 1 January

Prices:
Meals: a la carte 19.70/31.00

4.5mi Southwest of Worcester by A44 and A4103; from Bransford follow signs to Powick. Parking.

Typical Dishes

Quail with Haggis, whisky sauce

Saddle of venison, raspberry sauce

Chocolate and date pudding

Clent

002 Bell & Cross

Holy Cross, Clent DY9 9QL

Tel.: (01562) 730319 - Fax: (01562) 731733
Website: www.bellandcrossclent.co.uk

    VISA

Banks Original, Banks Bitter, Hooky, Timothy Taylor Landlord

A pretty garden and a little terrace make this pretty, early-19C inn a natural choice for summer days, but it's far from just a fair-weather pub. Five charmingly petite rooms and a traditional tap room – with a listed bar, no less – are so cosy that you'll be tempted to linger over that last drink, and attentive young staff certainly make you feel welcome. A tasty seasonal menu, with blackboard specials, is devised in part by the England football team's chef-by-appointment, who takes charge in the kitchen when not putting fire in the bellies of Sven's Men. Diners without a big match after lunch should let the training regime slide and treat themselves to the delicious cooking.

Food serving times:
Monday-Saturday:
12pm-2pm, 6.30pm-9.15pm
Sunday: 12pm-2.30pm,
7pm-9pm
Closed 25 December
Prices:
Meals: a la carte 22.00/25.00

Mid-way between Stourbridge and Bromsgrove; Clent is signed off Northbound A491; the pub is on the left hand side in Holy Cross. Parking.

Typical Dishes

Ham hock parfait, red pepper salsa

Roast Cornish cod, minted peas

Raspberry pannacotta

Cutnall Green

003 The Chequers

Kidderminster Rd, Cutnall Green WR9 0PJ
Tel.: (01299) 851292 - Fax: (01299) 851744
Website: www.chequerscutnallgreen.co.uk

Hook Norton, Timothy Taylor Landlord, Ruddles Bitter

This half-timbered roadside pub isn't too much to look at, but inside it's a different story. The bar boasts modern décor in traditional surroundings, typified by sandblasted pale beams, tiled floor and leather tub chairs. There's an adjacent, most welcoming Garden Room: lilac soft furnishings and a plush sofa, surrounded by hanging tankards. Richly coloured walls with wine-themed paintings invoke a modern country style. The pub's owner is Roger Narbett, who's chef to the England football team, but expect more than pasta or chicken: menus boast great choice from traditional favourites to up-to-the-minute and highly interesting. Service is invariably courteous, efficient and enthusiastic.

Food serving times:
Monday-Sunday:
  12pm-2pm, 6.30pm-9.15pm
Closed 25 December
Prices:
Meals: a la carte 21.50/25.95

3mi North of Droitwich Spa on A442.
Parking.

Typical Dishes

Tomato, pumpkin and sweet
potato soup

Grilled calves liver and mash

Chocolate brownie, Cointreau
ice cream

Leintwardine

004 Jolly Frog

The Todden, Leintwardine SY7 0LX

Tel.: (01547) 540298 - Fax: (01547) 540105

     VISA

Hobsons Town Crier - reviewed every 3 months

Run with personality and imagination, the Jolly Frog is the kind of place that rewards a little light curiosity, hidden around the next hedgerow bend in the gentle folds of Herefordshire. Once inside, you'll discover four cosy adjoining rooms and a conservatory with a fascinating collection of rustic bits and pieces, a library of over 850 cookery books and a small shop, but the cuisine itself more than holds the attention, spanning a commendably well-priced table d'hôte menu, an extensive choice of shellfish and interesting specials-board diversions: enthusiastic staff take the time to put you in the picture and remain quick off the mark with smooth and effective service. Though less French than the name might imply, it's informal, cosy, casual and true to its surroundings.

Food serving times:
Tuesday-Saturday:
12pm-2.30pm, 6pm-9pm (last orders)
Sunday: 12pm-2.30pm
Closed 25 December
- Seafood specialities -
Prices:
Meals: 16.50 (lunch) and a la carte 30.00/40.00

Typical Dishes

Fish soup

Fillet of brill, beetroot jus

White chocolate and cardamom pannacotta

7mi West of Ludlow on A4113. Parking.

Ross-on-Wye

005 ## The Lough Pool Inn

Sellack, Ross-on-Wye HR9 6LX

Tel.: (01989) 730236 - Fax: (01989) 880055
e-mail: david@loughpool.co.uk - Website: www.loughpoolinn.co.uk

 Wye Valley Best, Butty Bach, Adnams Explorer, Theakstons XB, Old Speckled Hen, Butcombe

This 16C black and white timbered inn is in a wonderfully rural spot tucked away among the country lanes of Herefordshire - an ideal location for garden and terrace dining in the summer months. It's a solid traditional establishment with exposed stone, flag flooring and lots of space to wander around with a pint of local ale. No trouble in spotting the dining areas: they're painted bright yellow with red cedar-stained pine flooring. Menus change frequently, depending on ingredients. The Lough Pool serves excellent modern style cooking where good local produce is unerringly to the fore: look out for the blackboard specials.

Food serving times:
Monday-Sunday:
   12pm-2.15pm, 6.30pm-9pm
Closed 25 December; also dinner Sunday and all day Monday November and January
Prices:
Meals: a la carte 16.00/30.00

Typical Dishes

Hereford Hop cheese soufflé

Rabbit in red wine, fresh linguini

Dark chocolate fondant, pistachio ice cream

3.25mi Northwest of Ross-on-Wye; turn right off A49 (Hereford) and follow signs for Hoarwithy. Parking.

Stoke Prior

006 Epic

68 Hanbury Rd, Stoke Prior B60 4DN
Tel.: (01527) 871929 - Fax: (01527) 575647
e-mail: epic.bromsgrove@virgin.net - Website: www.epicbrasseries.com

 VISA **AE** **MC**

 Selection of 6 or 7 ales changing every 2-3 weeks

The only remnants here of its days as a roadside pub are the tiled floor and odd rafter. Otherwise this stylish establishment has benefited greatly from a major facelift and extensions. At the centre, a large modern bar with comfy sofa lounge area. All around, an airy dining space with lots of glass, brick and wood, which has been cleverly worked into the modern design. The overall feel is one of effortless style, accentuated by comfortable seating at smart wood tables with good accessories. Menus are large and dominated by popular modern classics at reasonable prices. Service is efficient from staff who are used to being busy.

Food serving times:
Tuesday-Saturday:
12.30pm-2.30pm,
6.30pm-9.30pm

Prices:
Meals: 12.95 (fixed price lunch) and a la carte 19.00/29.00

Typical Dishes

Lobster and basil ravioli

Fillet of beef, shallots and red wine sauce

Mango and passion fruit parfait

2.25mi Southwest of Bromsgrove by A38 and B4091; pub is on the right after traffic lights. Parking.

Titley

007 The Stagg Inn 🛏

Titley HR5 3RL

Tel.: (01544) 230221 - Fax: (01544) 231390
e-mail: reservations@thestagg.co.uk - Website: www.thestagg.co.uk

 Hobsons Best Bitter, Town Crier or Old Henry, Black Sheep

In the delightful surroundings of the Welsh Marches stands this nationally renowned whitewashed landmark. A carefully cultivated network of local suppliers, a real regard for quality and exemplary belief in value for money have all contributed to its singular success. You can eat in three different areas: the cosy bar, the dining room with chunky wooden tables, or, assuming the weather is clement, the rear garden. Menus change every five or six weeks, but the cooking itself, assured and original with a hint of classic French flair, is a model of consistency, allowing fresh, natural flavours to shine through. Comfortable, softly lit surroundings and pleasant, intelligent service, contribute to a really memorable meal. If you wish to prolong the Stagg experience, there are two rooms above the pub, and more in the quieter part-Georgian vicarage down the road.

Food serving times:
Tuesday (except at bank holidays when open Monday instead) to Saturday:
12pm-2pm, 6.30pm-9pm
Sunday: 12pm-2pm
Closed first 2 weeks November, 25-26 December, 1 January, 1 week in Spring, May Day Monday
Prices:
Meals: a la carte 23.00/29.00
🛏 **6 rooms :** 50.00/110.00

3.5mi Northeast of Kington on B4355. Parking.

Typical Dishes

Scallops, celeriac purée

Fillet of Herefordshire beef, horseradish mash

Crème brûlée

Trumpet

008 **The Verzon**

Hereford Rd, Trumpet HR8 2PZ

Tel.: (01531) 670381 - Fax: (01531) 670830
e-mail: info@theverzon.co.uk - Website: www.theverzon.co.uk

 No real ales offered

S tanding just back from the main road, this attractive part-Georgian house gives no hint of its stylish modern interior. Deep leather sofas and armchairs are set invitingly around a comfortable bar with exposed brick walls; beyond is a spacious restaurant. You can eat in either, and the choice runs from a lunchtime sandwich to the full three courses of a modern menu, a concise list of classics balanced by dishes with a more original touch. Whether The Verzon is more of a pub or a bar-brasserie is a tricky question, but it's hardly likely to stop you enjoying it, particularly on a fine summer evening: its big deck terrace, under broad sunshades, gives wonderful views of the Herefordshire countryside. Large and stylish bedrooms are available.

Food serving times:
Monday-Sunday:
12pm-2pm, 7pm-9.30pm
Prices:
Meals: 19.00 (lunch) and a la carte 20.00/30.00
8 rooms: 65.00/150.00

3 1/4mi Northwest of Ledbury on A38. Parking.

Typical Dishes

Scallops, lemongrass dressing

Fillet of Herefordshire beef, wild mushroom ravioli

Rhubarb and saffron soufflé

Ullingswick

009 ### Three Crowns Inn

Bleak Acre, Ullingswick HR1 3JQ

Tel.: (01432) 820279 - Fax: (08700) 515 338
e-mail: info@threecrownsinn.com - Website: www.threecrownsinn.com

VISA

Hobsons Best and a selection of guest ales from Wye Valley

On one of Herefordshire's many quiet roads stands this red brick, timbered establishment blending in perfectly with its rural setting. You step straight into a wonderfully beamed bar boasting exposed brickwork and a cosy wood counter with benches and pews strewn around. Hops dangle from the rafters, sepia prints hang on the walls: all in all it's thoroughly pleasant and deserving of its loyal local following. The restaurant was refurbished to double its size in 2005, so more diners can now appreciate what's on offer. Keenly-priced food has a rustic, robust quality and tasty, local produce is proudly in evidence, not least vegetables and herbs from the kitchen garden. If you wish to prolong your stay in this hidden-away gem, there is a luxurious bedroom suite in which to enjoy a peaceful country repose.

Food serving times:
Tuesday-Sunday:
   12pm-2.30pm, 7pm-10pm
Closed 2 weeks after lunch on 24 December
Prices:
Meals: 14.95 (set price lunch) and a la carte 14.95/24.75
1 room : 75.00/95.00

1.25mi East of the village on unsigned country lane. Parking.

Typical Dishes

Leek and potato soup, smoked haddock

Crisp belly of pork, cider jus

Gratin of rhubarb, strawberry sorbet

Weobley

010 The Salutation Inn

Market Pitch, Weobley HR4 8SJ

Tel.: (01544) 318443 - Fax: (01544) 318405
e-mail: salutationinn@btinternet.com - Website: www.thesalutationinn.co.uk

 VISA AE MO

Goff's Jouster, Wye Valley Butty Bach, Spinning Dog Hereford Light Ale

An old country pub through and through, this 16C cider house, in the heart of this pretty Herefordshire village, truly looks and feels the part: crooked timbers are hung with jugs, hop-bines and horse-brasses, blue and white china plates are ranged along the mantelpiece. The traditional partition of lounge and public bar is still in evidence too: one pleasant corner of the pub is set as a formal dining room, with candles and neat, white tablecloths, although the same menu is served throughout. The sound and classically based cooking seems in tune with the atmosphere of the place. Tidily kept bedrooms, some in traditional floral patterns, are kept in good order.

Food serving times:
Closed 25 December
Prices:
Meals: a la carte 18.00/30.00
4 rooms : 53.00/86.00

Typical Dishes

Char grilled asparagus brochetta

Roast rump of Welsh lamb

Trio of crème brûlée

8mi South West of Leominster by A44 and B4230. Parking.

Yarpole

011 **The Bell Inn**

Green Lane, Yarpole HR6 0BD
Tel.: (01568) 780359

Timothy Taylor, Wye Valley, Old Hooky Bitter

Temptingly set between Leominster and Ludlow, the black-and-white timbered Bell Inn, first mentioned in the Domesday Book, promises delightful rustic ambience and it does not disappoint. The Bell does not try to be a gastropub but operates in traditional style, under the unerring eye of Claude and Claire, who also own the Michelin-starred Hibiscus in Ludlow. An impressive interior takes its cue from heavy beams, horse brasses, open fires and rural ornaments and pictures. Adjoining is a very characterful converted barn dining room boasting high, raftered ceilings, heavy wood tables and original stone cider press. Drinkers are catered for in a separate bar and snug. Well-paced, friendly service is a given here. Sizable menus feature British pub classics, while French influences and modern styles slide easily into the mix. Seasonal Herefordshire ingredients are to the fore; cooking is hearty and robust. You'd expect nothing less!

Food serving times:
Tuesday-Sunday and public holiday Monday:
   12pm-2.30pm, 6.30pm-9.30pm

Closed Monday unless public holiday

Prices:
Meals: a la carte 22.00/27.50

4mi North of Leominster by B4361 and minor road West. Parking.

Typical Dishes

Cornish crab cakes

Cassoulet of Gressingham duck

Sherry trifle

Atcham

012 The Mytton and Mermaid

Atcham SY5 6QG

Tel.: (01743) 761220 - Fax: (01743) 761292
e-mail: admin@myttonandmermaid.co.uk - Website: www.myttonandmermaid.co.uk

Woods Shropshire Lad and 2 guest ales

This redbrick, ivy-clad inn was built in 1735 and stands proudly on the banks of the Severn, opposite the National Trust's Attingham Park. The quirky bar is named after local 19C squire Mad Jack Mytton, who'd appreciate the warm, friendly atmosphere that prevails here. There's a log fire, sofa and large tables where you can linger over lunch or dinner. The easy-going restaurant – which has a separate identity but is really in the same room – sports polished tables and menus full of good, traditional dishes that change with the seasons. The relaxed style carries over into a pleasant riverside drawing room and a series of stylish, individually decorated bedrooms with antique and modern furniture.

Food serving times:
Monday-Saturday:
  12pm-2.30pm, 6.30pm-10pm
Sunday: 12pm-3pm,
              6.30pm-10pm
Closed 25 December
Prices:
Meals: a la carte 21.00/30.00
18 rooms : 75.00/155.00

Typical Dishes

Asparagus and goat's cheese terrine

Pork chop, pear and sage potato cake,

Warm chocolate pudding

3mi Southeast of Shrewsbury on the B4380 Ironbridge rd. Parking.

Brimfield

013 **The Roebuck Inn**

Brimfield SY8 4NE

Tel.: (01584) 711230
Website: www.roebuckinn.com

Banks Best Bitter and weekly changing guest ales

It takes something special in the gastronomic stakes to be especially noticed in the Ludlow area, and the mustard-coloured Roebuck Inn comes up with the goods – or, rather, the inventive menus. Slap bang in the middle of an attractive village just south of the famous town, it's every inch the epitome of a classic country pub, filled with rustic objects, curios and polished older wood furniture in the bar areas - the pubby rear bar is more food oriented. A spick-and-span dining room has felt the benefits of tender loving care. Dishes are likewise freshly inspired; there's a light lunch menu, full menu and blackboard specials too. Sleep overnight in homely bedrooms.

Food serving times:
Monday-Sunday:
    12pm-2.30pm, 7pm-9pm
Closed 25-26 December
Prices:
Meals: a la carte 22.00/29.00
 3 rooms : 45.00/80.00

4.5mi South of Ludlow; signed off A49. Parking.

Typical Dishes

Scallops, carrot and cumin purée

Roast rump lamb, spring vegetable and thyme broth

Lemon tart

Brockton

014 The Feathers Inn

Brockton TF13 6JR

Tel.: (01746) 785202 · Fax: (01746) 785202
e-mail: kayiatou@hotmail.com

Hobsons Best, Shropshire Lad

Wenlock Edge, in the heart of the Shropshire countryside, is a popular spot for walkers, and word-of-mouth has contributed to this attractive part 16th century pub becoming one of their more favoured watering holes. The owner/chef cut his teeth in well-thought-of London establishments and dining is to the fore here, with the constantly changing blackboard menus providing interesting modern English dishes underpinned by local produce, such as Shropshire partridge or beef. Ambience is ideal: the characterful interior boasts a tiled floor, white washed stone walls, beams, and vast inglenooks with wood-burning stoves. Lots of little areas surround the central bar so a cosy feel snuggles within the rusticity. If anyone feels like splashing out, there are various examples of local artwork for sale lining the walls. The newly opened bedrooms will be welcome to tired walkers.

Food serving times:
Saturday-Sunday:
12pm-2pm, 6.30pm-9.30pm
Tuesday-Friday:
6.30pm-9.30pm

**Closed 26 December
to 3 January; also Mondays
and all Bank Holidays**

Prices:
Meals: 14.95 (set price dinner) and a la carte 14.95/40.00 (Saturday-Sunday only)

Typical Dishes

Oxtail with potato gnocchi

Grilled sole, lemon and parsley butter

Lemon tart, raspberry sorbet

5mi Southwest of Much Wenlock on B4378. Parking.

461

Burlton

015 **The Burlton Inn**

Burlton SY4 5TB

Tel.: (01939) 270284 - Fax: (01939) 270204
e-mail: bean@burltoninn.co.uk - Website: www.burltoninn.co.uk

 4 different constantly changing real ales from local breweries

This 18C Shropshire stalwart knows how to pack 'em in – so much so that early in 2004 some bigger, better adjustments and refurbishments gave the old place more room to breathe. Nothing of the buzzy, bustling, pubby atmosphere has been lost, though, and the Burlton is unfailingly popular with the huntin', shootin' and fishin' locals. Window boxes and hanging baskets decorate the outside in summer and in colder weather, the compact, raftered bar crackles along in sympathy with the log fire. The food – like the real ale generously stocked – goes down a treat, oiled by smooth service from a polite, friendly crew. It's rustic food, home-cooked and fresh. In the rear annexe, smart and spacious bedrooms complete the picture – make sure you don't miss out on the first rate breakfasts.

Food serving times:
Monday-Saturday:
   12pm-2pm, 6.30pm-9.45pm
Sunday: 12pm-2pm,
                       7pm-9.30pm

Closed 25-26 December,
1 January and lunch Bank
Holiday Monday

Prices:
Meals: a la carte 16.70/29.85
6 rooms : 50.00/90.00

Typical Dishes

Thai mussels

Wild boar sausages, mustard mash and onion gravy

Chocolate torte

8mi North of Shrewsbury on A528.
Parking.

Marton

016 The Sun Inn

Marton SY21 8JP

Tel.: (01938) 561211
e-mail: info@suninn.biz - Website: www.suninn.biz

  VISA

 Hobsons Best Bitter and guest ale in summer months - Woods, Salopian, Six Bells breweries

The simply styled Sun with its neat and tidy stone facade is a credit to this quiet Marches village on the English-Welsh border. The owners previously ran a restaurant in the New Forest and their cooking experience shows to good effect, even down to tasty home-made bread. Light snacks are available all day in the rather spartan little front bar while dinner is served in the recently refurbished dining room, now resplendent in pine. The chef makes a point of using local ingredients and the well-prepared cooking, nourishing and enjoyable, has a real flavour of the season to it. Genial service from the experienced young owners helps things along nicely, as do the extensive selection of wines by the glass and real ales. An ever-increasing number of regulars and visitors who've picked up on the Sun - often by word of mouth - are proof positive of its widening appeal.

Food serving times:
Tuesday: 7pm-9.30pm
Wednesday-Saturday:
12pm-2pm, 7pm-9.30pm
Sunday: 12pm-2pm
(booking essential)
Prices:
Meals: a la carte 15.00/30.00

Typical Dishes

Crayfish and avocado salad

Pastrami spiced pork, apple and horseradish

Chocolate and Baileys mousse

8.5mi Southeast of Welshpool on the B4386. Parking.

Munslow

017 ## The Crown Country Inn

Munslow SY7 9ET

Tel.: (01584) 841205 - Fax: (01584) 841255
e-mail: info@crowncountryinn.co.uk - Website: www.crowncountryinn.co.uk

 Holdens Black Country and Golden Glow, John Roberts Clerics' Cure and Woods' and Hobsons' beers

Quite how old the Crown really is, no-one really knows, but it was already long-established when it served as a "hundred house" for travelling magistrates. Warm and characterful, it certainly has all the hallmarks of a charming old rural inn, with stout beams propping up its cosy taproom, a well-stoked fire and trains of hops dangling from the woodwork. Its cuisine is not bound by tradition, though: light but still substantial modern dishes are served in the bar at lunch, while the evening menu is planned and prepared with a dash of imagination. Local vegetables, rare-breed meats, a fine English cheeseboard and even local spring water demonstrate a taste for regional produce. The large garden and terrace are popular with walkers from nearby Wenlock Edge.

Food serving times:
Tuesday-Saturday:
    12pm-2pm, 6.45pm-9pm
Sunday: 12pm-2pm,
                6.30pm-7.45pm

Closed 25 December

Prices:
Meals: 16.50/15.00 (set price Sunday lunch/dinner) and a la carte 20.00/29.00

3 rooms : 45.00/70.00

Typical Dishes

Leeks with smoked salmon

Chicken breast, girolle and chive sauce

Milk chocolate pavé, poached cherries

On the B4378 between Much Wenlock and Craven Arms. Parking.

Newport

018 The Fox

Pave Lane, Chetwynd Aston, Newport TF10 9LQ

Tel.: (01952) 815940 - Fax: (01952) 815941
e-mail: fox@bruningandprice.co.uk - Website: www.fox-newport.co.uk

Timothy Taylor Landlord, Thwaites Original, Shropshire Lad and guest beers - Kelham Island Pale Rider, Bathams Best, Arizona

Bright and uncluttered, the Fox has a welcoming feel to it. The old pattern of nooks, parlours and lounges has been opened up and the well-chosen furnishings, though mostly restored or reclaimed, fit this more modern layout very well. A collection of framed fashion-plates and cigarette cards, rural scenes and period caricatures run the length of the walls and into the more intimate rooms off to the sides. It's nearly always possible to find a quieter corner somewhere, but the Fox really excels at the big get-together. Long dining tables are perfect for eating out in eights and tens: family brunches on a Sunday or an evening catching up with friends. A sizeable menu of modern classics is delivered with friendly efficiency. Big rear terrace and garden.

Food serving times:
Monday-Saturday:
12pm-10pm
Sunday: 12pm-9.30pm
Closed 26 December
Prices:
Meals: a la carte 16.95/32.15

Typical Dishes

Grilled black pudding, celeriac mash

Shoulder of lamb, carrot and swede mash

Sticky toffee pudding

1.5 mi South of Newport by A41 (Wolverhampton rd). Parking.

Norton

019 **Hundred House** 🛏

Bridgnorth Rd, Norton TF11 9EE

Tel.: (01952) 730353 - Fax: (01952) 730355
e-mail: reservations@hundredhouse.co.uk - Website: www.hundredhouse.co.uk

Heritage Traditional Beer, Saddlers Best Bitter, Old Ale Guest Bitter

You know you've arrived somewhere with a hugely individual character when you arrive at Hundred House. The extensive rear herb garden is a particular joy and supplies the kitchen with much delightful produce, not least the delectable soft fruit for dessert, or the dried flowers that cascade from beams. The inn has its origins in the 14C and, in the best sense, it shows: rafters, quarry tiled floors, open fires and venerable dark oak. After a hike along the Wrekin has bolstered a hearty appetite, you can eat almost anywhere. Lovely bedrooms offer a boundless variety of country comforts and character features – including half testers, four posters and swings in some of the rooms!

Food serving times:
Monday-Saturday:
   12pm-2.15pm, 6pm-9pm
Sunday: 12pm-2.15pm
Closed or accommodation
25 and 26 December

Prices:
Meals: a la carte 24.00/35.00
🛏 **10 rooms :** 85.00/125.00

Typical Dishes

Blinis of salmon, crab and prawn

Rack of lamb, chorizo and roast peppers

Pears poached in red wine

7 mi. South of Telford on A 442.
Parking.

Shrewsbury

020 The Armoury

Victoria Quay, Welsh Bridge, Shrewsbury SY1 1HH

Tel.: (01743) 340525 - Fax: (01743) 340526
e-mail: armoury@brunningandprice.co.uk - Website: www.armoury-shrewsbury.co.uk

 ♀ 🥢 **VISA** **AE** **MC**

 Rooster, Outlaw, Salopian Gold

This 18C former warehouse has a fascinating history: built for military use, it's done service as a bakery and a World War II convalescent home, and even been moved brick by brick to this spot in sight of the old bridge, where it cries out for a bankside terrace to enjoy the summer sunshine. Inside, gilt-framed mirrors, engravings and Edwardiana cover the brick walls, yard upon yard of old books are rivalled only by row upon rows of malts and liqueurs behind the bar, and a huge ceiling and tall arched windows make the open-plan room feel light and spacious. Lots of big tables, with a hotch-potch of second-hand chairs, make it ideal for a big get-together: its great popularity means there's usually a buzzy atmosphere, and the daily changing menu of modern favourites offers something for everyone.

Food serving times:
Monday-Saturday:
12pm-9.30pm,
Sunday: 12pm-9pm
Prices:
Meals: a la carte 19.00/30.00

Typical Dishes

Black pudding with cider and mustard mash

Rump steak, hand-cut chips

Sticky toffee pudding

By the Welsh Bridge. ⟩

Alrewas

021 **The Old Boat**

Kings Bromley Rd, Alrewas DE13 7DB
Tel.: (01283) 791468
e-mail: mikegething@hotmail.com

 Marstons Pedigree

Tucked away at the edge of the village, the easiest way to find the Old Boat is almost certainly from the canal. Though they've raised the tone since navvies and barges made this their drinking haunt, some of their customers still come by water, pottering up in their narrow boats. Anyone with an aversion to maritime knick-knacks might fear the worst at the sight of a massive anchor attached to the wall, but inside it's as much like an informal restaurant as a pub, with chunky wooden chairs and tables dotted around. Food is a big part of what they do here and regulars who come for a well-kept Burton beer may be tempted to stay for lunchtime sandwiches, set price and à la carte menus or something from an impressive variety of specials, either classic or modern in style. Friendly service.

Food serving times:
Monday-Saturday:
12pm-2pm, 6pm-9pm
Sunday: 12pm-8pm
Prices:
Meals: a la carte 20.00/30.00

4.5 mi Northeast of Lichfield by A38. Parking.

Typical Dishes

Twice baked goat's cheese soufflé

Shank of lamb, bubble and squeak

Lemon tart, raspberry sorbet

Wrinehill

022 The Hand and Trumpet

Main Road, Wrinehill CW33 9BJ
Tel.: (01270) 820048

 VISA

Woodland's Oak Beauty, Deuchar's IPA, Titanic Mild, Timothy Taylor's Landlord

The ancient village of Wrinehill (mentioned in the Domesday Book) has made a smooth transition into the 21C with this handsomely refurbished and sizable country pub. You're immediately struck by the delightful decked terrace, overlooking duck pond and gardens. On a warm day, you might just fancy plonking yourself down here and admiring the view, but then you'd be doing the stylish interior a disservice. The well-stocked bar has a shiny tiled floor with kilims lending a rather exotic touch, and the classy feel continues into the main dining area, where book shelves and rustic prints create just the right mood of relaxation to enjoy a leisurely lunch or dinner. Menus cover a tried-and-tested country route, with traditional dishes very much to the fore. There's a wide range of wines by the glass and draught real ales to wash it all down with. Incidentally, don't miss the pub's website, complete with a superb history of the area.

Food serving times:
Monday-Saturday:
12pm-10pm
Sunday: 12pm-9.30pm
Closed 25-26 December
Prices:
Meals: a la carte 20.00/25.00

Typical Dishes

Pigeon, pheasant and venison pie

Roast belly pork, cider gravy

Bara brith with toffee apples

6mi West of Newcastle-under-Lyme by A525 and A531. Parking.

Alveston

023 The Baraset Barn

1 Pimlico Lane, Alveston CV37 7RF

Tel.: (01789) 295510 - Fax: (01789) 292961
e-mail: barasetbarn@lovelypubs.co.uk

Mitchells and Butlers Brew 99

The historic structure of the old barn is still apparent in the lofty ceilings and rich, golden beams, but the main impression of this very contemporary pub is of one stylish setting after another: a smart lilac-and-white lounge conservatory, a main dining area in brick, pewter, oak and crushed velvet, an intimate rear mezzanine, and a dark, moody cigar bar for savouring an after-dinner drink and clustering round the log burner. A modern British and Mediterranean menu changes a couple of times a year: favourite signature dishes, grills, steaks, and their popular lobster and chips remain ever-present and sum up the bold, fresh culinary style. Bright, prompt service is the other key ingredient in a pleasant, unhurried lunch or evening out.

Food serving times:
Monday -Saturday:
12pm-2.30pm,
6.30pm-9.30pm
Sunday: 12pm-4pm
Closed 25 December
Prices:
Meals: 14.00 (set price lunch) and a la carte 20.00/40.00

2mi East of Stratford- upon- Avon on B4086. Parking.

Typical Dishes

Smoked haddock rarebit

Pork belly, trotter and fillet with cinnamon sauce

Chocolate fondant

Ardens Grafton

024 The Golden Cross

Wixford Road, Ardens Grafton B50 4LG

Tel.: (01789) 772420 - Fax: (01798) 491358
e-mail: steve@thegoldencross.net - Website: www.thegoldencross.net

 Purity (local brewer), Hooky Best Bitter, Revd James, Bombardier, Deuchars IPA

Popular destinations in this part of the world are not confined to nearby Stratford, as witnessed by the large number of satisfied visitors enjoying the ambience of this slickly run pub. It has a very pleasant feel, both inside and out. A large rear garden and terrace is ideal for summer dining; the roomy interior has a distinctly rural character, typified by the exposed beams, open fire and scrubbed wooden tables and chairs. A separate dining room gives off a more formal air; à la carte menus bear the hallmarks of modern British tastes and are very freshly prepared with vibrant use of local ingredients; the blackboard daily specials offer a distinct seasonal base.

Food serving times:
Monday-Friday:
    12pm-3pm, 5pm-11pm
Saturday: 12pm-2.30pm, 6pm-9.30pm
Sunday: 12pm-4pm
Prices:
Meals: 12.95 (Sunday lunch only) and a la carte 16.00/25.00

Typical Dishes

Home tea smoked duck salad

Guinea fowl with roast pear, ginger and chilli jus

Sticky toffee pudding

5mi South West of Stratford-upon-Avon by A46. Parking.

Armscote

025 **The Fox & Goose Inn** 🛏

Front St, Armscote CV37 8DD

Tel.: (01608) 682293 - Fax: : (01608) 682293

e-mail: email@foxandgoose.co.uk - Website: www.foxandgoose.co.uk

Hook Norton Best Bitter

The blacksmith who once worked here at his forge would be amazed at its 21C transformation. The Fox and Goose embraces modernity but doesn't forget its past. Flagstones, wooden pews and a log fire all have pride of place here. They syncopate smoothly with an upmarket ambience elsewhere in the pub. The small bar has warm red walls; they're cream in the larger, stylish eating area. Imaginative and traditional blend cleverly in the cooking stakes: you might try roast lamb shoulder with rosemary and redcurrant jus; or poached smoked haddock with spinach, poached egg and chive sauce. Service is helpful and attentive; bedrooms, eccentrically styled, are named after Cluedo characters - candlestick and lead piping not included, thank goodness...

Food serving times:
Monday-Sunday:
   12pm-2.30pm, 7pm-9.30pm
Prices:
Meals: a la carte 20.00/30.00
🛏 **4 rooms :** 50.00/120.00

Typical Dishes

Grilled Cornish sardines with lime

Herefordshire beef fillet, Dauphinoise potatoes

Trio of miniature crumbles

2.5 mi North of Shipston-on-Stour by A3400. Parking.

Aston Cantlow

026 The King's Head

21 Bearley Rd, Aston Cantlow B95 6HY

Tel.: (01789) 488242 - Fax: (01789) 488137
e-mail: info@thekh.co.uk - Website: www.thekh.co.uk

 Abbot, Purity Gold, Brew 11

This is a pub that's used to welcoming Stratford overspill, those who need a little respite from the intensity of Shakespeare's birthplace. It's a 15C whitewashed inn with black timbers set in a pretty village, with pleasant terrace and garden for summer visitors. The interior oozes charm with several cosy areas to choose from. There's a crackling log fire, low ceiling and polished flag flooring, plus rustic benches next to window tables, where you can watch the world go by. The attractive restaurant has a modern country style, reflecting the modish appeal of the menus, whose influence ranges from British and Mediterranean to the downright exotic (as in chilli and lime chicken kebabs with peanut dressing). Expect great service, too, generally with an Antipodean accent.

Food serving times:
Monday-Saturday:
  12pm-2.30pm, 7pm-10pm
Sunday: 12.30pm-3pm
Closed 25-26 December
and 1 January
Prices:
Meals: a la carte 18.00/27.00

3mi South of Henley-in-Arden, off B4089. Parking.

Typical Dishes

Duck, wild mushrooms and Puy lentils

Pork tenderloin, celeriac, potato gratin

Dark chocolate & orange

Farnborough

027 The Inn at Farnborough

Farnborough OX17 1DZ

Tel.: (01295) 690615

e-mail: enquiries@innatfarnborough.co.uk - Website: www.innatfarnborough.co.uk

No real ales offered

The historic village of Farnborough is home to two distinctive buildings: the National Trust owned Farnborough Hall and this Grade II listed 17C inn, at the heart of the community for nearly 400 years. Expectations are fully endorsed upon crossing the threshold. A homely interior is dressed in full sympathy with the age of the building: there's a warm glow from the open fire, flag stoned floor and country knick-knacks. A homely bar offers a promising selection of real ales and diners will appreciate the frequently changing menus; much time and effort goes into sourcing local ingredients, resulting in carefully prepared, tasty dishes with a modern flourish. Upstairs, in a sharp break from the rural treats below, is an eye-catching private meeting room with a zebra-striped ceiling.

Food serving times:
Monday-Sunday:
12pm-9.30pm
Closed 25 December
Prices:
Meals: 10.95/12.95
(2 and 3 course lunch or dinner) and a la carte 18.00/30.00

6mi North of Banbury on A423. Parking.

Typical Dishes

Duck and foie gras terrine

Roast monkfish, tiger prawns & ratatouille

Hot chocolate fondant

Great Wolford

028 ## The Fox & Hounds Inn 🛏

Great Wolford CV36 5NQ

Tel.: (01608) 674220
e-mail: info@thefoxandhounds.com - Website: www.thefoxandhounds.com

✂=room **VISA** **MC**

Hook Norton Best, Butcombe, Bass

It takes something special to catch the eye in an area as rich in delights as the Cotswolds, but this 16C inn passes the test with flying colours. It's located in the heart of a delightful village, its honey coloured exterior luring the visitor into a series of hugely characterful rooms with bags of period appeal, typified by exposed beams with hop bines, an ancient bread oven, lovely open log fire and solid stone floor. Select from a good array of wines and local real ales and dine at candlelit tables; there's a daily changing blackboard menu of well executed, hearty, fresh fare, that puts many local ingredients to good use. In warmer months, make for the summer terrace. Stay overnight in cosy, well-kept bedrooms.

Food serving times:
Tuesday-Friday:
12pm-2pm, 7pm-9pm
Saturday-Sunday:
12pm-2.30pm,
6.30pm-9.30pm
Closed 1st 2 weeks in January
Prices:
Meals: a la carte 18.50/30.00
🛏 **3 rooms :** 50.00/80.00

Typical Dishes

Brie and bacon parcels

Medallions of wildebeest, wild mushrooms

Brioche bread and butter pudding

4 mi Northeast of Moreton-in-Marsh by A44. Parking.

Henley-in-Arden

029 **Crabmill**

Preston Bagot, Claverdon, Henley-in-Arden B95 5EE

Tel.: (01926) 843342 - Fax: (01926) 843989
e-mail: thecrabmill@aol.com - Website: www.thecrabmill.biz

Tetleys, Wadworth 6X, Greene King Abbot Ale

A delightful rural hideaway, but one which doesn't quite leave its urbane smartness behind: a surprisingly spacious contemporary interior mixes smooth blond wood with ancient cross-beams and wattle walls, the warmth of a real fire and squishy tan leather sofas, so comfortable they demand a real battle of wills for a trip to the bar. A touch of brasserie style comes across in the competent cooking, with dishes like roast pigeon breast and mash, or pepper sirloin and chips, but it's the kind of food you can linger over, and you may find that hearty ramble up and down the Warwickshire hills being put back by another round. The staff look almost as nonchalant as the customers – the emblemed T-shirts are the clue – but provide prompt and conversational service with that noticeable bit extra. Justifiably popular, so consider booking.

Food serving times:
Monday-Sunday:
  12pm-2.30pm
Monday--Saturday:
  6.30pm-9.30pm
Closed 25 December
(booking essential)
Prices:
Meals: a la carte 22.00/32.00

Typical Dishes

Lamb's Kidneys, apple and black pudding

Seabass, rösti and crab bisque

Poached pear, chocolate shortbread

1mi East of Henley-in-Arden on A4189. Parking

Ilmington

030 **The Howard Arms**

Lower Green, Ilmington CV36 4LT

Tel.: (01608) 682226 - Fax: (01608) 682226
e-mail: info@howardarms.com - Website: www.howardarms.com

*Hook Norton 303, Everards Tiger, Purity EEBU, Timothy Taylor
Landlord, Butcombe Bitter, Shakespeare Brewery Noble Fool*

Wander in to this charming 16C inn for a quiet lunchtime pint and you may be surprised by the buzz of activity, but there's usually room for everyone in a spread of smartly kept rooms and snugs, decorated with prints, portraits and old photographs. Cheerful local staff are used to being busy and will talk you through the large weekly menu chalked up above the fireplace. Classic country cooking, done well, takes in dishes like steak and ale pie, pork in sage, honey and cider and pigeon with carrot and ginger purée. Three well-fitted bedrooms with an agreeable mix of antiques and country fabrics all share a view of the village green: if you do decide to stay, don't miss the famous paintings and porcelain at nearby Upton House, a stroll around the enchanting Hidcote Manor Gardens or a trip to Stratford-upon-Avon.

Food serving times:
Monday-Thursday:
    12pm-2pm, 7pm-9pm
Friday-Saturday:
    12pm-2pm, 7pm-9.30pm
Sunday: 12pm-2.30pm,
                6.30pm-8.30pm

Closed 25 December

Prices:
Meals: 21.00 (Sunday lunch only) and a la carte 21.00/28.00
3 rooms : 85.00/130.00

Typical Dishes

Kedgeree with poached duck egg

Guinea fowl, salsa verde

Chocolate & ginger mousse, white chocolate ice cream

4 mi Northwest of Shipston-on-Stour. Located in the centre of the village. Parking.

Lower Quinton

031 **The College Arms**

Lower Quinton CV37 8SG

Tel.: (01789) 720342 - Fax: (01789) 720392

e-mail: mail@collegearms.co.uk - Website: www.collegearms.co.uk

    VISA **M©**

 Hook Norton, Hooky Best, Purity Ales Pure Gold

Henry VIII once owned this place, so current incumbents Mr and Mrs Love inherited an establishment where feasting was hardly a new concept. England's portliest monarch would have approved, because food's still considered mighty important here, with two restaurants and one private dining room taking pride of place. A mix of modern and traditional dishes offers much choice and flexibility in surroundings with bags of character, tailor-made for relaxation: exposed beams, crackling fire, solid stone floors and solid part-16C walls. The pub is set on the northern edge of the Cotswolds and visitors don't need much temptation to stay overnight: four bedrooms, recently refurbished, are smart and cosy.

Food serving times:
Monday-Saturday:
12pm-2pm, 7pm-9pm
Sunday: 12pm-2pm
Prices:
Meals: 17.00 (set price lunch and dinner) and a la carte 20.00/35.00
4 rooms : 55.00/70.00

5mi South of Stratford-upon-Avon by A3400, B4632 and minor road east. Parking.

Typical Dishes

Ham hock, smoked pineapple & crispy quail's egg

Braised ox cheek, root vegetables

Pear 'Belle Hélène'

Tanworth-in-Arden

032 **The Bell**

The Green, Tanworth-in-Arden B94 5AL

Tel.: (01564) 742212

e-mail: ash@realcoolbars.com - Website: www.thebellattanworthinarden.co.uk

 VISA

Timothy Taylors Landlord, Black Sheep Bitter, Purity Gold

A very handily located pub, only 20 minutes from Stratford and five minutes from main motorway access, The Bell sits proudly in its pretty village location, close to an 11C church and providing sustenance to the occasional summer invasion of Morris dancers. Its premises embrace a recently added delicatessen and post office; a good deal of time, effort and money has been invested in the pub, too, and there's now a pleasing rustic-contemporary mix with a spacious, popular bar and an intimate main dining room that boasts squashy leather sofas and polished wooden tables. The wide ranging menus cover an interesting modern range: for instance, you might order baby Thai fish and oatmeal cakes with ginger and tomato sauce, followed by Moroccan chicken, couscous and raita. The modern theme is continued with designer-led bedrooms.

Food serving times:
Monday-Saturday:
    12pm-2pm, 6.30pm-9pm
Sunday: 12pm-2pm
Prices:
Meals: 10.50 (set price dinner) and a la carte 15.00/25.00
9 rooms : 55.00/110.00

4.5mi North West from Henley-in-Arden by A3400 and Tanworth Road. 5 minutes from main motorways. Close to church. Parking.

Typical Dishes

Arabic mezza

Lamb shank, colcannon mash, redcurrant jus

Kirsch marinated cherries, vanilla ice cream

Welford-on-Avon

⟨033⟩ The Bell Inn

Binton Rd, Welford-on-Avon CV37 8EB

Tel.: (01789) 750353 - Fax: (01789) 750893

e-mail: info@thebellwelford.co.uk - Website: www.thebellwelford.co.uk

Wadworth 6X, Old Hooky, Flowers OB, Hobsons Best, Fuller's London Pride, Calways Five

Visitors fanning out from Stratford strike lucky when they come across this part 17C redbrick inn. If it's the summer months, they can flop down at The Bell's enticingly attractive wood-furnished outside terrace with its array of hanging baskets. Or step inside, any time of year, and admire the flagged and beamed bar, glowing fire and rustic knick-knacks. Various other rooms mean there's space to breathe in here, with a range of tables, chairs and pews to stretch out at: the recently refurbished glass roofed dining room is maybe the most stylish place to eat. Local produce is very much to the fore, with local suppliers' names printed on the back of the menus. These offer a good balance of modern British and classic cuisine. They change a couple of times a year, and are supplemented by an extensive range of daily specials.

Food serving times:
Monday-Thursday:
        11.30am-2.30pm, 6pm-9.30pm
Friday-Saturday:
  11.30am-2.30pm, 6pm-10pm
Sunday: 12pm-9.30pm
Prices:
Meals: a la carte 18.15/25.85

Typical Dishes

Melon, prawn and red pepper tian

Paprika chicken, chorizo and prawn paella

Sticky toffee pudding

4mi West of Stratford-upon-Avon by B439 and a lefthand turn South. Parking. ➤

Barston

034 The Malt Shovel

Barston Lane, Barston B92 0JP

Tel.: (01675) 443223 - Fax: (01675) 443223
Website: www.themaltshovelatbarston.com

   VISA **AE**

 Brew XI, Old Speckled Hen, Fuller's London Pride

East of the M42 and right out into the countryside, this well-managed rural pub is worth having up your sleeve for a city getaway; you shouldn't expect to have it all to yourself – it's not a ticking-clock-snoozing-dog local – but the bustling atmosphere is at least half the pleasure. Lunchtime in particular tends to be busy, so get there early to be sure of a table. The terrace at the back, overlooking a large lawned garden, makes for pleasant al fresco eating. With its banquettes, colourful paintings, big metal-topped bar and busy kitchen on view behind glass, the main part of the pub has made a subtly modern style its own, without losing too much of its country character: the same could be said for its robust cooking which features daily fish specials and uses seasonings from the pub's own herb garden.

Food serving times:
Monday-Saturday:
12pm-2.30pm, 7pm-9.30pm
Closed 25 December
and 1 January
(lunch bookings not accepted)
Prices:
Meals: 25.00 (fixed price dinner) and a la carte 18.85/30.85

Off the A452 just South of Hampton-in-Arden: follow signs for Barston village; pub is on left hand side to the West of the village. Parking.

Typical Dishes

Seared scallops, white shallot purée

Sea bass, butternut squash and lime yoghurt

Vanilla pancakes, pear and

Chadwick End

035 The Orange Tree

Warwick End, Chadwick End B93 0BN

Tel.: (01564) 785364 - Fax: (01564) 782988
e-mail: theorangetree@lovelypubs.co.uk - Website: www.orangetreepub.co.uk

IPA, Abbots, Tetleys

Bay trees adorn the entrance to this smart pale-green painted pub conversion with definite restaurant sensibilities. Though pubby in style, the Orange Tree attracts ladies who lunch and sits firmly in the country dining league. Sumptuous leather sofas, cushioned chairs and banquettes beckon you into a contemporary sub-divided lounge and bar with views into the kitchen area. Unless you're making your way outside to the attractive terrace, settle down at one of the varnished wooden tables, and select a dish from the simple, up-to-the-minute menu which concentrates on oven-fired pizza, pasta and grills.

Food serving times:
Monday-Saturday:
  12pm-2.30pm, 6pm-9.30pm
Sunday: 12pm-2.30pm
(booking essential)
Prices:
Meals: a la carte 25.00/32.00

Typical Dishes
Asparagus and serrano ham
Lamb rump, roast minted pears
Baked cheesecake, white chocolate & cranberries

On A4141 midway between Solihull and Warwick. Parking.

Hampton-in-Arden

036 **The White Lion**

10 High St, Hampton-in-Arden B92 0AA
Tel.: (01675) 442833 - Fax: (01675) 443168

room *VISA*

> *Brew 11 Black Sheep and changing guest ales*

Set in a leafy village opposite the church, and very handy for the NEC in Birmingham, this 17C pub has Grade II listed status; surprisingly, though, when you step through the front door, there's an appealing rusticity on show, exemplified by stripped pine floors, pale beams and fresh flowers. The cosy front bar is where the locals gather, impressed by a fine range of real ales on offer; a separate side bar boasts welcoming, modern touches. To the rear, soft, neutral colours announce the dining room where dinner is served, a stylish place to eat, with ranks of mirrors and smart Lloyd Loom chairs. Well cooked, interesting dishes offer a predominantly light touch, full of Italian elements, but reaching further afield for added inspiration in other dishes. The comfortable bedrooms – 4 in the pub and a further 4 in the outside annexe – reflect the simple, modern style of the restaurant.

Food serving times:
Monday-Saturday:
 12pm-2.30pm, 6.30pm-10pm
Sunday: 12pm-3pm
Prices:
Meals: 22.95 (set price dinner if requested) and a la carte 19.50/23.95
🛏 **8 rooms :** 49.00/59.00
☕ 7.50

> In the centre of the village. Parking. **〉〉**

Typical Dishes

Smoked salmon and spinach Florentine

Roast duck, blackberry and Port jus

Pineapple tart Tatin

Lapworth

037 Boot Inn

Old Warwick Rd, Lapworth B94 6JU
Tel.: (01564) 782464 - Fax: (01564) 784989
e-mail: bootinn@hotmail.com - Website: www.thebootatlapworth.co.uk

Timothy Taylor's Landlord, Old Speckled Hen

Who'd believe Birmingham's just 10 miles up the road? Take a step outside the pretty village of Lapworth and discover this wonderfully rustic inn that pre-dates the adjacent Grand Union Canal by a few hundred years. It boasts a rabbit warren of beamed rooms to lunch in, the slightly gnarled tables adding to the charmingly frayed-round-the-edges feel. The Boot gets busy, so book or arrive early, and don't look for an area set for dining, as cutlery arrives after you've ordered. There's a wide mix of styles from classic rustic pub fare to dishes with a decided European and Oriental influence - whatever takes your gastronomic fancy. As well as the bars, you can eat in a timbered upstairs dining room or on the terrace.

Food serving times:
Monday-Sunday:
12.30pm-2.30pm,
6.30pm-10pm
Closed 25 December
(booking essential)
Prices:
Meals: a la carte 21.00/32.00

Typical Dishes

Baltic plate
Shepherd's pie, glazed carrots
Plum tart Tatin, cinnamon and vanilla ice cream

2mi Southeast of Hockley Heath on B4439; on the left hand side just before the village. Parking.

Sutton Coldfield

038 ## The Cock Inn

Bulls Lane, Wishaw, Sutton Coldfield B76 9QL

Tel.: (0121) 313 3960
Website: www.cockinnwishaw.co.uk

Hook Norton, Tim Taylors, Pedigree

Traditional on the outside, splendidly modern within. There's a confident, stylish ambience here, reflected in the buzz of the place. It's light and airy with wooden flooring and carvings and modern wood tables with discreet spot lighting. Some areas boast burgundy walls featuring framed wine labels; logs line another wall. There's a relaxing lounge area by the bar, and a cigar bar (apparently rather exclusive at weekends) opens onto a beer garden. Menus are original: they change seasonally, and have a section of little dishes alongside the well established grill rotisserie. The robust, modish cooking is mainly British, but other more eclectic elements vie for attention. All this, within minutes of the roaring M6 toll!

Food serving times:
Monday-Saturday:
   12pm-2.30pm, 6pm-9.30pm
Sunday: 12pm-6pm
Prices:
Meals: a la carte 18.50/31.00

7mi East of Sutton Coldfield just off A446 following signs over M6 toll road to Wishaw and Grove End. Parking.

Typical Dishes

Mushroom and smoked goat's cheese

Salmon and Parma ham, pesto

Dark chocolate pot, praline

*Y*orkshire, for many, means the
countryside: a mind's-eye landscape
of fells and fields spreading out from
the Pennines, neat Dales villages above the
Wharfe and the Swale, and Aysgarth Falls
and Hardraw Force in all their secluded
beauty. But the Ridings also lay claim to
the genteel charm of Harrogate and Ripon,
the striking ruins of Fountains Abbey and
Rievaux and the unexpected brilliance of
Vanburgh's Castle Howard, to say nothing
of York, its medieval walled town and its
awe-inspiring Minster. Industrial change
has left its mark in the pit towns and the
Steel City of Sheffield, but also in Leeds'
rejuvenated centre and at Saltaire, the 19C
mill village where Bradford-born David
Hockney's gallery is housed. The counties'
pubs range from the proudly classic to
the ceaselessly inventive, each striking its
own balance with the famous local love of
tradition: roast beef and Yorkshire pudding
may have been adopted by the rest of
Britain, but this is still the place to go for
Wensleydale cheese, York ham, moorland
game and parkin, the rich spiced oatmeal
cake baked specially for Bonfire Night!

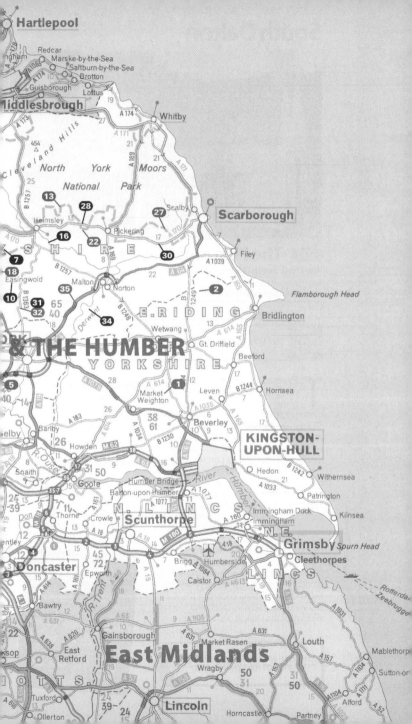

South Dalton

001 The Pipe and Glass Inn

West End, South Dalton HU17 7PN

Tel.: (01430) 810246
Website: www.pipeandglass.co.uk

 Daleside, Wold Top, John Smiths, and other changing guest beers

The pretty hamlet of South Dalton was abuzz in March 2006: James McKenzie's new 'project' was up-and-running. Ex-head chef of the much-heralded, Michelin-starred Star Inn at Harome, James was now bringing his talents to bear at this once neglected pub. Optimism was not misplaced. James and his partner Kate had invested a lot of time and effort into the Pipe and Glass, and the results were impressive: hand made chunky wooden tables, stripped wood floors and coir carpets, sleek lounge with low-back leather sofas, framed menus on rustic walls. So much for the décor. What about the food? Served either in snug bar or dining room, it's a well-honed mix of tasty modish dishes on a daily changing blackboard menu, the seasonal ingredients proudly bearing an East Riding provenance. Kate's cheery persona underpins the warm and welcoming service. Locals and foodies alike know this really is one to watch.

Food serving times:
Tuesday-Saturday:
12pm-2pm, 6.30pm-9.30pm
Sunday: 12pm-4pm
Closed 25 December
and 2 weeks in January
Prices:
Meals: a la carte 20.00/30.00

5mi North West of Beverley by A164, B1248 and side road West. Parking.

Typical Dishes

Homecured bresaola

Hay baked chicken, creamed leek & ham hock

Ginger burnt cream and rhubarb

Thwing

002 The Falling Stone

Main St, Thwing YO25 3OS
Tel.: (01262) 470403

🍷 ✂ ✂ *VISA* **MC**

 Mars Magic, Wold Gold and Falling Stone and one guest beer

Named after a meteorite which dropped from the skies here many years ago, The Falling Stone is the life-and-soul of this sleepy East Riding hamlet. A warm atmosphere extends from the greeting bestowed by Fudge, a delightfully friendly mastiff, to the blissfully informal and snug sitting areas with their range of low-level leather sofas, tea lights and open fire. This is a pub that takes its beer seriously: there's a fine selection of local ales from the Wold Brewery. Things are a little more formal in the linen-clad dining room, though rustic décor reminds you that this is the heart of the country and not a chic part of town. Menus change daily and start from a classical French base; they're ordered from a blackboard above the crackling fire.

Food serving times:
Wednesday-Friday:
6pm-10pm
Saturday-Sunday:
12pm-2.30pm, 6pm-10pm
Prices:
Meals: a la carte 18.00/25.00

Typical Dishes

Risotto of local crab, tomato, basil & Parmesan

Wild bass, sauce vierge

Mascarpone and vanilla cheesecake

9mi West of Bridlington by B1253 and minor road North. Parking. >

Asenby

003 Crab and Lobster 🛏

Dishforth Rd, Asenby YO7 3QL

Tel.: (01845) 577286 - Fax: (01845) 577109
e-mail: reservations@crabmanor.co.uk - Website: www.crabandlobster.co.uk

 John Smiths Cask, Skipton Golden Pippin and Skipton 1816

As atmospheric in its own way as the nearby North York Moors, this bizarrely adorned thatched pub displays lobster pots, pews, a dentist's chair, rocking chair and fairground horses in its midst, but there's nothing eccentric in its widely acclaimed menus. A large conservatory, called the Pavilion, and terrace have been added, and there's also an atmospheric, pubby styled brasserie, plus a softly lit, formal restaurant. Together they concentrate primarily on one type of dish: seafood, with the same menu served in all the different areas – the result is locally acclaimed dishes. The rooms are set in a part-Georgian manor house next door, new wooden log cabins and converted outbuildings: each of them individual, some with their own hot tub.

Food serving times:
Monday-Sunday:
12pm-2.30pm, 7pm-9.30pm
- Seafood -
Prices:
Meals: 14.50/17.50 (set price lunch) and a la carte 24.30/37.95
🛏 **14 rooms :** 150.00/200.00

Typical Dishes

King scallops, chorizo scone

Cod with juniper, potatoes and belly pork

Assiette of desserts

5.25 mi Southwest of Thirsk by A168. Parking.

Aysgarth

004 George and Dragon Inn 🛏

Aysgarth DL8 3AD

Tel.: (01969) 663358 - Fax: (01969) 663773
e-mail: info@georgeanddragonaysgarth.co.uk - Website: www.georgeanddragonaysgarth.co.uk

Cask, Theakstons, Black Sheep, Emmerdale

With its proximity to the impressive Aysgarth Falls and the Dales Countryside Museum at Hawes, as well as its setting in the heart of Wensleydale, this traditional family pub packs an instant punch. There's a pleasant terrace with thatched umbrellas, and, inside, a snug little bar highlighted by a crackling fire and fine array of Yorkshire ales. The feel for local produce extends to lunchtime sandwiches with, typically, Nidderdale salmon and Swalesdale cheddar. More substantial old favourites like Wensleydale pork sausages and mash or fish and chips make a reassuring appearance alongside more ambitious fare: tuck into this lot in either the airy Victorian styled dining room, or the open dining area with its display of wine knickknacks on the walls. There are seven comfy bedrooms; remember to book in advance – with its lovely scenery and superb walks, this is a popular spring and summer destination.

Food serving times:
Monday-Sunday:
12pm-2pm, 6pm-9pm
Closed 2 weeks in January
Prices:
Meals: 25.00 (set price dinner) and a la carte 15.00/25.00
🛏 **7 rooms :** 36.00/79.00

Typical Dishes

Scallops, horseradish rösti and salsa

Fillet steak, Lyonnaise potatoes

Chocolate fudge truffle

7mi West of Leyburn by A684. Parking.

Bilbrough

005 The Three Hares Country Inn

Main St, Bilbrough YO23 3PH

Tel.: (01937) 832128

e-mail: threehares@ukf.net · Website: www.thethreehares.co.uk

 John Smiths Cask, Timothy Taylor Landlord, Black Sheep Bitter and 1 changing guest ale

This immaculately whitewashed village pub feels miles away from the eager crowds of summer visitors to York; it's a great escape, certainly, but serves Bilbrough itself well enough, too. Traditional on the outside, the ambience inside is modern and fresh. The small bar area has rafters and exposed brickwork and is great for a cosy, informal lunch of sandwiches and salads. Two other rooms provide something of a contrast for those evening visitors with heartier appetites: here is a neat and tidy, linen-clad restaurant. Bar and dining room menus vary quite considerably: if you've chosen the latter, you'll have more ambitious options to choose from. Either way, service is smooth and polite.

Food serving times:
Tuesday-Saturday:
   12pm-2.30pm, 7pm-9pm
Sunday: 12pm-2.30pm
Prices:
Meals: a la carte 16.00/26.00

Typical Dishes

Rillette of duck

Baked Whitby fish pie

Bakewell tart, raspberry pannacotta

5 mi Southwest of York off the A64. Parking.

Burnsall

006 The Red Lion

Burnsall BD23 6BU

Tel.: (01756) 720204 - Fax: (01756) 720292
e-mail: redlion@daelnet.co.uk - Website: www.redlion.co.uk

Timothy Taylor Landlord, Theakstons Best, Black Bull and changing guest beers

From its haunted medieval cellars to the sedate comfort of the sitting room, history is ingrained in every nook and creaking beam of this creeper-clad inn on the River Wharfe. The 16C bar does a pleasantly busy trade in sustaining and enjoyable lunches by the fire. They'll gladly lay a table for dinner here too, but the restaurant, its windows overlooking the green and river, adds a further touch of formality and old-world service. A countryman's pub at heart, the Red Lion has its own trout and grayling waters and access to enviable grouse beats, so naturally fish and game, not to mention fine local lamb, are well represented on a extensive, classic menu with a light modern lift. Bedrooms boast sloping floors, open fires and Victorian brass bedsteads.

Food serving times:
Monday-Sunday:
    12pm-2pm, 7pm-9.30pm
Prices:
Meals: 22.95/32.95 and a la carte 25.00/35.00
14 rooms : 60.00/150.00

3mi Southeast of Grassington by B6265 West and B6160 South. Parking.

Typical Dishes

Red Lion Provencal fish soup

Sea bass, celeriac mash and tomato chutney

Lemon tart and lemon sorbet

Byland Abbey

007 **The Abbey Inn**

Byland Abbey YO61 4BD
Tel.: (01347) 868204 - Fax: (01347) 868678
Website: www.bylandabbeyinn.com

⟨≈rest⟩ **VISA**

 Black Sheep and Byland Brew

A charming, ivy-clad, part 17C country inn with a unique monastic connection: the story goes that Ampleforth monks helped to restore the old house using the old stones of the dilapidated abbey opposite. Its main rooms are full of character, as you might expect, their old beams and stonework still in place – one is open plan with an atrium roof, which works surprisingly well. Hearty, traditional cooking revolves around classic favourites supplemented with modern dishes and daily specials. Comfortable and handsomely furnished bedrooms are particularly fine, with plenty of thoughtful little extras; two rooms enjoy views of the enchanting Early Gothic abbey ruins.

Food serving times:
Monday: 6.30pm-9pm
Tuesday-Saturday:
12pm-2pm, 6.30pm-9pm
Sunday: 12pm-2pm
Closed 24-25 December
Prices:
Meals: a la carte 20.00/30.00
3 rooms : 95.00/155.00

Typical Dishes

Scallops with salmon ravioli

Herb crusted lamb,
Dauphinoise potatoes

Summer berry & mint
terrine

6mi Southwest of Helmsley by A170 and minor road South; opposite the ruins of Byland Abbey. Parking.

Carlton-in-Coverdale

008 Foresters Arms

Carlton-in-Coverdale DL8 4BB

Tel.: (01969) 640272 - Fax: (01969) 640272
e-mail: chambersmic@hotmail.co.uk - Website: www.the-foresters-arms.co.uk

   *VISA*

John Smith's Cask, Black Sheep Bitter, Wensleydale

Between the moor and the river Cover, the quiet Dales village of Carlton is an ideal place to get away from it all. There's a pleasantly unhurried mood in the two beamed and flagged rooms of its pub (a third room, the formal dining room, also opens for dinner), and ramblers can retrace the day's walk in the maps and prints which cover the walls; there's also seating outside if you want to take your beer out into the sun. Sound cooking on a traditional base goes well with a pint and certainly gets the locals' approval. If the pictures in the bar give you an appetite for more of the great outdoors, drive north to Aysgarth and its beautiful triple flight of waterfalls, made famous by the film Robin Hood, Prince of Thieves. Three pleasant cottagey bedrooms have been comfortably refurbished by the exacting young owners.

Food serving times:
Wednesday-Saturday:
   12pm-2pm, 6.30pm-8.30pm
Sunday: 6.30pm-8.30pm
Closed lunch, Tuesday-Thursday, November-April
Prices:
Meals: a la carte 15.50/27.60
3 rooms : 65.00/79.00

Typical Dishes
Mini potato and Lincolnshire poacher rösti
John Dory, cucumber and Nölly Prat
Baked rhubarb & custard

4.5 mi Southwest of Middleham by Coverdale rd. Parking next to pub in village car park. ➤

Constable Burton

009 Wyvill Arms

Constable Burton DL8 5LH
Tel.: (01677) 450581 - Fax: (01677) 450829

 🛆 ♈ ⤶rest **VISA** **AE** **M⑥**

Black Sheep, Theakstons, John Smith's and rotating guest ales:
Copper Dragon, Hydes, Hambleton

Abbeys and castles – Jervaulx, Richmond, Bolton – are all within a 10-mile radius of this early 20C pub, situated on a busy road in a small village on the eastern edge of the Dales. There are some traditional elements here – the odd beam, a stone bar area, plenty of memorabilia – but the real attraction for visitors and walkers wearied by a hike in the surrounding countryside is the good choice of ales and locally renowned dishes, steaks being a speciality. There's a blackboard menu which holds some interest, or just enjoy hearty cooking that makes the most of Yorkshire produce in the formal dining room, informal flag-floored bar dining area or the small, cosy bar. Bedrooms are neat, tidy and bright as is the small garden with its wishing well focal point.

Food serving times:
Monday-Sunday:
12pm-2pm, 6.30pm-9pm
Prices:
Meals: a la carte 20.00/29.00
🛏 **3 rooms :** 50.00/75.00

Typical Dishes

Fresh figs with goat's cheese
& Parma ham

Roast suckling pig, mustard
mash

Creme brûlée

3.5mi East of Leyburn on A684.
Parking.

Crayke

010　The Durham Ox

Westway, Crayke YO61 4TE

Tel.: (01347) 821506 - Fax: (01347) 823326
e-mail: enquiries@thedurhamox.com - Website: www.thedurhamox.com

  rest   **VISA**

> *Theakston's Best Bitter and guest beers - Henry's IPA and Cooper's Butt*

Seasonal Modern British cooking is the order of the day here: blackboard daily specials offer a satisfying selection which combines the robust and the sophisticated, sometimes in the same dish. A smartly set yet cosy dining room is convivial enough, but the real heart of this personally run pub is the charming main bar, with its inglenooks, open fires, gnarled beams and three centuries of character; diners are made to feel very welcome in both. A small shop at the entrance sells local deli produce and out in the converted farm buildings, attractive country-style rooms manage to marry period-style furnishings with mod cons like music systems or spa baths. A real local favourite on all counts.

Food serving times:
Monday-Friday:
　12pm-2.30pm, 6pm-9.30pm
Closed for food
25 December
Prices:
Meals: a la carte 20.00/33.00
8 rooms : 60.00/80.00

Typical Dishes

Beef carpaccio

Roast monkfish, chorizo and pancetta

Rhubarb & ginger crumble and egg custard

2 mi East of Easingwold on Helmsley rd. Parking.

Dalton

011 **The Travellers Rest**

Dalton DL11 7HU
Tel.: (01833) 621225

♀ *VISA* Ⓜ©

Black Sheep Best Bitter

A traditional looking, ivy-clad pub in a tiny hamlet well off the beaten track - for anyone wanting to get away not just from the roar of the city but even from the quiet murmur of the town, this could be the place. It looks like a traditional pub inside as well as out, consisting of a bar lounge with open fire and bric-a-brac, and another room with simple wood tables, chairs and benches. But there's also a linen-laid restaurant available for dinner, where the locals tend to turn out in force, and the reason is simple: the food's good – the blackboard menu's eclectic and traditional with modern twists, and it's decent value, too. Unpretentious, with personable and friendly service.

Food serving times:
Tuesday-Saturday:
   12pm-4.30pm, 7pm-9.30pm
Monday: 12pm-4.30pm
Closed 25-26 December
and 1st January
Prices:
Meals: a la carte 15.95/24.00

Typical Dishes
French farm salad
Cajun chicken, almond and ginger
Lime cheesecake with fresh fruits

7.5 mi Northwest of Scotch Corner by A66. Parking.

East Witton

012 The Blue Lion

East Witton DL8 4SN

Tel.: (01969) 624273 - Fax: (01969) 624189
e-mail: bluelion@breathemail.net - Website: www.thebluelion.co.uk

 Theakstons, Black Sheep, Riggwelter

On the edge of the Yorkshire Dales, this 18C one-time coaching inn reigns supreme. It's appealing all round, from the 18C style wood floors and crimson ceiling to the old, faded pictures, open fires and beams with entwined dried flowers – and that's just the restaurant. Pop across to the bar and the character shows no sign of flagging. Or rather, the flagging spreads out right there beneath your feet. It underpins two rooms that boast a bubbly and appealing atmosphere. Wooden booths, pubby knick-knacks, simple tables and chairs and a large, self-assured, modern blackboard menu – served throughout the establishment – entice diners in large numbers: the place has a strong local reputation. No-one seems in a rush: many are staying in the comfy, individually decorated bedrooms

Food serving times:
Monday-Saturday:
  12pm-2.15pm, 7pm-9.30pm
Sunday: 7pm-9pm
Closed 25 December
(booking essential)
Prices:
Meals: a la carte 19.00/31.00
15 rooms : 57.50/79.99

Typical Dishes

Whitby crab and beetroot salad

Confit of duck, wild mushroom, chestnut and bacon risotto

3mi Southeast of Leyburn on A6108.
Parking

Fadmoor

013 The Plough Inn

Main Street, Fadmoor YO62 7HY

Tel.: (01751) 431515

VISA ⓂⒸ

Black Sheep Best, Tetleys Cask

This neatly-kept little pub on the edge of the North York Moors has a solidly earned reputation and bustling atmosphere. Its position overlooking the village green guarantees a good smattering of walkers, and the friendly welcome ensures word-of-mouth is always positive. There's a characterful interior, a cheery balance between the rustic and the elegant: coir floors, sturdy range doubling as open fire, yellow walls, rich furnishings. Sit at simple wooden tables and chairs in the bar or head instead for a cosy, formally-laid rear dining rooms. Home cooking is to the fore, with the emphasis on fish and seafood. The same extensive menus are served throughout: a neat blend of the traditional with the more contemporary.

Food serving times:
Monday-Sunday:
  12pm-1.45pm,
  6.30pm-8.45pm

Closed 25-26 December and 1 January
(booking essential)

Prices:
Meals: 12.95 (set price 2 course lunch and dinner) and a la carte 17.95/27.00

Typical Dishes

Black pudding, tomato coulis and salad

Gressingham duck, mandarin & brandy sauce

Lemon and lime tart

2.25 mi Northwest of Kirbymoorside. Parking.

Ferrensby

014 ## The General Tarleton Inn 🛏

Boroughbridge Rd, Ferrensby HG5 0PZ

Tel.: (01423) 340284 - Fax: (01423) 340288
e-mail: gti@generaltarleton.co.uk - Website: www.generaltarleton.co.uk

🍷 ✗ **VISA** **AE** **M©**

🍺 *Black Sheep Best Bitter, Timothy Taylor's Landlord*

The extended 18C pub, surrounded by North Yorkshire countryside, remains as characterful and well run as ever. Neatly painted beams, old stonework and open fires, not to mention a small collection of humorous prints and period pictures on some of the walls, all bring out the convivial character of the place, although the atmosphere is substantially more formal in the dining room. Blackboard specials, early evening menus and Sunday fish suppers suggest a kitchen happy to experiment and accommodate while keeping the winning combination of affordable prices and flavourful, well-judged British cooking, based on quality local produce. Polite service makes for a really enjoyable lunch or evening out.

Food serving times:
Monday-Saturday:
  12pm-2.15pm, 6pm-9.15pm
Sunday: 12pm-1.45pm
Prices:
Meals: 18.95/29.50 (Sunday lunch only, dinner Monday-Saturday) and a la carte 20.00/32.00
🛏 **14 rooms :** 85.00/120.00

Typical Dishes

Tomato tart, goat's cheese, rocket & pesto

Confit of Dales lamb, thyme & tomato jus

Yorkshire rhubarb trio

From A1 at Boroughbridge, take A6055 road towards Knaresborough; the inn is on the right hand side. Parking.

Galphay

015 ## Galphay Inn

Galphay HG4 3NJ

Tel.: (01765) 650133 - Fax: (01765) 658992
e-mail: info@galphayinn.co.uk - Website: www.galphayinn.co.uk

 VISA **MC**

 Black Sheep Bitter, Timothy Taylor's Landlord

Appealing and unfussy, the steady cooking at the Galphay Arms never strays far from its traditional roots, but makes good use of regional ingredients and brings out the flavours of the season with simplicity and clarity: you can't go far wrong with anything on this menu, washed down with a glass of red or a Yorkshire ale. Choose one of the neatly set, marble-topped tables to one side, or a firelit bar in true country style with wood-panelled walls, heavy wooden tables and a collection of hunting prints on the walls. All in all, a proper village pub with a relaxing, homely feel, for which the personable owners can take much of the credit.

Food serving times:
Wednesday-Monday:
  12pm-2.30pm, 6pm-9.30pm
Prices:
Meals: 15.95 and a la carte
19.00/26.00

4.5mi West of Ripon by B6265.
Parking.

Typical Dishes

Mushrooms with spinach, blue cheese & pinenuts

Duck, honey and pink peppercorn sauce

Sticky toffee pudding

Harome

016 The Star Inn 🛏️

High St, Harome YO62 5JE

Tel.: (01439) 770397 - Fax: (01439) 771833
e-mail: starinn@btopenworld.com - Website: www.thestaratharome.co.uk

 VISA 〽️

 Copper Dragon, John Smiths, Black Sheep, Theakston's and various guest ales

You'll need a hearty appetite as well as a fine palate to get the most from this deliciously characterful, 14C thatched inn at the tip of the North York Moors. The aptly named pub not only provides an utterly charming dining room, but also superb, rich dishes, prepared with balance and panache, that show pride in its Yorkshire roots. The bar loses nothing by the dining room's starring role; it boasts Mousey Thompson's famous furniture and antiques, as well as solid stone floors, walls filled with period knick-knacks, beam-and-plank ceiling, big log fire, and daily papers and magazines. As if that weren't enough, there's a cosy coffee loft in the eaves, an organic deli selling all manner of delicious goodies, al fresco options in garden or on front terrace, and contemporary bedrooms for overnighters in converted outbuildings across the road.

Food serving times:
Tuesday-Saturday:
11.30pm-2pm,
6.30pm-9.30pm
Sunday: 11.30pm-2pm
Closed 25 December,
2 weeks in spring, bank holidays
(booking essential)

Prices:
Meals: a la carte 35.00/50.00
🛏️ **11 rooms :** 140.00/210.00

2.75 mi Southeast of Helmsley by A170. Parking. ➤

Typical Dishes

Fried Scarborough woof & scallops, ketchup

Roe deer & shepherd's pie

Yorkshire rhubarb

Hetton

017 ## The Angel Inn

Hetton BD23 6LT

Tel.: (01756) 730263 - Fax: (01756) 730363
e-mail: info@angelhetton.co.uk - Website: www.angelhetton.co.uk

VISA AE MC

Timothy Taylor Landlord, Black Sheep Bitter

This hugely characterful pub started brewing and serving beer to cattle drovers 300 years ago. If they returned now, they'd probably recognise the same unimproved oak beams, nooks and crannies, but there's now a formal restaurant as well as a bar. The snug warren of rooms is invariably packed, so try to get there early to bag a table. Otherwise, wander around and admire the rural prints, old menus and various awards displayed around the walls. The wooden bar displays well-priced blackboard specials, made up of classic and original dishes, some taking inspiration from France and Italy. Ingredients are mostly drawn from nearby sources: meats from the Dales, Lancastrian sausages and cheese, and fish from Fleetwood. Herbs are even more indigenous: from The Angel's own back garden. The pub's smart bedrooms are set in converted farm buildings across the road.

Food serving times:
Monday-Saturday:
6pm-9.30pm
Sunday: 12pm-1.45pm
Closed 25 December,
1 January
(booking essential)
Prices:
Meals: 16.50/19.25 (dinner early bird menu) and a la carte 20.00/34.50
5 rooms : 130.00/190.00

Typical Dishes

Yorkshire cheese soufflé

Goosenargh duck, fig and onion compote

Rhubarb three ways

5.75mi North of Skipton by B6265. Parking.

Husthwaite

018 **The Roasted Pepper**

Low St, Husthwaite YO61 4QA

Tel.: (01347) 868007 - Fax: (01347) 868776
e-mail: info@roastedpepper.co.uk - Website: www.roastedpepper.co.uk

  VISA

No real ales offered

Turn off the A19 on your way to the North York Moors for an interesting culinary diversion. In the pretty little village of Husthwaite stands this immaculately whitewashed Victorian pub, given a 21C wash and scrub-up: this amounts to an interior best described as sunny, with a bright, contemporary red and yellow palette given full reign. The 19C hasn't been totally forgotten, though – the original brick and tile flooring is still intact. There's a small bar with a couple of tables for drinkers; it all starts to get serious with the dining area, where heavy wood tables and chairs lend the air of a restaurant. Menus are keenly priced and have a distinctly Mediterranean theme, with tapas a key component. There's also a terrace which is popular in summer months.

Food serving times:
Tuesday-Saturday:
   12pm-2.30pm, 7pm-9.30pm
Sunday: 12pm-2.30pm
Prices:
Meals: a la carte 15.00/25.00

Typical Dishes

Tapas

Roast rump of lamb, sweet potato & parsnip potato cake

Raspberry cranachan

Between Thirsk and Easingwold off A19. Parking.

Kirk Deighton

019 **The Bay Horse Inn**

Main St, Kirk Deighton LS22 4DZ

Tel.: (01937) 580058

 VISA

Black Sheep, Cumberland Ale, Timothy Taylor Landlord, John Smith Cask

Pop up the road from Wetherby and you'll come upon a pub that's really making a name for itself locally. The Bay Horse is a busy place. Those in the know don't just come for the selection of real ales, good as it is. Nor for the spacey, eclectic interior bursting with country curios, such as fishing rods on the ceiling and charming old sepia prints on the walls. They don't even make the trip to stock up on homemade jams and pickles, though this is part of the appeal. They come mostly for the great food: local reputation is ensuring the Bay Horse is earning its spurs as a dining destination pub. Yorkshire ingredients are put to appealing use on a set menu with traditional undercurrent or daily specials board where local pheasant and mallard are typically popular choices, backed up by welcoming service from keen staff.

Food serving times:
Tuesday-Saturday:
   12pm-2.15pm, 6pm-9.15pm
Sunday: 12pm-2.15pm
Monday: 6pm-9.15pm
(booking essential)

Prices:
Meals: 13.95 (2 course lunch and dinner) and a la carte 17.50/30.00

Typical Dishes

Home smoked salmon

Saddleback pork, pears and crackling

White chocolate tart, blackcurrant sorbet

1.5mi North of Wetherby by B6164. Parking.

Langthwaite

020 The Charles Bathurst Inn

Langthwaite DL11 6EN

Tel.: (01748) 884567 - Fax: (01748) 884599
e-mail: info@cbinn.co.uk - Website: www.cbinn.co.uk

  VISA

> *John Smiths Best Bitter, Theakstons Best Bitter, Black Sheep Best and Riggwelter*

High in the windswept hills of Arkengarthdale, the well-run 18C inn is named after the old lord of the manor, whose "CB" monogram was stamped on the local lead from which he made his fortune: any cross-country ramble – and there are plenty – is likely to skirt more than one of his long-disused mines. Wood floors, open fires and photos of Herriot country add greatly to the charm of a neatly kept bar, which is perfect for a quiet pint or two, but owes much of its strong local reputation to its half-modern, half-traditional menu, painted afresh every day on two broad mirrors: there's more choice, and more demand, in the evenings. Spacious, individually decorated bedrooms with period pine furniture are good to come back to after a long day's walk.

Food serving times:
Monday-Sunday:
12pm-2pm, 6.30pm-9pm
Closed 25 December
Prices:
Meals: a la carte 17.50/30.00
18 rooms : 85.00/105.00

3.25mi Northwest of Reeth on Langthwaite rd. Parking.

Typical Dishes

Avocado and crab filo basket

Venison sausage, truffle mash & wild berry sauce

White chocolate crème brûlée

Leyburn

021 The Sandpiper Inn

Market Pl, Leyburn DL8 5AT

Tel.: (01969) 622206 - Fax: (01969) 625367
e-mail: hsandpiper99@aol.com - Website: www.sandpiperinn.co.uk

Black Sheep Best, Emmerdale, Copper Dragon

A pub ideally placed for weary ramblers making their way from the Dales, this converted 16C stone house could just as easily be missed by them, as it's tucked away at one end of the market square and needs to be sought out. The effort's not wasted. Downstairs is a traditional pub, divided into cosy alcoves nestling under dark beams, with a log fire lighting the way. In the simply stylish – though rather subdued - dining room, it's bare wood tables by day, but linen at night. Good value blackboard menus offer rich pickings in the form of traditional dishes, with local produce to the fore. For those who really are too weary, there are two comfy bedrooms upstairs and a new third room in a converted cottage across the road.

Food serving times:
Tuesday-Saturday:
 12pm-2.30pm, 6.30pm-9pm
Sunday: 12pm-2pm,
  7pm-9pm

Closed 25 December
and 1 January

Prices:
Meals: a la carte 20.00/30.00
3 rooms : 65.00/90.00

Typical Dishes

Mosaic of game

Roast sea bass, spaghetti of courgette, basil and spinach

Trio of puddings

In town centre. Limited parking available in the Market Place.

Marton

022 ## The Appletree

Marton YO62 6RD

Tel.: (01751) 431457 - Fax: (01751) 430190
e-mail: appletreeinn@supanet.com - Website: www.appletreeinn.co.uk

     VISA

 John Smiths Cash, Suddaby's Double Chance, York Yorkshire Terrier, Wold Top Falling Stone and 3 regularly changing guest ales

Spacious, warm and comfortable, a typical Yorkshire inn run by a friendly couple and set in a quiet village on the banks of the Seven, where the river runs down to the Vale of Pickering. In a rustic interior of exposed brick and timbers, well-spaced tables through three adjoining rooms mark this out as a dining pub first and foremost, so it's no surprise to find a touch of rather proper formality in the service. The cooking, too, works in its presentational flourishes, but it's not without its traditional, homespun side as well, with beef to the fore.

Food serving times:
Wednesday-Saturday:
  12pm-2pm, 6.30pm-9.30pm
Sunday: 12pm-2pm,
                  7pm-9pm

Closed 25 December
and 2 weeks January
Prices:
Meals: a la carte 20.00/35.00

Typical Dishes

Whitby crab cheesecake
Confit belly pork, black pudding
Double chocolate mocha tart

5mi west of Pickering by A170.
Parking.

Middleham

023 The White Swan 🛏

Market Pl, Middleham DL8 4PE

Tel.: (01969) 622093 - Fax: (01969) 624551
e-mail: whiteswan@easynet.co.uk - Website: www.whiteswanhotel.co.uk

 Black Sheep Best Bitter, Black Sheep Ale, John Smith's Cask Bitter, Theakstons Best Bitter

In a town now best known for its racehorses, where Richard III's white boar standard once flew from the now-ruined castle, The White Swan proves there's no accounting for some choices of pub names. A pleasant but unremarkable part of the market place, the old coaching inn saves the best for inside: the stone-floored bar with stove and inglenook is inviting enough, but the two cosy little rooms at the back are even nicer on a cold evening, and the neatly decorated bedrooms could be useful for an overnight stop. A sound, locally sourced English menu sticks to what it knows best with no over-reaching modern flourishes, preferring trusty favourites. Run with quiet Yorkshire competence, it's a real asset to the town.

Food serving times:
Monday-Sunday:
12pm-2.30pm,
6.30pm-9.30pm
Closed dinner 25 December
Prices:
Meals: 13.95 (set price lunch) and a la carte 15.00/25.00
🛏 **17 rooms :** 55.00/99.00

Typical Dishes

Confit of duck and bacon salad

Chicken with mozzarella and sundried tomatoes

Iced liquorice terrine

1mi from Leyburn on A6108. Parking in the Market Place.

Osmotherley

024 **The Golden Lion**

6 West End, Osmotherley DL6 3AA

Tel.: (01609) 883526

Timothy Taylor Landlord or Golden Best, Hambleton Best Bitter or Goldfield, NYB Co Fools Gold, Deuchars IPA

f you're walking the Cleveland Way, this old stone faced pub is like manna from heaven – it turns up right there on the path, so if you pay a visit, you're likely to meet fellow hikers. It's nothing very special to look at, and the interior isn't too much more than white walls and a few old pews, but the mix of ramblers, locals and those in search of a decent meal keeps the atmosphere lively and friendly. What draws the dining fraternity here are the simple, well-constructed, keenly priced dishes that consistently hit the spot. Tried-and-tested meals are prepared with real care; extensive menus offer hearty fuel for heading to the hills.

Food serving times:
Monday-Sunday:
12pm-3pm, 6pm-9pm
Closed 25 December
Prices:
Meals: a la carte 15.00/25.00
3 rooms : 80.00

Typical Dishes

Smoked haddock risotto

Pork with Parma Ham and Marsala sauce

Bakewell tart and custard

6 mi Northeast of Northallerton by A684. Parking in village.

Osmotherley

025 The 3 Tuns

9 South End, Osmotherley DL6 3BN

Tel.: (01609) 883301 - Fax: (01609) 883988

e-mail: enquiries@3tunsrestaurantco.uk - Website: www.3tunsrestaurant.co.uk

 rest **VISA**

 Timothy Taylor's Landlord, Black Sheep Bitter

Set in a pretty village, this is an unassuming pub on first sight – the modern sign outside is the first hint at the sympathetic refit that's taken place indoors. Pale oak panelling lightens rather than darkens the bar and restaurant, and combines surprisingly well with the retro design – there's more than a touch of re-interpreted Rennie Mackintosh in the pub's style. Three bedrooms in the pub and four in the cottage next door – formerly the village bakery – have been designed with similar care: they're comfortable and nicely maintained. Though you can wander in for a drink – and people do – the focus here is on food, served in a neatly set back room and also out on the front and back terraces, with modern menus which are a touch popular in places, as well as offering some more original dishes.

Food serving times:
Monday-Sunday:
12pm-2.30pm,
5.30pm-9.30pm

Prices:
Meals: a la carte 16.50/30.00
7 rooms : 55.00/75.00

Typical Dishes

Mussels, spicy tomato sauce

Halibut, cucumber and onion

Rhubarb sponge & custard

6mi Northeast of Northallerton by A684. Parking in village.

Ramsgill-in-Nidderdale

026 **Yorke Arms**

Ramsgill-in-Nidderdale HG3 5RL

Tel.: (01423) 755243 - Fax: (01423) 755330

e-mail: enquiries@yorke-arms.co.uk - Website: www.yorke-arms.co.uk

    VISA **AE** **①** **M③**

Black Sheep Special

Set in unspoilt countryside near Gouthwaite reservoir, this part 17C, delightfully ivy clad former shooting lodge is quite simply one of England's most charming inns. Handsomely styled with carved wooden furniture, antiques, oriental rugs and bright, gilt-framed oils, two welcoming dining rooms feel closer in atmosphere to a country house than a village pub, and the formal, structured service is that of a restaurant rather than an inn, but as a dining experience it's calm, refined and, at its best, quite delightful. Precise and consistent seasonal cooking balances classical style with a subtle regional identity. Good value lunch Monday to Saturday and you can make the most of a lovely riverside terrace and gardens, or flop onto the squashy sofas in the lounge. Superlative, stylish and contemporary bedrooms have been recently refurbished.

Food serving times:

Monday-Saturday:
    12pm-2pm, 7pm-9pm

Sunday: 12pm-2pm

Accommodation rates include dinner

Prices:

Meals: 21.00/50.00 (set price lunch and dinner) and a la carte 30.00/50.00

13 rooms : 120.00/ 240.00

5 mi Northwest of Pateley Bridge by Low Wath rd. Parking.

Typical Dishes

Morel tart, artichoke and fennel

Roast turbot, white truffle risotto

Apple Bavarois

Sawdon

027 The Anvil Inn

Main St, Sawdon YO13 9DY

Tel.: (01723) 859896

Website: www.theanvilinnsawdon.co.uk

 VISA **MC**

 Black Sheep Best and 2 other guest ales from local breweries - Wold Top and Copper Dragon

Twenty years ago, you would have found blacksmiths working in this solid stone building. Now the atmosphere is more sedate, though much evidence of former days lives on: an old furnace, bellows, tools and the original anvil are all in situ. Close by, in the village of Sawdon, stunning views over Dalby Dale prevail, and the rustic charm of the inn – all candle-lit tables, country style paraphernalia and log-burning stove - loses nothing by comparison. Yorkshire ales are pulled in the locals' bar and the intimate dining room is like a home-from-home. Mark, one of the owners and also the chef here, trained at local college and his roots are in evidence with seriously considered, good value dishes using dishes primarily sourced from the nearby moors and dales. And the portions are good, too!

Food serving times:
Tuesday-Saturrday:
    12pm-2pm, 6.30pm-9pm
Sunday: 12pm-3pm
Closed 25 December
Prices:
Meals: a la carte 14.35/21.65

12mi South West of Scarborough by A170 to Brompton and minor road north. Parking.

Typical Dishes

Aromatic crispy duck

Chicken, Wensleydale and ham

Orange, pinenut & honey semifreddo

Sinnington

028 Fox and Hounds 🛏

Main St, Sinnington YO62 6SQ

Tel.: (01751) 431577 - Fax: (01751) 432791
e-mail: foxhoundsinn@easynet.co.uk - Website: www.thefoxandhoundsinn.co.uk

Theakston's Best Bitter, Cask, Black Sheep Special

Drive four miles out from the attractive market town of Pickering and you arrive in sleepy Sinnington on the river Seven, at the southern end of the North York Moors. The Fox And Hounds, an attractively extended 18C coaching inn, is the pivot around which community life revolves. Its characterful front bar is beamed and panelled in ancient oak, with old artefacts and a woodburner. Flop down there or retreat to the smart residents lounge with a pint of local ale. The restaurant, housed in a rear extension, has smart, linen-clad tables; the impressive menu is served in both dining areas. Bedrooms are neat and tidy with a cottagey feel and style.

Food serving times:
Summer: Monday-Sunday:
12pm to 2pm, 6.30pm-9pm
Winter: Monday-Sunday:
12pm to 2pm, 7pm-9pm
Closed 25-26 December
Prices:
Meals: a la carte 20.00/28.00
🛏 **10 rooms :** 49.00/120.00

Just off A170 between Pickering and Kirkymoorside. Parking.

Typical Dishes

Confit duck, mango & cashew nuts

Guinea fowl, wild mushroom jus

Bread and butter pudding

Skipton

029 The Bull

Broughton, Skipton BD23 3AE

Tel.: (01756) 792065 - Fax: (01756) 792065
e-mail: janeneil@thebullatbroughton.co.uk - Website: www.thebullatbroughton.co.uk

Bull Bitter, Copper Dragon

D on't let the busy A59 send you roaring off into the Pennines without a stop at this delightful country pub, located within the grounds of Broughton Hall Country Park Estate amid 3000 Yorkshire acres. It's a lovely old building which has been carefully refurbished to bring out the open log fire, rustic décor and intimate seating areas. The greetings are effusive, even from the pub cat. A selection of hand-drawn cask ales is always available, but pride of place-mat goes to the Bull's own beer brewed specially for them. The relaxing feel stretches to the dining rooms which envelop you in a web of warm stone. Chef makes good use of ingredients close to hand with produce from the Dales never far from your knife and fork; the pub's "everything home-made" credentials are worn as a badge of honour.

Food serving times:
Monday-Thursday:
12pm-2pm, 6pm-9pm
Friday-Saturday:
12pm-2pm, 6pm-9.30pm
Sunday and Bank holiday Mondays:
12pm-6pm
Prices:
Meals: a la carte 15.00/24.00

3mi West of Skipton town centre on A59. In the grounds of Broughton Hall Country Park Estate. Parking.

Typical Dishes

Fishcakes, Café de Paris mayonnaise

Sausages & mash

Chocolate tart

Snainton

030 **Coachman Inn** 🛏️

Pickering Road West, Snainton YO13 9PL

Tel.: (01723) 859231 - Fax: (01723) 850008
e-mail: james@coachmaninn.co.uk - Website: www.coachmaninn.co.uk

🍺	*Wold Top*

The very image of a Georgian posting inn, the Coachman stands on the edge of the North York Moors and must have been a welcome sight to travellers on the York to Scarborough road. Inside, a modern dining room has a view over the lawn – if you're planning on a formal meal, this is probably better, not to mention more spacious, but the little bar takes some beating for warmth and character. Cushioned pews, old elm tables, framed prints, hunting curios and a stuffed otter called Tarquin all, in their way, add to the traditional cosiness, and the friendly atmosphere deserves pointing out. Modern British cooking incorporates Yorkshire-reared meats, locally landed fish, and a few other specialities like Dales goat's cheese. Individually styled bedrooms.

Food serving times:
Tuesday-Saturday:
          12pm-2pm, 7pm-9pm
Sunday: 12pm-2pm
Closed Monday
Prices:
Meals: a la carte 14.00/25.00
🛏️ **2 rooms :** 40.00/66.00

Typical Dishes

Home-made soup

Sirloin steak, beetroot & horseradish cream

Bread and butter pudding

0.5 mi West by A170 on B1258. Parking.

Sutton on the Forest

031 The Blackwell Ox Inn 🛏

Huby Rd, Sutton on the Forest YO61 1DT
Tel.: (01347) 810328 - Fax: (01347) 812738
e-mail: info@blackwelloxinn.co.uk - Website: www.blackwelloxinn.co.uk

 VISA **MC**

John Smith's Cask, Black Sheep Bitter

If it's heaving in York and you're stuck for a place to wine, dine and rest your weary bones, then you could do a lot worse than head north a few miles to the picturesque village of Sutton on the Forest and try your luck at this recently enlarged country inn and restaurant, where you'll be immediately enticed by the sight of cosy sofas in the open-fired bar. But do stir yourself, as food is the main emphasis here. The two dining rooms are set out with formal linen-clad tables, yet intimate enough to feel snug. Menus are based upon the southwest of France and the Catalan region of Spain, so expect tapas at one end of the culinary range, big cassoulets and rich Catalan stews at the other. Good value daily changing midweek set-price menus are another attraction. And for those weary bones, five comfy, individually decorated rooms are on offer.

Food serving times:
Monday-Sunday:
    12pm-2pm, 6pm-9.30pm
Prices:
Meals: 10.50/13.50 (set price lunch and dinner menu) and a la carte 17.50/27.50
🛏 **5 rooms :** 95.00

Typical Dishes

Duck & watercress salad

Monkfish and oxtail, salsify & girolles

Chocolate pudding, pistachio parfait

8mi North of York by B1363. Parking. ▶

Sutton-on-the-Forest

032 Rose & Crown

Main St, Sutton-on-the-Forest YO61 1DP

Tel.: (01347) 811333 - Fax: (01347) 811333

e-mail: andymiddleton@btconnect.com

Black Sheep Best, Timothy Taylors Landlord, Old Speckled Hen, Theakstons and many more guests ales

Everyday pub name, exceptional pub cooking typical of a carefully sourced and precisely prepared repertoire that's won plaudits around the county and beyond and has a loyal following of locals and other regulars. There's a lovely enclosed rear terrace and lawned garden and the smart, modern feel is softened slightly in a cosily rustic interior: it's unobtrusively stylish but still feels relaxed. Service is smooth and attentive without ever seeming stifling. The little seating and dining areas add a touch of intimacy, while the firelit bar, and the fair-minded value-for-money ethic, are in the best Yorkshire tradition. Small, but frequently changing wine list.

Food serving times:
Tuesday-Saturday:
    12pm-2pm, 6pm-9.30pm
Sunday: 12pm-2pm
Closed 25 December and
first 2 weeks in January
Prices:
Meals: a la carte 15.00/35.00

Typical Dishes

Shetland mussels

Sea bass, creamed leeks & shrimp butter

Syrup rice pudding, banana

On B1363 North of York. Parking.

West Tanfield

033 ## The Bruce Arms

Main St, West Tanfield HG4 5JJ

Tel.: (01677) 470325

e-mail: geoff@brucearms.com - Website: www.brucearms.com

room — ~~ — *VISA* — MC

> *Theakstons Best, Black Sheep Bitter*

This thriving little Yorkshire pub looks no great shakes from the outside, set as it is on a roundabout, despite the rather fetching creepers. Inside, though, a mini success story unfolds. Dating from 1820, it crams in timber beams, log fire, heaps of local memorabilia, and a good local ale on tap. In 1997, it re-styled itself as a bistro and its well-prepared, interesting dishes get the thumbs-up from all comers. Enjoy pre-dinner drinks in the leather furnished seating area just inside the entrance, then settle down for a meal in the cosy dining room, or on the vine covered terrace in warmer weather. Refurbished bedrooms offer rustic charm.

Food serving times:
Tuesday: 6.30pm-9.30pm
Wednesday-Saturday:
  12pm-2pm, 6.30pm-9.30pm
Sunday: 12pm-2pm
Closed Monday
Prices:
Meals: 12.95 and a la carte 12.95/28.50
2 rooms : 60.00/80.00

Between Masham and Ripon on A6108. Parking.

Typical Dishes

Serrano ham & pear, Hazlenut dressing

Nidderdale duckling, rhubarb sauce

Soft chocolate cake

Westow

034 The Blacksmiths Inn ⊨

Main St, Westow YO60 7NE

Tel.: (01653) 618365 - Fax: (01653) 618394
e-mail: info@blacksmithsinn.co.uk - Website: www.blacksmithsinn.co.uk

   rest **VISA** **MC**

John Smiths Cask, Tetleys Cask, Timothy Taylor Landlord,

Although it's fair to say that the Blacksmiths Inn is a modern dining pub, the move has taken it closer to, not further from, its country roots. There's a quiet glow from the wood-burning stove, and framed pictures, postcards, cartoons, Yorkshire landscapes and other themed artwork cover the walls. The local connection rings particularly true in the two trimly set dining rooms: vegetables from the pub's own farm, home-ground flour, and local sloe berries – in gin, jam, even chutneys and chocolates - play their part in a couple of specials and a concise, modern menu which changes by the week. Drinkers are made very welcome in the front lounge, with bowls of rustic, home-made nibbles like parsnip crisps and crackling set out on the bar. Knowledgeable and thoroughly pleasant service. Beamed, cottage-style bedrooms furnished in dark wood.

Food serving times:
Wednesday-Friday:
6pm-9pm
Saturday: 12pm-2pm, 6pm-9pm
Sunday: 12pm-3.30pm
Closed 1 week in January

Prices:
Meals: 14.95 (set price early bird dinner) and a la carte 21.40/30.95
⊨ **6 rooms :** 40.00/70.00

6.5 mi Southwest of Moulton off the A64 past Kirkham Priory. Parking.

Typical Dishes
Yorkshire Blue cheese beignet
Sirloin steak, triple cooked chips
Sticky date & walnut pudding

Whitwell-on-the-Hill

035 ## The Stone Trough Inn

Kirkham Abbey, Whitwell-on-the-Hill YO60 7JS

Tel.: (01653) 618713 - Fax: (01653) 618819
e-mail: info@stonetroughinn.co.uk - Website: www.stonetroughinn.co.uk

    VISA **MC**

Tetley Cask, Theakstons Old Peculiar, Black Sheep Best Bitter, Timothy Taylor Landlord, Suddaby's Golden Chance and guest

A truly idyllic spot on a summer's day – the Stone Trough Inn is close to the ruins of 12C Kirkham Abbey and the long bend of the River Derwent. The pub itself is newer than it might first seem, and the skillful and sympathetic reconstruction looks still more authentic from the inside; a charmingly rustic, heavily beamed bar built of Yorkshire stone is full of little nooks and snugs. You can dine here, choosing from a varied selection of Modern British dishes and blackboard specials, or take your drinks through to the restaurant, which actually feels more like a big farmhouse kitchen, complete with pine tables and chairs.

Food serving times:
Tuesday-Saturday:
   12pm-2pm, 6.45pm-9.30pm
Sunday: 12pm-2.15pm
Closed 25 December
Prices:
Meals: a la carte 23.00/26.00

5mi Southwest of Malton off A64 following signs for Kirkham Priory. Parking.

Typical Dishes

Salmon and crab cakes

Rack of Flaxton lamb, Dauphinoise potatoes

Iced Grand Marnier parfait

Sheffield

036 Lions Lair

31 Burgess St, Sheffield S1 2HF
Tel.: (0114) 263 4264 - Fax: (0114) 263 4265
e-mail: info@lionslair.co.uk - Website: www.lionslair.co.uk

Black Sheep, Tetleys

The centre of Sheffield may not be the automatic choice for those in search of cosy rusticity, but this neat little pub hidden away in the heart of the city provides a number of pleasant surprises. It boasts a lovely enclosed rear terrace with the added attraction of stylishly-nautical decking where summer barbeques and live music rustle the Yorkshire air and a snug interior dining room with leather banquettes, open fires, a pleasing mix of tables and popular, wide-ranging menus which are unfussy and freshly prepared, with dishes heavily influenced by the patron's French roots.

Food serving times:
Monday-Sunday:
12pm-3pm, 5pm-7pm
Closed 25 December
and 1 January
Prices:
Meals: a la carte 7.50/10.50

Typical Dishes

Spicy chicken wings

Cumberland sausage, Cheddar and leek mash

Chocolate cake

South of City Hall, off Parker's Pool. Parking in street outside or public parking nearby.

Totley

037 ## The Cricket

Penny Lane, Totley Bents S17 3AZ

Tel.: (0114) 236 5256

e-mail: enquiries@the-cricket.com · Website: www.the-cricket.com

  rest

 Stones Best Bitter, Black Sheep

Among the copses and fields, where Sheffield's outermost suburbs blend into countryside, you'll find the home ground of Totley Cricket Club and, next to it, the trimly kept Cricket Inn. A traditionally informal bar is filled with the team's memorabilia; bats and bails, team photos, shots of cavalier strokemakers and hurricane 'quicks' all reflect the first love of the White Rose county. Nourishing and enjoyable food, prepared with culinary good sense, is served here: the formal restaurant, with a menu to match, opens in the evening and for Sunday lunch; service is polite and friendly throughout. Afterwards, you could always stroll to the boundary and see if you can spot the next Trueman, Boycott or Vaughan…

Food serving times:
Tuesday-Saturday:
 12pm-2.30pm, 6pm-10pm
Sunday: 12pm-2.30pm
Closed 25 December and mornings October to April
Prices:
Meals: a la carte 14.00/30.00

Typical Dishes

Honey roast ham terrine

Confit of duck, parsley mash

Prune and Armagnac rice pudding

At the South end of the village: turn into Lane Head Road and go down the hill into Penny Lane. Parking.

Addingham

038 **The Fleece**

154 Main St, Addingham LS29 0LY

Tel.: (01943) 830491
e-mail: chris@monkmansbistro.fsbusiness.co.uk

 Black Sheep Bitter, Tetleys Cask, Timothy Taylor Landlord

This good-looking, ivy-clad pub sits on the busy main street in Addingham, close to the southern 'gateway' to the Yorkshire Dales National Park. Its pleasing features extend across the threshold, where can be found open fires to entice chilled walkers on cold days, a solid stone floor, and rustic walls filled with country oriented prints, oils and general knick-knacks. It's all overseen in a very personally run style by the charming owner, and the homely ambience extends to the dining area, which boasts 1930s style tables. There's an appealing mix of dishes from the blackboard menu, the repertoire covering anything from classic and traditional pub dishes to more contemporary offerings, all served in generous portions.

Food serving times:
Monday-Saturday:
12pm-2.15pm, 6pm-9.15pm
Monday-Saturday: 12pm-2.15pm, 6pm-9.15pm
Sunday: 12pm-8pm
Prices:
Meals: a la carte 15.00/25.00

On the busy through road in the centre of Addingham. Parking.

Typical Dishes

Woodpigeon & prune salad

Fleece seafood stew

Rhubarb & ginger crème brûlée

Halifax

039 Shibden Mill Inn

Shibden Mill Fold, Halifax HX3 7UL

Tel.: (01422) 365840 - Fax: (01422) 362971
Website: www.shibdenmillinn.com

Shibden Mill Bitter, Theakstons XB, John Smiths and 2 rotating guest bitters

Only a mile or two outside the centre of Halifax, and the landscape of the Shibden Valley already feels properly rural. The old millpond has long since run dry, and the formal split-level dining room gives away little of the mill's history, but there's a more authentic country feel to the main bar. With a pleasantly haphazard mix of landscape prints, plates and bottles for decoration, it's spacious but still intimate, and frankly the more inviting choice, although the frequently changing menu, served throughout, has more in common with restaurant dining. Served in hefty pub portions, the rather complex dishes bear the hallmarks of fashionable cooking over the last decade and reveal a solid background in the Modern British kitchen. Individually styled rooms, being refurbished one by one, make this a useful overnight stop.

Food serving times:
Monday-Sunday:
    12pm-2pm, 6pm-9.30pm
Prices:
Meals: a la carte 16.95/27.45
12 rooms : 68.00/130.00

Typical Dishes

Wood pigeon, beetroot risotto

Venison, vanilla mash and chocolate sauce

Chocolate three ways

2.25 mi Northeast by A58 and Kell Lane (turning left at Stump Cross Pub), on Blake Hill Rd. Parking.

Marsden

040 Olive Branch

Manchester Rd, Marsden HD7 6LU

Tel.: (01484) 844487
e-mail: mail@olivebranch.cuk.com - Website: www.olivebranch.uk.com

Olive Branch Special, Holme Valley Brewery

Three wonderfully cosy rooms – feeling almost like interlinking snugs – together with the rear contemporary restaurant make up the heart of this part 16C former cattle-drover's inn that matches exposed brick, pine antiques and framed sepia photographs with a light dash of modernity. Add to this the personable approach of the owners and its easy to see why the Olive Branch's reputation reaches well beyond Marsden itself. Up on the wall, large Post-it notes announce menu changes at the rate of a departures board: this might disconcert any chronically indecisive diners, but speaks well for the freshness of the diverse and tasty cooking. Flavourful seafood specialities are guaranteed, in any case, along with other contemporary country dishes. Comfortable, smart and stylish bedrooms. Moorland and canalside walks.

Food serving times:
Wednesday-Friday:
  12pm-2pm, 6.30pm-9.30pm
Saturday: 6.30pm-9.30pm
Sunday: 1pm-8.30pm
Closed 26 December and
first 2 weeks January
Prices:
Meals: 18.50 (set price lunch)
and a la carte 22.50/37.00
🛏 **3 rooms :** 55.00/70.00
🍽 10.50

1 mi Northeast on A62. Parking.

Typical Dishes

Loch Fyne scallops, garlic butter and Gruyère cheese

Steak pie

Treacle and lime tart, crème anglaise

Rishworth

041 The Old Bore

Oldham Rd, Rishworth HX6 4QU

Tel.: (01422) 822 291

e-mail: chefhessel@aol.com - Website: www.oldbore.co.uk

 VISA ⓜⓒ

Old Bore Bitter, Timothy Taylor's Landlord and guest beers - Moorhouses, Eastwood, Senders Copper Dragon

Here's a handy tip for drivers barrelling along the M62: do yourself a favour and turn off at J22 for a spot of R&R at the nearby Old Bore. Recently transformed, it's now a very characterful place to be. Outside, there's a pleasant terrace with stone walled border and good rural views. Inside, the relaxing main bar with its open fire and exposed rafters is an ideal place to wind down – there's a good selection of real ales and plenty of top-notch wines by the glass. Wine takes a front seat here, or at least a prominent place on the main dining room walls, which are filled with memorabilia relating to the grape. Another dining room puts the emphasis on deer antlers, just to remind you that, despite motorway proximity, this is really the heart of the country. Menus are most appealing. A strong local base underpins both the varied selection of blackboard daily specials or richly interesting dishes from the a la carte.

Food serving times:

Tuesday-Friday:
12pm-2.15pm, 6pm-9.30pm

Saturday: 12pm-2.15pm, 6pm-10pm

Sunday: 12pm-4pm, 6pm-8pm

Closed 25 December and 2 weeks in January

Prices:
Meals: 9.95/12.95 (set price 2 course lunch/dinner) and a la carte 18.95/40.00

Typical Dishes

Potted ham and crispy belly pork

Beef Bourguignon and mash

Trio of Yorkshire rhubarb

6mi South West of Halifax by A58 and A672. Parking.

Silsden

042 The Grouse at Silsden

Keighley Rd, Silsden BD20 0EH
Tel.: (01535) 657788 - Fax: (01535) 655742

Timothy Taylor Golden Best and Best Bitter; also Timothy Taylor 'Ram Tam' in winter

A buzzy pub, busy and popular, and refurbished in late 2003, at the bottom of the town: in the latter part of the 18C, there were three cottages here but for many years it's served as an inn. As you approach, the modernisation is apparent, announced by frosted glass and aubergine coloured signs. Inside, halogen lighting, wood floors, muted tones and stark browns reflect the zeitgeist. David, the manager, and Matthew, the chef, are brothers whose teamwork gels smoothly. Not a pub popular with drinkers, diners order drinks at the small bar and eat at the uncovered tables; light lunches give way to handsomely endowed dinners, whose more formal character still manages to satisfy the local demand for steaks.

Food serving times:
Tuesday: 6pm-9.30pm
Wednesday-Saturday:
    12pm-2pm, 6pm-9.30pm
    (10pm Saturday)
Sunday: 12pm-2pm
Closed 1 week in February
Prices:
Meals: 9.95/14.95 (set price 2 course lunch/3 course early dinner Tues-Thurs) and a la carte 18.00/25.00

4mi North of Keighley by A629 and A6034. Parking at rear.

Typical Dishes

Mussels, saffron cream

Rump of lamb, Mediterranean vegetables

Ginger cake with ice cream

Sowerby Bridge

043 The Millbank

Mill Bank Road, Sowerby Bridge HX6 3DY

Tel.: (01422) 825588

e-mail: eat@themillbank.com - Website: www.themillbank.com

    VISA MC

Tetley Bitter, Timothy Taylor Landlord

Here's a proper pub with wooden floors and exposed stone in an invigorating position in the Pennines. It caters just as readily for drinkers as for those who've come in to eat, even though its contemporary interior and modern artwork certainly put it firmly into the dining pub league. Chunky wooden tables and chairs, a ready warmth of service, allied to interesting modern cooking, guarantee customers from far and wide, and booking is essential. Dine in the conservatory for beautiful countryside views; a neat little terrace helps take the strain. Place your order with the smartly uniformed staff - whatever you choose from the menu, there's guaranteed good food at a modest price. Well-kept bedrooms add to the inn's reputation.

Food serving times:
Monday: 6pm-9.30pm
Tuesday-Saturday:
  12pm-2.30pm, 6pm-9.30pm
Sunday: 12pm-4.30pm,
                  6pm-8pm

Closed first week January
and 2 weeks October
(booking essential)

Prices:
Meals: 11.95 (2 courses with coffee) and a la carte 18.50/34.50

Typical Dishes

Foie gras brûlée

Loin of rabbit, confit leg, creamed cabbage

Chocolate fondant cake

2.25 mi Southwest by A58. Parking on the road in front of the pub.

Thunderbridge

044 **Woodman Inn**

Thunderbridge HD8 0PX

Tel.: (01484) 605778 - Fax: (01484) 604110
e-mail: thewoodman@connectfree.co.uk - Website: www.woodman-inn.co.uk

  rest *VISA* **MC**

 Tetleys Bitter, Timothy Taylor's Landlord, Barnsley Bitter

Take the road south from Huddersfield and you're soon in 'Last of the Summer Wine' country, the ideal setting for this 19C inn of Yorkshire stone which, nearly a decade ago, was extended by the owners to include the adjacent old weavers' cottages. Thus was created a host of well thought out bedrooms, the perfect final destination after an invigorating day in the nearby Southern Pennines. Bar and restaurant – set away from the bar on the first floor – are of more recent vintage, having both been refurbished in 2003. You can eat formally, at linen-clad tables, in the latter, while scrubbed tables and a more free and easy ambience set the mood for dining in the rest of the pub. Tasty, unfussy dishes appear on an appealing menu that utilises freshly prepared, local ingredients in a traditional manner

Food serving times:
Monday-Saturday:
  12pm-3pm, 6.30pm-9pm
Sunday: 12pm-6pm
Prices:
Meals: 10.50 (set price lunch) and a la carte 14.00/20.00
🛏 **12 rooms :** 45.00/65.00

5.75mi South East of Huddersfield by A629, after Kirkburton follow signs to Thunderbridge. Parking.

Typical Dishes

Honey and sesame king prawns with pillau

Venison and red wine sausage

Apricot and almond cake

Walton

045 **The Fox and Hounds**

Hall Park Road, Walton LS23 7DQ
Tel.: (01937) 842192

 VISA **MC**

 John Smith Cask, Black Sheep, Timothy Taylor Landlord

The same team that breathed recent life into the Bay Horse up the road in Kirk Deighton is also creating a stir at The Fox and Hounds, tucked away in a sleepy little West Yorkshire village east of Wetherby. You'll feel snug as soon as you enter the cosy bar, a stuffed fox tucked up in a basket typifying the relaxed mood. Pleasant country décor includes framed sepia prints, dried flowers and hop bines. Sit at rustic pine tables and tuck into very good value, wide ranging set menus underpinned by a solid Yorkshire base, served by an invariably cheerful and knowledgeable local waiting team. There are daily blackboard specials, too, and everything on them is home made, from rustic breads through to ice creams.

Food serving times:
Monday-Saturday:
12pm-2.15pm, 5pm-9pm
Sunday: 12pm-2.15pm
(booking essential)
Prices:
Meals: 13.95 (2 course lunch or dinner) and a la carte 17.50/30.00

Typical Dishes

Fresh mussels, coconut & coriander

Chateaubriand, Bearnaise sauce

Passion fruit crème brûlee

3mi East of Wetherby by minor road; between A659 and B1224. Parking.

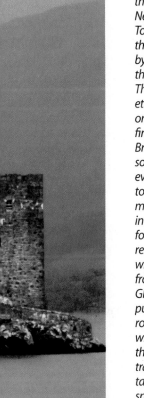

*W*indswept peaks and misty lochs from the pages of Burns and Scott or the urban grit of modern film and fiction? Visitors could be forgiven for wondering what to expect in this country of contrasts, but it's all here: the wild beauty of Wester Ross and the Neoclassical elegance of Edinburgh's New Town, the fishing villages of the East Neuk, the lush gardens of Inverewe, warmed by the Gulf Stream in the west, as well as the vibrance of straight-talking Glasgow. This is a land where tradition can mean etiquette and fellowship on the first tee or the raw energy of Shetland's Viking fire festival, centuries of pre-eminence in British science and letters, or a turbulent social history which has left its mark on every part of life. There's a difference in town and country pub culture, too. Perhaps more than anywhere else in Britain, inns in the countryside are often the centres for a widespread community: pub, hotel, restaurant and even shop in one, with a wise word behind the bar on anything from fishing lures to football scores. In Glasgow and Edinburgh, however, dining pubs are only a tiny part of a busy year-round cultural life, which hits fever pitch with the creativity and sheer variety of the summer festivals. One thing is for sure, traditional inns and modern gastropubs take equal pride in their national specialities: smoked or fresh salmon and trout, Loch Linnhe prawns, seafood soups like Cullen Skink and Partan Bree, prime beef, Highland game and haggis.

Balmedie

001 Cock and Bull

Ellon Rd, Blairton, Balmedie AB23 8XY

Tel.: (01358) 743 249 - Fax: (013580 742466
Website: www.thecockandbull.co.uk

Directors', Old Speckled Hen

"Where ancient meets modern without so much as a jolt," it says in the Cock and Bull's promo blurb. And that's just the half of it. This former shepherds' watering hole looks over fields to the North Sea. Inside, there are three distinct areas: two of them, the lounge/bar and the restaurant, are delightfully atmospheric, cluttered with artefacts (some African themed), old record players, sewing machines, posters and fabrics (plus anything else you might care to mention). Open fires complete a feast for the eyes and the senses. A more contemporary conservatory with polished wood tables and chairs completes the picture. Extensive menus cover the full range from 'popular pub fare' to 'fine dining', as well as heartily ample one-course dishes with Scottish produce to the fore. Service is very friendly from staff used to being run off their feet.

Food serving times:
Monday-Sunday:
12pm-9pm
Prices:
Meals: a la carte 18.00/28.00

6mi North of Aberdeen by A90. Parking.

Typical Dishes

Scallops, black pudding, tomato chutney

Thai marinated duck breast, ginger dressing

Berry crème brûlée

Netherley

002 The Lairhillock Inn

Netherley AB39 3QS

Tel.: (01569) 730001 - Fax: (01569) 731175
e-mail: lairhillock@breathemail.net - Website: www.lairhillock.co.uk

> *Timothy Taylor Landlord, Courage Directors, Belhaven Sandy Hunters, Isle of Skye 'Lairies Ale'*

Beautiful Deeside country stretches away to either side, and the Granite City is only a 15-minute drive, but tearing yourself away from a ramble in the hills is not an altogether bad idea when the wonderfully atmospheric front snug bar is the destination. A former coaching inn, the Lairhillock remains the beating heart of the community, and the snug exerts a gravitational pull. It's an invariably busy and friendly bar, but if you find the bustle too much, then there are other areas to discover: there's a lounge with an altogether more relaxed and traditional feel, and a conservatory with a view of the countryside. Here or in the more formal dining room is the place to dig into a good choice of satisfying, rustic dishes chock full of Scottish produce: Gourdon langoustines, salmon from the Dee and Don, Highland venison and boar, and Shetland mussels.

Food serving times:
Monday-Thursday:
12pm-2pm, 6pm-9.30pm
Friday-Saturday:
12pm-2pm, 6pm-10pm
Sunday: 12pm-2pm,
5.30pm-9pm

Closed 25-26 December and 1-2 January

Prices:
Meals: 12.95 (set price lunch Sunday only) and a la carte 15.50/22.50

15mi South of Aberdeen by B9077 and B979. Parking.

Typical Dishes

Cullen skink

Grilled venison escalopes, wild mushroom

Dark chocolate terrine

Bridgend of Lintrathen

003 The Steading

**(at Lochside Lodge and Roundhouse restaurant) Angus,
Bridgend of Lintrathen DD8 5JJ**   Tel.: (01575) 560340 - Fax: (01575) 560251
e-mail: enquiries@lochsidelodge.com - Website: www.lochsidelodge.com

Inveralmond Ossians or Inveralmond Thrapledouser

The more informal counterpart to the Roundhouse restaurant, the Steading's name is a reminder of its humble origins as an old farm building. The original stone walls are now decorated with all sorts of agricultural tools, rural fitments, and some country sports memorabilia, some of the mystery items look like they might fall into all three categories. Cushioned pews are pulled up to solid wood tables and a brasserie style lunch menu is served along with the same menu on offer in the Roundhouse restaurant at dinner. If you're just after a drink, there's a little bar to one side, with newspapers and magazines within easy reach of the leather seats. Four pine-fitted bedrooms, in the converted hayloft, all have a dash of tartan or floral colour and plenty in the way of thoughtful, homely touches.

Food serving times:
Tuesday-Saturday:
           12pm-1.30pm,
           6.30pm-8.30pm
Sunday: 12pm-1.30pm
Closed 25-26 December and 1-21 January
Prices:
Meals: a la carte 16.00/32.00
6 rooms : 45.00/85.00

Typical Dishes

Dunsyre blue cheese brûlee

Lamb's liver, chive mash

Lemon tart, lemon curd ice cream

8mi West of Kirriemuir by B951. Parking.

Crinan

004 Crinan (Bar) 🛏

Crinan PA31 8SR
Tel.: (01546) 830261 - Fax: (01546) 830292
e-mail: nryan@crinanhotel.com - Website: www.crinanhotel.com

 rest *VISA* ⓜⓒ

🍺 *Fyne Ales Piper's Gold*

Superbly located in a commanding position with exceptional views of Loch Crinan and Sound of Jura, this elegant, whitewashed building has picture windows that let guests take in superb views of fishing boats chugging out towards the Hebrides. Naturally enough, the bar has a nautical theme, while there are two homely lounges to sit and watch the world go by. There's a Gallery bar, too, which overlooks the loch. With all this natural beauty in abundance, make sure you get to eat where you can take in the vista. The split-level restaurant is smart with linen clad tables, and the menus have an interesting, modern feel to them. Try, maybe, roast scallops, cauliflower puree and raisin vinaigrette for starters; skate salad with haricot vert, or fillet of beef, cubed celeriac and red wine jus for a main. Stay in pleasant, bright bedrooms.

Food serving times:
Monday-Sunday:
12pm-2.30pm, 7pm-9pm
(8.30pm in winter)
Closed Christmas
Accommodation rates include dinner
Prices:
Meals: a la carte 19.85/30.85
🛏 **20 rooms :** 85.00/260.00

6mi Northwest of Lochgilphead by A816 and B841; at the end of Crinan canal on the edge of Loch Crinan. Parking.

Typical Dishes

Smoked Rothesay salmon, horseradish cream

Rib eye steak, duck fat chips

Apple crumble

Kintyre - Kilberry

005 ## Kilberry Inn 🛏

Kintyre-Kilberry PA29 6YD

Tel.: (01880) 770223

e-mail: relax@kilberryinn.com · Website: www.kilberryinn.com

 VISA **M©**

🍺 *Vital Spark, Piper's Gold, Highlander*

Between the wooded heights and the widening Sound of Jura stands a whitewashed cottage on a long country road. It's as simple as you could wish: a parlour for lunch and dinner and a little beamed lounge in stone and pine, with local landscapes on the walls, a fire in the hearth and local whiskies behind the bar. The blackboard menu changes every day, but the fortifying home cooking always has a real local flavour to it and the ingredients are all found close to home. It's the efforts of the staff that really make the place, though, with a nice, upfront informality setting the tone. The three bedrooms are cosy and usefully equipped: you'll need a good night's sleep before touring Arran or following the Islay and Jura whisky trail!

Food serving times:
Tuesday-Sunday:
12.30pm-2.30pm,
6.30pm-9.30pm
Closed January to mid-March; also Monday-Thursday, November-December

Prices:
Meals: a la carte 18.70/29.10
🛏 **3 rooms :** 39.50/45.00

Typical Dishes

Loch Fyne langoustines

Cod roasted with plum tomatoes & chorizo

Chocolate crème brûlée

15mi West of Tarbet by B8024. Parking.

Strachur

006 The Creggans Inn 🛏

Strachur PA27 8BX

Tel.: (01369) 860279 - Fax: (01369) 860637
e-mail: info@creggans-inn.co.uk - Website: www.creggans-inn.co.uk

🍷 ⚊rest *VISA* ⓜⓒ

Deuchars IPA, Greene King IPA, Bitter and Twisted, Timothy Taylor Landlord, Fuller's London Pride, Fyne Ales Pipers Gold

The enviable delights of Loch Fyne in wild and remote Argyll and Bute provide a haunting and spectacular backdrop to this whitewashed, roadside inn. The Creggan has a well-established and hard-earned local reputation, built up by years of smoothly run service. There's a cosy bar and small wicker-chaired conservatory, and two lounges, one of which has a fine outlook. You can eat at the bar, or the spacious dining room with its wood floor and warm colour scheme. Dishes are flavoursome and full of fine Scottish ingredients. Walks in the area are guaranteed to bring on a very restful state, and the Creggan comes up trumps with delightful, cottage style bedrooms.

Food serving times:
Monday-Sunday:
   12pm-2.45pm, 7pm-8.45pm
Closed 25-26 December
(bar lunch)/dinner
Prices:
Meals: 32.00 (set price 4 course dinner) and a la carte 18.00/30.00
🛏 **14 rooms :** 75.00/130.00

Typical Dishes

Loch Fyne Oysters

Fillet of beef with leeks and wild mushrooms

Sticky toffee pudding

21mi East and South of Inveraray by coast road A83 and A815. Parking and 2 moorings for boats.

Tayvallich

007 Tayvallich Inn

Tayvallich PA31 8PL

Tel.: (01546) 870282 - Fax: (01546) 870354
e-mail: rfhanderson@aol.com - Website: www.tayvallich-inn.com

 VISA AE ① ⓂⒸ

 Loch Fyne Ales: Pipers Gold, Maverick

In glorious isolation stands Tayvallich in the Sound of Jura. It's a little coastal hamlet with cosy harbour and Gulf Stream-nourished palm trees close to the shores of Loch Sween; the Tayvallich Inn, quite rightly, is the hub of the community. Believe it or not, it was the local bus garage until the early 1970s, when it was converted into its present incarnation. It has an enviable lochside setting and a smart whitewashed exterior with pleasant summer decking at the front. Inside, at the large bar in plump cushioned chairs, is a great place to mingle with the locals. Next door the pine furnished dining room has windows on three sides for the views, and interesting menus, which rely on fresh supplies of prawns, scallops and the local catch to underpin creative dishes.

Food serving times:
Monday-Sunday:
12pm-2pm, 6pm-9pm
Closed 25 December; also November-March, Monday-Wednesday
Prices:
Meals: a la carte 20.00/30.00

Typical Dishes

Crab, fennel and apple risotto

Scallops in lemon & butter

Strawberries in balsamic, vanilla mascarpone

12mi West of Lochgilphead by A816, B841 and B8025; on west shore of Loch Sween. Parking.

Swinton

008 The Wheatsheaf 🛏

Main Street, Swinton TD11 3JJ

Tel.: (01890) 860257 - Fax: (01890) 860688
e-mail: reception@wheatsheaf-swinton.co.uk - Website: www.wheatsheaf-swinton.co.uk

Deuchars IPA, Broughton Reiver

This cosy, attractive village inn on the Scottish borders has a welcoming stone façade, but the main delight here comes when you step through the entrance into the firelit bar with its fine array of real ales and wander through to the adjoining rooms whose nooks and crannies throw up subtle changes of character. The stylish restaurant is well renowned locally. It sources fresh seafood from Eyemouth Harbour, just 12 miles away, as well as borders beef, lamb and organic pork from local, traditional butchers. For dinner, you might try peppered breast of Gressingham duck in a thyme scented sauce with pink peppercorns, or baked fillet of local salmon with tarragon and prawns.

Food serving times:
Monday-Sunday:
  12pm-2pm, 6pm-9pm
Closed 25-27 December;
also Sunday evening
December, January
and February
Prices:
Meals: a la carte 22.00/35.00
🛏 **7 rooms :** 67.00/102.00

Typical Dishes

Smoked haddock, salmon and
dill fishcake

Rack of lamb with a basil
and mustard crust

Chocolate brownie

6mi North of Coldstream by A6112.
Parking.

547

Sorn

009 **The Sorn Inn** 🛏

35 Main St, Sorn KA5 6HU
Tel.: (01290) 551305 - Fax: (01290) 553470
e-mail: craig@sorninn.com - Website: www.sorninn.com

 VISA

> *No real ales offered*

This traditional, family run whitewashed inn nestles enviably in the heart of the Ayrshire countryside. There's a small bar which is popular with locals and which offers the "Chop House" menu of steaks and simpler dishes. The real hub of the inn, though, is the rear dining room clothed in smart linen-clad tables and with a small lounge offshoot. It specialises in modern British cooking that's particularly good value for the accomplished cooking on offer, which specialises in using locally sourced meat, fish and game. Worth looking out for are breast of pigeon on sarladaise potato, bok choi, light Madeira and juniper berry jus, or sea trout on crushed new potatoes, pea and mint velouté. To round things off, there are four simple but modern and comfy bedrooms with showers and even DVD players.

Food serving times:
Tuesday-Saturday:
    12pm-2pm, 6.30pm-9pm
Sunday: 12.30pm-6.30pm
Closed 2 weeks mid January
Prices:
Meals: 14.95/24.50 (set price lunch/dinner) and a la carte 16.50/24.50
🛏 **4 rooms :** 40.00/90.00

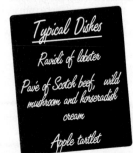

Typical Dishes

Ravioli of lobster

Pavé of Scotch beef, wild mushroom and horseradish cream

Apple tartlet

2mi East of Catrine by B713. Parking. >

Glasgow

010 **Babbity Bowster**

16-18 Blackfriars St, Glasgow G1 1PE

Tel.: (0141) 552 5055 - Fax: (0141) 552 7774

Deuchars IPA, Peter's Well and a regularly changing guest ale

A well-regarded Glasgow favourite in a carefully renovated townhouse, more informal than the neo-Classical façade might lead you to expect. Simple gingham-clothed tables and sketches and photos of city life set the tone in a laid-back, open-plan bar, where a short lunchtime menu of warming, substantial dishes includes Cullen Skink and stovies – meat and potato casseroles – as well as French bistro standards and croques monsieur. Upstairs, the restaurant's evening menu is a touch more formal but every bit as robust and tasty, choosing Scottish produce for its oat-crusted venison or sea bass in brandy butter. Oh, and the origin of the name? An old country dance which, like all the best folk songs, has at least two risqué interpretations to it. The friendly staff are happy to oblige with an explanation, or maybe even a rendition…

Food serving times:
Monday-Sunday:
12pm-10pm
Closed 25 December
Prices:
Meals: a la carte 12.95/25.85

Typical Dishes

Scallops with red pepper

Saddle of red deer

Clootie dumpling with toffee sauce

In city centre North of the Central railway station.

Glasgow

011 **Rab Ha's**

83 Hutcheson St, Glasgow G61 1LH

Tel.: (0141) 572 0400 - Fax: (0141) 572 0402
e-mail: management@rabhas.com - Website: www.rabhas.com

VISA **AE** **MC**

No real ales offered

Built on the New World tobacco trade, the exchanges, halls and warehouses of Merchant City are finding a new lease of life as shops, living space and, yes, gastropubs. After the magnificence of Hutcheson's Hall and the Victorian City Chambers around the corner, Rab Ha's rather blank façade looks like a bit of a let-down. Inside, though, it's far more inviting, lively and modern and, on a cold night, discreetly cosy: there's a bit of relaxed 'take-us-as-you-find-us' about the place, but if anything the service is actually more efficient and friendly for it. As students and local businessmen squeeze onto chairs and benches, you can clink lagers and weigh up a bar menu running from Thai curry to haggis with the trimmings. A more formal restaurant selection is more likely to take in cod with leek and tomato or beef in thyme and port sauce.

Food serving times:
Monday-Sunday:
12pm-10pm ; restaurant:
from 5.30
Closed 25 December
Prices:
Meals: 19.95 (set price dinner) and a la carte 15.00/25.00
4 rooms : 65.00/75.00

Typical Dishes

Haggis, neeps and tatties

Roast saddle of Rannoch Moor venison

Apple and prune sabayon tart

In city centre Southwest of George Square. Parking in the street or in Glassford Street NCP car park.

Achiltibuie

012 Summer Isles (Bar) 🛏

Achiltibuie IV26 2YG

Tel.: (01854) 622205 - Fax: (01854) 622251
e-mail: info@summerisleshotel.co.uk - Website: www.summerisleshotel.co.uk

   VISA **MC**

 Deuchar's IPA, Hebridean Gold, Isle of Sky Red Cuillin, Young Pretender

An idyllically named establishment for an idyllic setting – this super bar and hotel faces the eponymous isles, far away from the madding crowd at the end of a 20 mile single track road. The bar is the 'village pub', attached to the hotel but separate from it. Its simple, rustic ambience is perfect for the setting: sit in wooden booths and take in the wild, untouched landscape. You'll dine on seafood platters and rustic dishes such as casseroles and lamb shank; in the summer, don't miss the chance to eat al fresco. If you plump for the hotel, you'll be sampling precisely judged cuisine which has earned a Michelin Star for its excellence. There's every chance you'll stay the night: look forward to bedrooms ranging from simple and restrained to smart and sophisticated.

Food serving times:
Monday-Sunday:
   12pm-3pm, 5.30pm-8.30pm
**Closed 1 November
to 30 March**
Seafood - (bookings not accepted)
Prices:
Meals: a la carte 10.50/25.00
🛏 **13 rooms :** 78.00/192.00

Typical Dishes

Locally smoked salmon

Aberdeen Angus sirloin steak

Platter of 3 fine cheeses

15mi Northwest of Ullapool by A835 and minor road west from Drumrunie. Parking.

Applecross

013 **Applecross Inn** 🛏

Shore St, Applecross IV54 8LR

Tel.: (01520) 744262 - Fax: (01520) 744400
e-mail: applecrossinn@globalnet.co.uk - Website: www.applecross.uk.com

 VISA MC

 Isle of Skye Brewery: Red Cuillin, Young Pretender, Blaven

Not only one of the most remote pubs in the UK, but one of the trickiest to drive to as well – nevertheless, a visit to this cheerful hostelry, with stunning views to Skye's Cuillin Hills, is a truly rewarding experience. Approach via the hair-raising 'Pass of the Cattle', or the 24 mile single track road from Shieldaig: neither journey will be forgotten in a hurry. The inn is an old fisherman's cottage on the side of the loch. Its no-nonsense bar has pine panelling, exposed stone and lots of windows affording properly breathtaking views. Seafood, from extremely local sources, is the backbone of the menus: it's very fresh and certainly the thing to choose, though, local venison or sausages are also on the list. It gets busy, so be early or book! If you can't face the return journey just yet, they have bright and comfy bedrooms.

Food serving times:
Monday-Sunday:
12pm-9pm
Closed 25 December
and 1 January
(booking essential)
Prices:
Meals: a la carte 15.00/25.00
🛏 **7 rooms :** 80.00/90.00

From Kishorn via the Bealach nam Bo (Alpine pass), or round by Shieldaig and along the coast. Parking. >

Typical Dishes

Applecross Bay prawns

King scallops and crispy bacon on rice

Local cheeses from the West Highland dairy

Badachro

014 Badachro Inn

Badachro IV21 2AA

Tel.: (01445) 741255 - Fax: (01445) 741319
e-mail: lesley@badachroinn.com - Website: www.badachroinn.com

Crofter Pale Ale, Brewhouse Special

Probably rather easier to get to by boat than by car, this pleasant little whitewashed pub has rather wisely invested in two moorings for visiting yachts. It's in a delightfully sheltered and remote location, right on the seashore of this small inlet, close to a little group of local houses. A cosy, lawned area with tables sits adjacent to the water. Inside, it's equally compact and traditional, with an open fire, beams, minuscule bar and local maritime charts on the walls. The nicest place to eat is the conservatory, with Loch Gairloch lapping its sides. Go for dishes from the daily changing menus featuring local seafood: all very fresh, simply prepared, and, in the majority of cases, homemade. Or take your lunch on a sunny day onto the 'terrace' and watch the world go quietly by – perfect!

Food serving times:
April-December:
  Monday-Sunday: 12pm-3pm, 6pm-9pm
January-March:
  Monday-Sunday: 6pm-9pm
Closed 25 December
Prices:
Meals: a la carte 12.00/22.00

Typical Dishes

Smoked salmon with home-made bread

Gairloch prawns, salad and dip

Cranachan with shortbread

6mi South of Gairloch by A832 and B8056. Parking and 2 moorings for boats.

Cawdor

015 Cawdor Tavern

The Lane, Cawdor IV12 5XP

Tel.: (01667) 404777 - Fax: (01667) 404777
e-mail: cawdortavern@btopenworld.com

VISA AE ⓓ Ⓜ

Tradewinds, Cairngorm Stag

Only a few miles from Loch Ness and Moray Firth, this country inn has a tourist attraction of its own – it's only five minutes from the local castle. In fact, its links in this respect go somewhat deeper than mere proximity: it's set within the Cawdor Estate, in what used to be the joiner's workshop for the castle itself. It's now a very personally managed pub, and the owners run a tight ship. There are three separate rooms: one with pool table, one for smokers, and one for non-smokers, and old oak panelling from the castle can be found here. Well-marshalled young staff serve a wide ranging menu with plenty of choice, featuring top-notch local fish, game and meats.

Food serving times:
Monday-Saturday:
　　12pm-2pm, 5.30pm-9pm
Sunday:　　12.30pm-3pm,
　　　　　　5.30pm-9pm
Closed 25 December and 1 January
(booking essential Saturday-Sunday)
Prices:
Meals: a la carte 16.95/24.50

Typical Dishes

Black pudding, haggis and white pudding

Loin of lamb with garlic & bacon, rosemary jus

Bramble custard tart

5mi South of Nairn by B9090. Parking. ❯❯

Glenelg

016 Glenelg Inn

Glenelg IV40 8JR

Tel.: (01599) 522273 - Fax: (01599) 522283

e-mail: christophermain7@glenelg-inn.com - Website: www.glenelg-inn.com

VISA AE MC

 No real ales offered

Idyllically set off the beaten track in its own extensive grounds in a quiet hamlet by the lochside, this cosy inn was, in a previous incarnation, a couple of wee cottages. The Inn gloriously overlooks Glenelg Bay and the Isle of Skye. There's a very pubby bar, full of character: the locals have an amiable habit of turning it into the centre of the universe. It also boasts a beamed ceiling, dark wood panelling, and plenty of local photos on the walls. Blackboard menus offer a tried-and-tested, classic selection, utilising much local produce, of which fish and seafood are the speciality. If you're staying overnight, you can look forward to comfy, individually decorated bedrooms, followed by great Highland breakfasts in the morning.

Food serving times:
Monday-Sunday:
12.30pm-2pm, 7.30pm-9pm
Closed Christmas
Closed Sunday dinner to non residents - (booking essential) - accommodation rates include dinner

Prices:
Meals: 10.00/35.00 (set price bar meal/dinner)
7 rooms : 40.00/160.00

Typical Dishes

Seafood chowder
Char-grilled fillet of venison
Local cheeses

South of Kyle of Lochalsh: 10mi by toll bridge, A87 Southwest, minor road to Kylerhea and ferry or 20mi by A87 Southeast. Parking.

Kylesku

017 Kylesku 🛏

Kylesku IV27 4HW

Tel.: (01971) 502231 - Fax: (01971) 502313
e-mail: info@kyleskuhotel.co.uk - Website: www.kyleskuhotel.co.uk

 rest **VISA** Ⓜ©

No real ales offered

With its genuinely unforgettable view of Loch Glencoul and the mountains, the temptation would be to keep all knowledge of Kylesku to yourself. The heart of the discovery is the old hotel itself, with a very comfortable lounge in pretty patterns, and simple bedrooms, but for anyone not staying, the bar's the place to be. It's got a nice, down-to-earth feeling to it: there's a pool table, all sorts of countryside objects ranged along the wall, and a stove burning all through the long Highland winter. A blackboard menu with a strong seasonal character concentrates on the local speciality: good, just-landed shellfish in simply prepared, nicely judged dishes. Tasty and fresh, and as authentic as you could wish for.

Food serving times:
Monday-Sunday:
 12pm-2.30pm, 7pm-8.30pm
Closed mid-October to end February
Prices:
Meals: 29.00 (set price dinner) and a la carte 15.00/25.00
🛏 **8 rooms :** 50.00/80.00

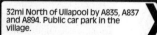
32mi North of Ullapool by A835, A837 and A894. Public car park in the village.

Typical Dishes

Venison terrine with Cumberland sauce

Grilled langoustine with garlic mayonnaise

Bread and butter pudding

Plockton

018 Plockton

41 Harbour St, Plockton IV52 8TN

Tel.: (01599) 544274 - Fax: (01599) 544475
e-mail: info@plocktonhotel.co.uk - Website: www.plocktonhotel.co.uk

 Hebridean Gold, Young Pretender, Deuchars IPA

Fine views of Loch Carron are a more than adequate reason to visit this attractive little National Trust village near the Kyle of Lochalsh. The eponymous inn – a delightful pair of wee cottages on the lochside – is the place to indulge the views while supping a pint with the locals, who flock here. The bar's the centre of activity, but if you're after a quieter environment, then you can retreat to the small rear terrace or the recently installed restaurant, where it's quite possible you'll be able to order a corn on the cob, alongside an impressive list of local seafood. Plockton isn't renowned for its road network, so for those making the wise move of staying overnight, there are plenty of recently refurbished, well-kept, comfy bedrooms to tempt you.

Food serving times:
Monday-Sunday:
12pm-2.15pm, 6pm-9pm
**Closed 25 December
and 1 January**
Prices:
Meals: a la carte 15.00/35.00
🛏 **15 rooms :** 45.00/100.00

5mi North of Kyle of Lochalsh.
Parking 100 yards away.

Typical Dishes

Char grilled local
langoustines

Seared scallops

White chocolate cheesecake

Plockton

019 Plockton Inn

Innes Street, Plockton IV52 8TW

Tel.: (01599) 544222 - Fax: (01599) 544487
e-mail: stay@plocktoninn.co.uk - Website: www.plocktoninn.co.uk

 rest **VISA** **MC**

> *Abbot Ale, Old Speckled Hen, Fuller's London Pride, Marstons
> Pedigree and others in rotation*

In the middle of a pretty harbour town on Loch Carron, this neighbourhood favourite without airs and graces is the place to come for good, unfussy seafood: platters of simply prepared shellfish and tasty dishes of locally landed fish are definitely the speciality, but they also do a good homemade hamburger! If you feel like some after-dinner entertainment, there might be a traditional music session in the bar next door. They also offer neat bedrooms in bright patterns; five of them are to be found in the annexe across the road.

Food serving times:
Monday-Sunday:
  12pm-2.30pm, 6pm-9pm
  (later in summer; earlier in winter)
Closed 25-26 December
Prices:
Meals: a la carte 14.00/22.00
14 rooms : 40.00/80.00

Typical Dishes

Seafood platter

*Pheasant with apricot and
pistachio stuffing*

Lemon and ginger crunch pie

5mi North of Kyle of Lochalsh.
Parking.

Waternish

020 **Stein Inn** 🛏

MacLeod Terr, Stein. Isle of Skye, Waternish IV55 8GA

Tel.: (01470) 592362

e-mail: angus.teresa@steininn.co.uk - Website: www.steininn.co.uk

✸✕ **VISA** **M©**

Reeling Deck, Blaven, Deuchars IPA, Red MacGregors Northern Light, Skye Ale, Old Speckled Hen

In a breathtakingly beautiful spot on Loch Bay, the oldest inn on Skye is run with great warmth and dedication by a chatty husband and wife team. At the heart of the place is a tiny pine-clad locals bar and a lounge with rough stone walls, tall settles and an open fire; it's good for soup, sandwiches and a local ale, but it would be a shame not to try something more substantial in the little dining room – well-prepared seafood dishes, like fresh prawn tails and halibut and chips, are the pick of a tasty menu which also includes Highland venison. But for pure relaxation and peace of mind, take one of their 90 malts down to the grassy bank or the benches looking west over the bay and watch the sun set beyond the headland. Guests staying in the cosy, well-kept bedrooms – a snip at the price – can compare the view in the morning.

Food serving times:
Monday-Sunday:
12pm-4pm, 6pm-9.30pm
(6.30pm-8pm in winter)
Closed 25 December and 1 January
- Seafood specialities -
Prices:
Meals: a la carte 12.75/22.00
🛏 **5 rooms :** 26.00/72.00

22mi West of Portree by A87, A850 and B886; on the shore of Loch Bay. Parking.

Typical Dishes

Scallops rolled in oatmeal

Highland venison pie

Local cheeses

Howgate

021 The Howgate

Penicuik, Howgate EH26 8PY

Tel.: (01968) 670000

e-mail: peter@howgate.com - Website: www.howgate.com

 VISA AE ① M©

No real ales offered

What was at one time a stabling facility for race horses, and more recently a dairy producing Howgate cheeses, is now a characterful establishment with two distinct areas. There's a tartan carpeted bistro with bar, open log fire and stone walls with framed newspaper articles, that specialises in simple, tried-and-tested dishes; and then there's the formal restaurant, which serves slightly more adventurous cuisine, but generally covers well-rehearsed, traditional territory. Menus are generous and extensive: daily specials, which range from home-made fishcakes to dishes with locally sourced beef, lamb and venison, should appeal to those who appreciate more traditional favourites.

Food serving times:
Monday-Sunday:
  12pm-2pm, 6pm-9.30pm
Closed 26 December
and 1 January
Prices:
Meals: a la carte 15.00/35.00

5mi South of the Edinburgh Ring Road (A720) by A702 and A703. Parking.

Typical Dishes

Pigeon on crispy bacon and black pudding

Fillet steak, hand-cut chips

Banoffee bread and butter pudding

Ardeonaig

022 **Ardeonaig**

South Loch Tay, By Killin, Ardeonaig FK21 8SU

Tel.: (01567) 820400 - Fax: (01567) 820282

e-mail: info@ardeonaighotel.co.uk - Website: www.ardeonaighotel.co.uk

 rest **VISA**

No real ales on tap

This family-run inn has its origins in the 17C, standing serenely in a wooded meadow on the south shore of Loch Tay. Its tranquil aspect is enhanced with a large garden – an ideal spot to relax in – or the library, which offers fine views. The homely, snug bar has walls filled with fishing memorabilia, and if you wander into the welcoming dining room you'll understand why: freshwater fish is a key element to the menus, alongside interesting dishes with a South African influence: the owner himself is a Springbok. There's also an enclosed courtyard, which, on a sunny day, is an ideal place to dine. Afterwards, delight in Highland walks or a slow drive alongside the Loch.

Food serving times:
Monday-Sunday:
    12pm-3pm, 7pm-10pm

Accommodation rates include dinner, bed and breakfast

Prices:
Meals: 26.50 (set price lunch/dinner) and a la carte 26.50/37.50

 20 rooms : 135.00/180.00

6mi East of Killin on south shore of Loch Tay. Parking.

Typical Dishes

Scallops, herb & tomato butter sauce

Lamb, rosemary and pinenut crust

Chocolate mielie meal

Glendevon

023 ## Tormaukin Country Inn

Glendevon FK14 7JY

Tel.: (01259) 781252 - Fax: (01259) 781526
e-mail: enquiries@tormaukin.co.uk - Website: www.tormaukin.co.uk

*Harviestoun Bitter & Twisted, Inveralmond Thrappledowser,
Timothy Taylor's Landlord*

This extended 18C drovers' inn is tucked away in the picturesque "hidden glen" of Glendevon, with the Ochil Hills providing a splendid distant backdrop. Although a roadside establishment, it still manages to convey a character in sympathy with its surroundings. There's rustic charm in abundance: beams, flagged floors, plush softly lit bar, and log fires. A handy place for the golfing community, who create a pleasant feel, mingling with walkers and locals. You can eat in the atmospheric bar or cosy restaurant. Menus have earned a deserved standing locally: a smooth mix of popular Scottish favourites with more modern options. Ramblers – or golfers – too tired to continue can stay in comfortable bedrooms.

Food serving times:
Monday-Friday:
12pm-2.30pm,
5.30pm-9.30pm
Saturday-Sunday:
12pm-9.30pm
Closed 2nd week January
Prices:
Meals: a la carte 16.85/30.00
12 rooms : 55.00/95.00

Typical Dishes

Scallops, chorizo and lemon parsley butter

Haunch of venison, root vegetables

Brioche and butter pudding

22mi Southwest of Perth by M90 to Junction 7, A91 and A823. Parking.

Kippen

024 The Inn at Kippen

Fore Rd, Kippen FK8 3DT
Tel.: (01786) 871010 - Fax: (01786) 871011
e-mail: info@theinnatkippen.co.uk - Website: www.theinnatkippen.co.uk

Harviestoun Bitter and Twisted, Caledonian Deuchars

Spacious, contemporary and open-plan, this fully refurbished village inn may not be quite what you were expecting. High-backed leather chairs and banquettes, smart glassware and casually uniformed staff set a determinedly modern tone, but it's not all out-with-the-old: framed black-and-white photos from the early 1900s show a very different way of life in this town on the edge of the Gargunnock Hills. The same wide choice is available at lunch and dinner, in the dining rooms and the rear bar, and ranges from surefire pub standards to slightly more elaborate restaurant dishes, still with a robust and straightforward style. Decorated in co-ordinated colours, the four bedrooms, named after local parishes, have a comfortable country feel to them.

Food serving times:
Monday-Sunday:
  12pm-2.30pm, 6pm-9.30pm
Closed 25 December
and 1 January
Prices:
Meals: a la carte 16.00/40.00
4 rooms : 50.00/80.00

9mi West of Stirling by A811 and B822. Parking.

Typical Dishes

Arbroath smokie pate

Aberfoyle venison, chocolate jus

Stem ginger and treacle pudding

Linlithgow

025 The Chop and Ale House 🛏

Champany, Linlithgow EH49 7LU

Tel.: (01506) 834532 - Fax: (01506) 834302

e-mail: reception@champany.com - Website: www.champany.com

Belhaven Best

A restaurant within a restaurant, the intimate Chop and Ale House does away with most of Champany Inn's formality. Ancient exposed stone, closely set tables and a crackling log fire can't have changed much since this was the inn's public bar, while bridle bits and equestrian bric-à-brac mirror the muted prints of local squires and their prize horses. Forget dropping in for just a pint – it's cosy and relaxing, but it's just not that kind of place – but do come for well-sourced cooking, all appetising and popular with a strong Scottish flavour and a few unexpected variations. Aberdeen Angus steaks, hearty burgers and sausages, as well as piquant pickled herrings, are served with quiet professionalism by a friendly team.

Food serving times:
Monday-Thursday:
   12pm-2pm, 6.30pm-10pm
Friday-Sunday:
                12pm-10pm
Closed 25-26 December
and 1 January
Prices:
Meals: a la carte 17.95/29.50
🛏 **16 rooms:** 115.00/ 135.00

2.5mi Northeast of town centre by A803; at the Champany Inn. Parking.

Typical Dishes

Home-smoked chorizo sausage

Aberdeen Angus ribeye steak

Malted waffles, vanilla ice cream

"Hiraeth" – the longing for home – and pride in the life of the nation take their source in many parts of Welsh identity. Unity is rooted in the very language of the Cymry, or "comrades", and the strength of community famously finds its voice in the songs of an eager rugby crowd. But above all, love of Wales is inseparable from a love of the land itself. The emblematic peaks of Snowdon and Cadair Idris and the steep streets of the Rhondda live long in the memory, but the full picture is wide enough to take in Lleyn's hidden coves and holy islands, the craggy stacks of the Pembrokeshire coast, the dominating towers of King Edward's castles and the fantasia of Portmerion, a playful dreamscape of domes and colonnades. Though long overlooked, Welsh cuisine is now making up for lost time and offering a taste of home, from rare delicacies like Wye and Usk salmon to world-famous lamb, Caerphilly, cawl cenin – a leek soup – and the humble Bara Brith; increasingly diverse real ales, and even Welsh whisky, mean there's always something new to try: Iechyd da!

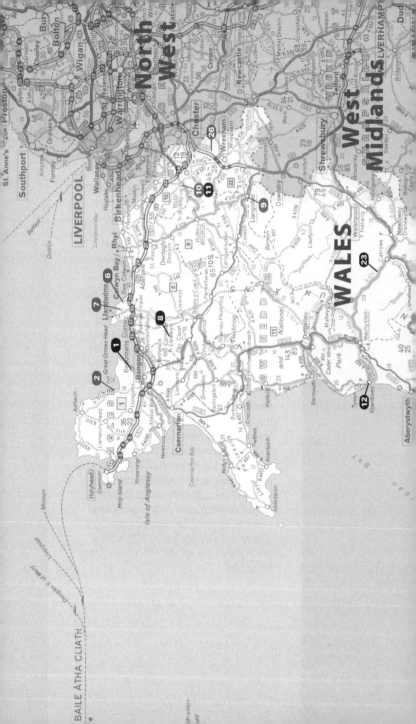

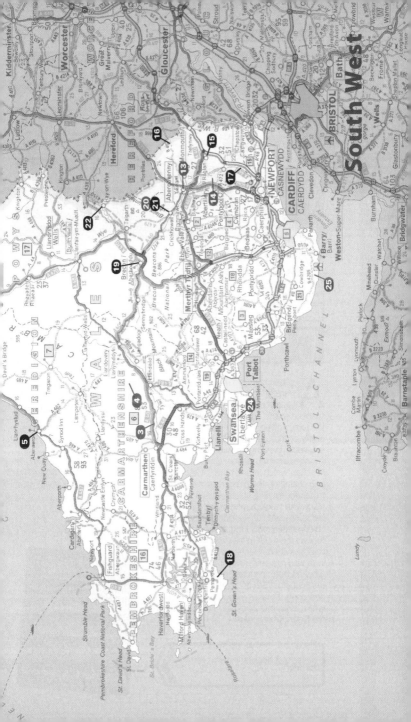

Beaumaris

001 Ye Olde Bull's Head Inn

Castle St, Beaumaris LL58 8AP

Tel.: (01248) 810329 - Fax: (01248) 811294
e-mail: info@bullsheadinn.co.uk - Website: www.bullsheadinn.co.uk

  room **VISA**

Draught Bass, Hancocks and 1 weekly changing guest ale

A classic market town inn and a good start for anyone crossing the Menai Strait for the first time – smart and spacious rooms are nicely maintained, but the same right-minded professionalism is in evidence throughout and a devoted following gives the restaurant an even stronger local reputation. Unlike the well-kept bar, which retains much of its old-style pub character, the brasserie has been tastefully restyled; an airy and comfortable place with seagrass matting, neat linen, soft lilac tones and lights around the sand-coloured beams. Sound, tasty cooking follows the modern lead and dishes like scallops with puy lentils and chorizo or beef with wild rice and shallot tarte Tatin are whisked from the kitchen by an efficiently drilled team. With its ample modern bedrooms it makes a good base from which to explore Anglesey, Snowdonia and the North Wales coast.

Food serving times:
Monday-Saturday:
12pm-2pm, 7pm-9.39pm
Sunday: 12pm-2pm, 6pm-9pm
Closed 25-26 December and 1 January
Prices:
Meals: a la carte 13.50/21.50
13 rooms : 75.00/100.00

Typical Dishes

Welsh mutton broth

Grilled black bream, parsley veloute

Warm rhubarb yoghurt cake

On the east side of the town centre. Parking.

Red Wharf Bay

002 Ship Inn

Red Wharf Bay LL75 8RJ

Tel.: (01248) 852568
e-mail: nfk1@btconnect.com - Website: www.shipinnredwharfbay.co.uk

    VISA **MC**

Adnams, Brains, Tetleys, Black Sheep, Hob Goblin, Deuchar's IPA

The neat, white-painted Ship Inn is a welcome enough sight in itself, but what makes it really special is its fabulous view: down on the shore of Red Wharf Bay, it looks out across the sands, over every play of afternoon light on the water and out to the galloping "white horses" in the open sea. In the height of summer, an empty table on the large terraces won't be free for long, but if you can tear yourself away, take a look inside. Pews and benches line the bare stone walls, which have gathered a collection of old beer adverts, pub mirrors and photographs to go with their nautical bric-a-brac, while the dining room provides a more formal setting on Saturday nights. A large menu offers anything from a lunchtime sandwich to sea bass on herb rösti or grilled pork with mustard sauce and apple compote.

Food serving times:
Monday-Friday:
12pm-2.30pm, 6pm-9pm
Saturday-Sunday:
12pm-9.30pm

Prices:
Meals: a la carte 15.00/28.00

2.5 mi Southeast of Benllech by A5025. Parking. ➤

Typical Dishes

Gratin of Conwy mussels

Shoulder of Welsh lamb, rosemary potatoes

Tim's sticky toffee pudding

Nantgaredig

003 Y Polyn

Nantgaredig SA327LH

Tel.: (01267) 290000

e-mail: ypolyn@hotmail.com - Website: www.ypolyn.co.uk

Tomos Watkins: OSB, Cwrw Hâf and Cwrw Bra 4

Only a short drive from the National Botanic Gardens, this modest roadside pub doesn't look particularly eye-catching at first, but its interior gives a very different impression. Attention to detail and a love of food are clear to see in the fresh, bright interior, decorated with cookbooks, framed menus and pictures of the world's famous chefs, and in the relaxed and assured service. The food itself shows similar care and effort: classic rustic dishes – from French and Welsh traditions – are prepared to show local ingredients at their best and bring out their wholesome and natural flavours. You're welcome to stop for just a drink, though, and settle down in one of the bar's easy chairs: the pub was actually built over a stream, which was used to cool the beer in the old days.

Food serving times:
Tuesday-Friday:
      12pm-2pm, 7pm-9pm
Saturday: 7pm-9pm
Sunday: 12pm-2pm

Closed 1 week at Christmas and 2 weeks in September or October

Prices:
Meals: 26.50 (set price dinner) and a la carte 20.00/26.00

Typical Dishes

Organic pork rillettes

Osso bucco, risotto Milanese

Warm treacle tart, vanilla ice cream

5mi East of Carmarthen on A40. From Nantgaredig South 1mi by B4310 on B4300. Parking.

Salem

004 **The Angel Inn**

Salem SA19 7LY
Tel.: (01558) 823394

 **VISA** **MC**

Reverend James and weekly changing guest beers

You'll find the welcome extended here to be as wide as the village of Salem is small; the owners took over in 2002 and their infectious enthusiasm has helped build a solid local following. Get here down a narrow road; you can't miss it, it's next to the chapel. Sink into one of the bar lounge sofas and place your order; there's a blackboard menu at lunchtimes and a more elaborate, printed a la carte in the evening. It's a spacious place, the Angel, and the sympathetic extension that is the restaurant offers large, well spaced tables, a wood floor and a subtle Victorian or Edwardian feel. By now, you'll have come to anticipate the warm, chatty service. What might surprise you are the rather complex dishes, featuring a host of local ingredients. Menus might include cannelloni of crayfish tails, Welsh spring lamb or Usk Valley venison.

Food serving times:
Tuesday-Saturday:
12pm-2pm, 7pm-9pm
Closed 1 week January
Prices:
Meals: a la carte 20.00/35.00

3mi North of Llandeilo by A40 off Pen y bane road. Parking.

Typical Dishes

Swansea Bay Thai curried mussels

Rump of Welsh lamb, beetroot and raisin jus

Hot chocolate fondant

Aberaeron

005 Harbourmaster

Quay Parade, Aberaeron SA46 0BA

Tel.: (01545) 570755

e-mail: info@harbour-master.com - Website: www.harbour-master.com

Buckley's Best, Brains SA

Appealingly situated on an attractive quayside in West Wales, this listed building is painted in deep, bold blue and was, indeed, the harbourmaster's home nearly 200 years ago. It's a fine place to relax and watch the sun set over Cardigan Bay, or, if you're feeling more energetic, to take a bracing walk along the coastal path at the front door. You can eat in the bar with the locals, or in the smart, nautically themed restaurant, which specialises in local produce with a pronounced seafood bias: feast yourself on locally caught lobsters, crab, seabass and mackerel. Beef and lamb are from the land surrounding Aberaeron. For another option of watching the setting sun, climb the listed Georgian spiral staircase and stay in one of the stylish and individual bedrooms.

Food serving times:
Tuesday-Saturday:
          12pm-2pm, 6pm-9pm
Sunday: 12pm-2pm
Monday: 6pm-9pm
Closed 24 December
to 10 January
Prices:
Meals: 16.50 (set price lunch)
and a la carte 21.00/30.00
9 rooms : 55.00/120.00

Typical Dishes

Carpaccio of Black beef

New Quay lobster, skinny fries, basil Hollandaise

Lime and honey pannacotta

In town centre overlooking the harbour. Parking.

Colwyn Bay

006 Pen-y-Bryn

Pen-y-Bryn Rd, Upper Colwyn Bay, Colwyn Bay LL29 6DD

Tel.: (01492) 534902 - Fax: (01492) 536127
e-mail: penybryn@brunningandprice.co.uk - Website: www.penybryn-colwynbay.co.uk

> 6 guest ales: Timothy Taylor's Landlord, Thwaites Braed 'r' Bryn, Flowers Original, Phoenix Arizona, Wye Valley Butty Bach

This purpose-built 1970s pub, on the road past the local zoo, really doesn't promise too much but hold your horses (and your elephants and leopards). Inside there's something of a transformation, with very spacious and comfortable surroundings forcing you to change your perspective. There are oak wood floors, polished tables and tasteful décor, comprising a host of old pictures of the promenade and local scenes, sporting fixtures, shops etc; one wall's packed with books and there's a real fire. To the rear is a garden with benches, and a fine view of the bay is possible from here and from some inside vantage points as well. A young, enthusiastic team runs the place, preparing an extensive menu, printed and replicated on a large blackboard. Welsh cooking combines with a tasty international dishes, plus good pub staples. Carefully prepared, generous portions all round.

Food serving times:
Monday-Saturday:
12pm-9.30pm
Sunday: 12pm-9pm
Closed dinner 25-26 December and dinner 1 January
Prices:
Meals: a la carte 17.00/24.00

1 mi Southwest of Colwyn Bay by B5113. Parking.

Typical Dishes

Smoked trout mousse

Spicy Moroccan lamb casserole

Bara Brith bread and butter pudding

Glanwydden

007 Queens Head

Glanwydden LL31 9JP

Tel.: (01492) 546570 - Fax: (01492) 546487
e-mail: enquiries@queensheadglanwydden.co.uk - Website: www.queensheadglanwydden.co.uk

 Weetwoods Eastgate, Weetwoods Ambush

If popularity is the yardstick of a good pub, then here is a league champion. Holiday-makers frequent this smart, cream painted pub in droves and most of them are within the premises as there are only a few tables dotted around the tarmac outside. It's a cosy, comfortable place (if you can get a seat) with the traditional appeal of low beamed ceilings, polished wooden tables, burgundy velour sofas and walls decorated with old maps and locally inspired paintings. Menus fit neatly into the tried-and-tested category but they contain plenty of local ingredients and are invariably well cooked. Dishes you might find are goat's cheese and onion tart, baked haddock with salad and bread, and homemade sticky toffee pudding. Despite the numbers, service is notably efficient.

Food serving times:
Monday-Sunday:
  12pm-2pm, 6pm-9pm
Closed 25 December
Prices:
Meals: a la carte 18.00/25.00

Typical Dishes

Crispy duck leg, sticky onions

Baked cod, Welsh rarebit

Fresh fruit Pavlova

3 mi Southeast of Llandudno by A470 off Penthyn Bay rd. Parking.

Tyn-y-Groes

008 The Groes Inn

Tyn-y-Groes LL32 8TN

Tel.: (01492) 650545 - Fax: (01492) 650855
e-mail: enquiries@thegroes.com - Website: www.groesinn.com

  VISA **AE** **①**

Tetley, Burton Ale, Great Orme

O n the eastern edge of the Snowdonia National Park and south of Conwy, this lays claim to being the oldest pub in Wales, and it bears its age with great charm, character and no little sense of style. There are lovely bar areas finished with great taste: historic bric-à-brac, beamed ceilings, polished oak furniture, relaxing garden and fine views. A cloth-clad dining room and conservatory are the places to dine: you'll find popular, tried-and-tested menus making good use of ingredients from North Wales. There are stylish bedrooms, furnished with fine fabrics; many boast superb countryside views; some have balconies and two have the added distinction of a terrace.

Food serving times:
Monday-Sunday:
        12pm-2pm, 6pm-9pm
Prices:
Meals: 16.95/28.00 (set price lunch/dinner) and a la carte 15.00/30.00
14 rooms : 79.00/175.00

Typical Dishes

Butternut squash and sage ravioli, green Tuscan oil

Conwy River salmon

Groes ice creams

2mi from Conwy Castle by B5106 towards Trefriw; the inn is on the right. Parking.

Llangollen

009 The Corn Mill

Dee Lane, Llangollen LL20 8PN

Tel.: (01978) 869555 - Fax: (01978) 869930
e-mail: cornmill@bandp.co.uk - Website: www.cornmill-llangollen.co.uk

 🍴 🍷 ✗=rest 🚫 **VISA** **AE** **M©**

 Flowers IPA, Phoenix Arizona, Deuchar's IPA, Wapping Stout, Oakham JHB

A cleverly restructured conversion with a strong imprint of original industrial chic: joists span the spacious rooms over three levels, wooden cogs and drivewheels are braced to the rafters of the bar, period prints of riverbank landscapes hang on rough, limewashed walls and glass blocks, set into the floor, give glimpses of the old workings of the mill. Best of all, a decked terrace juts out over the fast-flowing river Dee, and on still summer days you may just hear the restored steam engines chugging up the hill to Carrog. Bold and generous cooking adds a few international influences to a British base and offers plenty of choice, including lighter bites and a big sharing platter of starters. In July, the International Eisteddfod's fringe festival of arts and world music centres on the theatre around the corner.

Food serving times:
Monday-Saturday:
                12pm-9.30pm
Sunday: 12pm-9pm
Closed 25-26 December
Prices:
Meals: a la carte 15.00

Typical Dishes

Tuna steak, chilli dressing

Grilled pork chop, apple and mint mash

Sticky toffee pudding

Short walk from railway. Public parking.

Mold

010 Glas Fryn

Raikes Lane, Sychdyn, Mold CH7 6LR

Tel.: (01352) 750500 - Fax: (01352) 751923
e-mail: glasfryn@bandp.co.uk - Website: www.glasfryn-mold.co.uk

 VISA **AE** **MC**

> *Thwaites Original, Timothy Taylor's Landlord, Flower's Original, Bryn (local), Deuchar's, Weetwood Ales, Shropshire Gold*

This large, extended, red-brick pub, handily placed for visitors to the North Wales coast and Chester, presents a solid and conventional face to the world with a pleasant terrace and garden. In contrast the inside is altogether different; its modern feel is lent character by lots of old bottles, sepia photos and shelves of books, all of them lovingly kept and neatly exhibited. Institutions of local prominence are based nearby, so expect to rub shoulders at the bar with actors, lawyers, farmers, technicians and theatre-goers. It's a busy place with friendly service. There's a good choice of food with a global influence and the menu, both printed and on the blackboard, reflect traditional and modern tastes.

Food serving times:
Monday-Saturday:
                    12pm-9.30pm
Sunday: 12pm-9pm
Closed 25-26 December
Prices:
Meals: a la carte 15.95/29.70

Typical Dishes

Marinated king prawn salad

Chicken and ham pie, cabbage and mash

Hot waffles with honeycomb ice cream

1 mi North by A5119 on Civic Centre rd. Parking.

Mold

011 The Stables (at Soughton Hall)

Mold CH7 6AB

Tel.: (01352) 840577 - Fax: (01352) 840872
e-mail: info@soughtonhall.co.uk - Website: www.soughtonhall.co.uk

 VISA

Plassey Bitter

Where do you go for a decent pint in an extravagant 18C Italianate mansion? The summer house? The servants' quarters? Not quite. As relaxed and unfussy as the house is grand, the converted stable block gets slap-bang down to earth with a rustic interior of old brick and bare beams: horses' names on brass stable-plates, set into the tables, are a light-hearted touch. The approach to dining is just as informal: take your pick from sandwiches and light dishes or more substantial mains, some on the specials board - Welsh rarebit pork on a mound of apple and mustard mash sums up the generous country style here. There's also an interesting wine shop upstairs, which can only help to boost an excellent local following.

Food serving times:
Monday-Sunday:
 12pm-2.30pm, 6pm-9.30pm
(booking essential)
Prices:
Meals: a la carte 24.20/31.40
15 rooms : 130.00/180.00

Typical Dishes

Crab and spring onion cakes

Roast monkfish, olive and Parmesan potatoes

Chocolate fondant pudding

2.5 mi North by A5119 on Alltami Rd.
Parking

Aberdovey

012 **Penhelig Arms**

Aberdovey LL35 0LT

Tel.: (01654) 767215 - Fax: (01654) 767690
e-mail: info@penheligarms.com - Website: www.penheligarms.com

3 permanent and 2 weekly changing ales: Reverend James, Old Speckled Hen, Young's Special, Butty Bach, Evan Evans Cwrw

In the 1700s The Little Inn was a quaint meeting place for locals in this beautiful part of West Wales. Three centuries later residents and visitors are still coming, but the inn itself has grown out of all proportion, and the Penhelig Arms, now handsomely extended, looks out over the waters of the Dyfi Estuary. On one side is the Fisherman's Bar, where the locals gather round a log fire in the winter months. When it's warmer, you can go and sit at the sea wall. A separate dining room boasts bay views, sympathetically painted light blue walls and a laid back feel. Here and in the bar the walls are hung with contemporary Welsh art. The same menu is used throughout the house. Rustic and classic pub cooking is prepared from local produce, the fish dishes reflecting the latest catch. Some of the stylish modern bedrooms have balconies, others open onto terraces.

Food serving times:
Monday-Sunday:
12pm-2pm, 7pm-9.30pm
Closed 25-26 December
(booking essential)
Prices:
Meals: 18.00/28.00 (set price lunch/dinner Sunday only) and a la carte 17.50/25.75
16 rooms : 49.00/130.00

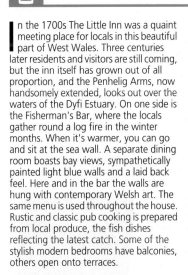

Typical Dishes

Grilled red mullet, Thai noodles

Black sea bream roasted with Anglesey sea salt

Baked cheesecake

On A493. Parking.

Abergavenny

013 The Hardwick

Old Raglan Rd, Abergavenny NP7 9AA

Tel.: (01873) 854220 - Fax: (01873) 854623
e-mail: stephen@thehardwick.co.uk - Website: www.thehardwick.co.uk

 Ruddles Best, Webb's Brewery No 2, Rhymney Brewery : Bevan's Bitter and Rhymney Bitter, Felin Foel, Double Dragon

Modern signage is the only real hint at what to expect here. The rest of the exterior – roughly textured in white – is rather plain and unassuming. Venture inside, though, and you instantly get a good feel. The middle room is where you're drawn to: it has original beams, a wood burner and, the key element, a convivial atmosphere. Its unfussy décor feels very natural and uncluttered, providing the perfect backdrop for appreciating where the Hardwick's real talent lies: the kitchen. Chef (and owner) Stephen won a Michelin star at the famous Walnut Tree, and he knows his suppliers well. Menus evolve with the seasons, and their extensive range veers from classic British to modern European: the cooking's neat, wholesome and unafraid to throw in some powerful flavours. Desserts, helpfully, come in two sizes and there's a good variety of bottled local beers to try.

Food serving times:
Tuesday-Saturday:
12pm-3pm, 6.30pm-10pm

Sunday and Bank Holiday Monday: 12pm-3pm

Closed 25 December, dinner 26 December, 22-30 January and 2-9 October

Prices:
Meals: a la carte 23.45/29.85

Typical Dishes

Crisp belly of pork, lemon and capers

Wild boar sausage and mash

Panettone brûlée pudding

2mi South East by A40 and B4598. Parking.

Nant-y-Derry

014 **The Foxhunter**

Nant-y-Derry NP7 9DN

Tel.: (01873) 881101 - Fax: (01873) 881377
e-mail: info@thefoxhunter.com - Website: www.thefoxhunter.com

 VISA

Bath Ales (Fem, Festivity, Wild Hare), Brains SA, Old Speckled Hen, Marston's Pedigree

An unlikely change of use by any standards: what started life as Victorian station master's house is now a pleasant, quietly prospering pub-bistro, with appetite-awakening food-themed prints and huge arrangements of lillies taking the place of leaves on the line. Stripped back to its basics – exposed timbers and original brickwork – it looks the picture of carefully styled gastropub, though the well-separated, bare wooden tables untypically allow their diners plenty of space. Alongside British dishes there is a wide-ranging choice with roots in rustic European cuisine. The pleasant service reflects the all round charm of this personally-run pub restaurant.

Food serving times:
Tuesday-Saturday, Mothering Sunday and some other Sundays:
12pm-2.30pm, 7pm-9.30pm
Closed 25-26 December and 2 weeks February

Prices:
Meals: 20.00 (set price lunch) and a la carte 20.00/30.00

Typical Dishes

Scallops, bacon, horseradish & black pudding

Home-cured salt beef, choucroute

Rich chocolate pot

6.5mi South of Abergavenny by A4042 and minor road. Parking.

Raglan

015 The Clytha Arms

Raglan NP7 9BW
Tel.: (01873) 840206 - Fax: (01873) 840204
e-mail: theclythaarms@tiscali.co.uk

🛏️ 🍷 ✗rest 🚭 **VISA** **AE** **①** **⑩©**

> Bass, Hook Norton, Felinfoel, traditional cider and regularly
> changing guest ales

This relaxed and unassuming country pub is one for the traditional, 'everyday hero' category. Under the roof of the old dower house, you'll glimpse a few framed prints, a dartboard and skittles and the gleam of bar taps through a crowd of chatting locals, while the broad inglenook in the comfy lounge bar next door comes complete with a drowsy pub cat. Though the menu of familiar standards, served in the more formal dining room, is prepared with due care and attention, the food at the Clytha Arms is really at its most appealing when it forgets its restaurant manners. With greater simplicity of presentation come direct and refreshing flavours, so find a seat on the refectory benches in the bar and tuck in to the generous servings. The set menu is good value or you can try the eclectic internationally influenced monthly selection; tapas are served at the bar. The comfortable bedrooms on the upper floor are individually styled.

Food serving times:
Tuesday-Sunday:
12.30pm-2.15pm,
7pm-9.30pm
Sunday: 12.30pm-2.15pm
Monday: 7pm-9.30pm
Prices:
Meals: 19.95 (set price lunch/ dinner) and a la carte 28.00/ 28.00
🛏️ **4 rooms :** 60.00/100.00

3mi West on the Clytha road (Old Abergavenny Road). Parking.

Typical Dishes

Mixed grill of shellfish

Teriyaki fillet of beef

Iced Tequilla souffle with mocha sauce

Skenfrith

016   The Bell at Skenfrith

Skenfrith NP7 8UH

Tel.: (01600) 750235 - Fax: (01600) 750525
e-mail: enquiries@skenfrith.co.uk - Website: www.skenfrith.co.uk

Freeminer Bitter, Timothy Taylor's Landlord, Kingstone Brewery,
Golden Valley

Our 2007 Pub of the Year is set in the Monmouthshire countryside. After a tour of the three border castles in the Monnow valley, be sure to visit this lovely pub: an overnight stay is highly recommended too. It's located by the river with flocks of sheep in the surrounding fields. A stylish country flavour imbues all areas: there's a stone floor, roaring log fire, bare wooden tables and chairs and lots of black-and-white photos of the locality in yesteryear. You can relax in comfy sofas or on the beautiful garden terrace. Everything, everywhere is spotlessly kept. A fresh, local and organic emphasis informs the menus, which adhere to a traditional base with modern overtones, and keen, friendly service can be relied upon. The inn's main strength, though, is its bedrooms; these are exceptional, from the inclusion of DVDs to luxurious toiletries, and practically define the term "country style".

Food serving times:
Monday-Sunday:
  12pm-2.30pm, 7pm-9.30pm
Closed 2 weeks late January to early February
Closed Monday November to March

Prices:
Meals: 21.50 (set price lunch Sunday only) and a la carte 25.00/30.00

8 rooms : 75.00/180.00

11 mi West of Ross-on-Wye by A49 on B4521. Parking.

Typical Dishes

Terrine of feta cheese & poppy seeds

Brill, tomato polenta, spinach and caviar sauce

Marmalade soufflé

Tredunnock

017 The Newbridge 🛏

Tredunnock NP15 1LY

Tel.: (01633) 451000 - Fax: (01633) 451001
e-mail: thenewbridge@tinyonline.co.uk - Website: www.thenewbridge.co.uk

 🍴 ⚔room 🚫 **VISA** **AE** ① **M©**

🍺 *Hancock's HB and 1 guest beer*

The fast-flowing River Usk is the sprightly neighbour to this smartly gabled, cream painted pub which, to complete the rural picture, overlooks a winding country road and, of course, the bridge. Inside, there's a lovely open, spacious feel with stylish contemporary touches sprinkled all around. The dining element here is strong and the prevailing ambience suggests restaurant at least as much as pub. A curved iron staircase connects two levels of chunky wood tables and chairs. Lots of blackboard specials to peruse - lunch is particularly good value. The cooking is modern and quite adventurous but not over embellished; the fish is delivered from Cornwall and other ingredients are equally carefully sourced. Afterwards, you can stay in state-of-the-art bedrooms where no expense has been spared.

Food serving times:
Monday-Sunday:
    12pm-3pm, 7pm-9.30pm
Closed 26 December
(booking advisable)
Prices:
Meals: a la carte 20.00/32.00
🛏 **6 rooms :** 110.00/150.00

Five minutes drive from the centre of Caerleon, on the banks of the River Usk. Parking.

Typical Dishes

Seared scallops red wine syrup

Saddle of Bwlch venison

Chocolate fondant, marmalade ice cream

Stackpole

018 **The Stackpole Inn** 🛏

Jasons Corner, Stackpole SA71 5DF

Tel.: (01646) 672324 - Fax: (01646) 672716
e-mail: info@stackpoleinn.co.uk

 VISA **MC**

 Felinfoel Double Dragon, Felinfoel Best Bitter, Brain's Reverend James and changing guest ales

A real fixture of the landscape, this rural pub feels as if it might almost have grown up out of the Pembrokeshire countryside: sturdy wooden slabs frame the bar-room, hops stretch their shoots towards the courses of bare brick and pint glasses shine on a Welsh slate bar. The owner, a natural hostess, superintends service with great warmth of personality; with her son in charge of the kitchen, it's a co-operative family effort. His straightforward, modern-classic cooking draws on seasonal Welsh ingredients to flavourful effect: winter in particular brings fortifying plates of warming and unfinicky country food like poached chicken with vegetable broth. There are now four bedrooms for those who would like to stay overnight.

Food serving times:
Summer: Monday-Sunday: 12pm-2pm, 6.30pm-9pm
Winter: Tuesday-Saturday: 12pm-2pm, 6.30pm-9pm
Sunday: 12pm-2pm
Prices:
Meals: a la carte 16.50/26.50
🛏 **4 rooms :** 35.00/60.00

Typical Dishes

Thai style fish cakes

Medallions of Welsh black fillet steak

Fresh raspberry brûlée

5mi South of Pembroke by B4319. Parking.

Brecon

019 **The Felin Fach Griffin** 🛏

Felin Fach, Brecon LD3 0UB

Tel.: (01874) 620111 - Fax: (01874) 620120
e-mail: enquiries@eatdrinksleep.ltd.uk - Website: www.eatdrinksleep.ltd.uk

 🖥 ♈ 🍷 ⅍room **VISA** Ⓜ️ⓒ

Tomos Watkins OSB, Evan Evans Dewi Sant, Evan Evans (various ales) and seasonal ales when possible

The wonderfully relaxed atmosphere starts in the open bar of this converted farmhouse: antiques and reclaimed furniture, bright modern colours and sofas by the log fire make this an easy place to feel at home in. It's the same story in the spacious bedrooms, all in light, restful tones, which prove that you can banish twee or designerish clutter and still have thoughtful extras close to hand: each has fine linens, European and Indian furniture and a selection of good books. Well-balanced cooking in a modern style makes intelligent use of local ingredients; classic or kitchen garden menus accompany the main choice at supper. Arrive early if you would like to eat on the terrace as its capacity is not infinite. Cocktails are a speciality and only a very tasty breakfast, fresh from the Aga, could possibly tempt you out of the wonderfully comfortable beds!

Food serving times:
Tuesday-Sunday and Bank Holiday Mondays:
12.30pm-2.30pm, 6.30pm-9.30pm
Other Mondays:
6.30pm-9.30pm
Closed 25-26 December
Prices:
Meals: 27.90 (set price dinner) and a la carte 17.00/30.00
🛏 **7 rooms :** 67.50/125.00

Typical Dishes

Portland dressed crab

Loin of local Welsh lamb, braised haricot blanc

Bitter chocolate tart

4.75 mi Northeast of Brecon by B4602 off A470. Parking.

Crickhowell

020 Nantyffin Cider Mill Inn

Brecon Rd, Crickhowell NP8 1SG

Tel.: (01873) 810775

e-mail: info@cidermill.co.uk - Website: www.cidermill.co.uk

Felinfoel Double Dragon, Henry's IPA, Wadsworth 6X, Uley Old Spot, Old Rosie cider

This hugely characterful 16C cider mill in the heart of the Brecon Beacons is difficult to miss: apart from being a distinctive mill by a busy crossroads, it's painted in an evocative pink wash. Inside, the characterful features remain: its working parts are still in situ, and two snug bars boast open fires, comfy country style seating and an interesting mix of antiques and curios. This was one of the first Welsh gastropubs, and a slightly more formal dining room is furnished with the original mill and press as well as cloth-clad tables. The blackboard menus change frequently and, apart from quite rightly highlighting cider, feature fish and game with some prominence. The kitchen proudly advertises its use of seasonal and very local ingredients from a local farm. The set menu is good value and lunch particularly popular.

Food serving times:

Tuesday-Sunday and Bank Holiday Monday:
12pm-2.30pm,
6.30pm-9.30pm

Closed Monday except Bank Holidays; also dinner Sunday September to April

Prices:

Meals: 12.95/16.95 (set price lunch and dinner) and a la carte 12.95/30.00

Typical Dishes

Baked Welsh goat's cheese

Confit of home reared lamb, herb mash

Sticky toffee pudding,

1.5 mi West of Crickhowell on A40. Parking.

Crickhowell

021 ## The Bear

High St, Crickhowell NP8 1BW

Tel.: (01873) 810408 - Fax: (01873) 811696
e-mail: bearhotel@aol.com - Website: www.bearhotel.co.uk

 Bass, Reverend James, Ruddles Best and Directors

In a small town in the Black Mountains, The Bear is a traditional coaching inn dating from 1435 with bags of charm and character. The snug bar at the front, with its open fire and beams, leads into an area of nooks and crannies and the lounge: lots of rafters, comfy armchairs, antique settles, and a window seat letting you see what's happening in the market square. Don't miss out on eating here; two separate dining rooms are handsome enough on their own, with plenty of antiques and curios, but when you add the delicious food they serve – classically based with first-rate local ingredients – then you should see why the place is perennially busy. Appetising, modern bar-bistro dishes use similarly fresh produce to flavourful effect. There's also a welcoming summer garden, and bedrooms are plush and spacious.

Food serving times:
Monday-Sunday:
12pm-2pm, 7pm-9.30pm
Closed 25 December to non-residents
Prices:
Meals: a la carte 20.00/30.35
32 rooms : 65.00/150.00

In the town centre. Parking.

Typical Dishes

Homemade soup
Fresh salmon fishcakes & new potatoes
Apple and wimberry pie

Hay-on-Wye

022 Old Black Lion

26 Lion St, Hay-on-Wye HR3 5AD

Tel.: (01497) 820841 - Fax: (01497) 822960
e-mail: info@oldblacklion.co.uk - Website: www.oldblacklion.co.uk

☐ ☐ ☐ **VISA** **M③**

Wye Valley Brewery, Brain's Reverend James

K now your JK Rowling from your DH Lawrence? After a busy round of book bazaars and seminars in the bibliophile's capital of Britain, head for dinner at this part 13C and 17C inn. The main bar is long on charm and character, lit by a real log fire: you could settle in comfortably with a pint and a good page-turner at any time, and though there's a separate formal dining room, you can choose a table and eat here, too. A dependable traditional menu holds one or two light variations, but the list of chalkboard specials is arguably the better choice – honest, tasty and prepared with good culinary understanding. Immaculate bedrooms, some in the adjacent block, are far better than the average pub, but it goes without saying that you'll have to reserve in good time for the Festival.

Food serving times:
Monday-Sunday:
  12pm-2.30pm, 6.30pm-9pm
Closed 24-26 December
Prices:
Meals: a la carte 19.40/28.50
☐ **10 rooms :** 50.00/85.00

Typical Dishes

Confit of duck, plum sauce

Herb crusted rack of lamb, rosemary lamb jus

Bread and butter pudding

In the town centre. Parking. ▶

Pontdolgoch

023 The Talkhouse 🛏

Pontdolgoch SY17 5JE

Tel.: (01686) 688919

e-mail: info@talkhouse.co.uk - Website: www.talkhouse.co.uk

 🍷 ⚥✗ 🍴✗ **VISA** Ⓜ©

No real ales offered

A cosy, unassuming exterior gives little away about the stylish goings-on inside this 17C former coaching inn tucked away on a quiet road in rural mid-Wales. It's full of charm, with lots of curios, knick-knacks and antiques adorning the rustic-styled bar, where you can slump into plush sofas in front of the log fire. French windows lead onto a lovely terrace and gardens for al fresco dining on warmer days. Eating here is a treat: considerate, personal service strikes just the right balance and a wide-ranging menu has a well-executed touch, as reassuringly local produce comes together to create well-honed seasonal dishes. There are bedrooms too: an immaculate trio with a welcoming, individual style.

Food serving times:
Tuesday-Saturday:
           12pm-1.30pm,
           6.30pm-8.45pm
Sunday: 12pm-1.30pm
Closed first 2 weeks of January
Prices:
Meals: a la carte 21.95/29.50
🛏 **3 rooms :** 70.00/95.00

Typical Dishes

Toasted Pantysgaw Goat's cheese, Carmarthen ham

Local Welsh fillet of beef, horseradish rösti

Vanilla pod crème brûlee

1.5 mi Northwest of Caersws on A470. Parking.

Llanrhidian

024 The Welcome To Town

Llanrhidian SA3 1EH

Tel.: (01792) 390015 - Fax: (01792) 390015
e-mail: enquiries@thewelcometotown.co.uk - Website: www.thewelcometotown.co.uk

No real ales offered

The Welcome to Town is more of a goodbye to the city – if you're in need of the perfect mid-week escape, a ten-mile drive takes you out into the rural peace of the Gower peninsula and straight to the front door of this old pub, where the owner's enthusiasm and experience is writ large…in the framed certificates and awards decorating a traditionally styled dining room. Able, pleasant service, with the formality of a restaurant, strikes the right note, while locally influenced cooking brings out appealing, seasonal flavours, a considered, rather classical approach underpinning it all. The specials board changes by the day, and it's worth asking about their good-value lunches.

Food serving times:
June-August:
Monday-Sunday:
12pm-2.30pm, 7pm-9.30pm
Sept-May: Tuesday-Saturday:
12pm-2.30pm, 7pm-9.30pm
Sunday: 12pm-2.30pm
Closed 25-26 December,
1 January and last 2 weeks in
February
Prices:
Meals: 13.95/32.50 (set price
lunch and dinner) and a la carte
15.95/41.00

Typical Dishes

Scallops, tomato and vanilla relish

Best end of local lamb, pea purée

Pear and blueberry sable

10.5 mi West of Swansea by A4118 and B4271. Parking.

East Aberthaw

025 The Blue Anchor Inn

East Aberthaw CF62 3DD

Tel.: (01446) 750329 - Fax: (01446) 750077
Website: www.blueanchoraberthaw.com

 Wye Valley Pale Ale, Brains Bitter, Wadworth 6X, Theakstons Old Peculiar

Part of the original 14C thatched pub succumbed to fire in 2004, but the Blue Anchor has now been rebuilt and restored in sympathy with its old charm. In summer it is bright with overflowing hanging baskets. Inside, the warren of little firelit rooms and massive walls in local stone give it plenty of character. It's still cosy, effortlessly pleasing and, once you get comfortable, very hard to leave, but the chatty staff wouldn't dream of hurrying you along. As you might expect, there's an extensive menu built on sound, homely foundations; restorative, traditional dishes seem to go down well with the locals. In the evening there is a choice between the popular bar menu or dining upstairs in the restaurant, where an Asian edge in some dishes complements the prime Welsh beef and other seasonal local specialities.

Food serving times:
Monday-Saturday:
    12pm-2pm, 7pm-9.30pm
Sunday: 12pm-2.30pm,
        7pm-9.30pm

Prices:
Meals: 17.95 (set price dinner) and a la carte 13.00/25.00

Turn at the cement factory and follow the road for approximately 1 mile. Car park opposite the pub.

Typical Dishes

Thai fish cakes

Wild sea bass, sauce vierge

Welsh farm house cheeses

Gresford

026 Pant-yr-Ochain

Old Wrexham Rd, Gresford LL12 8TY

Tel.: (01978) 853525 - Fax: (01978) 853505

e-mail: pant.yr.ochain@brunningandprice.co.uk - Website: www.pantyrochain-gresford.co.uk

Timothy Taylor's Landlord, Caledonian, Deuchar's IPA, Weetwood Old Dog, Spitting Feathers, Old Wavertonian

This pub enjoys a pleasant setting just outside the village. To get an idea of its vintage, look at the Tudor wattle and daub walls and timber in the alcove behind the inglenook fireplace. The Pant isn't just rather old, it's also rather vast, with several rooms running off the main bar. Overall it's smart yet rustic, enhanced by lake views and a small model railway in the grounds. Its library bar has some dining tables, plus a good view of the lake, which makes it the pick of the rooms in which to eat. The daily-changing menu is a printed sheet duplicated on the blackboard with a good choice of traditional and modern dishes ranging from light to very substantial; the cooking is robust and bold. This is a very well regarded place locally and its bustling atmosphere just adds to the experience.

Food serving times:

Monday-Saturday:
12pm-9.30pm

Sunday: 12pm-9pm

Closed 25-26 December
(booking essential)

Prices:

Meals: a la carte 16.95/25.00

Typical Dishes

Mushrooms with Welsh rarebit

Game and steak suet pudding, red cabbage

Bread and butter pudding

3.5 mi Northeast of Wrexham by A483 on B5445. Then 1 mi South from Gresford. Parking.

*W*ith over a third of the country's population living in and around, Belfast is truly the focus of Northern Irish life. As the only city in Ireland to feel the rise and heavy fall of Britain's industrial empire, it has worked bravely to re-establish itself with a busy cultural life and a wave of new building, and perhaps it is in part the attitudes in the rest of Britain and Ireland that make us look elsewhere for easier symbols and images of the country. Though less intensely marketed than the Southern Ireland experience, the six counties contain some of the finest landscapes in the island. The incredible, innumerable columns of the Giant's Causeway, formed 60 million years ago by volcanic eruptions, attract thousands of visitors every year, while to the east lie the quiet, wooded bays of the Antrim coast and the deep inland glens. The beautiful Mourne and Sperrin Mountains stand as great Ulster landmarks, while Lough Neagh, the largest body of fresh water in the British Isles, lies in repose, a vast blue mirror in the heart of the province: here you'll find the working landscapes and the working people richly explored in Seamus Heaney's poetic memories of his youth. From the cultivated splendour of Mount Stewart Gardens or Castle Coole to the earth-magic of Beaghmore, from the whale-backed islands of Strangford Lough to the leaping salmon and pike in Lough Erne, a feeling for the natural world of Northern Ireland goes straight to the heart.

Belfast

001 The Errigle Inn

312-320 Ormeau Rd, Belfast BT7 2GE

Tel.: (028) 9064 1410 - Fax: (028) 9064 0772
e-mail: philip@errigle.co.uk - Website: www.errigle.com

 VISA **AE** **MC**

 No real ales offered

Seventy plus years in the business, this big, traditional Belfast bar remains a pub landmark in the city. Hungry newcomers can be forgiven for edging awkwardly around the maze of rooms at first: the no-nonsense Pinewood bar is really the locals' stamping ground for a beer and a smoke, but remember that the bustling Tom McGurran bar always keeps a little space for diners. For a bit more restaurant comfort, though, you're better off surrounded by handsome dark wood and green leather in the Oak Room, or in the dining room upstairs on a Friday or Saturday. Dinner dishes along traditional lines are tasty, generous and carefully prepared; the specials are more imaginative. Lunches from the Brunch Lite Bites menu tend to be more basic: baps, grills, pastas and that dietician's nightmare, the mighty Errigle Fry.

Food serving times:
Monday-Sunday:
                    12pm-10pm
Closed 25 December
Prices:
Meals: a la carte 12.70/25.20

South of the city centre by A24, over the river and past the park, on the lefthand side. Parking on the street.

Typical Dishes

Chicken liver pate

Lamb shank, parsnip mash

Caramel and pear crumble

Bushmills

002 The Distillers Arms

140 Main St, Bushmills BT57 8QE

Tel.: (028) 2073 1044 - Fax: (028) 2073 2843
e-mail: simon@distillersarms.com - Website: www.distillersarms.com

♈ *VISA* ⓜⓒ

Old Speckled Hen, White Star, Captain Smiths, Legbitter (all bottled)

The smart conservation village of Bushmills has its very own smart – and stylish – pub, set conveniently on the high street. Once home to owners of the local distillery, it's seen some very plush interior renovations creating an open-plan bar and comfortable lounge with shiny wood floors, elegant coolie lampshades and chunky brown leather sofas. The rear dining area is spacious enough for groups taking in the delights of the north Antrim coast and the menus are decidedly, sometimes ambitiously modern. Typically, you could try grilled fillets of sea bass with Asian spices, wilted greens, boiled potatoes and chilled tomato, garlic and anchovy sauce or pan-seared chicken supreme, aubergine, basil couscous, tomato and red onion salsa.

Food serving times:
Monday-Sunday:
12.30pm-3pm,
5.30pm-9.30pm
Closed Mondays in winter; closed for dinner weekends in winter
Prices:
Meals: a la carte 19.00/25.00

Typical Dishes

Whiskey cured salmon
Lamb shank, mustard mash
Irish cheeses with quince

Close to the Bushmills whiskey distillery. Parking. ▶

Annahilt

003 The Pheasant

410 Upper Ballynahinch Rd, Annahilt BT26 6NR

Tel.: (028) 9263 8056 - Fax: (028) 9263 8026
e-mail: pheasantinn@aol.com

 VISA **AE** **①** **MC**

No real ales offered

Even in midweek the little public bar is bustling by lunchtime: the old floorboards, mock Tudor windows and a smouldering peat fire suggest a place happy to keep 21C fads at arm's length, for the moment at least. Press through and find a table, either along the colourful banquettes or in one of the booths, and allow yourself an aperitif while you look through the menu. You'll have time for a half at least; the choice is vast – too wide, perhaps – but you're assured of generous helpings. Seafood, grills, and a completely international range of dishes are included on a list of tasty, no-nonsense classics, served up with brisk, capable cheeriness by a young bar team. Thursday evening is quiz night and on Friday there is live music by a variety of groups.

Food serving times:
Monday-Sunday :
   12pm-2.30pm, 5pm-9pm
Closed 25-26 December
and 12-13 July
Prices:
Meals: a la carte 20.00/40.00

1mi North of Annahilt on Lisburn rd.
Parking.

Typical Dishes

Pigeon & quail, sage and mushroom risotto

Venison, whiskey & bacon sauce

Sticky toffee pudding

Ballynahinch

004 The Primrose

30 Main St, Ballynahinch BT24 8DN

Tel.: (028) 9756 3177 - Fax: (028) 9756 5954

e-mail: info@primrosebar.co.uk - Website: www.primrosebar.co.uk

 No real ales offered

Nothing particularly draws you in to The Primrose, just one of a pretty average string of buildings along Main Street: only inside do you notice that little extra thought and effort that raises this small-town pub above the norm. Several small rooms around the double bar are all brightly decorated and feel surprisingly welcoming: you can expect an encouraging turn-out in the evening, and even at lunchtime there's a pleasant buzz of conversation from the locals, happy to have escaped the shop or the office for an hour or two. They come for burgers, steaks and baguettes, one or two daily specials or a list of well-presented dishes that includes internationally influenced choices – teriyaki beef or Indian-spiced lamb with chick peas – as well as classics like smoked salmon and prawn salad. Attentive service.

Food serving times:
Sunday-Thursday:
    12pm-2.30pm, 5pm-8pm
Friday-Saturday:
    12pm-2.30pm, 7pm-9pm
Sunday: 12.30pm-2.30pm,
    5pm-8pm

Closed 25 December
(bar meals Sunday-Thursday evenings)
Prices:
Meals: a la carte 13.50/25.00

In the town centre on the west side of the road. Parking on the street.

Typical Dishes

Chicken and peach salad

Grilled salmon with cockles & mussels, Pernod sauce

Baileys and white chocolate cheesecake

Bangor

005 Coyle's

44 High St, Bangor BT20 5AZ
Tel.: (028) 9127 0362 - Fax: (028) 9127 0362

 No real ales offered

Northern Ireland's most popular coastal resort deserves a great venue to eat and drink, and at Coyle's it's hit paydirt. There's no mistaking the pubby appearance: a black exterior, advertising real music and hard liquor! The ground floor bar keeps that image intact. It's intimate and friendly with a welcoming ambience, and, apart from the liquor, there's an up-to-date menu where classics meet dishes with an international accent. A board directs you upstairs for the restaurant proper. This comes as a bit of a surprise: there's a touch of the art deco/nouveau about it, with stained glass and old framed posters such as a '40s ad for Craven A cigarettes. Although the rather basic tables and chairs don't really do justice to their surroundings, the cooking ticks all the right boxes. It's a harmonious blend of safe, traditional styles with more ambitious, but well executed, dishes.

In the town centre. Pay and display parking 2min walk.

Food serving times:
Tuesday-Friday:
12pm-3pm, 5pm-9pm
Saturday: 12pm-3pm, 5pm-9.30pm
Sunday: 12pm-8pm
Closed 25 December
Prices:
Meals: a la carte 14.00/18.00

Typical Dishes

Strangford Lough mussels
Monkfish, cod and crab cake
Chocolate brownies

Donaghadee

006 **Grace Neill's**

33 High St, Donaghadee BT21 0AH

Tel.: (028) 9188 4595 - Fax: (028) 9188 9631
e-mail: info@graceneills.com - Website: www.graceneills.com

 VISA **AE** **MC**

No real ales offered

Reputed to be the oldest pub in Ireland, the 17C Grace Neill's has certainly seen some changes in its time. True, the traditional front bar, propped up on its massive timbers, looks as charming and timeless as ever; it's a place for slow pints and unhurried chat, with families snacking and drinking in the lounge. But at the back, the split-level brasserie is chic, formal and uncompromisingly contemporary: silk cushions, elegant storm lamps, subtle shades of chestnut and aubergine and banquettes à la parisienne. The seafood specials are always a good choice as they contain the prime catch of the day. For a good deal try the early evening meals for two which include wine. The service can get rather earnest and solicitous, but there's no mistaking the good intentions behind it.

Food serving times:
Monday-Thursday:
12pm-2.30pm, 7pm-9pm
Friday-Saturday:
12pm-2.30pm, 7pm-9.30pm
Sunday: 12pm-2.30pm,
5.30pm-8pm
Closed 25 December
Prices:
Meals: a la carte 17.00/21.50

Typical Dishes

Sautéed tiger prawns

Smoked haddock and spinach risotto

Bread and butter pudding

In town centre. Parking.

Donaghadee

007 Pier 36

36 The Parade, Donaghadee BT21 0HE

Tel.: (028) 9188 4466 - Fax: (028) 9188 4636
e-mail: info@pier36.co.uk - Website: www.pier36.co.uk

     VISA **AE** **MC**

No real ales offered

Never less than busy, this family-run harbourside pub is a real local favourite. The door opens into a thronging front bar, which manages to be comfortable and gloriously cluttered at the same time, while the semi-raised dining area, in stripped pine and bare brick, has an almost country-cottage feel to it – perhaps it's the smell of bread and home cooking from the stove. Chatty, well-marshalled bar staff keep things moving briskly, serving up enjoyable, ultra-simple seafood as well as tasty grills and slow-cooked roasts. It's not called Pier 36 for nothing, and a pre-dinner stroll along the waterfront can be a lovely way of sharpening the appetite. The comfortable bedrooms in crisp modern colours are a welcome addition to upstairs.

Food serving times:
Monday-Sunday:
12pm-9.30pm
Closed 25 December
- Seafood specialities -
Prices:
Meals: a la carte 10.00/40.00
4 rooms : 50.00/80.00

On the harbour front. Parking in the street.

Typical Dishes

Crab claw in coriander & hazelnut butter

Brill, rocket and red onion mash

Bread and butter pudding

Dundrum

008 Buck's Head Inn

77-79 Main St, Dundrum BT33 0LU

Tel.: (028) 4375 1868 - Fax: (028) 4481 1033
e-mail: buckshead1@aol.com - Website: www.thebucksheaddundrum.co.uk

 VISA **AE** **MC**

No real ales offered

Local watercolours on the brick walls lend a touch of intimacy and originality to this relaxing, everyday pub, which is popular with the locals for lunch and with walkers, who come for the high tea served in the early evening (5-6.45pm). Here you can choose informal eating or something closer to restaurant style. Consistent and simply presented cooking with a seafood base strikes an appealing balance between traditional pub meals and more elaborate styles. There's plenty to see and do after lunch, too: visit Dundrum's ruined castle or head south into the lovely rolling landscape of the Mourne Mountains, driving the picturesque coast road or striking out on foot along part of the Ulster Way, which passes a few miles from here.

Food serving times:
Monday-Sunday:
  12pm-2.30pm, 5pm-9.30pm
Closed 24-25 December and Monday October-March
- Seafood specialities -
Prices:
Meals: 25.50 (set price dinner) and a la carte 15.50/25.50

In the village. Parking on the street.

Typical Dishes

Monkfish, Dundrum Bay mussels and cider cream

Loin of venison on potato and leek rösti

Buttermilk pannacotta

Dundrum

009 Mourne Seafood Bar

10 Main St, Dundrum BT33 0LU

Tel.: (028) 4375 1377 - Fax: (028) 4375 1161

Website: www.mourneseafood.com

 VISA Ⓜ

No real ales offered

Standing over the road from the popular Buck's Head Inn, this rather untypical seafood bar was previously the current owner's home, and the name plaque 'Downshire Manor' can still be found on the front. He also runs an oyster and mussel farm in Carlingford Lough, source of many dishes here, while other produce is brought in from the local boats. Bob (the owner) is keen for people to try 'bi-catch' species rather than fish under pressure such as cod, and this simple, casual bar is a great place to give it a go: prices are reasonable and fair. There's a core menu: meanwhile, waiters take time to explain the six or seven daily blackboard specials. Wet fish is available to buy and chef is happy to suggest the best way to cook if asked. It's not just seafood on the menu here: locally reared chicken and steaks also make an appearance. An excellent local reputation is building, so, if it's summertime, do make sure you book first.

Food serving times:
Summer: Monday-Sunday: 12pm-9.30pm
Winter: Wednesday-Sunday: 12pm-9pm or earlier

- seafood - Booking essential in summer

Prices:
Meals: a la carte 18.00/28.00

In the village. Parking across the street and in the village.

Typical Dishes

Langoustine in garlic butter

Whole sea bass or grilled lobster

Crème brûlée

Hillsborough

010 **The Plough Inn**

The Square, Hillsborough BT26 6AG

Tel.: (028) 9268 2985 - Fax: (028) 9268 2472
e-mail: derekpatterson@hotmail.com - Website: www.barretro.com

🍷 ⚔ ⚔ **VISA** **AE** **①** **MC**

No real ales offered

In such a quiet town, The Plough Inn keeps itself surprisingly busy: there's a contemporary style first-floor bistro – Bar Retro – where families are welcomed with wraps, burgers and panninis, and the traditional main bar at the hub of things below. Here, the stripped floorboards and no-frills approach set a simple tone, but there are no complaints from a regular crowd of neighbourhood drinkers and diners, who can take their pick from a list of snacks and sandwiches or a broad, appealing menu with a sound Irish base: even by local standards, the portions are immense. Service may slow down a little as the lunchtime rush picks up, but the polite good humour never flags.

Food serving times:
Monday-Sunday:
    12pm-3pm, 5pm-9.30pm
Closed 25 December
Prices:
Meals: 14.95/21.95 (set price lunch/dinner) and a la carte 15.00/30.00

Typical Dishes

Mozzarella and Serrano ham

Scallops, ginger and fennel cream

Bramley apple pancaket

At the top of the hill in The Square. Parking. ➤

*W*ell deserving of its old epithet, 'The Emerald Isle', Ireland conjures up images of dewy fields and distant mountains. Wondrous, ever-changing cloudscapes do haul in rainfall on an almost industrial scale, accounting for the fresh atmosphere and luminous look of the landscape, but this picture of gentle, unpeopled tranquillity does no justice to the country's variety: sandy strands, flora-rich peatland and, at the westernmost edge of Europe, the natural phenomenon of the Cliffs of Moher, a five mile spectacular of shale and sandstone bounded by the Atlantic breakers and the Burren. Peaceful Cashel and Clonmacnoise evoke the spirit of Celtic Christianity and kingship, while the Republic's towns and cities throb with life, culture and chatter: Galway has grown into a bustling university and cathedral city alongside its thriving port while Killarney, near the wild south-west tip, has been attracting visitors for over 200 years. Dublin remains the heart of the nation, a fascinating focus of literary association with a vital blend of street, café, bar and restaurant life: the addictive craic of the "fair city" is played out to an accompaniment of Georgian elegance and the stunning background of the Wicklow Mountains. Away from the capital, too, friendly pubs serve up not only good stout and even better conversation, but also wholesome favourites like Irish stew, colcannon and coddle and imaginative new cuisine showcasing the finest produce the country has to offer.

Liscannor

001 Vaughan's Anchor Inn 🛏

Liscannor

Tel.: (065) 708 1548 - Fax: (065) 708 6977

 ✖ ✖ **VISA** **MC**

 No real ales offered

Conveniently placed for the cliffs of Moher and the beach, this is a long-standing pub, seriously well-regarded by the locals and now also offers accommodation. It boasts a charmingly unique interior: the front counter acts as a shop where you can buy corn flakes and coffee, while the walls are filled with fishing paraphernalia: nets, photos, ships' wheels and the like. Simple wooden tables make it seem like a bistro; a mix of simple and complex dishes means there's always something of interest on the menu. The more involved options might, include seared scallops on a bed of crisp-fried smoked haddock and scallion mash with a white wine sauce. It gets very busy, so be prepared to wait for your dish to arrive.

Food serving times:
Monday-Sunday:
12pm-9.30pm
Closed 25 December
- seafood -
Prices:
Meals: a la carte 25.00/36.00
🛏 **3 rooms :** 70.00/70.00

Typical Dishes

Foie gras two ways

Rack of lamb, fondant potato & vanilla parsnip

White and milk chocolate Porter cake

On coast road 1.5mi from Lahinch on main route to Cliffs of Moher. Parking. ▶

Newquay

002 Linnane's Bar

New Quay Pier, Newquay
Tel.: (065) 707 8120
e-mail: linnaneslobsterbar@hotmail.com

 VISA **AE** **D** **MC**

 No real ales offered

On the crags overlooking Galway Bay, this little white-painted pub is traditional, friendly and totally relaxed. If the clouds are setting in, you can always find a table in the modest bar, decorated with black and white photos, but if there's even a hint of sun, make straight for the lovely terrace overlooking the water. A concise, all-seafood menu, concentrating on prime fresh shellfish, keeps it delightfully simple; they're open all day in summer, so you can while away the afternoon with open sandwiches, chowders, lobster, scallops, oysters, chilled Sancerre and plenty of fresh sea air! There's more seafood for sale at the pier shop. If you can tear yourself away, drive through the strange, barren Tolkien-scape of The Burren to Lahinch beach or the breathtaking Cliffs of Moher.

Food serving times:
Monday-Sunday:
12.30pm-9pm
Closed 25 December and Good Friday
- Seafood -
Prices:
Meals: a la carte 17.95/38.95

Typical Dishes

Baked crab with Mary-Rose sauce

Scallops in a cream and wine sauce, wild rice

Dessert of the day

About 2mi off N 67 between Kinvara and Ballyvaughan. Parking.

Castletownshend

003 **Mary Ann's**

Castletownshend

Tel.: (028) 36146 - Fax: (028) 36920

e-mail: maryanns@eircom.net - Website: www.maryannsbarrestaurant.com

   VISA **MC**

 No real ales offered

First find this sleepy coastal village, then follow the row of terrace houses until you come to a pleasant little 19C pub. With over fifteen years' experience, the friendly owners are old hands by now, taking real pride in their tasty, traditional home cooking and preferring not to cut corners when it comes to the important things. There's a familiar ring to much of the large menu, as well as the blackboard specials – this is food to satisfy, rather than surprise or impress – but homemade soups, good homebaked rolls, local cheeses and their real speciality, seafood, are all clearly well above the norm. If it's sunny enough, the friendly people behind the bar will offer you a seat in the garden.

Food serving times:
Monday-Sunday:
  12pm-2.30pm, 6pm-9.30pm
Closed 24-26 December and last 3 weeks in January; also Monday November to March
(bookings not accepted)
Prices:
Meals: a la carte 20.00/45.00

Typical Dishes

Mini seafood platter

Fillet steak

Assiette of desserts

South of N71 between Rosscarbery and Skibbereen. Parking in main street.

Clonakilty

004 An Súgán

Wolfe Tone St, Clonakilty

Tel.: (023) 33498 - Fax: (023) 33825
e-mail: ansugan4@eircom.net - Website: www.ansugan.com

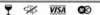 ♥ ✗ **VISA** ⓜⓒ

 No real ales offered

Personally run for ages, the unpretentious An Súgán welcomes hungry visitors as well as locals, dropping in to sink a pint and catch up on Clonakilty's news and current affairs. It's worth making time for a half in the characterful bar, all dark polished wood and frosted glass, before heading upstairs to the restaurant, decorated with memorabilia and old photos. A traditional blackboard menu doesn't try to reinvent the wheel, but offers sound, tasty home cooking with an appealing pub flavour: crisp, fresh prawn scampi are well worth trying. Relaxed and friendly service.

Food serving times:
Monday-Sunday:
    12.30pm-9.30pm approx
Closed 25-26 December and Good Friday
Prices:
Meals: 35.00 (set price dinner) and a la carte 22.00/35.00

Typical Dishes

Salmon and shrimp pate

An Súgán crab, tomato cream and mushroom sauce

Rich chocolate mousse

East of town centre. Parking in the street.

Kinsale

005 Dalton's

3 Market St, Kinsale
Tel.: (021) 4777957
e-mail: f.edalton@eircom.net

 No real ales offered

Moist, tasty crab cakes with pineapple salsa, chicken satay and Cajun popcorn prawns: here's a globe-trotting chef and landlord who is determined to bring a little unexpected variety to Kinsale's dining. A loyal local following suggests he must be doing something right, and while they still offer a good pie and pint for the traditionalist, it's the more ambitious dishes which set the place apart from the countless other pubs in town. It just goes to show that you can't go by appearances, for apart from the eyecatching purple façade, the line of bar stools, the tan banquettes, the tiled floor and the glowing fire are as traditional as the easygoing ambience and the cheerful welcome.

Food serving times:
Monday-Friday:
12.30pm-3.30pm
Saturday (summer only):
12.30pm-3.30pm
Closed 25 December and Good Friday
Prices:
Meals: a la carte 20.00/25.00

In town centre. Parking 2 minutes away in St Multose car park at top of road.

Typical Dishes
Seafood chowder
Crab cakes with fruit salsa and salad
Dark chocolate brownie cake with ice cream

Dublin

006 Clarendon Café Bar

32 Clarendon Street, Dublin D2
Tel.: (01) 679 2909 - Fax: (01) 670 6900

No real ales offered

The city's front-running gastro-pub, this sleek, metal-and-glass fronted destination has caused quite a stir since its refurbished doors were opened in 2004. Tourists, business suits, shoppers and, at nights, young clubbers all make a beeline for its shiny facade. You're free to eat or drink, and there are no 'time slots' weighing upon you. A distinct contemporary feel is adhered to so don't be surprised at sitting on chocolate leather boxes, augmented by a slight Moroccan edge courtesy of vivid scatter cushions. Tables are closely packed by the entrance; you might like to go upstairs and grab an intimate window table instead. The modern menus drift temptingly between casual favourites and serious restaurant dishes, all of which can be washed down with a choice from the extensive list of cocktails or wine by the glass.

Food serving times:
Monday-Thursday:
    12pm-3pm, 5pm-9.30pm
Friday-Sunday:
    12pm-6pm
Closed 25-28 December and 1-3 January
Bookings not accepted
Prices:
Meals: a la carte 20.00/35.00

In town centre, west of Grafton Street.

>>

Typical Dishes

Cod and chips in crispy beer batter

Shrimp and crab spring rolls, salsa

Warm chocolate brownie

Dublin

007 The Cellar Bar

Upper Merrion St, Dublin D2

Tel.: (01) 603 0600 - Fax: (01) 603 0700
e-mail: info@merrionhotel.com - Website: www.merrionhotel.com

  VISA

No real ales offered.

One of Dublin's favourite places for lunch is hidden away behind the elegant façade of an old Georgian town house, now the Merrion Hotel. The superbly restored wine vaults are now a smart destination bar by night, a bar-brasserie by day, and a city institution all round, so beat the lunchtime rush and find an alcove table under the brick and granite arches or pull up a spare stool at the long bar. Even on the busiest days, smiling, super-efficient bar staff keep things moving, serving up everything from hot roast beef sandwiches and Caesar salad to bacon and cabbage or Irish stew; plum frangipane tart with deliciously smooth ice cream is an occasional special and deserves to be tried.

Food serving times:
Monday-Saturday:
12pm-3pm, 6pm-10pm
Prices:
Meals: a la carte 30.00/45.00
143 rooms : 250.00/430.00

Typical Dishes

Foie gras with peach chutney

Irish West Coast seafood pie with lobster mash

Iced passion fruit parfait

At the Merrion Hotel; in town centre, between Merrion Square and St Stephen's Green. Parking available at a charge of 20 Euro per night.

Ballinasloe

008 **Tohers**

18 Dunlo Street, Ballinasloe
Tel.: (090) 9644848 - Fax: (090) 9644844

VISA M©

No real ales offered

A bustling market town like Ballinasloe ensures that this converted pub on the high street sees its fair share of local life: Tohers' ground floor bar is a buzzing place to be. It has a rustic charm befitting its proximity to the market square, and the marina is only a short walk away. Upstairs, the atmosphere's slightly more refined: three rooms make up the restaurant with its simple linen covered tables and understated rural décor. Menus contrast sharply: bar lunches are simple but tasty – everything from freshly baked baguettes to chicken fajitas – while upstairs in the evening, ambitious dishes with global inspiration make an appearance. Menus might include spring roll of gingered crab with a marinated carrot and fennel salad; or slow cooked Moroccan spiced lamb shank with lemon and garlic couscous.

Food serving times:
Monday: 12pm-3pm
Tuesday-Saturday:
12pm-3pm, 6pm-9.30pm
Closed 25-26 December and Good Friday; also 1 week in February and 2 weeks in October
Prices:
Meals: 38.00 (set price dinner) and a la carte 24.50/41.50

In town centre. On street parking.

Typical Dishes
Crispy calamari, sesame and soy dressing
Salmon fillet with herb crust
Warm brioche and butter pudding

Clonbur

009 Burke's Bar 🛏

Mount Gable House, Clonbur

Tel.: (094) 954 6175 - Fax: (094) 954 6290
e-mail: tibhurca@eircom.net - Website: www.burkes-clonbur.com

   VISA

 No real ales offered

etween two of Ireland's finest fishing waters, it's no surprise to find cabinets and cases displaying the ones that didn't get away. The brown trout in Lough Corrib and Lough Mask are legendary, the perch and pike no less so, and where better for food and drink after a long day out than this friendly pub, still owned by the Burke family. The tiny, unassuming shopfront opens up into a big, characterful bar and simply set rear dining room, as popular with the locals as with the anglers who flock to the West Coast in the height of the season. Simple, fortifying meals will set you up for the great outdoors: try cod and chips, a pint of stout and a generous slice of home-made apple pie.

Food serving times:
May-September:
  Monday-Sunday: 12pm-4pm,
  6.30pm-9pm
October-April:
  Monday-Friday: 1pm-4pm
Saturday-Sunday:
  12pm-4pm, 6.30pm-9pm
(live music Sunday)
Prices:
Meals: a la carte 23.00/40.00
🛏 **4 rooms :** 40.00/80.00

Typical Dishes

Baked mussels with herb crust and garlic

Irish stew

Homemade apple tart and cream

West of Cong. On street parking. ⟩

epublic of Ireland - Galway

21

Kilcolgan

010 **Moran's Oyster Cottage**

The Weir, Kilcolgan

Tel.: (091) 796113 - Fax: (091) 796503
e-mail: moranstheweir@eircom.net - Website: www.moransoystercottage.com

  VISA **AE** **MC**

No real ales offered

When you see the thatched roof of this pretty cottage, your mind might flash to a typical English country inn, but instead you're across the Irish Sea in a sleepy Galway village. Moran's is set in a delightful waterside location and you can watch the swans sail serenely past. Inside, this charming 18C building is full of nooks and crannies in the front bar. Settle down in one of the beamed snugs and parlours or go through to the very large dining area at the back where the walls are decorated with photos of famous customers. Local seafood dishes, unsurprisingly, make up the widely renowned menus: native oysters from their own oyster beds, lobster, mussels, crab salads, smoked salmon and seafood cocktails. Expect fairly fast and furious service from staff who are used to being busy.

Food serving times:
Monday-Sunday:
12pm-10pm
Closed 3 days at Christmas and Good Friday
- Seafood -
Prices:
Meals: a la carte 26.00/67.80

5 minutes from the village of Clarenbridge. Parking in road.

Typical Dishes

Seafood chowder
Seafood special
Baileys Cheesecake

Kinvara

011 Keogh's Bar

Main St, Kinvara

Tel.: (091) 637145 - Fax: (091) 637028
e-mail: keoghsbar@eircom.net - Website: www.kinvara.com/keoghs

 VISA **AE** **MC**

 No real ales offered

Kinvara is a pretty harbour village on the Galway coast, renowned for the quality of its Atlantic fishing catch. Gateway to the Burren, its colourful character is echoed in this bright yellow-fronted pub whose busy bar constantly buzzes to the sound of locals chattering over a pint of dark stout. At the back is a spacious, slightly more formal dining room, which still maintains a warm, pubby ambience. The Keoghs have been here for many years, and they serve simple, well-prepared and tasty dishes, based around the plentiful supplies of local seafood. On offer, typically, are prawns, salmon, crab, mussels and seafood chowder, cooked in a hearty and traditional style.

Food serving times:
Monday-Sunday:
12.30pm-10pm
Closed 25 December
Prices:
Meals: a la carte 18.40/28.00

In town centre. Parking. **》**

Typical Dishes

Chowder

Roast lamb with mint and potato mash

Bread and butter pudding with whiskey sauce

Cahersiveen

012 O'Neill's (The Point) Seafood Bar

Renard Point, Cahersiveen

Tel.: (066) 947 2165 - Fax: (087) 259 5345
e-mail: oneillsthepoint@hotmail.com

 No real ales offered

As the beautiful Ring of Kerry runs south, hold your course to the tip of the Iveragh peninsula: down at the quay, looking out across the harbour to Valencia Island, is a neatly kept little bar that's definitely worth going a little further for. Between them, a charming couple, owners of long standing, keep the place shipshape, pull the pints and prepare a short hot and cold supper menu of local seafood; all well chosen and as fresh as it comes, as you'd expect with a fish shed next door! It's a good place for a relaxed pint and a chat – there's no food at all at lunchtime – but if you arrive in the afternoon with time to spare, just take a seat on the little pavement terrace and wait for 6pm to roll around!

Food serving times:
Monday-Saturday:
12.30pm-3.30pm,
5.30pm-10pm
Sunday: 5.30pm-10pm
Closed Monday-Thursday November to March; also closed lunch April and October
- Seafood - (bookings not accepted)
Prices:
Meals: a la carte 35.00/40.00

Typical Dishes

Crab claws in garlic & olive oil, crushed chillies & fresh parsley

Pan-fried hake in garlic and olive oil with potato salad

West of Cahersiveen; follow the sign for the ferry. Parking.

Listowel

013 Allo's Bar

41 Church St, Listowel
Tel.: (068) 22880 - Fax: (068) 22803
e-mail: armel@easy.com

 VISA **AE** **MC**

No real ales offered

A discreetly set institution in the centre of Listowel, this is a wonderfully relaxed pub that proves very popular with locals and tourists alike. It's the other half of Allo's restaurant with rooms, the two gelling in a smooth and seamless symmetry. The bar is a narrow room with lots of original 19C charm. Walls feature exposed brick and the wooden bar and floor are thickly varnished; small booths and stools at the bar provide a most convivial and traditional feel. Menus change on a weekly basis and offer a good range of popular snacks and sandwiches alongside hearty daily specials. Booking really is a must, as it invariably gets packed here.

Food serving times:
Tuesday-Saturday:
12pm-9pm
Closed 25 December
(booking essential)
Prices:
Meals: a la carte 18.00/48.00
3 rooms : 45.00/100.00

Typical Dishes

Allos seafood chowder

Fillet of turbot, wild garlic mash

Dark chocolate pudding, hazelnut ganache

In town centre, off North corner of The Square. Parking in the road.

Carrick-on-Shannon

014 The Oarsman

Bridge St, Carrick-on-Shannon

Tel.: (071) 9621733 - Fax: (071) 9621734
e-mail: info@theoarsman.com - Website: www.theoarsman.com

 VISA **MC**

No real ales offered

No boating experience necessary, of course, but the town's club eights have been known to drop in, along with sea-anglers and tour rowers, back from a long day's pull up to Lough Key. They come for the spirited, upbeat atmosphere, light lunches and fresh, tasty dinners combining modern classics and a few popular Irish favourites; even when it's busy, alert and helpful staff will do their best find you a table in the main bar or up in the mezzanine, though propping up the bar for a half is no hardship here. Refurbished in traditional style, with some unlikely bits of bric-a-brac hanging from its exposed timbers and stone, it's an enjoyable place and worth seeking out.

Food serving times:
Monday-Saturday:
   12pm-4pm, 6.45pm-9.45pm
Closed 25 December and
Good Friday
Prices:
Meals: a la carte 32.00/48.00

Typical Dishes

Filo parcel of confit duck and foie gras

Fillet of pork in Parma ham, parsnip purée

Pear and pineapple dim sum

In town centre. Disc parking adjacent to pub.

Terryglass

015 The Derg Inn

Terryglass

Tel.: (067) 22037 - Fax: (067) 22297
e-mail: derginn@eircom.net - Website: www.derginn.ie

No real ales offered

Not, perhaps, typically pubby from the outside – sandwiched between the post office and Paddy's Bar – this is in fact an unmistakeable and friendly place once you're through the front door. Enthusiastically run by keen owners, it has wood and flagged floors, rafters, open fires and pot stoves; dotted round the central wood bar are chunky pine tables and an assortment of chairs, benches and pews, and there's outside seating in the summer months. As much local and organic produce appears on the menus as possible: classic Irish favourites alongside more modern dishes served in an invariably friendly manner. After which, all that remains is to take that brisk constitutional down to beautiful Lough Derg.

Food serving times:
Monday-Sunday:
11am-10pm
Closed 25 December and Good Friday
Prices:
Meals: a la carte 21.00/40.00

Typical Dishes

Monktail scampi in kataïfi pastry

Rack of lamb, mint and tomato chutney

Crème brûlée

Off R493; turn right at Paddy's Pub. Parking.

Dunmore East

016 The Ship

Dock Rd, Dunmore East

Tel.: (051) 383141 - Fax: (051) 383144
e-mail: theshiprestaurant@eircom.net

 VISA AE ⓪ ⓶ⓒ

 No real ales offered

A small, stone-built pub happily nestling in a pleasant fishing village, The Ship's corner position makes it one of Dunmore East's most recognisable institutions and it's well received locally. There's a strong element of delightful pubby character inside: big bar, polished wood floors, beams, pillars, and lots of open fires. Nautical memorabilia, too, is spot-on for the location. Sit down at simple tables and 'barrel' shaped chairs and tuck in to menus that are not, surprisingly, dominated by seafood: you'll find meat plays an equally prominent part in the soundly cooked range of dishes. Blackboard options, though, are firmly centred on fish specials.

Food serving times:
Monday-Sunday :
    1pm-4pm, 7pm-10pm
Closed Monday-Friday and dinner Sunday November-March
- Seafood -
Prices:
Meals: 28.00 (set price lunch) and a la carte 40.00/70.00

Typical Dishes

Scallops, salt cod brandade

Veal cutlet, Savoy cabbage & shitake

Chocolate tart, pistachio ice cream

On the hill, near the harbour. Parking in the street.

Lismore

017 Glencairn Inn

Lismore

Tel.: (058) 56232 - Fax: (058) 56232
e-mail: glencairninn@eircom.net - Website: www.lismore.com

room **VISA** **AE** **MC**

No real ales offered

This "pretty as a picture" cottage style inn is most homely: it even has a picket fence. A country pub writ large, it boasts everything from a little fire-lit bar to charming bedrooms with an old-world feel. The quaint bar is a good place to settle down with a pint of stout and enjoy freshly prepared dishes off a limited choice menu; or, if you prefer, the same options are on offer in a couple of small dining rooms, charmingly set up with a stylish country informality. The food is heartily rustic in nature: on the menu, you might find pot-roasted fillet of pork and apricots, or fish landed at Helvick, cooked in butter, olive oil and lemon juice. The owner is a talented artist, and it's easy to appreciate just how much of his inspiration has gone into the pub's appeal, not to mention his popular menus.

Food serving times:
Monday-Sunday:
12pm-2pm, 7pm-9pm
Closed Christmas week
Prices:
Meals: a la carte 40.00/60.00
5 rooms : 70.00/125.00

2mi west of Lismore on the road to Ballyduff and Glencairn. Parking.

Typical Dishes

Duck pâte
Fillet of turbot
Lemon and lime pudding

Carne

018 **The Lobster Pot**

Carne

Tel.: (053) 31110 - Fax: (053) 31401

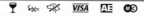

🍷 ⊗ ⊗ **VISA** **AE** **MC**

 No real ales offered

Engagingly quirky and genuinely welcoming, this personally owned seaside pub has been over 20 years in the making: it's now covered with old metal signs on the outside, and the intimate snugs and parlours are crammed with nauticalia and pasted with old posters and advertisements from days gone by. There's also a dining room at the back and, come the evening, they add an extensive list of grills, steaks and locally landed fish to the lunchtime chowders, salads and sandwiches. The real treat, though, is the huge seafood platter, an aquarium's worth of home-smoked salmon and mackerel, freshly dressed crab, poached salmon and prawns Marie Rose, served with bushels of salad. Try it with freshly baked brown scones and a glass of stout!

Food serving times:
Tuesday-Sunday and Bank Holiday Monday:
12pm-9pm
Closed 25 December and Good Friday; also month of January
- Seafood - check opening times in winter
Prices:
Meals: a la carte 30.00/60.00

South of Rosslare Harbour. Parking. ➤➤

Typical Dishes

Crab Mornay

Grilled Dover sole on the bone, tartare sauce

Sticky toffee pudding with caramel sauce

Arklow

019 Kitty's of Arklow

56 Main St, Arklow

Tel.: (0402) 31669 - Fax: (0402) 31553
Website: www.kittysofarklow.com

 VISA **AE** **①** **MC**

 No real ales offered

One of Arklow's most recognisable sights: that's the fondly regarded red building in the centre of the town. Locals flock here, and the downstairs bar is constantly bustling, the pints of stout flowing freely. It seems a shame to leave, but then again, there are two dining rooms upstairs, both rich in easy-going rustic character, decorated with everything from books and old farm equipment to pictures for sale. Arrive early for one of the most sought-after tables, which overlook the high street. Simple lunchtime menus range from panini to specials; in the evenings, more structured and elaborate options prevail; service is cheerful, efficient and as smooth as clockwork.

Food serving times:
Monday-Sunday:
12pm-5.30pm, 5.30pm-10pm

Prices:
Meals: 20.00/26.00 (set price lunch/dinner) and a la carte 26.00/40.00

Typical Dishes

Smoked salmon roulade

Wicklow rack of lamb

Homemade cheesecake

In the town centre. Public parking nearby.

Index of towns

633

A

B

C

T

V

W

Y

Also in the
Michelin Guide collection

eating
out in
pubs

Michelin Travel Publications

Michelin Travel Publications
Hannay House,
39 Clarendon Rd
Watford WD17 1JA
Tel: (01923) 205247
Fax: (01923) 205241
www.ViaMichelin.com
eatingoutinpubs-gbirl@
uk.michelin.com

Manufacture française des pneumatiques Michelin

Société en commandite
par actions au capital de
304 000 000 EUR.
Place des Carmes-Déchaux
63 Clermont-Ferrand (France)
R.C.S. Clermont-Fd B 855 200 507
© Michelin et Cie, Propriétaires-
Editeurs, 2006
Dépôt légal Septembre 2006
Printed in France 09-06

Typesetting:

Nord Compo, Villeneuve-d'Ascq
Printing and binding:
Clerc, St Amand-Montrond

Photography

Picture Editor: Eliane Bailly,
Stéphanie Quillon
Project manager: Alain Leprince
Agence ACSI – A Chacun Son
Image
242, bd. Voltaire– 75011 Paris

Location Photographs:

Jérôme Berquez, Frédéric Chales,
Ludivine Boizard, Jean-Louis
Chauveau/ACSI

Thanks to:

The Hinds Head, Bray-on-Thames
for the front cover images.

John Bigelow Taylor/Waddesdon,
The Rothschild Collection
(The National Trust) for the
image of The Five Arrows Hotel,
Waddesdon.

p 10: John A Rizzo/Photodisc
Vert/Getty Images

p 14: www.britainonview.com

p 190: britainonview/Rod
Edwards

p 444: britainonview/Martin
Brent

GREAT BRITAIN: Based on
Ordnance Survey of Great
Britain with the permission of
the controller of Her Majesty's
Stationery Office, © Crown
Copyright 100000247